BLOOD EXPIATION IN HITTITE
AND BIBLICAL RITUAL

SBL

Society of Biblical Literature

Writings from the Ancient World Supplement Series

Billie Jean Collins, Editor

Number 2

Blood Expiation in Hittite and Biblical Ritual
Origins, Context, and Meaning

Blood Expiation in Hittite and Biblical Ritual
Origins, Context, and Meaning

Yitzhaq Feder

Society of Biblical Literature
Atlanta

BLOOD EXPIATION IN HITTITE AND BIBLICAL RITUAL

Library of Congress Cataloging-in-Publication Data

Feder, Yitzhaq.
  Blood expiation in Hittite and biblical ritual : origins, context, and meaning / by Yitzhaq Feder.
      p. cm. — (Writings from the ancient world supplements / Society of Biblical Literature ; no. 2)
  Includes bibliographical references.
  ISBN 978-1-58983-554-2 (paper binding : alk. paper) — ISBN 978-1-58983-555-9 (electronic format)
  1. Blood in the Bible. 2. Blood—Religious aspects. 3. Ritual. 4. Hittites—Religion. I. Title.
  BS1199.B54F43 2011
  221.6'7—dc23
                              2011018656

Printed in the United States of America on acid-free, recycled paper
conforming to ANSI/NISO Z39.48-1992 (R1997) and ISO 9706:1994
standards for paper permanence.

∞

CONTENTS

ACKNOWLEDGMENTS

This book is a thoroughly revised version of my dissertation, submitted to the Bible Department of Bar-Ilan University in May 2009. I am indebted to the Keren Keshet Foundation for funding my doctoral research under the auspices of Bar-Ilan's Presidential Scholarship program.

I have been exceedingly fortunate to benefit from the council and example of two outstanding scholars: Prof. Rimon Kasher (Bar-Ilan University) and Prof. Itamar Singer (Tel-Aviv University). I must add that I am especially grateful to Prof. Singer for his unwavering and enthusiastic support even amidst the most challenging circumstances.

I was also uniquely privileged to have Dr. Yoram Cohen (Tel Aviv University) as one of the referees for my dissertation; the present manuscript has benefitted immeasurably from his incisive comments on both philological and theoretical issues. I would also like to thank Prof. Jared L. Miller (Universität München) for generously providing photos of several fragmentary Hittite texts and his insight on several points of interpretation. I am also grateful to the following scholars from Bar-Ilan University for their help and encouragement: Dr. Elie Assis, Prof. Ed Greenstein, Dr. Joshua Berman, Dr. Kathleen Abraham and Prof. Aaron Shemesh.

I would also like to thank Dr. Billie Jean Collins for her wise advice and dedication in preparing this work for publication.

On a personal note, I thank my parents for their love and support, and for always seeking to cultivate independence of thought, even at their own expense. This book is dedicated to them.

I also want to express my appreciation to Esty, my other half, for her unwavering support. Our children, Rachel and Pinhas Aaron, now ages 5 and 2.5 respectively, also have a share in this work. They have regularly reminded me of the tremendous capabilities of nonverbal communication and its relevance for the study of ritual.

Finally, I am most grateful to God, for providing me with the strength and inspiration to carry out this project, and for enduring its promethean pretentions.

אשר בידו מחקרי ארץ
ולגדלתו אין חקר
JERUSALEM, JANUARY 2011

ABBREVIATIONS

AB	Anchor Bible
ABoT	*Ankara Arkeoloji Müzesinde Boğazköy Tabletleri*
AfO	*Archiv für Orientforschung*
AHw	Wolfram von Soden, *Akkadisches Handwörterbuch*. 3 vols. Wiesbaden 1965–1981
Akk	Akkadian
AOAT	Alter Orient und Altes Testament
AOATS	Alter Orient und Altes Testament Sonderreihe
AoF	*Altorientalische Forschungen*
ANET	*Ancient Near Eastern Texts Relating to the Old Testament*. Edited by J. B. Pritchard. 3rd ed. Princeton: Princeton University Press, 1969
AuOr	*Aula Orientalis*
BASOR	*Bulletin of the American Schools of Oriental Research*
BDB	*Hebrew and English Lexicon of the Old Testament*. F. Brown, S. R. Driver, and C. A. Briggs. Peabody, Mass., 2003 (1906)
BF	Baghdader Forschungen
BiOr	*Bibliotheca Orientalis*
BJS	Brown Judaic Studies
BKAT	Biblischer Kommentar Altes Testament
CAD	*The Assyrian Dictionary of the Oriental Institute of the University of Chicago*
CBQ	*Catholic Biblical Quarterly*
CHD	*The Hittite Dictionary of the Oriental Institute of the University of Chicago*
ChS	*Corpus der hurritischen Sprachdenkmäler*
CBQ	*Catholic Biblical Quarterly*
Chr	Chronicles
COS	*The Context of Scripture*. 3 vols. Edited by W. W. Hallo and K. Lawson Younger. Leiden: Brill, 2003
CTH	*Catalogue des textes hittites*

DCH	*Dictionary of Classical Hebrew.* Edited by D. J. A. Clines. Sheffield: Sheffield Academic, 1993
DDD	*Dictionary of Deities and Demons in the Bible.* Edited by K. van der Toorn et al. Leiden: Brill, 1999
EA	El-Amarna
GBH	*A Grammar of Biblical Hebrew.* P. Joüon and T. Muraoka. Rome: Editrice Pontificio Instituto Biblico, 2006
GKC	*Gesenius' Hebrew Grammar.* Edited by W. Gesenius, E. Kautsch. Trans. by A. Cowley. Oxford 1983
GLH	*Glossaire de la langue hourrite.* E. Laroche. *RHA* 34–35 (1976–1977)
HALOT	*The Hebrew and Aramaic Lexicon of the Old Testament.* W. Baumgartner et al. Leiden: Brill, 1994
HAT	Handbuch zum Alten Testament
Heb	Hebrew
HED	*Hittite Etymological Dictionary.* Jaan Puhvel. Berlin-New York: De Gruyter, 1984–
HEG	*Hethitisches Etymologisches Glossar.* J. Tischler. Innsbruck, 1977–
HSS	Harvard Semitic Studies
HUCA	*Hebrew Union College Annual*
Hur.	Hurrian
HW	*Hethitisches Wörterbuch.* J. Friedrich. Heidelberg, 1952
HW²	*Hethitisches Wörterbuch.* J. Friedrich-A. Kammenhuber. Heidelberg: Winter, 1975–
ICC	International Critical Commentary
IDB	*Interpreter's Dictionary of the Bible.* Edited by G. A. Buttrick. 4 vols. Nashville, 1962
IEJ	*Israel Exploration Journal*
JANER	*Journal of Ancient Near Eastern Religion*
JANES	*Journal of the Ancient Near Eastern Society*
JAOS	*Journal of the American Oriental Society*
JBL	*Journal of Biblical Literature*
JCS	*Journal of Cuneiform Studies*
JHS	*Journal of Hebrew Scriptures*
JIES	*Journal of Indo-European Studies*
JNES	*Journal of Near Eastern Studies*
JNSL	*Journal of Northwest Semitic Languages*
JPS	Jewish Publication Society
JSOTSup	Journal for the Study of the Old Testament: Supplement Series
KBo	*Keilschrifttexte aus Boghazköy*

KHC	Kurzer Handkommentar zum Alten Testament
KUB	*Keilschrifturkunden aus Boghazköy*
LXX	Septuagint
m.	Mishna
MT	Masoretic Text
NABU	*N.A.B.U.—Nouvelles Assyriologiques Brèves et Utilitaires*
NA	Neo-Assyrian
NB	Neo-Babylonian
NASB	New American Standard Bible
NEB	New English Bible
NICOT	New International Commentary on the Old Testament
NIDNTT	*New International Dictionary of New Testament Theology*
OB	Old Babylonian
OBO	Orbis Biblicus et Orientalis
OTL	Old Testament Library
PEQ	*Palestine Exploration Quarterly*
RGTC	*Répertoire Géographique des Textes Cunéiformes*
RA	*Revue d'Assyriologie et Archéologie orientale*
RB	*Revue biblique*
RHA	*Revue Hittite et Asianique*
RlA	*Reallexikon der Assyriologie und vorderasiatischen Archäeologie*
RS	Ras Shamra
SAA	State Archives of Assyria
SB	Standard Babylonian
SCCNH	Studies on the Civilization and Culture of Nuzi and the Hurrians
SMEA	*Studi micenei ed egeo-anatolici*
StBoT	Studien zu den Boğazköy-Texten
StMed	*Studia Mediterranea*
Sum	Sumerian
TDOT	*Theological Dictionary of the Old Testament.* Edited by G.J. Botterweck et al.; trans. J. T. Wills and D. E. Green; Grand Rapids, Mich.: Eerdmans, 1977–2006
THeth	Texte der Hethiter
TLOT	*Theological Lexicon of the Old Testament.* Edited by E. Jenni and C. Westermann; trans. M. E. Biddle; Peabody, Mass.: Hendrickson, 1997
UF	*Ugarit-Forschungen*
VT	*Vetus Testamentum*
Weiss	*Sipra with Rabad's Commentary.* Edited by I. M. Weiss. New York: OM, 1946
WO	*Die Welt des Orients*

ZA	*Zeitschrift für Assyriologie*
ZAW	*Zeitschrift fur die Alttestamentliche Wissenschaft*
ZTK	*Zeitschrift für Theologie und Kirche*
ZVS	*Zeitschrift für vergleichende Sprachforschung*

NOTE ON TRANSLATIONS

All translations of Hittite or biblical texts are my own unless otherwise stated, though I have benefited from available translations and commentaries. Regarding Biblical texts, I have most consistently consulted the JPS translation and Milgrom's commentary on Leviticus.

INTRODUCTION

This study is about rituals and meaning. In modern academic research, it has become increasingly dangerous to mention these two terms in one breath. As will be shown in due course, the growing skepticism towards the notion of ritual meaning in current studies of ritual is an inevitable result of their tendency to treat its functions in highly abstract terms (e.g., as representative of social groupings or cognitive categories). In contrast, the present study seeks to determine the meaning of ritual in its concrete sociohistorical context. This approach is particularly appropriate for the rituals of the ancient Near East, which are most directly concerned with the needs of material existence, such as plague, illness, famine, infertility and the like.

In particular, this study examines the use of blood to purge the effects of sin and impurity in Hittite and biblical ritual. The idea that blood atones for sins holds a prominent place in both Jewish and Christian traditions. The present study traces this notion back to its earliest documentation. Our point of departure is the discovery of a set of rites documented in Hittite texts from the fourteenth to thirteenth centuries B.C.E., in which the smearing of blood is used as a means of expiation, purification,[1] and consecration. This rite parallels, in both its procedure and goals, the biblical sin offering. Expanding upon a proposal of the Hittitologist Volkert Haas, I will argue that this practice stems from a common tradition manifested in both cultures. In addition, this study aims to discover and elucidate the symbolism of this practice by seeking to identify the sociocultural context in which the expiatory significance of blood originated.

The first part of this study focuses on the relationship between the Hittite and Israelite sources. In order to understand the purpose of these rites properly, the texts from each culture are analyzed independently. In addition to analyzing the biblical texts in their canonical form, I will attempt to differentiate between

---

1. By the terms "expiation" and "purification" I am referring to processes for the removal of the effects of sin and ritual defilement, respectively. I will have more to say about these terms in depth later (see chapters 5–7).

1

earlier and later layers of the text, so as to trace the literary development of these sources and identify changing conceptions of the purpose of the sin offering.

The analysis of Hittite and Israelite sources leads to the identification of profound similarities in procedure, rationale, and circumstances of the rituals, only some of which will be mentioned in this overview. For example, the blood rites in both cultures consist of an act of smearing blood on an object, frequently cultic, as a means of removing metaphysical threats, such as sin and impurity, which will evoke divine retribution unless action is taken. The Hurro-Hittite blood rite—the *zurki*—is regularly accompanied by an offering of cooked fat, often from the same animal, called the *uzi* rite. This practice is strikingly similar to the sin offering, which involved the smearing and sprinkling of blood as well as the burning of its fat on the altar as a "pleasing aroma to YHWH" (Lev 4:31). Furthermore, the underlying dynamic of the Hittite and Israelite rituals are extraordinarily similar. In a dynamic that could be classified as form of metonymy, the ritual patron benefits from the expiatory rite by means of an associative connection between himself and the object. Moreover, the circumstances that require the performance of these rituals are nearly identical for both cultures, including expiation for unintentional sin, purification of a defiled temple, and the consecration of a new cult structure.

These striking parallels create a strong impression that the Hittite and Israelite blood rites stem from a common origin. This assumption is subjected to critical evaluation in ch. 3, where several additional points are raised in support of this conclusion. In particular, a comparison of blood rites from neighboring cultures from the ancient Near East and Mediteranean reveals that the latter differ from the Hittite and Israelite rites in their procedure and rationale. In further support of a common tradition, evidence is brought demonstrating the transfer of ritual traditions between the various ethnic groups of the Late Bronze Age Levant. Finally, an analysis of additional Hittite and biblical texts demonstrates the existence of parallels that extend beyond the blood rites themselves, narrowly defined.

The second part of this study attempts to reveal how the expiatory use of blood originated. In ch. 4, after outlining a theoretical critique of several dominant trends in the study of ritual symbolism, I argue that the function of rituals signs is not *arbitrary* but *motivated* by a sociohistorical context in which the relation between a sign and its function was understood as self-evident. This premise serves as a guideline for the subsequent analysis of the Hittite and biblical textual data of both cultures, revealing in both cases a relationship between the expiatory function of blood and beliefs associated with bloodguilt and revenge. In particular, an analysis of the relevant idioms in Hittite and Hebrew (*šarnink-* and *kipper,* respectively) reveals a pervasive belief in the necessity for making compensation for bloodguilt in order to avoid the imminent threat of divine retribution. Within this social context, blood served as a means of making restitution for guilt. This dynamic could then serve as a model for addressing other types of offenses vis-à-vis the gods, which were conceptualized in terms of a metaphorical scheme of guilt as debt.

If the two parts of the study are similar to parallel strands, one focusing primarily on historical questions and the other on symbolism, these lines of inqury finally converge in ch. 7. This chapter seeks to tie the loose ends and view some of the conclusions of the earlier chapters in a broader perspective. Specifically, it addresses questions pertaining to the origins of the blood rite and its transmission to Israel. Furthermore, it discusses the ramifications of our findings for modern critical theories of the Priestly source of the Bible. It also discusses the role of the sin offering's symbolism in shaping later Jewish and Christian metaphoric notions of sin and atonement and draws some fundamental conclusions regarding the relationship between the meaning and efficacy of ritual.

PART I

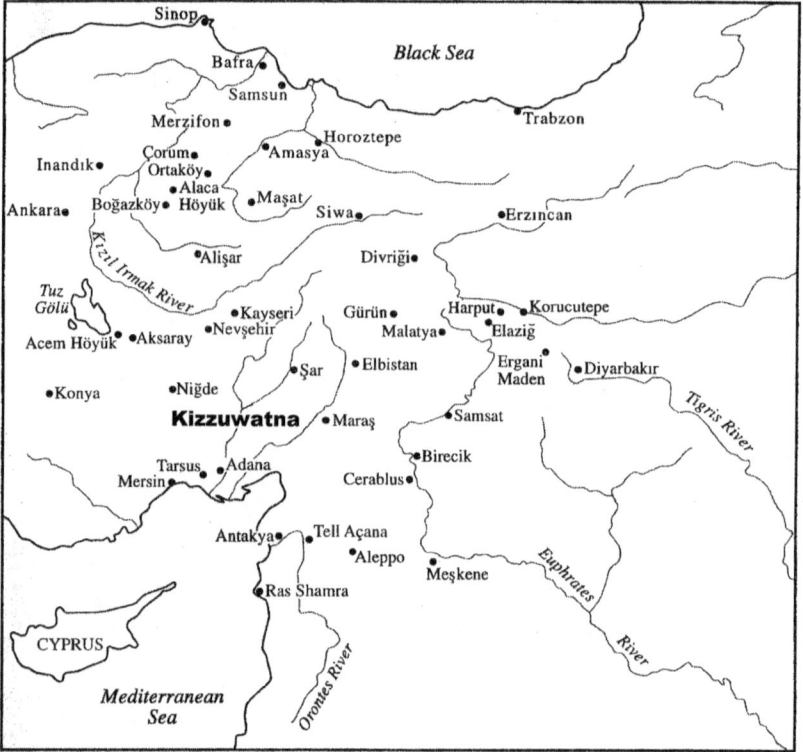

Map showing the location of Kizzuwatna. Adapted from Bryce,
Kingdom of the Hittites, xv.

1

THE HURRO-HITTITE *ZURKI* RITE

Though the compelling parallel between Hittite and biblical blood rites was noted sporadically throughout the twentieth century,[1] only in Haas's pioneering paper from 1990 did this comparison receive serious attention.[2] In this article, Haas amassed and summarized the relevant Hittite texts, concluding that the ritual use of blood in the Bible reflects a tradition preserved in these early sources.

Most of the texts in which this blood rite is attested were composed between the fourteenth and thirteenth centuries and reflect traditions from the region of Kizzuwatna (classical Cilicia) in southeastern Anatolia, bordering on northern Syria.[3] Most of these are written in the Hittite language, though some of them are in Hurrian. In general, the textual evidence from Kizzuwatna, as with that from Late Bronze Age sites in Syria (e.g., Ugarit, Alalaḫ, Emar), demonstrates a prominent role played by Hurrian ritual experts in transmitting the various ritual traditions throughout this region.[4]

Though ground-breaking, even Haas's study left many crucial questions for the interpretation of the blood rite unanswered. For example:

- What are the unifying themes in the rituals in which the blood rite appears?
- What is the role of the blood rite in the realization of the overall goals of the rituals in which it appears?
- Why was blood perceived as efficacious for the removal of sin and impurity over other *materia magica*?

---

1. Sommer and Ehelolf, *Das Hethitische Ritual des Papanikri*, 18; Kronasser, *Umsiedelung der Schwarzen Gottheit*, 56–58; Laroche, "Études de Linguistique Anatolienne," 99.

2. Haas, "Ein hurritischer Blutritus," 67–77.

3. For more discussion of the geography of Kizzuwatna, see below p. 232.

4. For more about the Hurrians, see Hoffner, "Hittites and Hurrians," 221–24.

In order to shed light on these issues, the present analysis will examine how the procedural aspects of the rite relate to its immediate goals and the overall aims of the rituals in which the blood rite is found.

SIN, IMPURITY, AND OTHER METAPHYSICAL THREATS

Hittite rituals are rooted in the assumption that adversity in human existence is symptomatic of a metaphysical cause, be it divine anger, black magic, or the like. By labeling these forces as *metaphysical*, I am attributing to the Hittites (as well as the Israelites) a belief in an unseen dimension that can dramatically influence phenomenal reality.[5] These elusive forces can be controlled, to some extent, through expiatory and purificatory rituals, which seek to avert the threat by addressing the inferred supramundane causes of the problem. However, since the exact cause of the danger, real or potential, remains in many cases indeterminate, the ritual participants must cover a broad spectrum of potential evil influences. Thus, the texts list numerous possible causes, which include such items as curse (*ḫurta*), bloodshed (*ešḫar*), oaths (*linga*) and impurity (*papratar*).[6]

Although these evil forces are themselves nebulous, they exert their negative influence by means of clinging to physical objects. This dynamic can be viewed as a type of *metonymy*, that is a relationship whereby one thing stands for another to which it is related (e.g., crown for monarchy). In this case, the defiled object was assumed to endanger its owner(s) by power of association. Fortunately, by virtue of the fact that the concretized form of the evil was bound to a material object, it could be eradicated by means of ritual techniques.[7]

A vivid illustration of these dynamics appears in the oracle inquiries of Tudhaliya IV, one of the last of the Hittite kings, who ruled near the end of the thirteenth century B.C.E.[8] These oracle inquiries paint a portrait of a ruler on the brink of paranoia who viewed his sovereignty as constantly threatened by the curses and sorcery of his political opponents and by divine retribution for the misdeeds of his predecessors. Such forces have defiled various symbols associated with the monarchy, requiring an appropriate purification ritual:

[*I*]*Š-TU* EME ᵐ*Úr-ḫi-*[ᵈU-*ub* DINGI]R.MEŠ LUGAL-*UT-TI* AŠ-*RI*ᴴᴵ·ᴬ
LUGAL-*UT-TI* ᴳᴵˢDAGᴴᴵ·ᴿᴬ˺ [*pá*]*r-ku-nu-an-zi* ᵈUTU-*ŠI-ia-za pár-ku-nu-*ᴿ*zi*˺

---

5. For a modern analogy, one may compare the relation between genotype and phenotype in genetics. For further discussion of the relation between these metaphysical beliefs and the perceived efficacy of ritual, see below, p. 152.

6. A perusal of any of these terms in the dictionaries yields numerous lists of this type. See also Janowski and Wilhelm, "Religionsgeschichte des Azazel-Ritus," 139–43.

7. See Janowski and Wilhelm, "Religionsgeschichte des Azazel-Ritus," 143–51.

8. CTH 569. Text Edition: van den Hout, *Purity of Kingship*.

[F]rom the curse of Urhi-[Tešub] they will [cl]eanse the [go]ds of kingship, the places of kingship (and) the thrones, and His Majesty will cleanse himself.[9]

Similar dynamics will be readily apparent in the various rituals that will be analyzed in the present study.

Thus, Hittite expiatory rituals are based on a paradoxical conception in which abstract threats are embodied in concrete objects. On one hand, in order to rationalize adversity, the Hittites were led to assume the existence of various nebulous forces of evil that exert their influence on human affairs. On the other hand, the need to eliminate these elusive forces was made possible by their concretization, that is, by their adherence to physical objects, which allowed them to be purged by the appropriate rituals.

Expiatory Rituals

Blood manipulations appear in several Kizzuwatnean birth rituals. The best preserved of these is the Ritual of Papanikri of Kummanni.[10] This ritual aims to neutralize the threat signaled by an ominous breaking of the birth stool, comprised of a basin with two pegs,[11] at the moment when the parturient is on the verge of giving birth. The first day of the ritual focuses on the removal of the defective birth stool and the construction of two new birth stools. A key passage reads as follows:

Obv. I

12 *nam-ma ḫar-na-a-ú Ú-NU-TE*^MEŠ*-ia ši-na-ap-ši-ia*
13 *pé-e-da-a-i na-at a-ra-aḫ-za dam-mi-li pé-di da-a-i*
14 *nu-za-kán* MUNUS-*TUM an-da-an-pát ḫa-a-ši* LÚ*pa-ti-li-iš-ša*
15 *A-NA* MUNUS-*TUM ki-iš-ša-an te-ez-zi ar-ḫa-wa-za*
16 *a-ri-ia I-NA* É*ka-ri-im-mi-wa-at-ták-kan ku-it*
17 *an-da ša-ga*^12*-a-iš ki-ša-at*

Then he (i.e., the *patili* priest) brings the birth stool and the equipment to the *šinapši*. He places them outside in a desolate place. The woman gives birth there inside. The *patili*-priest speaks thus to the woman: "Investigate by means of oracle the sign that occurred to you in the *karimmi*-Sanctuary."

---

9. KUB 50.6+ Rev. III, 48–50. Text and translation: van den Hout, *Purity of Kingship*, 188–89.

10. KBo 5.1 (CTH 476). Text: Strauß, *Reinigungsrituale aus Kizzuwatna*, 284–309.

11. For a description of the "birth stool," see Beckman, *Hittite Birth Rituals*, 102–4.

12. Contrary to the published collation KBo 5.1, the sign GA appears clearly in the photo, obviating the necessity for a correction (e.g., *CHD* Š, I:34; Strauß, *Reinigungsrituale aus Kizzuwatna*, 287).

18 *nu-za ar-ḫa a-ri-ia-zi nu-uš-ši ma-a-an* DINGIR-*LUM ku-iš-ki*
19 *kar-tim-mi-ia-u-wa-an-za na-an-za ši-pa-an-ti nam-ma* 2 ᴰᵁᴳDÍLIM.GAL
20 *ḫar-na-a-ú-wa-aš i-ia-zi* NA-AK-TÁ-MA-*ia-aš-ma-aš*
21 2 ᴰᵁᴳDÍLIM.GAL *i-ia-zi* 4 ᴳᴵˢGAGᴴᴵ·ᴬ-*ia i-ia-zi*

She consults an oracle: If any god is angry with her, she sacrifices to him. Then he[13] makes two basins (into) birth stools and a lid for (each of) them. He makes two basins and he makes four pegs.

22 *nu* 2 ᴳᴵˢBANŠUR *da-a-i nu-uš-ša-an* A-NA 1 ᴳᴵˢBANŠUR
23 1 ᴰᵁᴳDÍLIM.GAL *ḫar-na-a-ú-i* 2 ᴳᴵˢGAGᴴᴵ·ᴬ-*ia da-a-i nam-ma-ia-aš-ša-an*
24 A-NA 1 ᴳᴵˢBANŠUR 1 ᴰᵁᴳDÍLIM.GAL *ḫar-na-a-ú-i* 2 ᴳᴵˢGAGᴴᴵ·ᴬ-*ia da-a-i*

He takes two tables. On the first table, he places one basin for a birth stool and two pegs, then, on the second table, he places one basin for a birth stool and two pegs.

25 *nam-ma* IŠ-TU 2 MUŠEN *ḫar-na-a-ú-i* ᴳᴵˢGAGᴴᴵ·ᴬ-*ia ku-i-uš-ša*
26 *ar-ḫa-ia-an iš-ḫar-nu-ma-iz-zi u-uz-zi-ia-ia ḫar-na-a-ú*
27 *pí-ra-an* 2-ŠU IŠ-TU 2 UDU 4 MUŠEN-*ia ši-pa-an-ti*

Then he smears each birth stool and (its) pegs separately with the blood of two birds. And before the birth stool he offers a flesh-offering twice of two sheep and four birds.

28 *na-aš-ta* UDUᴴᴵ·ᴬ (erased MUNUS?) *mar-kán-zi ma-aḫ-ḫa-an-ma* ᵁᶻᵁÌ
29 *zé-e-a-ri nu zé-e-ia-an-ti-it ši-pa-an-ti*
30 *nu* DINGIRᴹᴱˢ 2 TÁ.ÀM *ku-lu-te-ez-zi*

Then they cut up the sheep. And as soon as the fat is cooked, he offers the cooked (fat). He performs the sacrificial routine twice for the gods.

---

13. As the Hittite language does not differentiate between male and female genders, it is conceivable that the parturient is responsible for constructing the new birth apparatus. However, the priest is clearly the primary actor for the vast majority of ritual actions. Furthermore, the physical condition of the woman at this point of the ritual would surely limit her functional capabilities.

The first group of ritual activities takes place near the *šinapši*, a cult structure in which most of this ritual's activities take place.[14] After the *patili*-priest[15] removes the broken birth stool to a desolate place (and thereby distances its dangerous contamination), he constructs two new sets of birth equipment. It can be assumed that the two sets correspond to the divine couple, Tešub and Hebat, who will be worshipped in parallel rites on subsequent days of the ritual. He places each birth stool on a separate table, and takes two birds and smears each birth stool separately with the blood of one bird.

The flesh offering (*uzi-*) appears in association with the blood rite in numerous Kizzuwatnean rituals, usually in the elliptical phrase: "*uzia zurkia šipanti*" (="he offers the flesh and blood").[16] The lexicographical text from Ugarit RS 20.149 establishes the sense of *uzi* as "flesh": [S]U (Sumerian) = *ŠĪRU* (Akkadian) = uzi (Hurrian) = šîru (Ugaritic).[17] The Hurrian term *uzi-* is apparently derived from Sumerian UZU, meaning "meat."[18] As astutely recognized by Strauß, the Papanikri Ritual provides the key to understanding this phrase, in particular regarding the procedure of the flesh offering.[19] In the *uzi*-rite, the priests cut up the animal (in this case, a sheep), and then present the cooked fat to the gods. Strauß' proposal finds further confirmation in the Šamuha Ritual, as we will see below.

It would seem that the statement in l. 27 that the flesh offering consists of two sheep and four birds assumes that the four birds used for the blood smearing are subsumed under the title flesh offering.[20] These four birds seem to be those that were used in the blood rite. Despite the fact that the text refers to the birds under the title of the flesh offering, it is doubtful that their fat was actually used in the rite. Besides the practical consideration that the amount of fat contained in a bird is negligible, the instructions in lines 28–29 refer only to the fat of the sheep.

---

14. For recent research on the *šinapši*, see the references provided by Singer (*Muwatalli's Prayer*, 56, n. 202) and Trémouille (*dHebat: Une Divinité Syro-Anatolienne*, 174–79).

15. For a description of the various functions of the *patili* priest, see: Beckman, *Hittite Birth Rituals*, 235–38 and Haas, *Materia Magica*, 13–14.

16. Regarding the *–a* ending of *u-zi*-ia, see Strauß, *Reinigungsrituale aus Kizzuwatna*, 92–93,112 and n. 444 with references.

17. See Nougayrol, "Textes Suméro-Accadiens," 232–33. Although originally published as [Z]U (= SÚ), it is better interpreted as the nearly identical SU sign. Cf. Huehnergard, *Ugaritic Vocabulary in Syllabic Transcription*, 46–47.

18. Laroche, "Études de Linguistique Anatolienne," 96, n. 30.

19. *Reinigungsrituale aus Kizzuwatna*, 95.

20. The combination of two birds and a sheep here should not be equated with the ritual of the third day for the purification of the child in which the two birds and a lamb are sacrificed as *waštul* ("sin"), *ḫaratar* ("transgression"), and *enumašši* ("conciliation") offerings respectively (II, 2–3). In this rite, the text states explicitly that these animals are burned, whereas in our case, the fat of the sheep is cooked.

As a result, the scribe's practice of referring to the animals used for the *uzi-* and *zurki-* rites together as a unit demonstrates that a formal unity exists between the independent yet intertwined *uzi* and *zurki* rites.

What is the immediate purpose of this ritual complex? Fortunately, the text provides an explicit answer. At the beginning of the ritual, a priest questions the parturient, beginning from the *a priori* assumption that she must have committed a transgression to anger a god. She must then perform an oracle inquiry to determine the identity of the god so that she can appease him/her via sacrifice (I, 14–17).

The awareness of sin emerges just as clearly from the priest's speech after the execution of the blood-smearing and flesh-offering rites. He declares:

41 *ma-a-an-wa AMA-KA na-aš-ma A-BU-KA ap-pé-ez-zi-az*
42 *ku-it-ki wa-aš-ta-nu-wa-an ḫar-kán-zi na-aš-ma-wa zi-ik*
43 *ka-a pa-ra-a ḫa-an-da-an-ni na-aš-ma za-aš-ḫi-it ku-it-ki*
44 *wa-aš-ta-nu-wa-an ḫar-ta nu ḫar-na-a-uš ḫu-u-ni-ik-ta-at*
45 GIŠGAGḪI.A-*ma-wa du-wa-ar-na-ad-da-at ki-nu-na-wa*
46 *ka-a-ša* DINGIR-*LUM* 2 TÁ.ÀM *šar-ni-ik-ta*[21]
47 *nu BE-EL* SÍSKUR *pár-ku-iš nam-ma e-eš-du*

"If your mother or father have committed some sin in the end, or you have just committed some sin as a consequence of divine intervention or in a dream, and the birth stool was damaged or the pegs were broken, O divinity, she has made atonement for her part two times."[22] Then the ritual patron shall be pure again.

The priest expresses two possible causes for the divine anger towards the parturient. Either the woman herself has committed a sin, or she is suffering for the transgression committed by her parents.

Several observations should be made regarding the loci of the blood manipulations, that is, the new birth stools. It would seem that these birth stools have no immediate functional purpose. First of all, the text states before the construction of the new birth stools: "The woman gives birth there inside" (14). Although this phrase could be interpreted in multiple ways,[23] it seems that the simplest reading yields that the construction of the new birth equipment takes place *after* the birth. Furthermore, the fact that the priest constructs two sets of birth equip-

---

21. Text: Strauß, *Reinigungsrituale aus Kizzuwatna*, 288.

22. For this understanding of *kāša,* see Rieken, "Hethitisch *kāša, kāšma, kāšat(t)a,*" 265–73.

23. For instance, the text could be merely specifying the location where she will give birth, namely in the *šinapši.* However, since the text does not mention labor at any other point, and since the child, with no prior introduction, is purified on the third day of the ritual, it would seem that this phrase is referring to the birth taking place.

ment indicates that their purpose is symbolic and not functional.[24] Finally, after the associated purification rites have been executed, the birth stools are handed over to the gods (39–40).

Consequently, we should interpret the ritual function of the birth stools symbolically. From the introduction to the ritual, which describes the breaking of the birth stool as a foreboding omen, our first inclination is to assume that the ritual is intended to prevent the danger posed to the woman and/or the child over the course of delivery. However, in light of the fact that the birth takes place before the ritual has essentially begun, it would seem that the purpose of the rite is to divert the danger posed to the child in the non-immediate future. Though the specific means of punishment has yet to be manifested, the reality of unatoned sin is nonetheless perceived as a vital threat. Therefore, it seems that the smearing of blood on the birth stools is intended to remove the woman's sin and thereby prevent it from being transferred to the child.

At this point, a comparison with the Mesopotamian Namburbi rituals is illuminating. Similar to the Papanikri Ritual, Namburbi rituals are employed to avoid the misfortune portended by an omen. Since the Namburbi rituals view the omen itself as an embodiment of the evil, one can eliminate the threat by destroying the omen.[25] This goal can be achieved by various methods, one of the most common of which is to transfer the evil to a clay model of the harbinger which is subsequently disposed of. Although the birth stool in the Papanikri Ritual is also a sign of divine anger and portends punishment, in contrast with the Namburbi rituals, the ritual does not identify the harbinger with the danger itself. Granted, the broken birthstool is disposed of at an uncultivated place (I, 13), but this action receives the most cursory mention in the text. The text focuses on the rites associated with the construction of the new birth stools, which are smeared with blood and ultimately dedicated to the gods. In this light, it becomes clear that the birth stools serve an appeasing function in the ritual. In reaction to the broken birth stool, which expresses the gods' anger towards the parturient, she dedicates the bloodied birth stools in order to demonstrate her desire to appease them. In other words, the medium that reveals the ominous judgment of the gods also provides the means by which the parturient can appeal to the gods and persuade them to change their decree.

The Šamuha Ritual[26] presents a procedure for removing curse from the royal couple and the temple. Unfortunately, we are still missing most of the text, pos-

---

24. According to this interpretation, the equipment on which the parturient gives birth is left unstated, a plausible assumption in light of the birth rituals' generally laconic treatment of the non-ritual aspects of the birth process.

25. See Maul, *Zukunftsbewältigung*, 10.

26. KUB 29.7+; CTH 480; edition: Lebrun, *Šamuha: Foyer Religieux*, 117–43.

sessing only the second tablet, which covers only days eleven through fifteen. Nevertheless, the tablet gives a clear indication of the ritual's vast complexity.

The preserved text opens with a series of rites that take place on the eleventh day by the gates of the temple intended to purify (*gangatai-*) the deity from curses related to the king. This situation is reminiscent of the omen reports of Tudhaliya IV cited above in which a curse against the king defiles the statues of his gods. Apparently, this process is not instigated by actual knowledge of such a curse, but rather, it comes as a response to either some desperate situation (e.g., plague, famine, or military defeat) or in reaction to some foreboding portent.[27]

The first part of the text relates to a series of manipulations of a *gangati* plant performed in the presence of the king himself and the queen's utensils (*UNŪT* MUNUS.LUGAL), which are intended to remove all of the curses from the deity and the royal couple. The fact that the king is present for the ritual while the queen is represented by her utensils is puzzling.[28] After several rites employing the *gangati* plant, the participants bathe and the temple is purified (Obv. 1–36).

On the the twelfth and thirteenth days, the officiant performs a similar series of rituals by the gates of the temple using *ali* wool and barley dough.[29] Here the text raises further possibilities for the origin of the evils:

Obv.

43 EGIR-*ŠU-ma* DINGIR-*LUM ḫu-u-ma-an-da-a-aš ḫu-u-ur-di-ia-aš ud-da-ni-i ku-i-e-eš ku-i-e-eš i-da-a-la-u-e-eš*

44 *an-tu-uḫ-[š]e-eš ta-pu-ša-kán ku-i-e-eš a-ra-aḫ-ze-ni* KUR-*ia pí-ḫu-da-an-te-eš*

45 *at-ta-aš-ša da-a-an at-ta-aš-ša ud-da-ni-i ŠA* BA.BA.ZA *iš-ni-it* SÍG*a-li-it-ta*

46 *ar-ḫa a-ni-ia-az-zi...*

---

27. This conclusion can be inferred from the use of the indeterminate pronoun *kuiški* in the following statement (Obv. 4–5): [*ma*]*n=wa* dUTU-*ŠI=kán kuiški ANA PĀNI* DINGIR-*LIM idalawani memian ḫarzi* ("If anyone has spoken evil before the deity against His Majesty...").

28. Initially, we might assume that the queen is unable to participate because she is ill, and this may even explain the reason for the ritual. However, the length and complexity of the ritual seem to imply a larger-scale threat to the country. In this context, it is worth noting that the text repeatedly utilizes the formula of "holding back/down" (EGIR-*an ḫarkanzi*) the queen's utensils. In contrast, it states unequivocally "but by no means is one to hold back/backwards the king's utensils" (*UNUT* LUGAL-*ma* EGIR-*an* UL *kuwatqa ḫarkanzi*). The lexical entries for the idiom *appa(n) ḫar(k)-* shed little light on the meaning of the rites. Cf. *HED* H, 145: "hold back, hold down, occupy"; *HW*[2] III/14: "dahinter aber halten" (p. 282) or "züruck(be)halten, besetzen" (p. 286).

29. For these rites, see Strauß, *Reinigungsrituale aus Kizzuwatna*, 56–60.

Then she cleans off the deity by means of barley dough and *ali* wool for the matter of all of the curses that any evil men in the proximity or those brought to a surrounding land (imprecated), and for the matter of a father or second father.[30]

These lines reinforce the conclusion that the dire situation that is facing the royal couple is not necessarily of their own device. They may be suffering from the curses of an enemy or from an offense against the gods left over by their fathers. The dough and wool rites are followed each day by the washing of the participants and the lustration of the temple (38–56).

On the evenings of the thirteenth and fourteenth days, rites are performed for the Night Goddess and the goddess Pirinkir. On the night of the thirteenth, the rites are performed on behalf of the queen's utensils, whereas those of the fourteenth are for the king. The Night Goddess, in the form of an image or symbol, is brought down to the "River of Pulling Up" (ÍD *šara ḫuitiawar*), where they perform *dupšaḫi*[31] rites. These involve drawing up the curses from the underworld and casting them into a fire (Obv. 58–Rev. 18).

On the evening of the fifteenth day, the blood-smearing rite (*zurkianza*)[32] is to be carried out as follows:

Rev.
21   *ne-ku-za me-ḫ[ur m]a-aḫ-ḫa-an a-pé-e-da-ni-pát* UD-*ti* MUL-*aš wa-at-ku-zi nu-uš-ša-an* DINGIR-*LUM a*[*-ni-ia-an-zi*]

22   *nu-uš-ša-an* A-[N]A PA-NI ÍD SÍSKUR *zu-ur-ki-ia-an-za du-up-*[*š*]*a-ḫi-ia-aš ḫu-ur-di-ia-aš š*[*i-pa-a*]*n-da-an-zi*

23   A-NA Ú-NU-UT MUNUS.LUGAL [*I*]Š-*TU* KU$_6$ SILÁ-*ia ši-pa-an-da-an-zi* ...[33]

30. For transcription and translation, see *HW*[2] A, 555. Puhvel, "Remarks on 'two'," 100–101) suggests that *dan attašš* (lit. "second father") is an idiom for grandfather. Cf. also *HEG* T, III:91.

31. For the obscure term *dupšaḫi*, see *HEG* T, III:453–54; Trémouille, *ᵈHebat: Une Divinité Syro-Anatolienne*, 179–83.

32. *zukiyanza* appears to be an accusative singular form, reflecting Luwian influence. See Miller, *Kizzuwatna Rituals*, 309 with references regarding *šarlatanza*. Cf. Strauß, *Reinigungsrituale aus Kizzuwatna*, 96, n. 368.

33. Lebrun 's edition (p. 123) adds a dividing line after line 23 that does not exist on the actual tablet.

> When it is evening of that day and a star appears, the deity [is cleansed].[34] Then f[a]cing the river they p[erf]orm the *zurki* rite of the *dupšaḫi*[35] of curse. For the utensils of the queen they perform the rite by means of a fish and a lamb...

The rites are performed facing the river, in the presence of the Night Goddess. The use of a fish for the *zurki* rite appears in two other texts associated with the Night Goddess (see below). Two possible explanations may be offered. On one hand, it can be interpreted as exhibiting an idiosyncrasy of the cult of the Night Goddess. Accordingly, the *zurki* rite, like the related *uzi* rite, should be viewed as sacrificial, and as such, it must be adjusted to the "taste" of the relevant god. On the other hand, Haas has identified a particular stream of ritual tradition, expressed in texts originating in the vicinity of Šamuha, in which fish serve as vehicles for disposing of impurity.[36] In this light, it is possible that the use of a fish in the *zurki* rite may serve a similar function of removing impurity. Whichever of these explanations is correct, the use of a fish for the *zurki* rite in the Šamuha texts provides clear testimony to the tendency of local customs and symbolic conceptions to influence the form in which a ritual tradition is accepted and expressed.

The ritual continues with a series of analogical rites to remove curse and impurity from the temple, god, and royal couple. In the first of these, the priestess takes a soda plant and grinds it into soap. She then compares the curse to a soda plant that grows rampantly within the temple. Thereafter she grinds the plant into soap, neutralizing the danger of the curse (Rev. 24–35).[37]

In the next phase of the rite, the officiant, while holding an onion, compares the evil to an onion which covers the temple with layer after layer of impurity. She then peels the onion to remove the threat from the temple (36–41). The ritual continues with several more symbolic acts sharing the overall goal of banishing the evil (42–66). These are concluded with the sending off of a cow, a female

---

34. Although *anniya*- in the sense "to clean off" is usually preceded by *arḫa* (e.g., Obv. 46 of this text, quoted above; see also *HW*² A, 86), this meaning seems to fit the context. oetze's translation "they w[ipe clean] the god" (*ANET*, 46) seems to reflect a reconstruction based on the verb *anš*- ("to wipe off") However, *anš*- is also usually preceded by *arḫa* (see *HW*² A, 95–96) and there is no further indication in the context of a wiping rite.

35. In this case of a genitival clause within another genitival clause, one might think to translate "the *zurki* of the curse of *dupšaḫi*." However, the numerous other instances in this text in which *hurtiaš* modifies *dupšaḫi*- (cf., e.g., Obv. 60, 64, 69) supports the present translation. The implication of this expression is that the *zurki* rite is a sub-rite of the greater framework established by the *dupšaḫi* ritual. So already Lebrun, *Šamuha: Foyer Religieux,* 137.

36. See Haas, *Materia Magica,* 491–94; Strauß, *Reinigungsrituale aus Kizzuwatna,* 199–201.

37. For an English translation of the series of analogical rites, see A. Goetze, *ANET*, 346.

sheep and a goat to carry away "evil speech" (*idalu uttar*), "perjury" (*NĪŠ* DIN-GIR-*LIM*),[38] and the "impurity of [cu]rse" (*ḫurtaiš* [*pap*]*ratar*).

The preserved text concludes with a sacrificial meal, prescribed as follows:

71   EGIR-*ŠU-ma-za* EN.SÍSKUR *IŠ-TU* NINDA.KUR.RA TUR GA.KIN
      TUR-*in šar-la-a-iz-zi*

72   EGIR-*an-da-ma zu-ur-ki-ia-aš* UZU *zé-e-ia-an-ti-it ši-pa-an-ti nam-ma*
      ar-na-mi-it-ti

73   *nu* DINGIR-*LUM IŠ-TU* KÙ.BABBAR *ga-an-ga-da-a-iz-zi Ú-NU-UT*
      EN.SÍSKUR -*in IT-TI* DINGIR-*LIM IŠ-TU* KÙ.BABBAR *ga-an-ga-da-a-iz-zi*

Then the ritual patron with a small flat bread and a small cheese performs a praise offering. Then he offers the cooked meat of the *zurki* offering. Then he *arnamittis*.[39] He purifies the deity by means of silver, and he purifies by means of silver the utensils of the ritual patron along with the deity.

Though a precise understanding of the statement *zurkiaš* UZU *zēyantit šipanti* has previously eluded commentators,[40] we may ascertain its meaning by taking the ritual as a whole. This statement describes the *uzi* rite to be performed with the flesh of the lamb and fish whose blood was used in the *zurki* rites mentioned previously (21–23).[41] This interpretation finds support in the reference to *uzi* and

---

38. This term also connotes the curse entailed with failure to fulfill the oath. See *CHD* L–N, sub *lingai*. Compare also Akk. *māmītu* and Heb. אלה. See Feder, "Mechanics of Retribution."

39. The obscure verb *arnamitti* is found exclusively in the Kizzuwatna corpus, nearly all of which are in rituals associated with the Night Goddess (KUB 29.4+ II, 34; KUB 29.7 Obv. 72; KBo 32.176 Obv. 6; Bo 4951 Rev. 12). Interestingly, it always follows the *uzi* and *zurki* rites. In our ritual, it is associated with the cooking of the meat of the sheep whose blood was smeared in the *zurki* rite. In the Walkui Ritual (Rev. 6; see below), the verb is accompanied by the instrumental phrase *IŠTU* BA.BA.ZA ("by means of porridge") and appears with the reflexive particle –*za*. In the Cult Expansion Ritual (II, 34; see below), it is stated that the ritual patron stands up (*šara tiyanzi*) immediately afterwards. Accordingly, this term may signify a food offering, appearing consistently after *šipanti*- ("to libate, offer"). Alternatively, it might denote "to participate in a sacrificial meal," which may even include partaking of the *uzi* offering. This possibility is supported by its appearance with the reflexive particle –*za*. Unfortunately, the only etymology that has been offered (see *HED* A, 162) does not fit the evidence, precluding for now a more definite translation. See further Kronasser, *Umsiedelung der Schwarzen Gottheit*, 49; Beckman, *Hittite Birth Rituals*, 129; Miller, *Kizzuwatna Rituals*, 304; Mouton, "Le rituel de Walkui," 86, n. 86.

40. For previous treatments, see Laroche,"Études de Linguistique Anatolienne," 96; Otten, *Materialien zum hethitischen Lexikon*, 12.

41. Perhaps this understanding underlies Lebrun's translation: "il effectue l'offrande du *zurki* de viande cuite" (*Šamuha: Foyer Religieux*, 132), though he does not elaborate in his

zurki rites from the first day of the Papanikri Ritual (I, 25–35), which explicitly states that the *uzi* rite is "performed by means of the cooked (fat)" (*nu zeyantit šipanti* [29]). Thus, this passage reinforces the conclusion that the *uzi* and *zurki* rites were considered a unit.

To summarize, the Šamuha Ritual provides further evidence of the use of blood smearing to remove evil. In this case, the evil is described primarily as a curse that threatens the royal couple and the temple. Though the text does not explicitly state which objects serve as loci for the blood smearing, the most likely candidates are images or symbols of the deities. As noted above, the ritual exhibits ambiguity regarding the origin of these curses, whether they derive from an act of the royal couple or come from further afield. This ambiguity is consistent with the belief in depersonalized forces of evil and the automatic retribution caused by it. As stated above, this objectified notion of evil opens the possibility for expiatory rituals that offer the counter mechanism by which such threats can be neutralized.

Like the Šamuha Ritual, the Ritual of Walkui[42] is also connected with the Night Goddess' cult. Despite the very partial preservation of the one tablet of this text, it makes a significant contribution to our understanding of the *zurki* rite. The beginning of the text reads as follows:

Rev.

1   *UM-MA* [m]*Wa-al-ku-i* [LÚ]SANGA *ŠA* DINGIR-*LIM MU-ŠI ma-a-an an-du-wa-ah-h*[*a-aš*]

2   *za-aš-hi-ia u-ru-ra-a-an* [SAR] *na-aš-ma* UZU.ŠAH *e-ez-za-zi na-aš-ma-aš-*[*ša-an*][43]

3   *pa-ra-a ha-an-da-a-an-ni-ma A-NA* UZU.ŠAH *an-da tar-na-at-ta-ri*

4   *na-aš-ma-kán I-NA* É.DINGIR-*LIM an-da pa-ra-a ha-an-da-a-an-ni A-NA* SAR[HI.A]

5   *u-ru-ra-a-*[*a*]*n*[SA][R] *an-da ú-e-mi-i-e-ez-zi nu zu-ur-ki-ia IŠ-TU* K[U$_6$]

6   *ši-pa-an*[-*ti a*]*r-na-mi-it-ti-ma-za IŠ-TU* BA.BA.ZA[44]

Thus speaks Walkui, the SANGA priest of the Night Goddess: When a person in a dream eats an *urura*-plant or pork, or by divine providence is exposed to pork, or, in the temple by divine intervention he finds an *urura*-plant among the plants, he performs a blood rite with a f[ish]. Then he *arnamitti*s with porridge.

---

commentary.

42. KBo 32.176 (CTH 496).

43. The reading and reconstruction of the last three signs follows Mouton, "Le rituel de Walkui," 86.

44. Text: Lebrun, "Un rituel de Walkui," 602–3. Cf. also Mouton's transcription ("Le rituel de Walkui," 86).

This ritual outlines the procedure for purification from the defilement that results from various forms of contact with cultically impure substances. The situations that require the performance of the ritual include the eating of pork or an *urura* plant in a dream. Though the use and consumption of pigs are well attested in relation to both the mundane and ritual spheres of Hittite culture, our text treats the pig as defiling.[45] Though not otherwise attested, the same was obviously true for the *urura* plant.

Interestingly, this text focuses on two situations in which the perpetrator has minimal volition: in a dream or by *parā ḫandatar,* a phrase that usually means "divine protection."[46] These cases can be summarized as follows:

in a dream:
    1)   eating a taboo food
by *parā ḫandatar*:
    2)   making contact with pig's meat
    3)   finding the *urura* plant in the temple

Regarding the first of these, Mouton suggests that the ritual reflects the belief that the eating of pork, even in a dream, can render a person impure.[47] Regarding *para ḫandatar,* she proposes that the Hittites believed that even if a person's actions stem from his own volition, misdeeds can only take place if he is abandoned, temporarily or permanently, by his protective deity.[48] According to this understanding, the sense of *para ḫandatar* in these contexts is the opposite of its usual sense of "divine protection" and refers to a situation whereby the gods abandon the human to his fate. Alternatively, one might understand these passages as referring to violations that occur as a result of divine orchestration. A suggestive biblical parallel to such an idea can be found in Exod 21:13–14: "The one who fatally strikes a man shall be put to death. But if he did not plan, and God caused it to happen by his (i.e., the accidental murderer's) hand, I will appoint for you a place to which he can flee." According to this latter interpretation, *para ḫandatar* might be best translated "divine compulsion."

However we may understand the underlying beliefs, it is clear that the ritual focuses on involuntary acts. For this reason, we might compare the usage of *para ḫandatar* in this text with the Western legal concept "Act of God," which refers to an uncontrollable event that can exempt a litigant from contractual respon-

---

45. For an analysis of the Hittites' ambivalent attitude towards the pig, see Mouton, "Le rituel de Walkui," 92–100 and Collins, "Pigs at the Gate."

46. This is an abbreviated form of *para ḫandandatar.* See *CHD* P, 130–33.

47. Mouton, "Le rituel de Walkui," 90, 101.

48. Mouton, "La différenciation entre rêve," 523–31. See also Kammenhuber, *Materialien zu einem hethitischen Thesaurus,* 140–52.

sibility. Although the import of these statements is not entirely clear, they may perhaps be construed as implying that the opportunity to make amends with the relevant deities would not be available had the transgression been committed brazenly.

Interestingly, the pair of terms "dream" and "divine providence" appears also in the Papanikri Ritual. As cited above (p. 12), the priest declares as follows:

> "If your mother or father have committed some sin in the end, or you have just committed some sin as a consequence of divine intervention or in a dream, and the birth stool was damaged or the pegs were broken, O divinity, she has made atonement for her part two times" (I, 41–46).

Though the Papanikri and Walkui rituals differ in that only Papanikri explicitly refers to transgression (*waštuwant*), both texts make clear that the primary remedy for the impurity/offense is the blood rite.

As a result, the Walkui and Papanikri rituals are concerned with the formal consequences of the act, whether defilement or sin, and not their internal motivations. As such, we find a certain similarity to the Šamuha ritual, which focuses on the effects of evil rather than its exact cause. However, in the case of Walkui, the offensive act is known, although it was committed involuntarily, while in the case of the Šamuha ritual, the presence of a curse is inferred from some external event, although its source remains indeterminate. In all of these texts, one of the primary means of eliminating these various forms of depersonalized evil is the blood rite.

PURIFICATION OF A DEFILED SANCTUARY

Blood-smearing plays a significant role in temple rituals from Kizzuwatna. For example, the ritual of the *purapši* priests Ammihatna, Tulbi and Mati, which describes the procedure to purify the temple after the discovery of a sacrilege committed there, requires a *zurki* rite as a step in reinitiating the temple for cult use.[49] The text defines its purpose as follows:

Obv. I
3   *ma-a-an-kán I-NA É.DIN[(GIR-LIM an-da šu-up-pa-i)]*
4   *pé-di it-ḫi-uš ku-iš-ki an-da ⌜ da-a- i⌝*

---

5   *na-aš-ma-kán ku-in im-ma a-pé-e-da-ni p[(é-)]di*

---

49. KBo 23.1+ (CTH 472). The first edition of this text was published by Lebrun ("Les rituels d'Ammihatna," 139–64). Recently, Strauß has republished the text (*Reinigungsrituale aus Kizzuwatna*, 253–71).

6   *mar-ša-aš-tar-ri-in an-da-an i-ia-zi nu ki-i* [(SÍS)KUR.]-*ŠU*[50]

If someone brings *impurity*[51] into a holy place inside the temple, or performs any kind of sacrilege inside that place—this is its ritual.

The ritual begins with the removal of two "icons of the Deity" (*BIBRU* DIN-GIR-*LIM*)[52] from the temple (Obv. I, 9–10). The ritual's treatment of these icons makes it clear that they considered vehicles of the divine presence. As will become clear below, these two vessels correspond to the divine couple Tešub and Hebat. Using flat breads, wine, oil, and red wool, the SANGA priest evokes the deity (apparently Tešub) from wherever he may have fled at the time when the impurity intruded upon the temple (19–25). Subsequently, "the chief pure woman of the temple"[53] performs a series of analogical rites in order to remove impurity from the icons (26–38). Then the icons are immersed in a river and anointed (39–44). At this point, a ^{LÚ}AZU priest waves a partridge (MUŠEN *ḪURRI*)[54] over the icons to absorb their defilement.[55] Then a big bird (MUŠEN. GAL)[56] is burned for "the way" as a burnt offering (*ambašši*),[57] apparently a gift

---

50. Text: Strauß, *Reinigungsrituale aus Kizzuwatna*, 258.

51. The meaning of the rare term *idḫiuš* is not clear. Haas (*Die hurritischen Ritualter-mini*, 80, n. 115) connects the term with the Hurrian stem *id-* (= "(zer)schlagen"; see Neu, *Das hurritische Epos der Freilassung*, 198).

52. Although *bibru* is frequently translated "rhyton," Güterbock has suggested that this term is applied to a wider array of iconic figures ("Hethitische Götterbilder und Kultobjeckte," 212–14.

53. *ŠA* É.DINGIR-*LIM šalli-<iš>* MUNUS-*za párkuiš*. Emendation according to KBo. 23.1 Rev. III, 2. See Strauß, *Reinigungsrituale aus Kizzuwatna*, 259 n. 99, who translates "eine hochgestellte reine Frau." In contrast, the present translation assumes that *šalliš* is referring to a defined position or status, i.e., "the chief pure woman of the temple," which is usually ortho-graphically represented by GAL in the first position (see *CHD* Š, 99–100). This interpretation could partially account for the peculiar word order and perhaps even the incongruent reading *šalli* in KBo. 23.1. Cf. Lebrun, "Les rituels d'Ammihatna," 156 who makes additional sugges-tions.

54. Hittite MUŠEN *ḪURRI* (=Sumerian: buru₅-ḫabrud-da^{MUŠEN}; Akkadian: *iṣṣūr ḫurri*) is probably a partridge, although some identify it with the sheldrake. In Mesopotamia, its appearance was understood to be a foreboding sign, which could require exorcistic Namburbi rites, but it also seemed to epitomize sexual potency, as can be ascertained from its use in šà.zi. ga rituals. See *CAD* I, 207–8 sub. *iṣṣūr ḫurri*; Veldhuis, *Religion, Literature, and Scholar-ship*, 231–33. In Hatti, it appears in oracle texts (see Kammenhuber, *Orakelpraxis, Träume und Vorzeichenschau*, 11) as well as in rites to remove impurity (see Haas, *Materia Magica*, 488–89; Strauß, *Reinigungsrituale aus Kizzuwatna*, 75–76). Cf. also *CHD* L–N, sub *laḫ(ḫ)anza(na)*.

55. For the waving ritual, see Strauß, *Reinigungsrituale aus Kizzuwatna*, 72–76.

56. Haas views this term as corresponding to either a goose or a duck (*Materia Magica*, 487–88).

57. For *ambašši*, see Haas, *Geschichte der hethitischen Religion*, 661–65; Schwemer,

offering intended to show appreciation to the path that led the deity back, here conceived of in a deified form (48–50). Now the action returns to the temple. As the icons are reinstalled next to the altar, the first day concludes with officiants performing two sets of *kupti* rites for the male and female gods of the *šinapši* (51–55).[58]

The second day of the ritual is fully devoted to the performance of the *uzi-* and *zurki-* rites (56–57). The text does not reveal any further details on these rites, neither which animal is used nor what is the target of the blood smearing. Nevertheless, based on the text's overall focus on the icons and on analogy to similar rituals (see below), it is probable that these vessels are the recipients of the blood. The only other activity of this day is the preparation of "waters of purification" in the evening by leaving them under the stars for the night (58–59).

On the third day, they perform the *gangati* rite for the deity. Then they wave various creatures—an eagle, a falcon, a lamb, a young goat, and a partridge as well as a *ḫušti* stone—over the icons. Then the "waters of purification" are used to wash the deity and sprinkle the temple (II, 1–5). Then two geese are burned as "anger" (*parliya*) and "sin" (*arniya*) offerings by the gates of the temple (7–8). Then they burn two big birds inside the temple for *duwantiḫia* and "reconciliation" (*enumašši?*)[59] and a lamb as a well-being (*keldi*) and burnt (*ambašši*) offering.[60] Then a goat is slaughtered for well-being (9–13). These offerings of the birds and the lamb are then repeated in a parallel manner beside the temple of Hebat (14–16). From the explicit reference to Hebat, we can extrapolate that the main god in the ritual is the goddess' spouse Tešub.

At this point, we can take a step back to determine the overall goals of this ritual and the *zurki* rite's place among them. The main purpose of the first day's rituals is to evoke the deity back into the icons and to then remove defilement (*papratar*) from him by means of various symbolic acts performed on the icons, thereby rendering the deity clean (*parkuiš*).[61] The *gangati* and *zurki* rites of the second day, which follow the reinstallation of the icons in the temple, seem to continue the process of purification of the first day. However, it may be justified to assume a subtle functional distinction between the activities of first and second days. Whereas the first day's rites focus on the removal of defilement

---

"Das alttestamentliche Doppelritual," 83–85; Strauß, *Reinigungsrituale aus Kizzuwatna*, 113–18.

58. For further discussion of *kupti* rites, see Strauß, *Reinigungsrituale aus Kizzuwatna*, 79–92.

59. For this rendering, cf. Haas and Wilhelm, *Riten aus Kizzuwatna*, 75–77; *HW*[2] E, 44.

60. For the latter two offerings, see Schwemer, "Das alttestamentliche Doppelritual," 81–116.

61. I, 30–31, 36–37, 46–47.

from the deity, which required the immediate removal of the icons from the sanctuary, the second day's purifications serve to reinitiate the icons and the sanctuary itself for cultic use. This distinction is reflected by the fact that the icons are returned to the temple for the second day's rites.

It is interesting to note that the catalog tablet KBo 31.4+ refers to a ritual from Kummanni authored by, among others, Mati and Papanikki.[62] Several scholars have identified this Papanikki with Papanikri.[63] The existence of numerous similarities between this ritual and the Papanikri Ritual strengthens the assumption that these texts originated within the same circle of Kummanni priests. In addition to the mention of rites that are characteristic of the entire Kizzuwatna corpus (e.g., *gangati, uzi-zurki* rites), the common elements include the mention of the *šinapši* and the performance of parallel rites for Tešub and Hebat.

RITUALS FOR ESTABLISHING NEW CULTIC STRUCTURES

Blood smearing not only serves as a means to remove objectified forms of evil such as sin, contamination and curse, but it is also used to consecrate buildings and objects for use in the cult.

The foundation ritual KBo 15.24+ describes the rites needed to prepare the locus of a new cult building. The most prominent of these is the depositing of cult figurines in the ground beneath the future structure's foundations.[64] By virtue of our knowledge of similar practices attested in ancient Mesopotamia from the third millennium B.C.E.[65] as well as the reference to Mesopotamian gods, we must regard this ritual as a Hittite adaptation of a Mesopotamian tradition.

At the beginning of the preserved part of the text, the ritual officiant sacrifices to a pit, which acts as the gatekeeper to and from the underworld, requesting that it not permit any infernal deities or dangerous forces from rising.[66] Then the officiant anoints with oil and libates wine at the locations on the ground which correspond to the future location of various cultic implements, including an altar and a table (II, 1–30).

---

62. Rev. V, 21'–28'. See Dardano, *Hethitischen Tontafelkataloge aus Ḫattuša*, 104. For the location of Kummanni, see below, p. 232.

63. For example, see Kümmel, "Kummanni," 335 and Trémouille, "Une objet cultuel," 74.

64. Text edition: Boysan-Dietrich, *Das hethitische Lehmhaus*, 60–76. Previous edition: Kellerman, *Rituels de Fondation Hittites*, 165–78.

65. See Ellis, *Foundation Deposits in Ancient Mesopotamia*, 131–38; Kellerman, *Rituels de fondation hittites*, 195.

66. Kellerman assumes that the offering is also meant to appease these deities (*Rituels de fondation hittites*, 193).

Subsequently, he creates four bronze statues of "the (divine) mistress who built the house" (^{d}NIN.É.MU.EN.DÙ) and a winged bull made of bronze (GUD-*i*[*a* x x x] *partauwarašit* ZABAR).[67] The four statues will be deposited in the ground at the four corners of the foundation together with fruits, grains, precious stones, honey, wine and other gifts. The bronze bull will be deposited under the place of the pillar (^{GIŠ}*šarḫuli*) (31–65).[68]

Then the officiant arranges a sacrificial meal in honor of the gods Ea, Gulla, Hebat and the mistress who built the house. On a wooden table located across from the "pillar," he sets up various breads, including ten "ear breads," which are then placed in the ears of the statues. At this point the text seems to state, in an only partially decipherable line, that these statues become "gods of the foundation."[69] If this reading is correct, we may interpret this statement as referring to the deification of the figurines. Subsequently, fruits, wine, beer and other items are offered to Ea (II, 66–III, 19).

The officiant then smears the cult objects with blood:

20   *na-aš-ta* 1 UDU *A-NA* ^{d}É-A *ši-pa-an-ti nu* 4 ALAM ZAB[AR
        ^{d}NIN.É.MU.UN.DÙ]
21   GUD ZABAR *a-ia-ak-ki-in-na iš-ḫar-nu-ma-a-iz-zi nu-k*[*án*
22   *šu-up-pa ḫu-i-šu* SAG.DU GÌR^{MEŠ} ^{UZU}GAB ^{UZU}ZAG.UDU *da-*[*a-i*
23   *na-at PA-NI* ^{GIŠ}BANŠUR ^{d}A-A *da-a-i*[70]

---

67. Although there is a small break between GUD and *partauwarašit*, which could open the possibility that the wings are attached to another creature, the appearance of GUD ZABAR below (III, 14, 21) strengthens the assumption that the bull is winged, as assumed by most translators (so Kellerman, *Rituels de fondation hittites* and Boysan-Dietrich, *Das hethitische Lehmhaus*; *CHD* P sub. *partawar*).

68. On this term, see Boysan-Dietrich, *Das hethitische Lehmhaus*, 83–84.

69. III, 19. I would suggest reading this line as: *na-at-za ša-am$^?$-ma-na-aš* DINGIR^{MEŠ} *ki-ša-an-*[*ta*]-*ri* ("Then they become gods of the foundation.") I am very grateful to Prof. Jared L. Miller for providing me with photos of this line and his helpful suggestions, especially the reading ŠA for the first sign of *šam(m)anaš*. The main difficulty is the reading of the second sign, understood here as AM. Regarding the last sign, I have followed Otten's collation, AŠ, although in the photos it resembles NI. Previous attempts to understand this line, besides being based on substantial emendations, are untenable on contextual grounds. Kellerman reads the second word as *ú$^!$-tum$^!$-*[*m*]-*a$^?$-na-aš* (*Rituels de fondation hittites*, 170). More comprehensible is Boysan-Dietrich's reconstruction: *ú$^!$-i$^!$-*[*l*]a-*na-aš* (p. 72). This reading would yield the translation: "They become gods of clay." Though attractive, this reading does not fit the signs, nor can it be reconciled with the fact that the figurines in the text are constructed from bronze, not clay!

70. Text: Boysan-Dietrich, *Das hethitische Lehmhaus*, 72. Though the text at this point is from Manuscript B (KBo 13.114), I have continued with the line numbering of Manuscript A (KUB 32.137+) along with Kellerman. Boysan-Dietrich arranges the text here according to B (III, 2–5).

> Then he slaughters 1 sheep to Ea. He bloodies the 4 bronze statues of the mistress who built the house, the bronze bull and the *AYAKKU*. He takes the raw sacrificial meat, the head, the legs, the chest and the shoulder, and he places them before the table of Ea.

Here the officiant smears with sheep's blood the cult images and the *ayakku*. *ayakku* is an Akkadian loanword that refers either to an important cult object or the sanctuary itself.[71] After the head, legs, shoulder and chest are presented to Ea, the heart and liver are cooked (24–26). In the following sacrificial meal, the officiant drinks three times to Ea, Kulla, and Hebat. Then he drinks three times to Ea and the divine mistress (27–41).

This ritual incorporates numerous elements from Mesopotamian religion. An examination of these elements may shed light on these rites. Although the sacrificial meal addresses several gods, it clearly focuses on Ea. Ea is associated in Mesopotamian mythology with wisdom and building. The otherwise unknown goddess ^dNIN.É.MU.EN.DÙ who serves as Ea's female counterpart in this ritual seems to be charged with securing divine protection for the new structure.

Furthermore, the term ^{NINDA}*hazizi* for "ear breads" is a loanword from the Akkadian *hasīsu*, which, like the Sumerian GEŠTU(G), denotes both "ear" and "wisdom."[72] In fact, Kellerman suggests that the insertion of these breads into the ears of the statues is intended to convey Ea's knowledge of building to these statues.[73] However, since these breads appear in diverse contexts, it is difficult to pin down their exact function here. For example, the breads appear in Babylonian elimination rituals which address Ea,[74] as well as in Hittite evocation rituals as a means of evoking various gods from the underworld.[75]

As a whole, this ritual seeks to protect the future temple from negative influences and secure the blessings of the gods. One of the critical means of guaranteeing the latter is by depositing deified figurines in the building's foun-

---

71. The Akkadian term is probably a Sumerian loanword, as it appears as a textual variant for É.AN.NA ("House of Heaven"). See most recently Beaulieu, "Eanna=Ayakkum in the Basekti Inscription," n. 36. In several texts, it appears in parallelism with temples. Furthermore, *ayakku* appears as an epithet for gods in the form ^dBelat-Ayakki in Hittite and NA texts. For sources, see *CAD* A, I, 224–25, which translates "(a structure in a temple)." Cf. *AHw* I, 24: "Heiligtum, Hochtempel (?)." Friedrich & Kammenhuber translate "Gegenstand im Tempel" (*HW²* A, 47). Cf. also Otten, "Bemerkungen zum Hethitischen Wörterbuch," 92.

72. See von Brandenstein, "Ein arisches und ein Semitisches Lehnwort," 58–62; *CAD* H, 126–27; *HEG* H, 233; *HED* H, 284–86. Cf. Laroche, *GLH*, 100.

73. Kellerman, *Rituels de fondation hittites*, 195–96.

74. For example, see the sources cited by Maul, "^{NINDA}GEŠTUG = *hasīsītu*," n. 7.

75. For example: KUB 15.35+ (CTH 716) iv 11–12.

dation. This action may seek to secure the presence of the divine mistress in the new structure, or at least to secure her blessing.

Like other aspects of this text, the blood rite seems to combine diverse ritual traditions. On one hand, the smearing of blood on the statues strongly resembles the Kizzuwatnean *zurki* rite of purification and expiation. On the other hand, the context of the rite seems more closely aligned with Mesopotamian foundation rituals. Interestingly, in the latter context blood libations are offered to the chthonic deities in order to appease them for the territorial intrusion caused by the process of digging into the ground and laying the foundations for the new structure.[76] For example, a letter to Essarhaddon mentions the smearing of the foundation stones with blood:

> 15 [*nu-uk x in*]*a* 1 KÙŠ-*a-a* 7 *pu-la-a-ni*
> 16 [*x x x x*] KAB *i-šak-ku-nu* UDU.NITÁ *ina* UGU-*ḫi*
> 17 [*i-ṭa-ab-b*]*u-ḫu da-a-mu ú-la-ab-bu-šu*
> 18 [*ina* ŠÀ *uš-še i-š*]*ak-ku-nu a-na ṣa-a-ti* UD-*me*

Seven foundation stones of x cubits will be placed [...right and l]eft, and a ram [will be slaught]ered upon them. They will be covered with blood, and placed [in the foundations] until far-off days.[77]

A similar rationale may be discerned in our Hittite ritual. If so, our ritual seems to reinterpret the form of the Kizzuwatnean blood rite, namely the smearing of a cult object with blood, in accordance with the function of blood in Mesopotamian foundation rituals. As will be argued in more detail below (p. 234), it appears that as the blood rite spread beyond its original Syrian milieu, it became subject to reinterpretation in light of divergent symbolic meanings attributed to blood in its new contexts.

The "Cult Expansion Ritual" for the Night Goddess (CTH 481) deals with the establishment of a new temple for her worship.[78] This goal is accomplished by the construction of a new gold statue of the goddess and dividing the divine presence so that it can dwell in both the old and new temples.

After a day of preparations, "waters of purification" (*šeḫeliaš widar*) are drawn and brought to the old temple where they are placed on the roof to pass the night. Then, using red wool and fine oil, they evoke the deity into the old temple from the seven paths, the seven footpaths, the mountain, the river, the steppe, the sky and the earth. This evocation channels part of the Night Goddess' presence

---

76. For relevant sources and references, see Ambos, *Mesopotamische Baurituale*, 70–71.

77. Text and Translation: Parpola, *Letters from Assyrian and Babylonian Scholars*, 292.

78. Text edition: Miller, *Kizzuwatna Rituals*, 272–97. Cf. also B. J. Collins's recent translation in *COS* 1.70:173–77.

into a woolen fabric called an *ulihi*, which is then bound to the deity's statue (55–74). As suggested by Miller, the *ulihi* may be the same as the red wool used to evoke the deity.[79] In the subsequent days of the ritual, the participants will perform further rites to summon the deity's presence into her statue. The deity's presence will then be divided and brought to the new temple.

The activities of the third day are described as follows:

II

14   *I-NA* UD 3^{KAM}-*ma ma-a-an lu-uk-kat-ta nu* EN SÍSKUR *ka-ru-ú-a-ri-wa-ar*

15   *hu-u-da-ak I-NA* É DINGIR-*LIM ú¹-iz-zi* MUL$^{HI.A}$ *nu-u-a a-ra-an-da*

16   *na-aš-ta še-he-el-li-ia-aš* A.A$^{HI.A}$-*ar šu-uh-ha-az kat-ta*

17   *ú-da-an-zi na-aš-ta* EN SÍSKUR *A-NA PA-NI* DINGIR-*LIM an-da*

18   *ú-iz-zi na-aš A-NA* DINGIR-*LIM UŠ-KE-EN na-aš* EGIR SISKUR *ša-ra-a hu-it-ti-ia-u-aš*

19   *ti-ia-zi na-aš-ta* ^{LÚ}SANGA DINGIR-*LAM a-a-pí-ta-az*

20   *ša-ra-a* 7-*ŠU hu-it-ti-ia-az-zi* EN SÍSKUR-*ia-kán*

21   7-*ŠU ša-ra-a hu-it-ti-ia-az-zi*

On the third day in the morning, the ritual patron comes immediately at dawn into the temple. While the stars are still standing, they bring down the waters of purification from the roof. Then the ritual patron comes in before the deity. He bows to the deity. He then proceeds with the ritual of pulling up. Then the priest evokes the deity upwards from the pit 7 times, and the ritual patron evokes (her) upwards 7 times.

22   *nam-ma-at-kán IŠ-TU* É DINGIR-*LIM I-NA* ^{É}*A-BU-US-SÍ pa-ra-a*

23   *ú-wa-an-zi nu I-NA* ^{É}*A-BU-US-SÍ* SÍSKUR *du-up-ša-a-hi-in*

24   *i-ia-an-zi A-NA* SISKUR *du-up-ša-hi-ti-i* 1 ^{NINDA}*mu-u-la-ti-in*

25   *da-a-an-zi a-aš-zi-ma-kán ku-iš* 1 ^{NINDA}*mu-u-la-ti-{x}-iš*

26   *na-an* ⌊EGIR⌋ SISKUR *du-up-ša-hi-ti-i šar-la-at-ti da-an-zi*

27   *nu A-NA* ⌊EN⌋ SISKUR *ku-wa-pí a-aš-šu na-aš a-pád-da pa-iz-zi*

28   *ma-ah-ha-an-m*[(*a*)] *a-pé-e-da-ni* UD-*ti ne-ku-uz me-hur*

29   MUL-*aš wa-at-ku-uz-zi nu* EN SÍSKUR *ka-ru-ú-i-li*

30   *I-NA* É DINGIR-*LIM ú-*[*iz*]-*zi na-aš A-NA* DINGIR-*LIM Ú-UL UŠ-KE-EN*

31   ⌊*na*⌋-*aš* EGIR SISKUR *zu-úr-ki-ia-aš* ⌊*ti*⌋-*ia-az-zi*

32   ⌊*nu* SÍSKUR⌋ *zu-*⌈*úr*⌉-*ki-aš IŠ-TU* ⌈KU₆⌉ *ši-pa-an-da-an-zi*

33   EGIR-*ŠU-ma* MÁŠ.TUR *na-aš-ma* SILA₄ *ši-pa-an-da-an-zi*

34   *nu* EN SÍSKUR *ar-na-mi-in-ti na-aš ša-ra-a ti-ia-zi*

---

79. See Miller, *Kizzuwatna Rituals*, 409–10. Cf. Kronasser, *Umsiedelung der Schwarzen Gottheit*, 45–46; Haas and Wilhelm, *Riten aus Kizzuwatna*, 171–72; Haas, *Geschichte der hethitischen Religion*, 505–6; Beal, "Dividing a God," 203.

Then they come out of the temple into the storehouse. In the storehouse they perform the *dupšahi* ritual. For the *dupšahi* ritual they take 1 *mulati* loaf, but the *mulati* loaf that remains they take back for the *dupšahi* (and) the praise ritual. The ritual patron may go wherever suits him. And when on the evening of that day a star appears, the patron comes into the old temple. He does not bow to the deity. He then proceeds with the ritual of blood. They perform the ritual of blood with a ⸢fish⸣. And afterwards, they slaughter a kid or a lamb. The ritual patron *arnamiti*s and stands up.

35   *na-aš* EGIR SÍSKUR *šar-la-at-ti ti-ia-⸤zi⸥ nu* SISKUR *šar-la-at-ta-aš*
36   *IŠ-TU* UDU *ši-pa-an-da-an-zi nam-m[a* E]N SÍSKUR *IT-TI* DINGIR-*LIM*
37   ⸤*IŠ*⸥*-TU* KÙ.BABBAR *ga-an-ga-⸢ti-ia-zi⸣-ia* ⸢*ga*⸣*-an-ga-da-an-zi*
38   E[(GIR-Š)]*U-⸤ma⸥* SILA₄ *am-ba-aš-ši-ti-i wa-ar-nu-wa-an-zi*
39   *nu* E[N SÍSK]UR *UŠ-KE-EN na-aš-za ar-ḫa I-NA É-ŠU pa-iz-zi*

Then he proceeds with the praise ritual and they perform the ritual of praise with a sheep. Then they purify the patron along with the deity using silver and *gangati.* But afterwards they burn a lamb as a burnt offering. The ritual patron bows, and he goes away to his house.

As in the Šamuha (Rev. 22–23) and Walkui rituals (Obv. 5–6), a fish is used here for the *zurki* rite.[80] As noted above, fish are frequently employed in the cults of the Night Goddess and Pirinkir.

Though not explicitly stated, it seems that this *zurki* rite involves the smearing of blood on the goddess' statue. This act is followed by the slaughter of a sheep or lamb, which is perhaps intended as the *uzi* offering. The slaughter is followed by the verb *arnamitti-*, which may signify an additional offering.[81] Then the deity and patron are purified by means of the *gangati* plant and silver.

On the nights of the third and fourth days, the officiants perform a set of ritual activities and offerings focusing on the goddess Pirinkir. After performing a ritual of well-being for Pirinkir on the roof of the old temple, they bring her down (apparently in the form of an astral disk)[82] and carry her inside the temple. Then they perform a ritual of well-being. Then the ritual patron "rewards" (*piyanāizzi*) the deity, the priest and the *katra* women. Then he bows and returns home (II, 40–III, 11).

A comparison of the evocation rites for the Night Goddess and Pirinkir yields an important insight into the significance of blood in this ritual. Whereas the text describes in some detail a series of rites intended to draw the Night God-

---

80. Miller, *Kizzuwatna Rituals*, 284, n. 435.
81. See above, n. 39.
82. See I,13.

dess up from the underworld (II, 14–21), the evocation of Pirinkir seems to be achieved by means of the rites performed on the roof of the temple (II, 40–III, 11).[83] In this light, one may interpret the smearing of the deity's statue with blood as a means of attracting her from the underworld. Such a usage of blood is consistent with the pervasive belief in Hittite, Mesopotamian, and Greek sources (among others), that the chthonic deities insatiablely crave blood. Alternatively, since the blood rite seems to follow the evocation sequences, the blood might better be viewed as an offering to greet the goddess upon her emergence from the underworld. This sequence in which the blood rite immediately follows evocations is repeated in two subsequent phases of the ritual (see below).

The ritual of the old temple is completed with the following rites and declaration, which have central importance for our overall understanding of the ritual:

III

23   a-pé-e-ma-kán ma-⌈aḫ⌉-ḫa-an I-NA É DINGIR-LIM ka-ru-ú-i-li-aš
24   SISKUR tu-ḫal-zi aš-⌈nu-zi⌉ nu-uš-ša-an Ì.DÙG.GA ᴳᴵˢtal-la-i
25   la-a-ḫu-u-wa-an-⌊zi⌋ nu PA-NI DINGIR-LIM ki-iš-ša-an me-ma-i
26   na-ak-ki-iš-⌊za⌋ DINGIR-LUM NÍ.TE-KA pa-aḫ-ši DINGIR-LIM-ni-ia-
      tar-ma-za-kán
27   šar-ri nu ⌊e⌋-da-aš-ša A-NA Éᴴᴵ.A GIBILᴴᴵ.A e-ḫu
28   nu-za na-ak-⌊ki⌋-i pé-e-da-an e-ep nu ma-aḫ-ḫa-an ⌊i⌋-ia-at-ta-ri
29   nu-za e-ni-⌊pát⌋ pé-e-da-an e-ep nam-ma-kán DINGIR-LAM ku-⌈ut⌉-ta-az
30   ar-ḫa IŠ-TU SÍG SA₅ 7-ŠU ḫu-it-ti-ia-an-zi
31   nam-ma-kán ú-li-ḫi-in ŠA Ì.DÙG.GA ⌊ᴳᴵˢ⌋ tal-la-i an-da ⌊da-a-i⌋

As soon as he finishes the tuḫalzi ritual in the old temple, however, they pour fine oil into a tallai vessel. Before the deity he speaks thus: "Esteemed deity, protect yourself but split your divinity. Come to the new temples! Take for yourself an honored place. And when you make your way, take that place." Then they pull the deity from the wall 7 times using red wool. Then he places the uliḫi in the talla vessel of fine oil.

In this unique passage, the priest implores the goddess to split her divinity so that she can inhabit both her old and new temples.[84]

Meanwhile, activities begin to take place also at the new temple. After a purification rite in which a sheep and another animal (broken text) are waved, the new statue of the goddess is brought into the new temple (17–22). At this point, the officiants perform another evocation ritual next to a river. The goddess

---

83. Although an offering of silver for an offering pit (api-) is mentioned in II, 57, nothing else is mentioned regarding its use or any other possible evocations from the underworld. On the chthonic aspect of the Night Goddess, see Miller, Kizzuwatna Rituals, 373–76.

84. For further discussion of this idea, see Beal, "Dividing a God."

is evoked from natural locations such as the mountain, sea, river, steppe, etc. as well as from geographical locations such as Babylon, Akkad, and Elam. Then they erect a tent where they set up a wickerwork table furnished with various food items as well as the *uliḫi*.

The *zurki* rite leads off the next series of activities:

III

56   *nu* SISKUR *zu-ur-ki-⌈ia⌉-aš IŠ-TU* MÁŠ.TUR *ši-pa-an-da-an-zi*

57   EGIR-*ŠU-ma šar-⌈la⌉-at-ta-an-za IŠ-TU* SILA₄ *ši-pa-an-da-an-zi*

58   EGIR-*ŠU-ma* SILA₄ ⌈*am*⌉-*ba-aš-ši wa-ra-a-ni* EGIR-*ŠU-ma A-NA* DIN-
      GIR-*LIM*

59   *IŠ-TU* LÚ ^{GIŠ}⌈BANŠUR⌉ TU₇^{ḪI.A} *ḫu-u-ma-an-da* 1 NINDA *a-a-an* {*ŠA*
      ½ GU₄}

60   *ŠA ½ ŠA-A-TI* ⌊1⌋ ^{NINDA}[GÚ]G 1 NINDA.KU₇ *ŠA* 1 *UP-NI* 1 ^{DUG}*ḫu-u-*
      up-pár KAŠ

61   1 ḪAB.ḪAB ⌊GEŠTIN⌋ *ú-⌈da⌉-an-zi nu A-NA* DINGIR-*LIM a-da-an-na*

62   *pí-an-zi nam-ma* ^{SÍG}*ú-li-ḫi-in I-NA* É EN.SÍSKUR

63   ^{GIŠ}*ar-kam-mi-it gal-gal-tu-u-ri-it pé-e-*⌊*da*⌋*-an-zi*

64   *nu-uš-ši* NINDA *EM-ṢU* GA.KIN.AG *pár-ša-a-an IN-BI*^{ḪI.A}-*ia*

65   *kat-ta-an iš-ḫu-u-wa-an-zi nam-ma* DINGIR-*LAM ḫu-u-uš-ti-it*

66   *ar-ḫa wa-aḫ-nu-an-zi nam-ma* DINGIR-*LAM I-NA* ^É*A-BU-US-SÍ a-ši-ša-*
      an-zi

Then they perform the blood rite with a kid. Then they perform the praise (rite) with a lamb. Then he burns a lamb as a burnt-offering. Then from the table man they bring to the deity all of the soups, 1 warm bread of ½ *upnu*-measure, 1 legume bread, 1 sweet bread of ½ *upnu*-measure, 1 *ḫuppar* of beer (and) 1 pitcher of wine, and they give to the deity to eat. Then they carry the *ulihi* to the house of the ritual patron with a harp and drum. Then beneath her they scatter sour-dough bread, crumbled cheese and fruits. Then they wave a *ḫušti* stone (over) the deity. Then they set the deity in the storehouse.

The absorption of the Night Goddess into the *uliḫi* is immediately followed by the *zurki* rite. Although not explicitly stated, we can assume that the blood is smeared on the *talla*-vessel, which holds the *uliḫi*.

Although the deity is evoked from numerous possible locations, it is significant that the rites take place next to a river, as rivers are oft treated in Hittite rituals as gateways to the underworld. Furthermore, this evocation of the deity is immediately followed by the blood rite. Consequently, this passage reinforces the interpretation suggested above that blood is being treated here as a welcoming feast for the Night Goddess upon her emergence from the underworld.

After additional offerings and a sacrificial meal for the goddess, the participants begin a festive procession to the house of the ritual patron, accompanied by food gifts and music. Since the old cult statue remains in the old temple and the new one is already in the new temple, there is little doubt that the text is using the term "the deity" in reference to the cloth *uliḫi*. After a waving rite with *ḫušti*-stone, the deity is brought to the storehouse of the new temple.

A burnt offering is then performed in the presence of the new cult statue in the new temple. Thereafter, the *ulihi* is attached to the statue. Interestingly, the text states explicitly that blood (*zurki*) and praise (*šarlatta*) rites do not take place at this point (IV, 1–7). This comment raises two important questions. First of all, why would we assume that these rites *should* take place in this situation? By comparing the other instances of these rites in the Expansion Ritual, we observe that they take place immediately after the evocation of the goddess and her absorption into an object. Here, the *uliḫi* that contains her presence is united with her cult statue; hence, we would think to perform the blood and praise rites. This answer brings us to the second question: why do they not take place? Apparently, the ritual postpones the rites until the point when the other *uliḫi*, which was brought from the old temple, is also united with the cult statue.

That evening "waters of purification" are placed on the roof of the new temple under the stars. On the following day, these waters are mixed with the fine oil from the *talla* vessel that holds the *uliḫi* from the old temple. The mixture is then used to wash the wall of the new temple. Through this act, the wall is made pure/holy (*nu kuza šuppiš*).[85] According to Beal's intriguing interpretation, this act has profound theological significance. In his view, the purpose of exposing the "waters of purifications" to the stars is to absorb the Night Goddess's essence from her astral aspect. Indeed, Beal notes that one of the evocations performed in the old temple was to summon the deity from the wall (III, 29–30). Therefore, the use of the *uliḫi*'s oil combined with the waters to wash the temple wall may actually be intended to transfer the deity's essence to the wall(s) of the temple.[86] At this point, the *uliḫi* that was brought from the old temple is tied to the headdress (*kureššar*)[87] of the new statue, completing the transfer of the divine presence (in its divided form) to the new temple.

The rites of the following day reach a climax with the blood-smearing rite:

IV
31 [*ma-a*]*ḫ-ḫa-an-ma I-NA* UD 2^KAM *ne-ku-uz me-ḫur* MUL-*aš wa-at-ku-zi*
32 [*nu*] EN SÍSKUR *I-NA* É DINGIR-*LIM ú-iz-zi na-aš* DINGIR-*LIM-ni* UŠ-KE-EN
33 [*nu I*]*T-TI* DINGIR-*LIM* GIBIL *ku-e* 2 GÍR^ḪI.A *i-ia-an nu a-pé-e*

---

85. For *šuppi*, see Wilhelm, "Reinheit und Heiligkeit," 203–5.
86. "Dividing a God," 207.
87. For this term, see *HED* K, 262–64; Haas, *Materia Magica*, 624–27.

34   [*da-a*]*n-zi nu A-NA* DINGIR-*LIM PA-NI* ^{GIŠ}BANŠUR *a-a-pí pád-da-an-zi*
35   [*na-aš*]-*ta* 1 UDU *A-NA* DINGIR-*LIM e-nu-ma-aš-ši-ia ši-pa-an-da-an-zi*
36   [*na-a*]*n-kán ḫa-at-te-eš-ni kat-at-an-da ḫa-ad-da-an-zi*
37   [SUD-*aš*]-*ma* x *ku-ut-ta-az Ú-UL e-eš-zi* ^{GIŠ}BANŠUR TUR-*ia*-⌐*aš-ša*⌐-*an*
38   [*ki-i*]*t-ta? nu* DINGIR-*LUM* GUŠKIN *ku-ut-ta-an Ú-NU-TE*^{MEŠ}
39   ⌐*ŠA*⌐ [DINGIR-*L*]*IM* GIBIL *ḫu-u-ma-an e-eš-ḫar-nu-ma-an-zi*
40   *nu* DINGIR [GIBI]L É DINGIR-*LIM-ia šu-up-pé-eš-zi* ⌐UZU⌐*I-ma*
41   *ar*-⌐*ḫa*⌐ *wa-ra-a-ni Ú-UL-at ku*-⌐*iš-ki*⌐ *e-ez-za-az-zi*

When a star appears on the evening of the second day, the ritual patron comes
into the temple and bows to the deity. They take the 2 knives that were made
with the new deity, and they dig an offering pit for the deity before the table.
Then they sacrifice 1 sheep to the deity for reconciliation and slaughter it down
into the pit. But the [evocation] from the wall does not take place. But a small
table is [plac]ed? there. The golden deity, the wall, and all of the equipment
of the new deity they smear with blood. He sanctifies the new deity and the
temple. But the fat is burned completely, nobody eats it.

After the ritual patron enters and acknowledges the presence of the deity in the
new temple by bowing, the participants dig an offering pit for the deity. From
here we might infer that, according to the Hittite conceptualization, the deity
maintains her presence in the netherworld simultaneously with her presence
in her temples and in the astral sphere at night. After a reconciliation offering
(*enumašši*), the wall, the cultic utensils, and the golden cult statue are smeared
with blood. The blood rite thereby serves to consecrate (*šuppeš-*) and initiate the
cult structure and apparatus for use.

In absence of an explicit statement in the text, we may assume that the blood
has been taken from the *enumašši* sheep. Likewise, the fat mentioned in the last
line of the text must refer to the same animal. In light of the use of the fat in the
uzi-zurki sequence of the Papanikri Ritual, the fat burning here should probably
be considered an *uzi* offering. This suggestion is corroborated by the fact that
the *zurki* rite is not depicted as such in this passage; rather, it is presented by the
verbal form *ešharnumanzi*. In any case, it is clear that the burnt fat is an offering
to the deity.

In summary, one finds in the Expansion Ritual two different functions attributed to the blood rite. Whereas in several cases it appears as an offering to the
Night Goddess in her chthonic aspect, the final passage attributes a purificatory
or consecratory effect to the rite.

SUMMARY

This survey of the rituals that include the blood-smearing rite has yielded several
significant insights. One observes several aspects that indicate a sacrificial nature

to the rite. First of all, the *zurki* rite is often paired with the *uzi* rite, and in many cases the blood and the flesh are derived from the same animal. Consequently, just as the *uzi* rite is a sacrificial offering that is offered by means of cooking the fat, so too, it may be inferred that the *zurki* rite was considered an offering, at least in some cases. Secondly, the animal chosen for the blood rite is sometimes idiosyncratic to the deity being worshipped. For instance, the blood rite for the Night Goddess involves a fish. This trait might further indicate that the blood was considered an offering.

The object that receives the application of blood varies, but we can make the general observation that the objects metonymically represent the beneficiaries of the ritual—both divine and human. Just as we find blood applied to cult statues and divine signs, the application of blood to the birth stool in the Papanikri Ritual removes transgression from the parturient and her child.

The purpose of the blood rite in numerous examples is to remove impurity and sin. Although the rituals of Papanikri and Walkui specify that the sin is involuntary, other rituals portray a less-defined notion of the evil being removed. The mechanism of metonymy described above allows the officiants to remove intangible forms of evil, including sin, impurity, and curse. Interestingly, we have no examples of the blood being applied to the body of a human being. However, some texts present additional functions for the blood rite. In the foundation ritual KBo. 15.24+, blood serves as a propitiatory gift to the infernal deities. Perhaps the most intriguing use of the blood rite is that found in the last passage of the Expansion Ritual KUB 29.4+, where blood is smeared on cult objects in order to consecrate them for ritual use.

Several tantalizing questions remain. What can be ascertained regarding the origin of the blood rite? What is the source of the expiatory power attributed to blood in these rites? These issues will be addressed in ch. 7, but first, let us examine the *zurki* rite's biblical counterpart.

2

THE BIBLICAL SIN OFFERING

Although blood appears in numerous cultic contexts in the Bible, only a few of the rites resemble the Hittite blood rite. The clearest parallel to the Hittite blood rite is found in the sin offering (חטאת/*ḥaṭṭat*) ritual, which corresponds with the Hittite practice both in its procedural aspects as well as the occasions that require its performance. But to avoid a biased interpretation of the Israelite evidence, we will postpone this comparison until after we have first examined the biblical sources on their own terms.

All of the ritual texts pertaining to the biblical sin offering can be attributed to one of the two Priestly sources: P(riestly) and H(oliness). The dating of these materials remains highly controversial. Through most of the twentieth century, scholarly opinion was sharply divided between those who date P in the exilic or post-exilic periods (Wellhausen), that is, the sixth century B.C.E. or later, and those who date them earlier (Kaufmann).[1] More recently, opinions have moderated somewhat, such that even advocates of a post-exilic dating acknowledge the existence of earlier traditions[2] and advocates of a pre-exilic dating (e.g., Milgrom, Knohl) concede the existence of exilic or post-exilic additions and redactions. Regarding the beginnings of the Priestly composition, opinions vary even among the early daters, spanning within the range of the tenth to sixth centuries B.C.E.[3] I will return to this debate in subsequent chapters, when I will be able to show how my findings bear on this discussion.

For the moment, it is more critical to distinguish between the two Priestly sources responsible for the sin offering rituals. Regarding the relative chronology

---

1. For a convenient survey, see Klingbeil, *Ritual of Ordination*, 70–97, esp. 72–73. For a more comprehensive account, see Krapf, *Priesterschrift und die vorexilische Zeit*.

2. Such a conclusion can hardly be avoided in light of the discovery of the Priestly Blessing of Num 6:24–26 on the scrolls from Keteph Hinnom, which originate from the pre-exilic period (see Kaiser, *Grundriss der Einleitung*, 60).

3. See, e.g., Knohl, *Sanctuary of Silence*, 200–224; Milgrom, *Leviticus*, 13–35; *Leviticus* 2:1361–64.

of H and P, the majority of scholars since the late-nineteenth century tended to view H as earlier. However, this consensus has changed in recent decades in the wake of Knohl's systematic argumentation for H's redaction of P.[4] The present investigation concurs with Knohl's view and adduces further support for it.

In light of the recognition of multiple literary layers comprising the Priestly texts, we will attempt to distinguish between earlier and later strata. At the same time, since a central aim of this study is to engage in a comparison with the Hittite evidence, and in acknowledgement of the conjectural nature of any dia-chronic reconstruction—empirically grounded is it may be, each biblical text will be introduced with a brief treatment of its canonical form.[5]

THE SIN OFFERING RITUAL TEXTS

THE SIN OFFERING RITES OF LEVITICUS 4–5

Synchronic Overview

The laws of the sin offering in Lev 4–5:13 outline the means by which the community or individual can remove the guilt caused by a minor transgression. We will use these passages as a point of departure, since they provide the most complete depiction of the procedure of the sin offering.

The quadripartite structure of Lev 4 establishes a correspondence between the type of ritual procedure and the identity and status of the transgressor(s). The first two of these four sections, pertaining to sins of the anointed priest (הכהן המשיח) and the entire assembly of Israel (כל עדת ישראל), require a manipula-tion of blood inside the Tent of Meeting. The following two cases, pertaining to sins of the chieftain (נשיא) or an individual (נפש אחת ... מעם הארץ) require a blood rite in the courtyard. The cases can be outlined as follows:

I. Tent Ritual
    1. Anointed priest, vv. 3–12
    2. Entire assembly, vv. 13–21
II. Courtyard Ritual
    3. Chieftain, vv. 22–26
    4. Lay individual, vv. 27–35

---

4. See Knohl, *Sanctuary of Silence*. For a history of research, see pp. 1–6. The earlier proponents of this latter order include Elliger, who associated H with the redaction of Leviticus (*Leviticus*, 14–20).

5. See also the detailed analyis of Gane (*Cult and Character*, 45–90).

The Tent Ritual. The two cases described in Lev 4:3–21 require a two-stage sin offering ritual, which involves blood manipulations inside the Tent of Meeting and in the Courtyard. The procedure is described as follows:

> [3]If the anointed priest does wrong to incriminate the people, he shall offer for the wrong he has done a bull of the herd without blemish as a sin offering to YHWH. [4]He shall bring the bull to the entrance of the Tent of Meeting before YHWH, lean his hand upon the head of the bull and slaughter the bull before YHWH. [5]The anointed priest will take some of the bull's blood and bring it into the Tent of Meeting. [6]The priest will dip his finger in the blood and sprinkle some of the blood seven times before YHWH against the veil of the shrine. [7]The priest will place some of the blood on the horns of the altar of perfumed incense, which is in the Tent of Meeting, before YHWH; and the rest of the bull's blood he will pour out at the base of the altar of burnt offering, which is at the entrance of the Tent of Meeting. [8]And all of the suet of the sin-offering bull he shall set aside; the suet that covers the entrails and all of the suet that is around the entrails; [9]the two kidneys and the suet that is around them, that is on the sinews, and the caudate lobe on the liver, which he shall remove with the kidneys—[10]just as it is set aside from the ox of the well-being offering. The priest shall turn them into smoke on the altar of burnt offering. [11]But the hide of the bull, and all its flesh, together with its head and shins, its entrails and dung—[12]all the rest of the bull—shall be taken away to a pure place outside the camp, to the ash dump, and burned with wood; it shall be burned on the ash dump.

After the hand-leaning rite and the slaughter of a bull at the entrance of the Tent, the anointed priest brings its blood into the Tent. He then sprinkles the blood seven times with his finger "towards/against the veil of the adytum" (את פני פרכת הקדש). As this equivocating translation indicates, it is not clear whether the blood should be sprinkled *on*, or merely *in the direction of*, the curtain.[6] Then the priest daubs the blood on the horns of the incense altar. He then exits the Tent and pours out the remaining blood on the base of the altar of burnt offerings. The suet is then removed from the carcass and offered to God on the altar of burnt offering, but the remaining flesh, bones, and skin are brought to a pure place outside the camp to be burnt.

---

6. For further discussion of the expression את פני פרכת הקדש among ancient and modern commentators, see Gane, *Cult and Character*, 72–80. In light of the absence of any mention of the incense altar in Lev 16, the purgation of the shrine described in Lev 16:16b may have been effected by the blood sprinkling on/towards the curtain. Of course, Exod 30:10, asserts that the incense altar was also purged, but, as recognized by many source critics, the latter verse is a gloss (see, e.g., Knohl, *Sanctuary of Silence*, 29). See also the diachronic analyses of Lev 4 and Lev 16 below, on pp. 38–43 and p. 77–97, respectively.

The Courtyard Sin Offering. The procedure of the courtyard sin offering is described as follows:

> [22]When the chieftain does wrong by violating any of YHWH's prohibitive commandments inadvertently, and he incurs guilt, [23]or he is informed of the wrong he committed, he shall bring as his offering a male goat without blemish. [24]He shall lean his hand on the goat's head, and it shall be slaughtered at the spot where the burnt offering is slaughtered, before YHWH: it is a sin offering. [25]The priest shall take some of the blood of the sin offering with his finger and put it on the horns of the altar of burnt offering; and (the rest of) its blood he shall pour out at the base of the altar of burnt offering. [26]All of its suet he shall turn into smoke on the altar, like the suet of the well-being offering. Thus shall the priest make expiation on his behalf for his wrong, that he may be forgiven.

After the hand-leaning rite and slaughter of the goat, a priest dips his finger in its blood and daubs it on the horns of the altar of burnt offerings. The remaining blood is poured out at the base of the altar. The suet is then burned on the altar as an offering. In contrast with the explicit instruction to burn the carcass which appears in the Tent offering (vv. 12, 21), the verses that describe the courtyard offering are silent regarding the means of disposing with the animal's flesh.

Diachronic Analysis

A chronological stratification of Lev 4 can be justified by several converging lines of analysis.[7] Let us begin with some of the evidence based on formal literary grounds. From a comparison of the subunits that comprise Lev 4, the section dealing with the chieftain (vv. 22–26) stands out for several reasons. For instance, in contrast to the other cases which begin with אם (vv. 3, 13, 27, 32), the case of the chieftain opens with אשר (v. 22). This anomaly raises the suspicion that the case of the chieftain served as the first case of the ritual text. Taken by itself, this argument could be parried by the assumption that the editor sought to distinguish between the first two cases, which involve blood rites inside the shrine (vv. 3–21), and the following cases (vv. 22–35), which begin with that of the chieftain, which take place in the courtyard.[8]

---

7. This analysis has benefited from that of Elliger (*Leviticus*, 53–68), but contains several revisions and additions. Cf. also Janowski, *Sühne als Heilsgeschehen*, 196.

8. See Milgrom, *Leviticus*, 246, 248–49 for rebuttals to some of Elliger's main arguments. Cf., however, 636–37, where Milgrom seems to accept to some degree the diachronic reconstruction of Janowski (*Sühne als Heilsgeschehen*, 227–47), which is itself based largely on Elliger's analysis!

However, two additional stylistic differences between the first two cases and the latter cases cannot be explained on such grounds. First of all, the first two cases include an additional clause describing the dedication of the animal containing the verb והקריבו ("he/they shall offer [3b, 14b]") that is absent in the subsequent cases.[9] Secondly, whereas the removal of the suet is described in vv. 22–35 by the verb סו"ר (יסיר\הוסר), this verb is replaced twice in vv. 3–21 with the verb רו"ם (ירים\יורם). This difference is particularly striking in light of the fact that both sections are explicitly dependent upon the instructions for the well-being offering in Lev 3 which employ סו"ר![10]

The distinction between רו"ם and סו"ר is particularly significant because one can plausibly explain an editor's substitution of the former for the latter. While either of these two verbs can be used with the meaning "to remove," they bear distinct connotations. Apparently, verses 22–35 preserve the original formulation, סו"ר, which is a direct reference to the laws of the well-being offering in Lev 3, which uses the verb סו"ר to describe the removal of the suet (vv. 4, 10, 15). However, סו"ר frequently bears a negative connotation, signifying a desire to distance an unwanted entity.[11] Notably, it is used repeatedly in the context of "turning away from evil" (סור מרע) throughout the psalmodic and wisdom literature.[12] In contrast, the verb רו"ם, which means literally "to lift up," bears a distinctly positive connotation. According to the metaphorical scheme that underlies biblical Hebrew (which might well be universal), the opposition "up"/"down" roughly corresponds to "good"/"bad."[13] Since the idiom "to lift up" evokes the privileged position of "up" in the biblical metaphorical conception, it is not surprising that the verb רו"ם and its nominal derivative תרומה are frequently used to describe sacrificial portions allotted to either God or the priesthood.[14] Accordingly, this terminology could be deemed more appropriate for describing the removal of the suet, which was considered God's portion of

---

9. Cf. Rendtorff, *Geschichte des Opfers*, 212–13.

10. The language of the well-being offering instructions is also preserved in v. 9b (יסירנה).

11. This negative connotation is extremely common for both the *qal* form, meaning "to turn away" (e.g., 2 Kgs 15:9, 24; Prov 16:6, 17) and the *hiphil*, "to remove" (e.g., Gen 35:2; Exod 23:25).

12. See, e.g., Isa 1:16; 59:15; Ps 34:15; 37:27; Prov 3:7; 4:27; 13:19; 14:16.

13. This privileged position of "up" vis-à-vis "down" is evident in the Bible's theological conception whereby God is found in high places (e.g., heaven, Mt. Sinai) as well as in its depiction of human interactions, according to which to be "on top" is considered to be a position of power and authority (e.g., Ps 27:6). Obviously, this same phenomenon is present in many languages, including English. See Lakoff and Johnson, *Metaphors We Live By*, 14–21.

14. For example, רו"ם is employed to describe the separation of God's portion (אזכרה) of the grain offering (Lev 2:9; 6:8). Likewise, the noun תרומה denotes the Israelites' contribution to the building of the Tabernacle (e.g., Exod 25:2–3) and the sacred portion of the priests (e.g., Lev 7:14, 32, 34; Num 5:9).

the offering and would explain why the author of vv. 3–21 would prefer to substitute ירים for יסיר. Consequently, these factors might indicate that the first two
sections of the chapter are secondary.

This impression is reinforced by aspects of the cultic terminology and praxis
mentioned, which are found exclusively in the first two sections. The most decisive of these elements is the incense alta,r which has long been recognized as a
relatively late stratum in the cultic texts of the Torah.[15] This argument is largely
based on the "out of place" reference to the incense altar in Exod 30:1–10 and
the mention of *"the* altar" (המזבח) in Lev 16:18, which employs the definite article in reference to the altar of burnt offerings, implying that the original form of
Lev 16 was oblivious to the existence of an incense altar.[16]

Moreover, the rites described in the first two sections involve a seven-fold
sprinkling of blood before the curtain (vv. 6, 17). In my analyses of Lev 8 and
Lev 14,[17] I will bring evidence regarding the secondary nature of the seven-fold
sprinkling in these chapters, which at least raises the possibility that this element
is part of an editorial layer of Lev 4 as well. Indeed, as recognized by Paran,
the seven-fold sprinkling is the seventh ritual act depicted in the sequence Lev
4:4–6, as well as in Lev 14:24–27.[18] In the latter case, the seven-fold sprinkling
appears at the center of a sophisticated introversion, which will be interpreted as
betraying the passage's redaction by H.[19]

Let us now turn to the cultic personalities and institutions mentioned in
Lev 4. The term הכהן המשיח ("the anointed priest") appears in this form or in a
paraphrase in the following sources outside our chapter: Lev 6:15; 16:32; 21:10;
and Num 35:25. All of these sources seem to be relatively late and may even be
attributable to H.[20] In passing, it should be noted that the lateness of this term

---

15. For a recent summary of the research regarding the relevance of the incense altar to
source criticism, see Gane, *Cult and Character*, 26–27.

16. This argument is based on the understanding that the altar mentioned in Lev 16:18
is the altar of burnt offerings, contrary to the opinion of the Rabbis that it is the incense altar
(*m. Yoma* 5:5). The lateness of references to the incense altar was already argued by Wellhausen (*Prolegomena zur Geschichte Israels*, 62–66; *Composition des Hexateuchs*, 137–39) and
Kuenen (*Origin and Composition of the Hexateuch*, 87, 312).

17. See below, pp. 46–48 and 65–67.

18. Paran, *Priestly Style*, 198–99.

19. These similarities despite the absence of distinctive H terminology in Lev 4:3–21
suggests one of the following explanations: 1) H tradents composed some texts in a language
similar to P (though this proposal threatens the empirical grounds for distinguishing these
layers); 2) alternatively, one may posit that the difference in cultic views (and by implication,
the chronological gap) between late P and H may have been negligible.

20. Regarding 6:15, Milgrom argues for the secondary nature of Lev 6:12–18aα and attributes this passage to H (*Leviticus*, 396; *Leviticus* 2:1343). Lev 16:32 is part of the H addition to
Lev 16 (see Knohl, *Sanctuary of Silence*, 27–29; on Num 35, see pp. 99–100).

should not be taken as an indication of the lateness of the practice of anointing priests in Israel, as has been argued by some scholars.[21] Since the anointment of political and cultic officials was a wide-spread practice in the Late Bronze Age, stretching from Anatolia to Canaan, we cannot view the anointment of Israelite priests as a late development.[22] Rather, it is more likely that the term "the anointed priest" reflects either a distinction between the anointment rite of the high priest and that of other priests or a change in practice at some historical point after which the anointment of all priests was discontinued.[23]

Unfortunately, the terms עדה and קהל employed in the following section (vv. 13–21) do not seem to provide a reliable basis for reconstructing a historical setting. Despite the attempts of Hurvitz and Milgrom to show the early provenance of the term עדה, largely based on the fact that this term is replaced by קהל in Ezekiel,[24] this argument is not conclusive in light of use of the term עדה by the fifth-century B.C.E. Jewish community at Elephantine.[25]

Turning to vv. 22–35, in light of the aforementioned arguments for this section's priority, let us examine the term נשיא (v. 22).[26] Milgrom has shown that the Tetrateuch and the book of Joshua employ this term in reference to the wilderness and conquest periods of Israelite history, whereas it is virtually absent in the biblical record of the monarchic period, until it reappears again in Ezekiel in reference to the Davidic monarch.[27] This data leaves us with two possibilities: either the use of נשיא in Lev 4:22 is an archaism employed by an exilic or post-exilic writer that refers to a ruler of monarchal or quasi-monarchal status,

---

21. For references, see Fleming, "Biblical Tradition of Anointing Priests," 401, n. 1.

22. Most pertinent is the anointment of priestesses documented in ritual texts from Emar. For discussion and references, see Fleming, ibid., 401–14.

23. Lev 6:13; 16:32 and Num 35:25 could be understood as indicating that only the high priest was anointed. In comparison, Lev 21:10 indicates that only the high priest received anointment on his head (cf. Exod 29:7; Lev 8:10–12). But this might well be an attempt of an H tradent to harmonize earlier contradictory traditions, which depict the anointment of all priests, with later traditions, which imply that only the high priest was anointed. At the same time, the existence of two separate rites, as depicted in Exod 29 appears to be an authentic tradition.

24. Hurvitz, "The Priestly Term 'Eda," 261–67; idem., Relationship between the Priestly Source, 65–67; Milgrom, "Priestly Terminology," 66–76.

25. See Levine, Leviticus, 202, n. 16. For further discussion and references, see: D. Levy and J. Milgrom, "עדה," TDOT 10:468–80; cf. the critical remarks of the editor, H. Ringgren, 480.

26. See also Duguid, Ezekiel and the Leaders, 11–18; H. Niehr, "נשיא," TDOT 10:44–53 and Rendtorff, Leviticus, 181–82.

27. Milgrom, Leviticus, 246–47. In an isolated usage from the post-exilic period, Sheshbazar is called הנשיא ליהודה (Ezra 1:8), which parallels the term פחה ("governor") in 5:14. For arguments against the possibility that P's usage is a retrojection of this post-exilic usage, see Duguid, Ezekiel and the Leaders, 16–18.

parallel to its usage in Ezekiel, or the term is an authentic reference to the pre-monarchic institution. The latter possibility is favored by the fact that the term in our passage, unlike Ezekiel, lacks the definite article -ה.[28] Furthermore, the structure of the chapter implies that the נשיא is the chieftain who represents his tribe. In fact, the references in Ezra 6:17 and 8:35 to sin offerings of twelve goats on behalf of the twelve tribes seems to be based on this interpretation.[29] This understanding would allow us to understand the structure of Lev 4 as reflecting a gradual progression from communal sins, being the most serious, to individual sins as follows:

- Sins of a national magnitude (High Priest, Assembly)
- Sins of a tribal magnitude (the Chieftain)
- Sins of an individual

Thus, the use of the term נשיא may reflect the origins of the text in a period where tribal leaders still wielded authority in Israelite society, a situation which disappeared rapidly upon the emergence of the monarchy.

Although kin-based structures (i.e., tribes) and certain local governing bodies, such as the "elders" (זקנים), continued to function after the establishment of the monarchy,[30] there is no reason to assume the continued existence of the נשיא after the establishment of the monarchy. This impression is strengthened by a case of inner-biblical exegesis. In Jezebel's plot to execute Naboth, she lays the following accusation against him: "You have cursed (lit. blessed) God and king" (ברכת אלהים ומלך), alluding to the law of Exod 22:27: "You shall not curse God, nor a chieftain of your people" (אלהים לא תקלל ונשיא בעמך לא תאר). In this allusion, the author of 1 Kgs 21:10 is extending the law of the chieftain in Exod 22:27 to apply to a king. This exegetical deduction would seem to correspond to a political development in which the king has usurped the role of the tribal chief.[31]

As a final observation, we should note the absence of any reference to the Tent of Meeting in vv. 22–35, which may indicate that these sections were not adapted to the priestly narrative.[32] Since the older stratum of Lev 4 (vv. 22–35)

---

28. Rendtorff, *Leviticus*, 182.

29. See Blenkinsopp, *Ezra-Nehemiah*, 130.

30. See Zevit, *Religions of Ancient Israel*, 616–21; Barmash, *Homicide in the Biblical World*, 46–49.

31. A similar inference is made by Niehr (*TDOT* 10:47).

32. Aside from the caution that should be exercised with any argument from silence, a further objection can be raised. Verses 26, 31 and 35 refer to the laws of the well-being offering that appear in Lev 3. Since the latter chapter contains several references to the Tent of Meeting (vv. 2, 8, 13), it would follow that Lev 4:22–35 must have been composed with the Tent of Meeting in mind. This objection can be addressed by assuming that the references to the Tent

shows no evidence of a centralized cult or national government, we must leave open the possibility that these instructions may have originated at a local altar. In light of our analysis of the term נשיא, it is possible that they originated during the period before the tribal chieftains ceded their authority to the monarchy. If these deductions are correct, it would appear that the addition of the first two sections of Lev 4, which deal with the sin of the anointed priest and that of the entire congregation, serve to transform the sociopolitical and cultic background of the chapter from rituals that take place at a local altar within the framework of a tribal confederacy to the unified cult of a national entity.

THE ORDINATION RITUAL OF EXOD 29 AND LEV 8

Synchronic Overview

Blood rites play an important role in the ritual for consecrating the Tabernacle and the priesthood. This ritual appears twice in the Torah, first as the Deity's instructions to Moses in Exod 29, and again in the account of their execution in Lev 8.[33] Scholars have come to various conclusions regarding the source-critical relationship between the two texts.[34] These issues will be discussed below. But since the discrepancies between the chapters have little bearing on the basic procedure, we will presently overview the ritual by taking both accounts of the ritual together.

The ritual action begins with the preliminary bathing of Aaron and his sons (Exod 29:4; Lev 8:6). Aaron is then dressed in his cultic attire and anointed (Exod 29:5–7; Lev 8:7–9, 13). At this point, there is a discrepancy between the two texts regarding the anointment of the cult appurtenances, a point which will be examined below. Thereafter, Aaron's sons don their priestly attire (Exod 29:8–9; Lev 8:13).

The first sacrifice is the sin offering (Lev 8:14–17; cf. Exod 29:10–14):

> [14]Moses presented the sin offering bull, and Aaron and his sons leaned their hands on the head of the sin offering bull, [15]and it was slaughtered. Moses took the blood and placed it with his finger on the horns around the altar, cleansing the altar; then he poured out the (remaining) blood at the base of the altar. Thus he consecrated it to make expiation upon it. [16]The suet and all the entrails and the caudate lobe of the liver and the two kidneys and their suet were taken up,

---

of Meeting in Lev 3 stem from its redaction, which adapted the pre-existing laws to the narrative context of P (so Elliger, *Leviticus*, 48–50).

33. For a thorough review of the research on this ritual, see Klingbeil, *Ritual of Ordination*, 56–96.

34. See Klingbeil, ibid., 104–7.

and Moses turned them into smoke on the altar. [17]But (the rest of) the bull—its hide, its flesh and its dung—were put to fire outside the camp, as YHWH had commanded Moses.

As expressed by the hand-leaning rite, this sin offering is brought on behalf of the priesthood. Unlike the ritual for expiating the high priest's sin (Lev 4:3–12), the present blood manipulation is performed only on the sacrificial altar in the Tabernacle courtyard. The suet is burned on the altar as an offering to the Deity, and the remains are burned outside the camp. Although the text seems to assert that the function of the blood daubing of blood on the altar's horns is to consecrate it (ויקדשהו לכפר עליו), we will demonstrate below that this interpretation is not the only one possible.

A ram is then sacrificed as a burnt offering (Exod 29:15–18; Lev 8:18–21). Then follows the unique rite of ordination (Exod 29:19–21; cf. Lev 8:22–24):

> [19]Then take the second ram, and let Aaron and his sons lean their hands upon the ram's head. [20]Slaughter the ram, and take some of its blood and put it on the lobe of Aaron's right ear of Aaron and on the lobe of his sons' right ears, and on the thumbs of their right hands, and on the big toes of their right feet; and dash the (remaining) blood on the altar round about. [21]Take some of the blood that is on the altar and some of the anointing oil, and sprinkle them upon Aaron and his vestments, and also upon his sons and his son's vestments. Thus shall he and his vestments be holy, as well as his sons and his sons' vestments.

This passage details two distinct acts—the daubing of blood on the priests' extremities and the sprinkling of blood and anointment oil on the priests and their clothes.

The function of these rites can be understood in at least two distinct ways. On one hand, Milgrom has argued that the blood daubing fulfills a purificatory role. First, he suggests that this rite should be seen as analogous to the rites for altar purification (Exod 29:36–37; Lev 8:15). In particular, this rite, which involves the daubing of blood on the priests' right ear, thumb, and big toe corresponds to the altar ritual of Ezekiel, which involves blood applications to the top, middle, and bottom of the altar (43:20). Just as these rites are explicitly designated to purge and purify, so too the daubing of the blood of the ordination ram here. Second, this blood rite is nearly identical to the application of blood of a guilt offering to the ear, thumb and big toe for the purification of the leper (Lev 14:10–18; see below). Third, in the context of the command for the priestly consecrands to eat its flesh with the accompanying breads, the text states: "those that are expiated by them shall eat them" (ואכלו אתם אשר כֻּפַּר בהם

[Exod 29:33]).[35] Based on these analogies, Milgrom deduces that the ordination ram is associated with purification.

At the same time, Gilders has pointed out that expiation is only one of blood's numerous ritual functions in the Israelite cult. One of its important uses is to index relationships between the ritual participants, the sancta and God.[36] For example, in Exod 24:6–8, Moses throws some of the sacrificial blood on an altar and the remaining blood on the congregation in order to seal a covenant between the Israelites and God. In reference to the priestly ordination ritual, Gilders has perceptively noted: "Since the ordination blood manipulations both establish an existential relationship between the Aaronids and the altar and distinguish the Aaronids from all other Israelites, it comes as little surprise to find that only Aaronids have access to the altar."[37] Such a role is more consistent with the function of the ordination ram as a whole, which seems to be a type of well-being offering.[38] Finally, it should be recognized that the only purpose ascribed to this series of rites is the statement that the priests have been sanctified (Exod 29:21; Lev 8:30).

The sanctification of the priests is achieved by virtue of the anointment oil, which is considered to be inherently holy (Exod 30:23–25), and the blood, which is endowed with contagious sanctity by virtue of its contact with the altar. According to the principle "whatever touches the altar shall be sanctified" (כל הנגע במזבח יקדש [Exod 29:37]), the blood transmits contagious sanctity from the altar to the priestly consecrands.[39]

Diachronic Analysis

At the beginning of its account of the Ordination Ritual, Lev 8 departs radically from the ritual instructions in Exod 29. In the midst of the latter's account of Aaron's anointment (Exod 29:7), Lev 8 inserts a detailed description of the anointment of the Tabernacle and all its appurtenances, enumerating the wash basin (כיר), its stand (כנו), the utensils (10–11), and singling out the altar for a seven-fold sprinkling. This procedure corresponds to Exod 40:9–11 (cf. Exod 30:26–29). Although Exod 29 does mention the anointment of the altar, it is

---

35. Milgrom, *Leviticus*, 528–29. Cf. also Ibn Ezra on Lev 8:23. This last point, rooted in the immediate context, crucial in light of the methodological strictures enumerated by Gilders (*Blood Ritual in the Hebrew Bible*, 98–103).

36. Gilders, *Blood Ritual in the Hebrew Bible*, 78–82.

37. Ibid., 103.

38. Cf. Noth, *Leviticus: A Commentary*, 72; Elliger, *Leviticus*, 119; Marx, *Les systèmes sacrificiels*, 172.

39. Ḥizzequni on Exod 29:21; Milgrom, *Leviticus*, 534.

only at the end of the ritual (v. 36). Furthermore, the anointment of the other appurtenances is not mentioned. As can clearly be observed in the following compartative table,[40] the text of Lev 8 contains an interpolation based on Exod 40:9–12, which has been inserted between Exod 29:7aα and β: [41]

Exod 29:7	Exod 40:9–13	Lev 8:10–12
7ולקחת את שמן המשחה 7Take the oil of anoint-ment	9ולקחת את שמן המשחה 9Take the oil of anoint-ment	10ויקח משה את שמן המשחה 10Moses took the oil of anointment
	ומשחת את המשכן ואת כל אשר בו וקדשת אתו ואת כל כליו והיה קדש and anoint the Tabernacle and everything in it, and consecrate it and all of its vessels, and it will be holy.	וימשח את המשכן ואת כל אשר בו ויקדש אתם and he anointed the Taber-nacle and everything in it and consecrated them.
	10ומשחת את מזבח העלה ואת כל כליו וקדשת את המזבח והיה המזבח קדש קדשים 11ומשחת את הכיר ואת כנו וקדשת אתו 10Anoint the altar of burnt offerings and all of its vessels; thus you will consecrate the altar and it will be most holy. 11Then anoint basin and its stand and consecrate it.	11ויז ממנו על המזבח שבע פעמים וימשח את המזבח ואת כל כליו ואת הכיר ואת כנו לקדשם 11Then he sprinkled on the altar seven times. He anointed the altar and all of its vessels as well as the basin and its stand to consecrate them.

---

40. This table is based on Milgrom, *Leviticus*, 514, but cf. already Elliger, *Leviticus*, 113.

41. Nevertheless, the sequence in Lev 8 still does not conform entirely to that of Exod 40:9–15 where the anointment of the Tabernacle precedes the washing of Aaron and his sons. In contrast, Lev 8:6–9 the washing and dressing of Aaron comes first, consistent with the sequence in Exod 29:4–6. Thus, we must assume that Lev 8 followed the order of Exod 29 originally and was secondarily harmonized with Exod 40:9–15. See also Milgrom, *Leviticus*, 513–15 and discussion below.

	12והקרבת את אהרן ואת בניו אל פתח אהל מועד ורחצת אתם במים 13והלבשת את אהרן את בגדי הקדש 12Bring Aaron and his sons forward to the entrance of the Tent of Meeting and wash them with water. 13Put the holy vestments on Aaron,	
ויצקת על ראשו and pour it on his head,		21ויצק משמן המשחה על ראש אהרן 12Then he poured the oil of anointment on the head of Aaron,
ומשחת אתו thereby anointing him.	ומשחת אתו וקדשת אתו וכהן לי anoint him and sanctify him to minister to me.	וימשח אתו לקדשו thereby anointing him to sanctify him.

The elegance of the interpolation in Lev 8:10–12 causes most readers to overlook the significant tension that exists between the accounts of Exod 29 and Exod 40. According to Exod 40:9–13 and Lev 8:10aβ–11, the anointment of the cultic appurtenances must be performed before the sacrificial rituals can take place. In contrast, the Exod 29 account mentions the anointment of the altar only at the end of the ritual (vv. 36–37) with no reference to the anointment of the other furnishings:

36ופר חטאת תעשה ליום על הכפרים וחטאת על המזבח בכפרך עליו ומשחת אתו לקדשו
37שבעת ימים תכפר על המזבח וקדשת אתו והיה המזבח קדש קדשים כל הנגע במזבח יקדש

36A sin offering bull you shall sacrifice each day for expiation; and you shall cleanse the altar by performing purification upon it, and you shall anoint it to consecrate it. 37Seven days you will perform purification on the altar and consecrate it, and the altar shall become most holy; whatever touches the altar will become sanctified.

This passage states clearly that the act of purgation takes place before the anointment, reflecting the rationale that first the altar must be purified before it can be sanctified. Hence, the terminology of holiness (קד"ש) is used to express the final crowning phase of the ritual process. On the other hand, Exod 40:9–13 (as well as the dependent interpolations in Lev 8) reflects an entirely different rationale for the anointment; namely, the anointment serves to ritualize the cult appurtenances, separating them from profane use and endowing them with cultic status.[42] Such a view reveals a strong motivation to distinguish clearly between the holy and the profane realms, and thus may perhaps betray the ideology of the Holiness Source.[43]

Let us turn now to the varying accounts of the sin offering. It is described in detail in Exod 29:10–14 and Lev 8:14–17. In addition, Exod 29:36–37 presents the law for offering a sin offering every day for seven days for the purification of the altar. These passages are compared in the following table:

Exod 29	Lev 8
<div dir="rtl">10והקרבת את הפר לפני אהל מועד וסמך אהרן ובניו את ידיהם על ראש הפר 11ושחטת את הפר לפני יקוק פתח אהל מועד 12ולקחת מדם הפר ונתתה על קרנת המזבח באצבעך ואת כל הדם תשפך אל יסוד המזבח 13ולקחת את כל החלב המכסה את הקרב ואת היתרת על הכבד ואת שתי הכלית ואת החלב אשר עליהן והקטרת המזבחה 14ואת בשר הפר ואת ערו ואת פרשו תשרף באש מחוץ למחנה חטאת הוא</div>	<div dir="rtl">14ויגש את פר החטאת ויסמך אהרן ובניו את ידיהם על ראש פר החטאת 15וישחט ויקח משה את הדם ויתן על קרנות המזבח סביב באצבעו **ויחטא את המזבח** ואת הדם יצק אל יסוד המזבח **ויקדשהו לכפר עליו** 16ויקח את כל החלב אשר על הקרב ואת יתרת הכבד ואת שתי הכלית ואת חלבהן ויקטר משה המזבחה 17ואת הפר ואת ערו ואת בשרו ואת פרשו שרף באש מחוץ למחנה כאשר צוה יקוק את משה</div>

---

42. This distinction has central importance for distinguishing between editorial layers of these chapters. At first glance, one might assume that the interpolator of vv. 36–37 to Exod 29 is the same redactor who added vv. 10aβ–11 to Lev 8 (H?). Such a proposal could find support in the fact that Knohl attributes Exod 29:38–46 to H (*Sanctuary of Silence*, 65), though he himself does not include vv. 36–37. However, this proposal does not convincingly explain the contradictions between Exod 29:36–37 and Exod 40:9–13 (as well as Lev 8:10aβ–11). Specifically, Exod 29:36–37 contradicts these passages in that a) the sin offering precedes the anointment of the altar, and b) the anointment of the altar alone is mentioned. The importance of these differences should not be treated lightly, since the interpolations to Lev 8, vv. 10aβ–11 and probably an emendation to v. 15, were intended to harmonize these two points with Exod 40.

43. See, e.g., Lev 11:47; 20:25–26. The relative lateness of Exod 35–40 was recognized long ago (see, e.g., Kuenen, *Origin and Composition of the Hexateuch*, 76–81). Although Knohl attributes these chapters to H (*Sanctuary of Silence*, 66–68), I presently withhold my judgment. In any case, one cannot rule out the possibility that the interpolation Lev 8:10aβ–11 reflects a redaction even later than Exod 35–40, which attempts to harmonize the earlier contradictory traditions.

36וּפַר חַטָּאת תַּעֲשֶׂה לַיּוֹם עַל הַכִּפֻּרִים **וְחִטֵּאתָ עַל**
הַמִּזְבֵּחַ בְּכַפֶּרְךָ עָלָיו וּמָשַׁחְתָּ אֹתוֹ **לְקַדְּשׁוֹ**:
37שִׁבְעַת יָמִים תְּכַפֵּר עַל הַמִּזְבֵּחַ וְקִדַּשְׁתָּ אֹתוֹ וְהָיָה
הַמִּזְבֵּחַ קֹדֶשׁ קָדָשִׁים כָּל הַנֹּגֵעַ בַּמִּזְבֵּחַ יִקְדָּשׁ:

10Bring the bull before the Tent of Meeting, and let Aaron and his sons rest their hands on the head of the bull. 11Slaughter the bull before YHWH, at the entrance of the Tent of Meeting, 12and take some of the blood of the bull and place it on the horns of the altar with your finger; then pour out the rest of the blood at the base of the altar. 13Take all of the suet that covers the entrails and the caudate lobe of the liver, and the two kidneys with the fat on them, and turn them into smoke on the altar. 14But the meat of the bull, its hide and its dung shall be put to fire outside the camp. It is a sin offering

14Moses presented the sin offering bull, and Aaron and his sons leaned their hands on the head of the sin offering bull, 15and it was slaughtered. Moses took the blood and placed it with his finger on the horns around the altar, **and cleansed the altar**; then he poured out the (remaining) blood at the base of the altar. Thus **he consecrated it to make expiation upon it.** 16The suet and all the entrails and the caudate lobe of the liver and the two kidneys and their suet were taken up, and Moses turned them into smoke on the altar. 17But (the rest of) the bull— its hide, its flesh and its dung—were put to fire outside the camp, as YHWH had commanded Moses.

36A sin offering bull you shall sacrifice each day for expiation; **and you shall cleanse the altar by performing purgation upon it**, and you shall anoint it **to consecrate it**. 37Seven days you will perform purgation on the altar and consecrate it, and the altar shall become most holy; whatever touches the altar will become sanctified.

When comparing the description of the execution of the sin offering rite in Lev 8:14–17 with the instructions which appear in Exod 29:10–14, two significant additions (emphasized here in boldface font) to the Lev 8 text come to light, which provide an interpretation of the blood rite. The first of these is the expression ויחטא את המזבח ("and [he] cleansed the altar"), which employs the *piel* transitive form of חט"א with the altar as direct object to express the idea that the altar itself is the beneficiary of the cleansing rite.[44] This syntactical form parallels the usage of כִּפֶּר with sancta as the direct object, which signifies the

---

44. See the detailed discussion of the חט"א *piel* form below, p. 99–105.

"purging" of these objects.[45] The latter כִּפֶּר formulas must be distinguished from the those used in earlier passages that utilize כִּפֶּר עַל with a person as the indirect object, which are glossed as "expiating on behalf of" the offerer.[46] As will be shown in additional examples, this new focus on purging objects appears in the later editorial layers of numerous Priestly texts.

The second interpretive addition to Lev 8:15 is found at the end of the verse. Here the result of the blood manipulation is summarized by the phrase "he consecrated it to make expiation upon it" (ויקדשהו לכפר עליו), which articulates unambiguously that the purpose of the rite is to sanctify the altar so that it can be used for future expiation rites.[47]

Some scholars understand these two interpretive phrases in Lev 8:15 as corresponding to the two types of blood manipulations; the daubing of blood (ויתן) serves to purify (ויחטא) the altar, while the pouring out (יצק) of the remaining blood on the altar's base effects its sanctification (ויקדשהו).[48] Although this view is syntactically justifiable, it must be rejected. First of all, there is no other evidence that the pouring out of blood on the altar's base sanctifies. Secondly, we must recognize that these interpretive "additions" to Lev 8 are, in effect, based on parallel expressions which appear in Exod 29:36 as part of the instruction to purge the altar for seven days:

Exod 29:36	Lev 8:15
ופר חטאת תעשה ליום על הכפרים	וישחט ויקח משה את הדם ויתן על קרנות המזבח סביב באצבעו
וחטאת על המזבח	ויחטא את המזבח ואת הדם יצק אל יסוד המזבח
בכפרך עליו	ויקדשהו
ומשחת אתו לקדשו	**לכפר עליו**

The formulation of Exod 29:36 reflects its view that the anointment with oil, whose function is to consecrate (לקדשו) takes place after the sin offering rite has purified the altar. This order was probably present in the original form of Lev 8:15, but the final redactor of the chapter has apparently rearranged this

---

45. For some examples of the *piel* forms כפר\חטא with a sanctum as the direct object, see Lev 8:15; 16:20, 33; Ezek 43:20, 22, 26; 45:18, 20.

46. E.g., Lev 4:26, 31, 35; 12:7–8; 14:18–20, 29, 31; 16:6, 11.

47. See Rashi; Ibn Ezra. It seems that the scholars who understand לכפר עליו as an instrumental expression "by making expiation for it" (e.g., NEB; cf. Janowski, *Sühne als Heilsgeschehen*, 230) are interpreting Lev 8:15 in light of Exod 29:36 (בכפרך). However, the differences between the two passages (see below) beg for caution. Furthermore, such an interpretation does not fit the syntax of Lev 8:15. See also Milgrom, *Leviticus*, 524–25.

48. E.g., Gorman, *Ideology of Ritual*, 86; Rendtorff, *Leviticus*, 280.

verse significantly. In its present form, Lev 8 reflects the view that the anointment of the altar is a prerequisite for its use in the cult; hence, the anointment takes place before the sacrifices (v. 10aβ–11). The final editor of Lev 8 has removed the anointment from the sin offering ritual sequence in v. 15 and combined the remaining elements in the expression ויקדשהו לכפר עליו. Thus, the statement of sanctification in Lev 8:15 (ויקדשהו) betrays its source in Exod 29:36 where anointment sanctifies the altar immediately after the blood manipulation.[49]

Further evidence for this conjectured reconstruction of Lev 8:15 can be mustered from the unusual use of the verb יצ"ק in reference to the pouring of blood. This verb is used by P regularly in reference to anointing with oil (e.g., Exod 29:7; Lev 2:1, 6; 14:15), but appears in only one other case in conjunction with blood (Lev 9:9). The editor seems to have deliberately substituted the verb יצ"ק in relation to pouring out the blood for the usual verb שפ"ך (e.g., Exod 29:12; Lev 4:7, 18, 25, 34) in order to hint at an analogy to the pouring (ויצק) of oil on Aaron's head (v. 12), which serves to sanctify him (לקדשו). The redactor has thereby compensated for his transfer of the consecrating act of anointing the altar from its original context (apparently after v. 15bα) to v. 11, by adding a consecrating act of pouring (יצ"ק).[50]

Now let us examine more closely the meaning of Exod 29:36. It is not clear whether the sin offering mentioned in v. 36 is the same as that mentioned in Exod 29:1, 10–14, which is designated for the expiation of the priests, or whether this verse is introducing an additional sin offering for the purification of the altar. In attempting to sort out these possibilities, Driver has identified several discrepencies between the two passages. For instance, the rationale given for the sin offering in v. 1 is the sanctification of the priests, whereas v. 36 focuses on the consecration of the altar. The rationale stated in v. 1 finds expression in the ritual action, particularly the the hand leaning rite (v. 10), which implies that the priests are intended to receive the benefit from the offering. Furthermore, the interpretive remarks in Lev 8:15, which ascribe the effect of purging the altar to the rite, are missing from the parallel in Exod 29:10–14 but parallel the terminology of v. 36.[51]

In addition to these distinctions, Noth makes an important structural observation. The command in Exod 29:35, which obligates the repetition of the ordination ritual over the course of seven days gives the impression of being the original conclusion for the chapter, ending with the summarizing command to

---

49. So Milgrom, *Leviticus*, 524.

50. While this reading could justify understanding the pouring out of the sin offering blood at the altar as an act of consecration, it would be more of a stylistic redactorial device than a genuine interpretation of ritual activity.

51. Driver, *Book of Exodus*, 324.

Moses "Ordinate them for seven days."[52] This instruction is paralleled by Lev 8:33–36, which depicts its fulfillment, concluding the chapter with the statement: "Aaron and his sons performed all of the things that YHWH had commanded through Moses" (36). On these grounds, Driver and Noth conclude that Exod 29:36 is a later addition that introduces a *second* sin offering whose purpose is to purge the altar.[53]

But this conclusion has its weaknesses. The most obvious of these is that Lev 8:15 combines the expressions of Exod 29:12 and 36 with the implication that they are referring to one and the same rite. Moreover, if Exod 29:36–37 is understood as referring to a second sin offering, this passage would contradict all known strata for these chapters, contradicting:

- Exod 29:1–35, which deals with making expiation for the priesthood, not purging the altar
- Lev 8:15, which recognizes only one sin offering
- Lev 8:10–12 (addition to Lev 8), which depicts the anointment before the blood rite

A much more satisfactory solution is that Exod 29:36–37 is, in fact, an addition, but that it is actually a reinterpretation of the sin offering described in vv. 10–14. This conclusion addresses all of the points listed above, and moreover, allows for this addition to be consistent ideologically with Lev 8 in its penultimate state, that is, before the gloss in vv. 10–12 referring to the preliminary anointing of the Tabernacle and all its appurtenances and the corresponding rearrangement of v. 15 described above.

This last observation provides a key to unraveling the literary history of Exod 29/Lev 8. Based on these ideological inconsistencies, I propose the following reconstruction:

---

52. Noth, *Exodus*, 232–33.

53. Cf. also Propp, *Exodus 19–40*, 469. Most commentators, ancient and modern alike, assume that there is one sin offering with a double function. An interesting exception is the Temple Scroll, which adduced two sin offerings, but one is for the priests and the other for the laity (XV, 16–18). See Milgrom, *Leviticus*, 523, 562.

Layer	Text	Ideological Positions
1 (P₁)	Exod 29:1–35	Sin offering for priests; no anointment of sancta
2 (P₂)	Exod 29:36–37; Lev 8	Sin offering purges altar; anointment of altar takes place after blood rite[54]
3 (H?)	Lev 8:10aβ–11, deletion of anointment from v. 15	Anointment of *all* sancta precedes sin offering rite, consistent with Exod 40:9–13

In summary, this diachronic analysis has shown that the original function of the sin offering ritual in Exod 29 and Lev 8 was to make expiation for the priests. Subsequent reinterpretations of the rite introduced the notion of purging the altar, expressed by the *piel* forms of כפ"ר and חט"א with the altar as the object.

EZEKIEL'S CONSECRATION RITUALS

Synchronic Overview

Ezekiel's temple vision (chs. 40–48) contains two blood rituals that aim to purify and consecrate the sacrificial altar (43:18–27) and the temple (45:18–22). The instructions for the altar ritual are as follows:

> [18]He spoke to me: 'O mortal, thus said the Lord YHWH: These are the laws of the altar on the day it is erected so that burnt offerings can be offered upon it and blood dashed upon it. [19]You shall give to the levitical priests who are the stock of Zadok, who are close to me—says YHWH—to minister to me a bull of the herd as a sin offering. [20]You shall take some of its blood and daub it on

---

54. There are several reasons for assuming that Lev 8 originally agreed with Exod 29:36–37 that the anointment of the altar takes place after the blood rite, but was subsequently adapted by the Layer 3 redactor (H?). First, even with the interpolation of vv. 10aβ–11, Lev 8 is not consistent with Exod 40:9–13 (see n. 41 above). Second, as argued above, the position of the verb קד"ש in v. 15 seems to hint at the original position of the anointment rite, occurring after the blood rite as in Exod 29:36. It is worth noting that both layers of redaction were relatively conservative in that they chose to leave Exod 29 intact, aside from the appendix in vv. 36–37. The redactors seem to have been guided by the assumption that it is sufficient to adapt the description of the *execution* of the ritual (i.e., Lev 8), such that, from an interpretive standpoint, the performance in Lev 8 would supersede the instructions of Exod 29. For this strategy, see also Milgrom, *Leviticus*, 17. It is possible that Lev 8 was originally consistent with Exod 29:1–35 (P₁), but this view would require a double redaction of v. 15.

its four horns and on the four corners of the base and on the rim round about; thus you will purify it and purge it. [21]Then you shall take the sin offering bull and burn it in the *guarded place*[55] of the temple outside the sanctuary. [22]On the second day you shall offer an unblemished goat as a sin offering, and they will purify the altar as they purified it with the bull. [23]Upon your completion of the purification, you shall dedicate an unblemished young bull of the herd and an unblemished ram from the flock. [24]You shall present them before YHWH, and the priests shall throw salt upon them and offer them as burnt offerings to YHWH. [25]Every day for seven days, you shall present a sin offering goat as well as a young bull of the herd and a ram from the flock that are unblemished-(these) they will offer. [26]Seven days they will purge the altar, thereby purifying it and ordaining it. And when these days are over, then from the eighth day onward the priests shall offer on the altar your burnt offerings and your well-being offerings, and I will extend my favor to you, says the Lord YHWH.

These instructions for the consecration of the altar are clearly based on the P tradition for the consecration of the priesthood. Ezekiel is here cast in the role of Moses, charged with initiating the cult.[56] However, this function is out of place and uncharacteristic of Ezekiel, and thereby leaves little doubt as to the dependency of this tradition on P.[57] This dependency is further exhibited by the seven-day scheme followed by the eighth day when the cult is officially inaugurated.[58]

The blood applications to the four horns of the altar, the four corners of its ledge (עזרה), apparently the upper one, and the rim (גבול) correspond to the altar's top, middle, and bottom respectively (cf. vv. 13–17).[59] This procedure is an expansion of P's procedure of applying blood to the four horns of the altar, whose purpose is to emphasize that the entire altar is purged.[60] Furthermore, a

---

55. According to the MT, the term מפקד הבית may be connected with שער המפקד, mentioned in Neh 3:31, which may have been located at the eastern side of the temple. The root פק"ד is associated with census-taking, but also with overseeing and guarding. See Block, *Book of Ezekiel*, 2:608; Kasher, *Ezekiel: Introduction and Commentary*, 2:841. Alternatively, the text could be amended to מוקד הבית ("place of burning"); cf. the note on the NJPS translation, citing Lev 6:2; Isa 33:14; Ps 102:4 (for the word) and Lev 4:12; 6:4 (for the place).

56. Block, *Book of Ezekiel*, 2:604, 607; Kasher, *Ezekiel: Introduction and Commentary* 2:834.

57. Zimmerli, *Ezekiel 2*, 432–33.

58. For further analysis of the similarities and differences, see Kasher, *Ezekiel: Introduction and Commentary 2*:844–46. See also below, pp. 57–60.

59. On the structure of the altar, see Dijkstra, "The Altar of Ezekiel," 27–32.

60. Some scholars (e.g., Block, *The Book of Ezekiel*, 2:608) have understood this rite in light of the expression על המזבח סביב ("on the altar round about"), which refers to the disposal of blood of certain offerings (e.g,. Exod 29:16, 20; Lev 1:5, 11). This proposal must be rejected for several reasons, the most obvious of which it that this expression never appears in connec-

parallel has been drawn between this rite and the blood applications to the ear lobe, thumb, and big toe of the priests in their ritual of ordination (Exod 29:20; Lev 8:23–24).[61] Though the meaning of such an analogy between priest and altar is not immediately clear, it may serve to emphasize the prophet–priest's interest in order and symmetry, whereby the priests and the altar must undergo parallel rites of passage in order to achieve cultic status.

A major difference seems to exist between the Torah's ordination ritual and Ezekiel's altar ritual. Whereas the former seems to be primarily a rite of passage by which the priesthood and altar are brought out of their mundane status and endowed with the requisite sanctity fitting for the service of the Deity, the text describing Ezekiel's altar ritual emphasizes its expiatory function. In fact, it is introduced with an exhortation in which the prophet makes clear that the blueprint for a new temple is no mere architectural matter:

> You, O mortal, describe the temple to the House of Israel and they will be ashamed of their sins and they will measure its design. And when they are ashamed of all that they have done, inform them of the plan of the temple and its layout, its exits and entrances—its entire plan and its laws, and all of the details of its plan, and its instructions. Write it before their eyes so that they will be careful to carry out its entire plan and its laws (43:10–11).

Ezekiel makes no false pretenses that the nation's sins can simply be forgotten. If the slate is to be wiped clean, this will need to be achieved internally as well as ritually.

Turning to the second relevant passage, Ezek 45 outlines a special ritual for the Passover festival and its elaborate preparations:

> [18]Thus said the Lord YHWH: On the first day of the first month you shall take an unblemished bull of the herd and decontaminate the Temple. [19]The priest shall take the blood of the sin offering, and apply it to the doorposts of the temple, to the four corners of the ledge of the altar, and to the doorposts of the gate of the inner court. [20]Thus you will do on the seventh day of the month to purge the Temple from (the defilement caused by) an unwitting or ignorant person. [21]On the fourteenth day of the first month you will have the Passover sacrifice, and during a festival of seven days unleavened bread shall be eaten. [22]On this day the chieftain will provide a bull as a sin offering on his own behalf and on behalf of the entire population. [23]And throughout the seven days of the festival he shall provide a burnt offering to YHWH—seven bulls and

---

tion with the sin offering, whose blood rite has a unique function.

61. See Zimmerli, *Ezekiel 2*, 433; Milgrom, *Leviticus*, 528–29.

seven rams, unblemished, each day for seven days—and a sin offering goat each day.

This passage introduces a purification scheme unknown from other biblical sources. On the first day of the first month—the first of Nissan—the Temple is to be purged by means of a sin offering. This purification is effected by the daubing of blood on the doorposts of the entranceway to the temple, on the four corners of the altar's ledge, and on the doorposts of the gate to the inner court—apparently the eastern gate which faces the altar.

According to the mt, this rite is to be repeated on the seventh day of the month of Nisan (v. 20). However, the Greek version reads: "in the seventh, on the first of the month," which would make the ritual semi-annual. Though there are merits to the Greek version,[62] the rationale provided in v. 20 for the rite, to remove the contamination caused by "an unwitting or ignorant person" (מאיש שגה ומפתי) is more understandable according to the mt, according to which the text outlines two stages of purifying the sanctuary in preparation for the Passover rite. Whereas the rite on the first of the month removes both intentionally and unintentionally caused forms of impurity, the repetition on the seventh day provides a back-up measure to purge any further impurity which was caused inadvertently thereafter.[63] Finally, on the fourteenth day of the month, on the day of the Passover festival, the chieftain (הנשיא) is commanded to bring a bull as a sin offering to expiate on behalf of himself and the nation (vv. 21–22).

Kaufmann has noted an illuminating contrast between this ritual and Lev 16, both of which aim to purge the Tabernacle of impurity and transgression. Whereas the P ritual focuses on the interior of the Tabernacle, particularly the blood rite in the adytum (Lev 16:14–16a)—that is, the place of the divine presence, Ezekiel's ritual does not penetrate beyond the inner court and focuses on

---

62. The rationale would be to create symmetry between the first and seventh months (see, e.g., Cooke, *Book of Ezekiel*, 502–3). This tendency is, in effect, evident in v. 25, in which the offerings of the Passover and the Festival of Tabernacles are made equivalent. In addition, the expanded formula, which restates the month in v. 21, בראשון בארבעה עשר יום לחדש ("on the fourteenth day of the first month"), could be seen as implying that the intervening verse, v. 20, was referring to a different month, namely the seventh.

63. One is hard pressed to understand why the semi-annual repetition reflected in the Septuagint would address only inadvertent sins (Milgrom, *Leviticus*, 282–83). Although it could be conjectured that the prophet foresees a future in which Israel will cease to sin intentionally (cf. 36:25, 33; 37:23), Kasher ("Anthropomorphism, Holiness and Cult," 200) points out that the cultic laws of chs. 40–48 undermine this possibility, reflecting a persistent awareness of the human tendency to sin (e.g., 44:6–45:10).

the exterior of the temple, particularly the doorposts of the two gateways leading to the inner court.[64]

Kasher explains this discrepancy as being consistent with Ezekiel's tendency to distance people from the locus of the divine presence,[65] but this explanation might not tell the whole story. It remains difficult to escape the suspicion that Ezekiel's radically different procedure, in which blood is applied to the doorposts of the Temple, reflects a tradition distinct from that of the Lev 16 blood rites. As will be shown below in a survey of Mesopotamian blood rites, the daubing of various substances, including blood, on doorposts appears in numerous Babylonian ritual texts, among them that of the new year festival (akītu).[66] As we will will see, the apotropaic function of these rites, which seek to prevent the entry of demonic forces into the temple or house, differs markedly from the rationale underlying the blood rites of the Hittite texts and P. Although Ezekiel's usage of כִּפֶּר and חִטֵּא shows linguistic continuity with the later priestly descriptions of purging sancta,[67] the form of the rites themselves, particularly the daubing of doorposts, indicates Babylonian influence. In particular, Ezekiel's introduction of a set of purification rituals in Nissan, which are similar to festivals that take place six months later on the first and tenth of Tishrei, respectively, makes them correspond roughly to the times of the semi-annual akītu festival.[68] As a result, there are numerous reasons to suspect that the blood rites in Ezekiel have been influenced by the prophet's historical circumstances.

Diachronic Analysis

Most of the scholars who have attempted to reconstruct the historical development of the sin offering ritual view the rituals in the book of Ezekiel as representative of the earliest phase of the ritual's development.[69] Aside from their general adherence to the classical critical view regarding the lateness of P, justification for this view is found in the lack of references to fat burning or the consumption of the leftover flesh. In addition to the evidence adduced in the previous section, the ensuing discussion will make even clearer that Ezekiel's

---

64. Kaufmann, *Religion of Israel*, 307–8.

65. Kasher, "Anthropomorphism, Holiness and Cult," 199–200. Regarding the Ezekiel's systematic distancing of people from the place of the divine presence, see pp. 197–201.

66. See Linssen, *Cults of Uruk and Babylon*, 184–244.

67. See pp. 48–50, 53; see also Feder, "*kuppuru, kippēr* and Etymological Sins," 542.

68. This argument is strongest if we accept the Greek version of v. 20. See Wagenaar, "Post-Exilic Calendar Innovations," 18–20. Preserving the MT's reading, this argument assumes that Ezekiel is taking for granted the existence of expiation rituals in Tishrei.

69. See, e.g., Rendtorff, *Geschichte des Opfers*, 222–26, 233–34, 249; Gese, *Atonement*, 102, 110–13; and Janowski, *Sühne als Heilsgeschehen*, 232–41.

depiction of the sin offering represents a relatively late phase in the development of the sin offering ritual.

As noted above, Ezekiel's ritual for the purgation of the altar (Ezek 43:18–27) is patterned after the priestly ordination described in the Torah (Exod 29; Lev 8). The analogy between the altar and the priesthood is manifested by Ezekiel's use of the expression ומלאו ידיו,[70] literally "and they will fill its hand(s)," to describe the ordination of the altar. This idiom is used numerous times throughout the Bible, both inside the cultic literature and outside it, to refer to the ordination of priests.[71] It is parallel to the Akkadian expression *mullû qātam* which also refers to the authorization or ordination of a person.[72] The use of this idiom in Ezekiel in relation to an inanimate object, i.e. the altar, has no parallel. Thus, the ritual of consecrating the altar in Ezekiel is clearly based on the precedent of priestly ordination found in the Torah.

Ezekiel's instructions for the purging of the altar indicate his awareness of P$_2$ additions to Exod 29 and Lev 8. First of all, the prophet's use of the *piel* forms of חט"א and כפ"ר in reference to the altar (v. 20, 22, 23, 26) matches the language of Exod 29:36 and Lev 8:15. Lest we attempt to explain away the similarity on the grounds that these are the standard cultic terms for purgation, we should note the following textual comparison:

Exod 29, 35: Seven days of priestly ordination	Exod 29, 37: Seven days of consecrating altar	Ezek 43, 26: Seven days of consecrating altar
ועשית לאהרן ולבניו ככה ככל אשר צויתי אתכה **שבעת ימים תמלא ידם**	**שבעת ימים תכפר על המזבח** וקדשת אתו והיה המזבח קדש קדשים כל הנגע במזבח יקדש	שבעת ימים יכפרו את המזבח וטהרו אתו ומלאו ידו (קרי: ידיו)

---

70. So the *qeri;* the *ketiv* reads ידו. The Septuagint and Peshitta indicate a reading of ידם, which would have the expression referring to the priests, thereby placing the idiom back in its normal usage. But the context deals only with the ordination of the altar; thus the MT should be maintained.

71. Exod 28:41; 29:9, 29, 35; 32:29; Lev 8:33; 16:32; 21:10; Num 3:3; Judg. 17:5, 12; 1 Kgs 13:33; Ezek 43:26; 1 Chr 29:5; 2 Chr 13:9; 29:31.

72. See references in Milgrom, *Leviticus*, 539. Cf. also Rupprecht, "Quisquilien zu der Wendung מלא את-יד פלוני," 73–93; Wallis, "'Hand füllen'," 340–49; L. A. Snijder, "מלא," *TDOT* 8:301–6.

Thus you shall do to Aaron and his sons, just as I have commanded you; **for seven days you will ordain them (lit.: 'fill their hands').**	**Seven days you will perform purification for the altar** and consecrate it, and the altar shall become most holy; whatever touches the altar will become sanctified.	Seven days they will purge the altar and purify it and ordain it (lit.: 'fill its hands').

From this comparison, it would seem that Ezek 43:26 combines the expressions from Exod 29:35b and 37a. Particularly striking is the similarity between the two instructions for purging the altar, especially between the expressions "for seven days ... you will perform purification for the altar and consecrate it" (שבעת ימים תכפר על המזבח וקדשת אתו) and "for seven days they will purge the altar and purify it" (שבעת ימים יכפרו את המזבח וטהרו אתו).

This literary dependency may contribute to establishing a chronological framework for the evolving rationales of the sin offering. Despite the fact that the Ezekiel passages are textually problematic and might well reflect multiple literary layers,[73] it appears nevertheless that, no matter how one would attempt to dissect the existing passages, it would not be possible to isolate a source that is not based on the aforementioned Priestly sources. More importantly, the rationale given for the sin offering in these passages corresponds to that of the later layers of the Priestly corpus, namely purging the altar, as expressed syntactically by כִּפֶּר and חִטֵּא with the altar as the direct object.[74]

A more serious problem is the lack of scholarly consensus regarding the authorship and provenance of Ezek 40–48. Although we cannot expect to settle this controversial issue here, it is worthwhile to note two fundamental grounds for granting an exilic provenance to these chapters, or at least their core. First, Greenberg has identified significant thematic and linguistic similarities that connect chs. 40–48 with the rest of the book—evidence that would support the assumption of their common authorship by the exilic prophet.[75] Second, we noted above two indicators of Babylonian influence on the sin-offering rituals: 1) the requirement for semi-annual purging rituals and 2) the apotropaic placement of blood on the gateways of the temple. If such arguments can be sustained, then we may be able to posit a *terminus ad quem* for the emergence of the notion of purging the sancta during the times of the Babylonian exile. In other words, the transition from the datival formulation כִּפֶּר עַל ("making expiation on behalf

---

73. See, e.g., Zimmerli, *Ezekiel 2*, 431–35.

74. See above, pp. 48–50.

75. Greenberg, "Ezekiel's Program of Restoration," 181–209.

of") to כִּפֶּר אֶת + direct object ("purging") seems to have taken place already in the preexilic period.

THE PURIFICATION OF THE LEPER

Synchronic Overview

Leviticus 13–14 deal at length with a skin disease called צרעת, which we will call "leprosy" for the sake of convenience.[76] A person who has been diagnosed with this disease is banished from the Israelite camp for an indeterminate period (Lev 13:46; Num 5:2). If the priest determines that the disease has abated, the leper must engage in a three-phase ritual of purification before being reintegrated into the Israelite community.

The first phase of the ritual is described as follows (Lev 14:1–9):

> [1]YHWH spoke to Moses, saying: [2]This shall be the ritual of the leper at the time of his purification. When it is reported to the priest, [3]the priest shall go outside the camp. The priest shall make an examination, and if the disease has abated from the patient, [4]the priest shall order that two pure live birds, a cedar wood, crimson (yarn) and hyssop be brought to the person being purified. [5]The priest shall order one bird to be slaughtered into an earthenware vessel over spring water. [6]He shall take the live bird, the cedar wood, the crimson yarn and the hyssop, and he shall dip them and the live bird in the blood of the bird that had been slaughtered over spring water. [7]He shall sprinkle seven times onto the one being purified from "leprosy," thus cleansing him, and he shall release the live bird in the open country. [8]The one being purified shall launder his clothes, shave off all of his hair and bathe in water, thus becoming pure. Then he may enter the camp, but he must dwell outside his tent for seven days. [9]On the seventh day, he shall shave off all of his hair—of his head, chin and eyebrows—indeed, he shall shave off all of his hair. He will launder his clothes and wash his body in water; then he shall be pure.

The ritual preserved in Lev 14 is not a ritual to remove the disease from the patient, though it may be originally based on such a ritual.[77] According to the ritual's present form, the activity begins only after the priest is convinced that the disease has abated, according to the criteria laid out in Lev 13.

---

76. Much research has been dedicated to the identity of צרעת, and it seems clear that it must be distinguished from leprosy (Hansen's Disease). See, e.g., Hulse, "The Nature of Biblical 'Leprosy'," 87–105; Stol, "Leprosy. New Light," 22–31; Milgrom, *Leviticus*, 816–18.

77. See Kaufmann, *Religion of Israel*, 107–8; Levine, *In the Presence of the Lord*, 83–85; Milgrom, *Leviticus*, 887–89.

The ritual involves two birds, one of which is slaughtered and the other sent off. Together they serve to remove and dispose of the impurity. The priest bundles the cedar stick and the hyssop together with crimson yarn. He uses this bundle to sprinkle the mixture of blood and spring water on the one being purified. The live bird is then dipped in the mixture of blood and spring water and freed to carry off the contamination to some distant place, never to return.

How are we to understand the function of blood in the sprinkling rite (v. 7)? At first glance, since the expression "thus cleansing him" (וטהרו) stated even before the live bird is sent off, we may infer that the blood has an inherent power to purify. However, the process can be understood differently. Clearly, the blood establishes a symbolic channel by which the contamination is transferred to the live bird, even in the absence of direct physical contact. More specifically, it acts as an *index*[78] which connects the live bird, which was previously dipped in the blood, with the patient who is now being sprinkled. As a result, once the impurity has been transferred to the live bird, the person is purified. Thus, the sending away of the bird is not required for the purification of the leper, but to distance the impurity from the camp. Even if we ascribe to the sprinkling a double function of cleansing and indexical transfer, it may be that the former is achieved by means of the spring water that was mixed with the blood.

The purified leper must then shave his entire body and bathe (v. 8). The act of shaving at the completion of a purification rite is reminiscent of Babylonian Namburbi rituals where the exorcistic rite is followed by the cutting of hair and fingernails.[79] The underlying rationale seems to be that once the source of the impurity has been removed, the patient can be cleaned of residual effects, which are perceived to cling to his hair and body. He may now return to the camp, but is required to dwell outside his tent for seven days, since he may still contaminate objects that are found with him inside an enclosure. At the end of these seven days, he must shave a second time, launder, and bathe (v. 9).

The next phase of the ritual is described as follows (Lev 14:10–20):

[10]On the eighth day he shall take two unblemished sheep and a one-year-old unblemished ewe, and three tenths (of an *ephah* measure) of semolina, a cereal offering mixed in oil, and one *log*-measure of oil. [11]The purifying priest shall set the one being purified and these (offerings) before YHWH at the entrance to the Tent of Meeting. [12]The priest shall take one sheep, and present it as a guilt offering along with the *log* of oil, and he shall elevate them as an elevation offering before YHWH. [13]The sheep should be slaughtered in the place where

78. For discussion of this term, see below, p. 61.

79. See Maul, "How the Babylonians Protected Themselves," 128. On biblical shaving rites in general, see Olyan, "What Do Shaving Rites Accomplish?," 611–22.

the sin offering and the burnt offering are slaughtered in the holy precinct, since the guilt offering is like the sin offering. It (goes) to the priest; it is most holy. [14]The priest shall take some of the blood of the guilt offering. The priest shall daub it on the lobe of the right ear of the one being purified, on the thumb of his right hand and on the big toe of his right foot. [15]The priest shall take the *log* of oil and pour it into the palm of his own left hand. [16]The priest shall dip his right finger in the oil that is in the palm of his left hand, and he shall sprinkle with his finger some of the oil seven times before YHWH. [17]Some of the remaining oil that is in his palm, the priest will daub on the lobe of the right ear of the one being purified, on the thumb of his right hand and on the big toe of his right foot, over the blood of the guilt offering. [18]The remainder of the oil which is in his palm, the priest will daub on the head of the one being purified. Thus the priest will make expiation on his behalf before YHWH. [19]Then the priest will perform the sin offering rite and make expiation on behalf of the one being purified for his impurity. Afterwards, he shall slaughter the burnt offering. [20]Then the priest shall offer up the burnt offering and the cereal offering on the altar; thus the priest shall make expiation on his behalf and he shall be pure.

Once a person has successfully freed himself from the defiling influence of the disease, he must be reintegrated into the cultic community and reestablish his standing before God. The first rite in this sequence involves the daubing of the extremities with blood and oil in a rite that is very similar to that performed on the priestly consecrands in Exod 29/Lev 8. The preparation for this rite requires that the guilt offering sheep and the *log* of oil are consecrated by means of an elevation rite (v. 12).

The guilt offering is slaughtered, and its blood is daubed on the right ear lobe, thumb, and big toe of the one being purified (v. 14). Then the priest sprinkles the oil seven times in the direction of the Tent, locus of the divine presence (v. 16). In contrast to the oil used in the priestly ordination, which is inherently holy by virtue of the fact that it was prepared according to the Deity's instructions (Exod 30:22–33), the oil in the present ritual requires a specific rite to endow it with the desired power. This oil is applied to the same body parts as the blood, and the remainder is then daubbed on his head (vv. 17–18a).

The series of rites concludes with a series of goal formulas that use the expression וכפר עליו in relation to the oil rite (v. 18) and the sacrificial offerings (vv. 19–20). The sense of כִּפֶּר in this context is not immediately clear.[80] One might assume that it refers to the expiation of sin, in keeping with the usual purpose of the guilt offering to redress guilt. Furthermore, the expiatory role of blood is reminiscent of the sin offering, although the latter's blood is never applied to a person. However, the context seems to emphasize impurity,

---

80. This term will be discussed in depth below, p. 167–96.

not sin.[81] Indeed, v. 20 concludes with a declaration that the person has now become pure (וטהר). Furthermore, the purificatory use of anointment rites is well-attested in ancient Near Eastern sources, though seldom acknowledged in biblical research.[82]

But this procedure may also be viewed as a ritual of aggregation, aimed at reintegrating the exiled leper back into communal life.[83] This process follows a gradated succession of stages, as can be shown by the following table:

Day	Level of Integration
1	Enables return to camp, though patient must dwell outside tent
7	Enables participation in following day's sacrificial ritual
8	Enables return to tent and resumption of normal cultic and communal life

As will be shown in the following section, this emphasis on reaggregation seems to stem from H's redaction of the chapter.

Diachronic Analysis

As recognized by Lund and developed by Milgrom, the ritual for the eighth day (vv. 10–20) is arranged as a complex introversion. The following is my translation arranged according to Milgrom's scheme:[84]

THE STRUCTURE OF LEV 14:11–20

A. [11]The *purifying priest* shall set the *one being purified* and these (offerings) *before YHWH* at the entrance to the Tent of Meeting.[12]The priest shall take one sheep, and present it as a guilt offering

B. along with the log of *oil,* and he shall elevate them as an elevation offering *before YHWH.* [13]The sheep should be slaughtered in the place where the *sin offering* and the *burnt offering* are *slaughtered,* in the holy precinct, since the guilt offering is like the sin offering. It (goes) to the priest; it is most holy.

---

81. Accordingly, this passage could be taken as support for the assertion that the term חטאת refers to a "purification offering," not a "sin offering." For a refutation of this contention, see below, p. 99–108.

82. See Yakubovich, "Were Hittite Kings Divinely Annointed?," 130–34.

83. Wenham, *Book of Leviticus,* 208. Gorman (*Ideology of Ritual,* 154, 172–79) does not use this term, recognizing that purification plays an equally important role, but nevertheless argues for reintegration as one of the main goals of the ritual complex.

84. See Lund, *Chiasmus in the New Testament,* 53–57; Milgrom, *Leviticus,* 846–48.

C. [14]The priest shall take some of the *blood of the guilt offering.*

D. *The priest shall daub it on the lobe of the right ear of the one being purified, on the thumb of his right hand and on the big toe of his right foot.*

E. [15]The priest shall take the log of *oil* and pour it into the *palm* of his own left hand.

X. [16]The priest shall dip his right finger in the *oil* that is in the *palm* of his left hand, and he shall sprinkle with his finger some of the *oil* seven times *before YHWH.*

E'. [17]Some of the remaining *oil* that is in his *palm,*

D'. *the priest will daub on the lobe of the right ear of the one being purified, on the thumb of his right hand and on the big toe of his right foot,*

C.' over the *blood of the guilt offering.*

B'. [18]The remainder of the *oil* which is in his palm, the priest will daub on the head of the one being purified. Thus the priest will make expiation on his behalf *before YHWH.* [19]Then the priest will perform the *sin offering* rite and make expiation on behalf of the one being purified for his impurity. Afterwards, he shall *slaughter* the *burnt offering.* [20]Then the priest shall offer up the burnt offering and the cereal offering on the altar;

A'. thus the *priest* shall make expiation on *his behalf* and he shall be *pure.*

The italics indicate the corresponding expressions. The sophistication in which dry technical instructions have been converted into a meaningful literary structure is nothing less than astounding. We can, however, discern some of the additions that were made in order to create this symmetry, for example, vv. 13 (B) and 17b (C').[85]

---

85. The secondary nature of 13b has commonly been recognized (e.g., Noth, *Leviticus: A Commentary*, 104, 109; Elliger, *Leviticus*, 175). The awkward syntax of v. 17aα, in which the direct object precedes the verb and subject, is also probably a result of the literary rearrangement of the text. See Milgrom, *Leviticus*, 848.

Milgrom cites an observation of D. P. Wright that "this introversion glosses over some jarring elements: for example 'before YHWH' appears not only in B, X, B', but also in A, and the priest's palm occurs not only in E, X, E', but also in B'." Milgrom then adds his own interpretive conclusion: "This passage is a clear indication that the large-scale chiastic structure was not perfected by the P school."[86] In my opinion, Wright's observations should be interpreted differently. First of all, I would attribute this introversion to H, as it is akin to those found in the Holiness Code, yet unlike the simple chiasms of P.[87] Secondly, we should recognize that these "jarring elements" could have been removed quite easily had the redactor so desired, especially considering the great care and stylistic acumen otherwise evident in the organization of this passage. Rather, it seems that the editor was here exercising conservatism in relation to his source materials, in that he sought to fashion the introversion by rearrangement of the materials and by additions, but with minimal deletions. Ironically, Milgrom himself has identified several H additions to Lev 14 and acknowledges H's redaction of this chapter.[88]

Nevertheless, I do posit that H has made a significant addition to the text, namely the seven-fold sprinkling before YHWH (v. 16), which serves as the nucleus (X) of the introversion. Indeed, as demonstrated above,[89] the seven-fold sprinkling in Lev 8:10aβ–11 is clearly a gloss, and H's religious ideology that apparently motivated the latter gloss seems to be present here as well. This recognition can provide a more convincing rationale for the sprinkling rite in Lev 14:16 than the conventional understanding that the purpose is to consecrate the oil for ritual use,[90] which is redundant in light of the prior elevation rite (v. 12).[91] As will become clear presently, the function of this sprinkling corresponds to a dominant theological concern that pervades H as a whole.

The placement of the seven-fold sprinkling "before YHWH" in the center of the chiastic structure of vv. 11–20 hints that the oil has more than just purificatory significance. Gorman has noted that elsewhere in the Bible (and beyond) anointment serves to signal a change of status. In particular, he draws an analogy

---

86. Ibid., 848. Milgrom is referring to H's affinity for complex introversions which he himself cites as a "literary artifice that holds better promise of yielding a distinction between P and H" (p. 39). For some examples, see pp. 39–42.

87. See ibid. 2:1319–23, 1330–32.

88. Ibid., 886–87. Cf. also Fishbane, "Biblical Colophons," 438–42.

89. See above pp. 46–48.

90. So, e.g., Vriezen, "Lustration and Consecration," 214; Noth, *Leviticus: A Commentary*, 109.

91. Milgrom (*Leviticus*, 854) notes the redundancy of the sprinkling rite, but his explanation that is a "booster" to reinforce the elevation rite is not convincing.

to the priestly anointment, commenting that the anointment in Lev 14 "effects and communicates the individual's passage into a restored social standing."[92]

Gorman's understanding can be refined if we consider with greater attention the semiotic dynamics of Lev 14:16. This sprinkling "before YHWH" establishes an indexical relationship between the oil and the divine presence, so that the subsequent sprinkling on the purified leper serves to establish a renewed connection between him and the Deity.[93] We should recall that God's presence in the midst of the Israelite camp is the rationale given by the Holiness Source for exiling the serious impurity bearers from the camp (Num 5:1–4). Thus, it would seem that H's structural reorganization of the text, with the resulting emphasis placed on the seven-fold sprinkling rite, is intended to stress that the person is being readmitted to dwell in proximity to God. Consequently, H has adapted a P ritual that had previously focused on purification and providing an added dimension (if not realigning it completely) to concentrate on reintegration into the sacred camp.

This rationale can also be posited for the sprinkling of the blood of the red cow towards the Tent of Meeting (אל נכח פני אהל מועד) in Num 19:4. The dominant view[94] that this sprinkling serves as a means of consecrating the blood for the production of the ash water fails to address why such a rite is unnecessary in other rites involving blood. In light of the parallel act with oil in Lev 14:16, we may provide a more precise answer. The sprinkling of the blood towards the Tent and the subsequent sprinkling on the impure person serves to establish an indexical connection whose purpose is to reintegrate the impurity bearer into the holy camp.[95]

The subsequent section (vv. 21–32), which makes provisions for an indigent leper, is also structured as a complex introversion and should also be attributed to H. Since the structure is very similar to that of vv. 11–18, there is no reason to

---

92. Gorman, *Ideology of Ritual*, 175. See also Schmitt, *Magie im Alten Testament*, 180; Marx, *Les systèmes sacrificiels*, 171, 174–75.

93. For an illuminating discussion of the notion of indexicality, particularly as it applies to Num 19, see Gilders, "Making Sense of a Biblical Ritual."

94. See, e.g., Vriezen, "Lustration and Consecration," 211, Noth, *Leviticus: A Commentary*, 39; Elliger, *Leviticus*, 69; Rodriguez, *Substitution in the Hebrew Cultus*, 124. In contrast, Kiuchi suggests that the lustration serves to protect the Tent from defilement (*Purification Offering*, 124).

95. True, this chapter nowhere states that the impurity bearer has been banished. In fact, it may imply the opposite, such that it would be consistent with P's ideology whereby only the leper is sent out of the camp, as opposed to H who also banishes people with genital eruptions or corpse impurity (Num 5:2). At the same time, certain verses (e.g., 10b–13) reflect a stylistic and ideological affinity to H. Nevertheless, since the view that failure to purify contaminates the Sanctuary, as stated in vv. 13, 20, is characteristic of H (see below pp. 93–95), this chapter must have been redacted by the latter (see Knohl, *Sanctuary of Silence*, 92–94).

analyze it in detail here.[96] We should note that, once again, the seven-fold sprinkling of the oil (v. 27) is located at the central focus point of the passage.

In summary, the purification rituals of Lev 14 have passed through several literary stages. In their original form, they seem to have resembled the goat rite of Lev 16 (see below) and may have been intended as healing rites. This early phase of the tradition will receive further attention below when we will investigate a number of parallels between specific Hittite rituals and their bniblical counterparts. In Lev 14's present form, the rites focus exclusively on purification from ritual defilement. The H redaction of this chapter adapted these texts to its theological conception by emphasizing the purpose of integrating the leper into the holy camp.

EATING THE SIN OFFERING'S MEAT

Synchronic Overview

In Lev 6, the priests are instructed that the leftover flesh from the courtyard sin offering should be given to the officiating priest for consumption (vv. 18–19; cf. 7:6–7):

> [18]Speak to Aaron and his sons thus: this is the law of the sin offering. The sin offering shall be slaughtered before YHWH, at the place where the burnt offering is slaughtered; it is most sacred. [19]The priest who offers it as a sin offering shall consume it; it shall be eaten in a holy place, in the courtyard of the Tent of Meeting.

From the wording of this rule, we might infer that the allocation of the flesh to the officiating priest was considered a prebend for his services in the ritual.

This impression is sustained further by a passage that describes the priestly portion of the most holy offerings:

> [8]YHWH spoke to Aaron: "Behold I have given you the supervision of my tithes for all of the sanctified offerings of the Israelites. I have given them to you as a perquisite and for your children as an eternal portion. [9]This will be yours of the most holy sacrifices from the fire, every offering, every grain offering, every sin offering and every guilt offering that they remit to me. It is most holy for you and your sons (Num 18:8–9).

---

96. See Milgrom, *Leviticus*, 859–63.

The wording of this passage, especially the use of the word תרומה ("contribution") implies that the consumption of the sin offering's flesh is perceived as a privilege.

However, there are reasons to view the consumption of the flesh as a means of eliminating the sin and impurity removed by the sin offering. The first piece of evidence is analogy. Whereas the courtyard sin offering is eaten by the priest, the Tent sin offering is burned outside the camp (Lev 6:23). It seems that the reason for the burning of the carcass in the latter case relates to its impurity, as can be deduced by the fact that the person who burns the remains of the Day of Atonement sin offerings must wash himself and launder his clothes, just as the person who leads the goat to Azazel (16:26–28).[97] Accordingly, one may deduce that just as the burning of the carcass serves as a means of disposing of evil, so too the consumption of the flesh. [98]

A more explicit testimony to this notion appears in the narrative depicting the aftermath of the divine fire that consumed Aaron's sons Nadab and Abihu (Lev 10:1–2). The discovery that Aaron and his remaining sons Elazar and Itamar did not eat the sin offering of the community (cf. 9:3) sparks Moses's anger:

> [16]Then Moses insistently inquired about the sin offering goat, and it had already been burned! He was angry with Elazar and Itamar, Aaron's remaining sons, saying: [17]"Why did you not eat the sin offering in the sacred precinct, because it is most holy, and He has assigned it to you to bear the sin of the congregation to effect expiation for them before YHWH. [18]Since its blood was not brought into the interior of the sacred precinct, you should have eaten it in the holy precinct, as I commanded." [19]Aaron spoke to Moses: "See, today they brought their sin and burnt offerings before YHWH and such things have befallen me! Had I eaten the sin offering today, would YHWH have approved?!" [20]Moses heard, and he approved (Lev 10:16–20).

Most of the scholarly debate regarding the function of the consumption of the sin offering flesh has centered on this passage. In a meticulous analysis of this

---

97. Wright, *Disposal of Impurity*, 130–31. Wright also cites Lev 6:20–23 (pp. 95–96 and 147–49) but these verses could be also explained by the notion of sancta contagion, as they employ the term יקדש ("become sanctified") not יטמא ("become defiled"). On this passage, see below.

98. According to Milgrom, the discrepancy in disposal method between the Tent and courtyard offerings stems from the fact that the Tent offerings expiate for transgressions of greater severity than the courtyard offerings; thus the sin that has been transferred to the animal's flesh is too potent for consumption (*Leviticus*, 263; cf. 639).

pericope, Gane has removed many of its ambiguities.[99] I will mention here only a few salient points.[100]

Moses's anger over the burning of the sin offering flesh is clear evidence of the belief that the consumption is an essential element of the expiatory process. True, some scholars interpret the clause "to bear the sin of the congregation" (לשאת את עון העדה) as referring to the priests' general obligation to make expiation on behalf of the nation, which entitles them to a prebend.[101] However, this view cannot be reconciled with a close analysis of the syntax and structure Lev 10:16–20, as will be presently shown.

The first important observation is that Moses's words are divided into a question (...מדוע) and a motive clause (beginning with כי), which serves to explain the question. Gane has shown that they are formed in a chiasmic structure, which can be shown (with slight adaptations) as follows:

A   Why did you not eat (מדוע לא אכלתם)
    B   the sin offering (את החטאת)
        C   in the sacred precinct (במקום הקדש)
        C'   because it is most holy (כי קדש קדשים הוא)
    B'   and it (ואתה)
A'   He has assigned to you (נתן לכם)

In this structure, A corresponds with A' in that both are addressed in the second person to Aaron and his surviving sons. The C elements correspond by their use of קד"ש derivatives. Most importantly for our analysis is the correspondence between B and B', whereby ואתה ("and it") corresponds to את החטאת ("the sin offering"). The chiastic structure serves to highlight the syntax of this verse, in

---

99. Gane, *Cult and Character*, 91–105.

100. It is worth noting two of the common objections to the contention that the priestly consumption of the sin offering flesh fulfills an expiatory function. First, some scholars have argued that since the meat of the sin offering is deemed "most holy" (6:18, 22; 10:17), it cannot bear impurity, e.g., Kurtz, *Sacrificial Worship of the Old Testament*, 228–30 and Dillman, *Exodus-Leviticus*, 463–64, but this argument is hardly convincing. Since the sin offering ritual shares numerous characteristics with the bird rite of Lev 14 and the goat rite of Lev 16, both of which involve the transfer of evil to an animal, it is logical to assume a similar dynamic is involved with the flesh of the sin offering. Second, there is no indication in Lev 10 that the failure to eat the offering undermined the preceding expiatory rites (Elliger, *Leviticus*, 139; Kiuchi, *Purification Offering*, 75).In fact, the appearance of the divine glory at the send of the ritual series is a clear indication of divine approval (Lev 9:24). However, this objection ignores that Lev 10:16–20 is a late harmonistic reinterpretation of Lev 8–9 (see below). For an alternative solution, see Gane, *Cult and Character*, 91–92.

101. von Hoffman, 281; Ehrlich, *Randglossen zur hebräischen Bibel* on Lev 10:17; Janowski, *Sühne als Heilsgeschehen*, 239; Kiuchi, *Purification Offering*, 46–52, 72.

which Moses provides a justification as to why God consigned *it*, namely the sin offering flesh, to Aaron and his sons for consumption. The upshot of these observations is that it is neither the performance of the sin offering ritual in general[102] nor the performance of the blood manipulation[103] that achieves the expiatory effects described in verse 17b, but rather the consumption of the flesh.[104]

Furthermore, B. Schwartz has demonstrated that the image of carrying sin (נש"א עון) has two main usages, both of which are extensions of the metaphor of sin as a burden.[105] When a person bears his own sin, he must take expiatory measures to remove his "burden" in order to avoid the otherwise inevitable consequences of his actions, usually death or extirpation (כר"ת). However, in some cases, a person of higher cultic status can relieve another's burden of sin, and in these cases נש"א עון means to "carry off."

For example, the priest's ability to bear the congregation's sins is expressed in relation to the golden frontlet (ציץ) that Aaron wears when performing his cult duties:

והיה על מצח אהרן ונשא אהרן את עון הקדשים אשר יקדישו בני ישראל לכל מתנת
קדשיהם והיה על מצחו תמיד לרצון להם לפני ה'

> It shall be on Aaron's forehead, that Aaron may bear the sin arising from the holy things that the Israelites consecrate from any of their sacred donations; it shall be on his forehead at all times, to win acceptance for them before YHWH (Exod 28:38).

Similarly, according to Num 35:9–34, unintentional murderers are released from the cities of refuge upon the death of the high priest (v. 32). This rule might be taken to imply that the high priest's death serves as a vicarious atonement. As noted above, the converse is also true. The transgression of the high priest can incriminate the nation (Lev 4:3). Thus, the priests' role is truly a mediating function; just as they serve as God's surrogates in bearing the sins of the people, they are at the same time acting as the nation's representatives before God.

Frequently, it is God himself who takes away the sin from a person (נשא עון),[106] but in some sources, such as Lev 10:17 we learn that the priests are authorized to act as divine representatives in removing sin. We may add to Gane's analysis by noting that an inclusio may also be perceptible in the subsequent explanation:

---

102. So, e.g., Janowski, *Sühne als Heilsgeschehen*, 239, n. 272.
103. So Kiuchi, *Purification Offering*, 49.
104. Gane, *Cult and Character*, 94–99.
105. Schwartz, "'Term' or Metaphor," 149–71; "Bearing of Sin," 3–21.
106. E.g., Exod 34:7; Num 14:18; Mic 7:18. See Schwartz, "Bearing of Sin," 9.

A   And it He has assigned it to you (ואתה נתן לכם)
B   to bear the sin of the congregation (לשאת את עון העדה)
B'   to effect expiation for them (לכפר עליהם)
A'   before YHWH (לפני ה')

The idea embodied in this structure is that God appointed the sin offering to the priests for consumption (A), so that they will bear the nation's sins (B), making expiation for them (B'), and thereby reconciling them with God (A'). The underlying message is that God has delegated the consumption of the sin offering to the priesthood so that they can act as his agents in making expiation for the people.[107]

Thus, we should understand the expression "to bear the sin of the congregation" here as referring to the priests' ability to unburden the transgressor of his sin and "carry it off."[108] Thus, Moses' accusation reveals the fact that the eating of the flesh serves to bear the offerers' sins, thereby making expiation on their behalf.

If the main purpose of eating the sin offering flesh is to dispose of the evil that has been removed from the sancta, why does Moses begin his rebuke by emphasizing its sanctity? Let us reexamine the law to which Moses is alluding, namely Lev 6:18–23:

[18]Speak to Aaron and his sons thus: this is the law for the sin offering. The sin offering shall be slaughtered before YHWH, at the place where the burnt offering is slaughtered; it is most holy. [19]The priest who offers it as a sin offering shall consume it; it shall be eaten in a holy place, in the court of the Tent of Meeting. [20]All that touch its flesh will be consecrated, and if its blood spatters on clothing, that which was spattered shall be laundered in a sacred area. [21]An earthenware vessel in which it was boiled will be broken, and if it was boiled in a bronze vessel, it will be scoured and rinsed with water. [22]Any male among the priests may eat it; it is most holy. [23]Any sin offering whose blood was brought into the Tent of Meeting to make expiation in the sanctuary will not be eaten, it shall be consumed in fire.

Within this passage, verses 18–22 can be taken as a discrete subunit unified by the fact that all of the rules stem from the sanctity of the offering. In fact, this unit is structured chiastically:

A   [18bβ]It is **most holy** (קדש קדשים הוא).

---

107. See in more depth, Gane, *Cult and Character*, 99–105.
108. See also Milgrom, *Leviticus*, 622–25.

B ¹⁹The priest who offers it as a purification offering shall consume it; it shall be eaten in a **holy** place (במקום קדש), in the court of the Tent of Meeting.

 C ²⁰All that touch its flesh **will be consecrated** (יקדש) and if its blood spatters on clothing, that which was spattered shall be laundered in a **sacred** area (במקום קדש).

 C' ²¹An earthenware vessel in which it was boiled will be broken, and if it was boiled in a bronze vessel, it will be scoured and rinsed with water.

B' ^{22a}Any male among the priests may eat it

A' ^{22b}It is **most holy** (קדש קדשים הוא).

This structure can be represented thematically as follows:

A 18bβ Declaration of "most holy" status
 B 19 Law of consumption
  C 20 Law of contact
  C' 21 Law of contact
 B' 22a Law of consumption
A' 22b Declaration of "most holy" status

After these rules pertaining to consumption, v. 23 states the divergent procedure for the sin offering of the Tent, which requires burning. It appears, therefore, that vv. 18bβ–22 were deliberately crafted to form a self-contained stylistic subunit. Not only is this unit framed by declarations of the sin offering's sanctity ("It is most holy"), the root קד"ש appears in these verses seven times.

The structure of this subunit can serve to clarify ambiguous aspects of its content. Despite the fact that the text attributes the requirement of washing to the offering's sanctity (vv. 20–21), many interpreters view the cleansing as evidence that contact with the sin-offering flesh defiles.[109] They raise the following question: if these objects are sanctified, why must they be washed or destroyed (in the case of earthenware vessels)—acts that are usually performed in response to impurity?[110] According to the rabbinic solution, the purpose of the cleaning or breaking is to prevent anyone from eating the remains (הנותר) of the offering after they have been rendered disqualified for consumption (פגול).[111] But this understanding is unlikely for the simple reason that this law is stated only in relation to the sin offering, whereas the laws of נותר and פגול pertain to other

---

109. See, e.g., Wright, *Disposal of Impurity*, 130–31.
110. Cf. Lev 11:32–33; 15:12.
111. See Rashi on v. 21 and Rashbam on v. 20. Cf. Lev 7:16–18.

offerings as well.[112] Alternatively, some modern scholars suggest that the sin offering flesh has an ambiguous status, vacillating between sacred and impure domains.[113] However, in light of the passage's emphasis on the root קד״ש, it is clear that that the author's views on the matter were anything but ambivalent. Based on the present form of the text, we should understand this passage as prescribing measures of desanctification aimed at preventing desecration of consecrated objects through their removal from the sacred precincts.

Nevertheless, the exaggerated emphasis on sanctity in this short passage raises the suspicion that this passage might be polemical. More to the point, the structure of the passage may be intended to convey a particular message, that is, that the laws detailed in verses 19–22a are governed by the elevated status of the offering as declared in its opening (18) and closing (22b). In other words, the careful stylistic organization of the passage may serve a rhetorical function. Namely, it addresses priests who may shy away from the consumption of the sin offering flesh for fear of its defilement, drawing an analogy to the Tent offering, which must be burned. Accordingly, the passage aims to convince the priestly audience that these measures are mandated by the holiness of the offering, not its impurity.

Another passage relevant to this discussion appears in the prophet Hosea's rebuke of the priests:

חטאת עמי יאכלו ואל עונם ישאו נפשו

They eat the sin(-offering) of my people and they long for their iniquities (4:8).[114]

---

112. The *Keli Yaqar* attempts to explain the rabbinic position as pertaining to the other most holy offerings, though the rabbis themselves seem to confine this law to the sin offering (*m. Zevahim* 11:1, 4; *t. Zevahim* 10:9). See also Milgrom, *Leviticus*, 404–5, who cites a similar view held by the Karaites. Indeed, there is no textual basis for applying this law to the other offerings.

113. Such an idea was particularly popular in anthropological writings from the beginning of the twentieth century that emphasized the alleged ambiguous relationship between sacred, taboo, and impure domains. See Durkheim, *Elementary Forms*, 415. On the previous page, Durkheim makes an oblique reference where he applies this idea to the Israelite sin offering. See also Robertson Smith, *Religion of the Semites,* 446–54, esp. 452. For a more recent expression of such an idea, see Milgrom, *Leviticus*, 403–6.

114. Scholars have offered several solutions to the problematic reading נפשו. If it is to be preserved on the basis of *difficilior lectio potior*, the pronominal suffix can be understood distributively as referring to each one of the priests (Kimchi). Alternatively, the text can be read נפשם in accordance with numerous manuscripts of MT. Finally, Gesenius suggests that the the suffix is a result of dittography, resulting from the *waw* which begins the following verse (GKC §145m). None of these options significantly affects the meaning of the verse. Regarding the expression נש״א נפש, its usage is dependent on whether it is followed by a person (or God) or

Anticipating of the Lutheran critique of indulgences, the eighth-century B.C.E. prophet attacks the priests for encouraging sin in order to derive personal benefit. Playing on the double meaning of the term חטאת ("sin"/"sin offering"), he accuses them of being nourished by the people's sin offerings.[115] Further, he claims, in a sarcastic play on the idiom נשׂא עון, that, instead of "bearing" the nation's sin, they long for its transgressions (ואל עונם ישאו נפשו).[116] In effect, Hosea is portraying a severe perversion of the priestly role in consuming the sin offerings, namely to act as divine surrogates in removing the sins of the nation. Thus, this verse testifies to an awareness of priestly traditions and terminology associated with the sin offering in the late-eighth century B.C.E.

This passage can also shed light on the exchange between Moses and Aaron in Lev 10. Moses's rebuke may be rooted in the suspicion that Aaron and his sons have deliberately disregarded the prohibition on mourning (vv. 6–7), and for that reason, they neglected to eat the sin offering (cf. Deut 26:14). Be that as it may, Moses's words reveal a distinctly legalistic focus, with his emphasis on the fact that the blood had not been brought inside the sacred precincts, evoking the cultic law of 6:23 (cf. 16:27). Such zealousness to detail is understandable when taking into account the background of the preceding events, in which Nadab and Abihu were annihilated when they "brought a strange fire before God that he had not commanded them," that is, they had deviated from the divinely authorized cult procedure.

Aaron's reply shows that Moses's suspicions were ill-founded. He refers back to the chain of events in which Nadab and Abihu were struck down by divine vengeance shortly after bringing their own expiatory offerings earlier that day (9:2–11), which were a prerequisite for them to serve as cultic representatives of the congregation.[117] Under these circumstances, he retorts, how could we expect to bear the sins of the nation by consuming their sin offering?[118]

---

by an inanimate object or idea. In the former case, it refers to placing one's reliance on another human or divine being; see, e.g., Deut 25:15; Ps 25:1. In the latter case, as in our verse, it refers to placing one's desire or expectation in something: see, e.g., Jer 22:27; Prov 19:18. Seebass, "נפשׁ," *TDOT* 9:507.

115. See Levine, *In the Presence of the Lord*, 107; Andersen and Freedman, *Hosea*, 358–59; Stuart, *Hosea–Jonah*, 79; Milgrom, *Leviticus*, 286–87. Not all commentators acknowledge that תאטה in this passage refers to the sin offering, arguing from the parallelism of חטאת\עון that it refers to sin. See, e.g., Harper, *Amos and Hosea*, 257–58. But translating the passage as a reference to "eating sin" is much less likely than "eating the sin offering." Furthermore, the usage of the terms נשׂ"א and עון can hardly be coincidental (see below).

116. See also Milgrom, *Leviticus*, 286–87.

117. Milgrom, *Leviticus*, 626.

118. See Ehrlich, *Randglossen zur hebräischen Bibel*, 37; Hoffmann, *Das Buch Leviticus* on 10:19–20.

Aaron, the high priest, recognizes the hypocrisy of the situation in which the priests would effect expiation for the nation, when they themselves have just evoked divine punishment. Although he had been previously been preoccupied with the technical aspect of the cultic law, Moses, the lawgiver, is now forced to concede the point.

This brief narrative episode challenges the dichotomy that is often purported to exist between formal ritualistic practice and internal personal religion. On one hand, pious intentions cannot justify innovations in the divinely commanded ritual system (vv. 1–2). On the other, adherence to the formal details of cult praxis cannot take the place of the priest's moral integrity (v. 19). These equally unyielding demands serve as the foundation for the Priestly ideal. As Hosea's rebuke demonstrates, such an ideal was often at odds with reality.

Diachronic Analysis

The explicit references to the priest's privilege and obligation to eat the remaining flesh of the sin offering surveyed above cannot but call our attention to the glaring absence of any reference to this consumption in the prescriptive (Lev 4–5:13) and descriptive texts (Exod 29; Lev 8–9), which preserve the details of particular ritual procedures. Indeed, the ritual texts associated with the consecration and inaugural rituals relate that, despite the fact that the blood rites were performed on the courtyard altar, the flesh of the sin offering was burned outside the camp with its hide and dung (Exod 29:14, Lev 8:17; 9:11). This procedure contradicts the law outlined in Lev 6:19–23 which allots the flesh of the sin offering to the officiating priest for consumption, except in cases where the blood was manipulated inside the shrine. While this discrepancy could potentially be explained by analogy to the prohibition that a priest should benefit from his own grain offering (Lev 6:16),[119] the absence of any reference to the priestly consumption of the flesh in Lev 4:22–35 undermines this view. At the least, one must assume that the disposal of the carcass was not of any major significance to the expiatory process. More likely, this text (as well as Exod 29 and Lev 8–9) reflect an alternative, possibly earlier, tradition according to which the flesh was not allocated to the priests.[120]

There are indications that both 6:18–23 and 10:16–20 were either composed or redacted by H. While neither of these two passages bears the distinctive ter-

---

119. See Ḥazzequni on Exod 29:14; Dillmann, *Die Bücher Exodus und Leviticus*, 463–64; Gane, *Cult and Character*, 89.

120. So, e.g., Rendtorff, *Geschichte des Opfers*, 222–26; Wefing, "*Entsühnungsritual am grossen Versöhnungstag*," 140–41; Janowski, *Sühne als Heilsgeschehen*, 237–38; Milgrom, *Leviticus*, 636–40.

minology of H, they show some stylistic affinities to this source, in particular the use of introversions. Moreover, the numerical scheme comprised of seven instances of קדֹשׁ in 6:18–22 may be taken as a trace of H's influence.[121] Since H's activity is evident elsewhere in Lev 6–7, such an attribution is not surprising.[122]

Regarding 10:16–20, we must be more cautious, as there are no overt indications of H's intervention. However, since this passage is based on 6:18–23, as reflected by the expression כאשר צויתי ("like I commanded" [v. 18]), we should leave the possibility open that this passage derives from the same source. Furthermore, we should note that the core Nadab and Abihu narrative of Lev 10 has been supplemented by a number of appendixes.[123] Since the passage that deals with the drinking prohibition (vv. 8–11) contains several literary characteristics of H,[124] one may suspect that the subsequent sections may have been composed or edited by the same source. In any case, even if Lev 6:18–23 and 10:16–20 are ascribed to P based on the lack of distinctive H vocabulary, they clearly emerged from a relatively late stratum.

This diachronic perspective may shed some light on the underlying message of the dialogue between Moses and Aaron in Lev 10:16–20. First, the passage acts as a midrash that seeks to remove the tension between the law of Lev 6:18–23, which mandates the priestly consumption of courtyard sin offerings, and the ritual of Lev 9 where the congregation's offering is apparently burned like that of the priesthood (vv. 11, 15).[125] Second, Moses's accusation provides a rationale for the eating of the sin offering that is not provided elsewhere in the cultic literature. The passage might serve a polemical function, namely to justify the eating of the sin offering flesh in response to P's contrary tradition to burn it. More specifically, the emphasis in these passages on the sanctity of the sin offering seems to reveal an intention to assuage priests' fear of defilement. In other words, these passages may be addressing the religious anxieties of the priests aroused in the wake of a cult reform that required eating instead of burning the flesh.[126]

---

121. On H's frequent use of schemes incorporating the number seven, see Milgrom, *Leviticus* 2:1323–25.

122. Knohl attributes the following to H: 6:10–11; 7:19b:22–36 (*Sanctuary of Silence*, 105; cf. 49–51). Besides the present pericope, Milgrom attributes 7:22–29a to H (*Leviticus*, 396, 426).

123. Elliger, *Leviticus*, 136.

124. See Knohl, *Sanctuary of Silence*, 51–52. Cf. Elliger, *Leviticus*, 134–35; Milgrom, *Leviticus*, 617. Knohl also attributes vv. 6–7 to H (68–69).

125. Elliger, *Leviticus*, 135–36.

126. This understanding is preferable to that of Milgrom (*Leviticus*, 635–640), which is based on several speculative presuppositions.

The reference in Hos 4:8 to the expiatory function of eating the sin offering raises some intriguing possibilities for placing this tradition in a historical context. In particular, it raises the possibility that the authors' of Lev 6:18–23 and Lev 10:16–20 (H?) were influenced by northern traditions.[127] It is interesting to note that another addition to Lev 10, verses 9–10, which can be more confidently attributed to H, warns the priests against drunkenness during their service. This concern also finds parallel in Hosea's accusations against the northern priesthood in that same chapter (4:11, 18). In this context, it is interesting to note the view held by some scholars that Hosea was a disenfranchised northern priest or at least affiliated with a priestly opposition group.[128] Though these connections between Hosea and H remain speculative and cannot be fully explored here, they raise the possibility that the eating of the sin offering may have been a northern tradition brought to Judah after the destruction of Samaria in 722 B.C.E.[129]

THE EXPIATORY RITUAL OF LEVITICUS 16

Leviticus 16 presents a complex synthesis of rites. Though these may have been independent originally, they are now integrated into a coherent scheme. The following analysis will examine the function of its individual rites and seek to identify the reinterpretations of these rites which are reflected in the secondary layers of the text.

Synchronic Overview

The blood rite is divided into three parts, which correspond to the divisions of the Tabernacle, namely, the adytum, Tent, and courtyard. These rites require a bull as a sin offering for the high priest and the priesthood and two goats for the congregation. A lottery determines which of the goats will be designated for YHWH and which is to be sent off to Azazel:[130] The bull and the goat assigned to YHWH are used for the blood rite that is performed inside the adytum:

---

127. Alternatively, it may also reflect the earlier Judean practice that was then changed by P. According to this possibility, despite the fact that Lev 6:18–23 and Lev 10:16–20 are relatively late, they may reflect a reactionary tendency that is challenging an earlier cult reform advocated by P.

128. See Wolff, "Hoseas geistige Heimat," 243–50; Cook, *Social Roots of Biblical Yahwism*, 231–66. It is interesting to add that Hosea's use of the term תורה (Hos 4:6; 8:12) in cultic contexts is reminiscent of the Priestly use of this term to designate cultic instructions.

129. See also Knohl's discussion of the historical background for the "Holiness School" (*Sanctuary of Silence*, 204–20).

130. Based on alternative readings in the other textual witnesses, such as עזזאל, most scholars view the MT reading עזאזל ("goat to go") as a later emendation and assume that Azazel

[11]Aaron shall bring forward his sin offering bull and make expiation for himself and for his household. He shall slaughter his sin offering bull. [12]He shall take a full pan of blazing coals from upon the altar that is before YHWH and two handfuls of finely ground perfumed incense, and he shall bring these inside the curtain. [13]He shall place the incense on the coals before YHWH, and the cloud of incense shall envelop the cover that is upon the testimony, lest he die. [14]He shall take from the blood of the bull and sprinkle with his finger on the eastern face of the *kapporet*, and in front of the *kapporet* he shall sprinkle some of the blood with his finger seven times. [15]Then he shall slaughter the people's sin offering goat and bring its blood inside the curtain and manipulate its blood like he did with the blood of the bull on the *kapporet* and before the *kapporet*. [16]Thus he will purge the adytum from the impurities of the Israelites and from the (defiant) transgressions of all their sins, and thus he will do to the Tent of Meeting that dwells among them in their impurities. [17]No one shall be in the Tent of Meeting when he comes to make expiation in the holy domain until he leaves, and he shall make expiation on the behalf of himself, his household and the entire congregation of Israel.

Donning special linen vestments, the high priest burns incense to prevent a potentially fatal sighting of the Deity in the adytum (cf. vv. 12–13). The blood rite consists of an act of sprinkling on the ark's cover and seven aspersions in the air before it, using the blood of the bull and goat. These acts purge the adytum of the Israelites' impurities and transgressions. These detailed instructions are followed by a laconic comment to repeat the procedure inside the Tent in v. 16b, which will be discussed below.

The third and final stage of the blood rite is described as follows:

[18]He shall go out to the altar that is before YHWH and make expiation upon it. He shall take some of the blood of the bull and some of the blood of the goat and apply it to the horns around the altar. [19]He shall then sprinkle on it some of the blood with his finger seven times and purify it and sanctify it from the impurities of the Israelites. [20]When he finishes purging the adytum, the Tent of Meeting and the altar, he shall bring forward the live goat.

---

is a proper name, signifying God's counterpart who receives Israel's iniquities. See Pinker, "A Goat to Go to Azazel." Cf. however, Janowski and Wilhelm's recent proposal that this term is a corrupted form of the Hurrian offering term *azus/zḫi*. According to this view, the term originally signified the type of offering, so that the goat for *azuz(ḫi)* paralleled the goat for *ḥaṭṭat* (See Janowski and Wilhelm, "Religionsgeschichte des Azazel-Ritus," and below, pp. 123–24).

As is clear from the verb "he went out" (ויצא), these verses deal with rites that take place at the sacrificial altar in the courtyard.[131] Through the acts of daubing and sprinkling of blood, the altar is purified.

The text now provides instructions for the rite to be performed with the live goat designated for Azazel:

> [21]Aaron shall lean his two hands on the head of the live goat and confess over it all of the iniquities of the Israelites and the (defiant) transgressions of all their sins. He shall place them on the head of the goat and send it off to the wilderness by means of a designated man. [22a]Thus the goat will carry on it all of the iniquities to a remote land.

After impurity and transgression have been removed from the sanctuary, the latter is transferred onto the live goat and banished from the Israelite settlement. It is instructive to compare this verse with the description of the effects of the adytum rite in v. 16:

Blood Ritual	Goat Ritual
[16]וכפר על הקדש מטמאת בני ישראל ומפשעיהם לכל חטאתם וכן יעשה לאהל מועד השכן אתם בתוך טמאתם	[21]וסמך אהרן את שתי ידו ידיו על ראש השעיר החי והתודה עליו את כל עונת בני ישראל ואת כל פשעיהם לכל חטאתם ונתן אתם על ראש השעיר ושלח ביד איש עתי המדברה [22]ונשא השעיר עליו את כל עונתם אל ארץ גזרה ושלח את השעיר במדבר
[16]Thus he will purge the adytum from the impurities of the Israelites and from the (defiant) transgressions of all their sins, and thus he will do to the Tent of Meeting that dwells among them in their impurities.	[21]Aaron shall lean his two hands on the head of the live goat and confess over it all of the iniquities of the Israelites and all of the (defiant) transgressions of all their sins... [22a]Thus the goat will carry on it all of the iniquities to a remote land.

From this comparison, we can see that the central role of "impurities" (מטמאת) in the adytum rite has been replaced by "iniquities" (עונת) in the goat rite.[132] This

---

131. So Ibn Ezra, against the rabbinic view that these verses refer to the incense altar inside the Tent (*Sipra*, Aharei Moth, Pereq 4, 8 [ed. Weiss, 79b]; *m. Yoma* 5:5; Rashi; Ramban). This conclusion is reinforced by v. 16, which refers to the completion of the rites to purge the Tent of Meeting, as well as by v. 20, which depicts the altar as distinct from the Tent.

132. This comparison probably underlies the Mishnaic distinction between the blood ritual, which atones for the intentional sin of contaminating the sanctuary, and the live goat ritual, which removes both major and minor transgressions (*m. Shavuot* 1:6).

distinction is continued in the subsequent verse of each passage, which mentions only the main category of evil: "impurities" (16b) versus "iniquities" (22a).

Since "iniquities" are not mentioned in relation to the blood rites of Lev 16, let us examine this term in more depth so as to appreciate the distinctive character of the goat rite. In cultic texts, עון denotes the culpability that a person must bear because he has either neglected to perform an expiation ritual or because the nature of the sin does not permit expiation. Likewise, the expression נש"א עון ("bear iniquity") usually refers to situations in which a person sins intentionally.[133] In such cases, there is generally no cultic remedy, and the person is condemned to annihilation. For example, Num 15 explictly states in relation to the brazen sinner: "that person will surely be cut off—his guilt is upon him" (הכרת תכרת הנפש ההוא עונה בה [v. 31]). The expressions נשא עון and עונה בה signify a situation where the person has not separated himself from his defiant act. Consequently, the weight of the act would cling to him and ultimately crush him.[134] Koch has perceptively noted that the impact of these formulas is parallel to that of the expressions דמיו בו (literally "his blood is on him")[135] or דמך על ראשך ("your blood is on your head").[136] These idioms refer to a situation where one is culpable for one's own demise.

Yet some sources, including Lev 16, reveal a means by which one could restore the possibility of expiating iniquities—verbal confession. For example, the pericope regarding the graduated sin offering (Lev 5:1–3) presents the law regarding a person who "bears guilt" for withholding testimony (v. 1). Although this transgression is undoubtedly intentional, he may bring a sin offering, provided that he first "confess over that matter in which he sinned" (והתודה אשר חטטא עליה). A more extreme example of this dynamic appears as part of the covenant curses in Lev 26. The latter chapter predicts that, after suffering the severest divine retribution, which will decimate the nation and cast them into exile, the survivors will finally begin to feel remorse:

40והתודו את עונם ואת עון אבתם במעלם אשר מעלו בי ואף אשר הלכו עמי בקרי
41אף אני אלך עמם בקרי והבאתי אתם בארץ איביהם או אז יכנע לבבם הערל ואז ירצו את עונם

> 40 But if they shall confess their iniquity and iniquity of their ancestors, in their trespass against me, and moreover, that they continued in opposition to me 41so that I, in turn, continued in opposition to them, and dispersed them in the land

---

133. E.g., Lev 5:1; 17:16; 19:8; 20:17, 19.

134. Schwartz, "Bearing of Sin," 9–10.

135. Lev 20:9, 11–13, 16, 27; Ezek 18:13.

136. 2 Sam 1:16 (*ketiv* דמיך). Cf. also 1 Kgs 2:32. See Koch, "Die israelitische Auffassung vom vergossenen Blut," 436–41.

of their enemies—if, then, their uncircumcised heart is humbled, and they shall atone for their iniquity.[137]

When the Israelites acknowledge responsibility for their sins, including those of their ancestors, and admit that they have brought the divine wrath upon themselves, God will renew his covenant with them.

The preceding observations can illuminate the role of confession in the goat rite of Lev 16. As is particularly clear from the passage in Lev 26, the term עונות can also refer to collective guilt left over by individual transgressors after their death. Accordingly, it is one of the functions of the high priest, the cultic representative of the Israelite corporate personality, to take responsibility for the "orphaned" sin through verbal confession and remove it from the community by means of the goat to Azazel.[138]

Diachronic Analysis

Even a cursory evaluation of this chapter reveals a number of tensions that defy harmonization. For example, the chapter opens with a warning cautioning Aaron from entering the sacred precinct "at any time" (v. 2), which implies that the following ritual addresses an emergency situation, yet the summary at the end of the chapter in vv. 29–34a fixes the date at the 10th day of the 7th month.[139] Through closer analysis, three literary layers can be identified, consisting of the primary ritual source and two subsequent redactions. The following analysis will attempt to delineate these materials and thereby reveal the distinct understandings of the ritual reflected in these distinct strata.[140]

Since the original ritual has been thoroughly integrated with later redactional layers, it is not possible to isolate this source. The separation of layers can be achieved only by isolating the redactional strata and analyzing the relation between them and the original (necessarily conjectural) ritual. Though the attribution of certain clauses to a particular stratum is tentative at best, I present

---

137. I understand the *yiqtol* form אלך as expressing that God's reaction is successive to (i.e., caused by) Israel's disobedience, expressed by the *qatal* in the phrase ואף אשר הלכו עמי בקרי of the previous verse. In other words, the Israelites are confessing that their punishment and exile were caused by their own actions. Cf. Milgrom, *Leviticus* 3:2332.

138. In this context we should recall that the term iniquities (עונות) is not mentioned in conjunction with the defilement of the sanctuary (vv. 16, 19). The origin of these iniquities must therefore be outside the Tabernacle, namely in the Israelite settlement at large.

139. This tension was already sensed by Rabbinic commentators. See Milgrom, *Leviticus*, 1012–13.

140. For overviews of these attempts, see Wefing, "*Entsühnungsritual am grossen Versöhnungstag*," 3–29 and Aartun, "Gesetz über den grossen Versöhnungstag," 74–76.

the following reconstruction in order to assist the reader in following my broader arguments regarding the different editorial agendas which have shaped the final form of Lev 16.[141]

Stratum	Content	Verses
1 (P_1)	A) Sin offering ritual with bull in adytum B) Ritual with two goats	A) $2^?$, 3–4, 6, 14*, 17 B) 7–10, 21—22*
2 (P_2)	• Integration of independent rituals • Application of new composite ritual to context of the sin of Nadab and Abihu and its aftermath • Specifically, the priesthood must be expiated on account of their sin, and the sanctuary must be purged of corpse impurity	1, 2bγ, 5, 11–16, 17bβ–19, 34b
3 (H)	• Setting a fixed date for the composite ritual • Attributing further significance to the ritual in conjunction with a systematic view of sin offering rituals • Specifically, the ritual provides the means for an annual purging of the sanctuary and expiation for the people's defiant acts	16aβ, 20a, 29–34a

As outlined in this table, the main guidelines for distinguishing between sources pertain to the distinct interpretations of the ritual expressed in them. Aside from the recognition of a primary layer (which itself may be composite—see below), which served as a basis for redaction, we must distinguish between the two layers of redaction of the chapter. The first of these sought to integrate these primary materials and framed them in reference to the Nadab and Abihu incident of Lev 10. Indeed, many scholars have recognized that Lev 16 was originally appended to the Nadab and Abihu narrative before the purity laws of Lev 11–15 were inserted between them.[142] The insertion of those chapters as well as the final redaction of Lev 16, which transformed the ritual into an annual day of expiation, should be attributed to H. A more detailed analysis of the literary and ideological basis for distinguishing between these layers will be discussed in the following sections.

---

141. The following diachronic analysis pays only cursory attention to vv. 21–28. The asterisks in the table refer to verses whose content seems to have existed in the original source but whose form has been reworked.

142. Noth, *Leviticus: A Commentary*, 117–18; Elliger, *Leviticus*, 12; Milgrom, *Leviticus*, 1011, 1061.

Stratum 1. There are several indications that the chapter is based on a unique and probably archaic ritual tradition. First of all, the chapter is characterized by idiosyncratic terminology, including *hapex legomena* such as איש עתי (v. 21) and ארץ גזרה (22). Most distinctive in this respect is the anamolous designation הקדש in reference to the adytum (2, 3, 16, 20, 23), in comparison to elsewhere in P and H, which employ this term in reference to the Shrine. Another possible indication of the relative earliness of the primary layer is the lack of mention of the incense altar (see below). Moreover, the reference to Azazel, whether the name refers to a demonic entity or an offering term,[143] may testify to the ritual's antiquity. Finally, the typological similarity to the bird rite of Lev 14 may also support this assumption.[144] These characteristics are crucial for the diachronic analysis of this chapter, since much of the description of the ritual procedure seems to have been reworked by Strata 2 and 3 editors.

An additional basis for distinguishing between Strata 1 and 2 can be established through analysis of the introduction to the chapter, which integrates the ritual instructions into the Priestly narrative. Specifically, it frames the reception of these instructions as taking place in the aftermath of the Nadab and Abihu incident:

¹וידבר ה' אל משה אחרי מות שני בני אהרן בקרבתם לפני ה' וימתו

²ויאמר ה' אל משה דבר אל אהרן אחיך ואל יבא בכל עת אל הקדש מבית לפרכת אל פני

הכפרת אשר על הארן ולא ימות כי בענן אראה על הכפרת

[1]YHWH spoke to Moses after the death of the two sons of Aaron when they approached YHWH and died. [2]YHWH said to Moses: Tell Aaron, your brother, that he must not enter at will into the holy precinct, inside the curtain, before the *kapporet* that is on the ark, so that he will not die, for by means of a cloud I will appear on the *kapporet*.

The relationship between the Nadab and Abihu incident described in Lev 10:1–7 and the opening verses of Lev 16 is at first glance perplexing, as numerous contradictions are immediately apparent. First of all, Lev 10:1 describes the transgression of Aaron's eldest sons as being that they "offered (ויקריבו) a strange fire before YHWH that he had not commanded them," thereby focusing the criticism on their offering. Similarly, the event is portrayed elsewhere in the Torah as occurring "by their offering (בהקרבם) a strange fire before YHWH" (Num 3:4; 26:61). In contrast, our chapter refers to their death which happened "upon their *approaching* בקרבתם)) YHWH" (v. 1). True, the ancient versions interpret the

---

143. See above, n. 130.
144. See below, p. 132.

infinitival *qal* form בקרבתם in light of the *hiphil* בהקרבם, which appears in the other sources, thereby harmonizing the sources so that all refer to the transgression of offering a strange fire.[145] However, this interpretation must be rejected, as it is contradicted by v. 2 which continues to refer to the dangers of *approaching* the adytum.

Second, a close reading of Lev 10:1–7 seems to reveal that Aaron's sons did not enter the sanctuary at all, and that they were struck down in the courtyard when a "fire came forth" (ותצא אש, v. 2), i.e., exited from the Tent. Ironically, the language employed here to depict God's rejection of their offering is the same as that used to describe the fire of God's acceptance, which consumed the Israelites' offerings in the immediately preceding account of the Tabernacle's cultic initiation (Lev 9:24):

ותצא אש מלפני ה' ותאכל על המזבח את העלה ואת החלבים וירא כל העם וירנו ויפלו על פניהם

Fire **came forth** from before YHWH and consumed the burnt offering and the fats on the altar, and the whole nation saw, cheered and fell on their faces.

From this parallel we may deduce that just as the latter burning took place at the altar of burn offerings in the courtyard, so too Nadab and Abihu were also consumed in the courtyard. In addition, Moses commands the Levites Mishael and Elzaphan to remove the corpses in v. 4. Since they are non-priests and hence forbidden to enter the shrine (cf. Num 18:4–5), we must conclude that the bodies lay in the courtyard.[146] Finally, v. 3 seems to imply that their death took place "before all of the people" (ועל פני כל העם), which would indicate that the deaths occurred in the only place where the people could assemble—the courtyard.[147] Thus, the allusion at the beginning of Lev 16 contradicts the simple understanding of 10:1–7.

A final tension between Lev 10:1–7 and Lev 16:1–2 pertains to the role of burning incense. Whereas Lev 10:1–7 views the illicit offering of Aaron's sons as the sole cause of their demise, Lev 16 focuses on the danger of approaching God. In this context, the incense offering serves to neutralize the threat. The

---

145. Not surprisingly, the Sipra (Aharei Moth, Parshatha 1, 2, ed. Weiss, 77a–b) records a disagreement whether the deaths occurred as a result of approaching (על הקריבה מתו) or as a result of their offering (על הקרבה).

146. In the Sipra, R' Eliezer views this latter argument as decisive proof that Aaron's sons died outside the Tent, but R' Aqiva maintains that they were killed inside but that their bodies were dragged out to the courtyard by means of iron spears (Millu'im Shemini 35, ed. Weiss, 48b; cf. Targum Pseudo-Jonothan on Lev 10:5). For further discussion, see Milgrom, *Leviticus*, 605–6.

147. See also Milgrom, *Leviticus*, 599–600.

juxtaposition of vv. 1 and 2 leads to the induction that if Aaron fails to observe the conditions of proper entry into the adytum, he will suffer the same fate as his sons.[148] More specifically, Aaron must not enter the adytum unless he creates a cloud of incense to shield his gaze from the divine presence.

What should we make of the unique understanding of the Nadab and Abihu episode as reflected in Lev 16:1–2? One might assume that the author of Lev 16:1–2 simply understood (or misunderstood) the text of Lev 10:1–7 in this manner. However, the systematic manner in which the elements of the narrative have been transformed to move the emphasis from the illicit offering to the misdeed of approaching the Deity seems to reflect a deliberate reworking of the narrative that aims to change its focus.

Alhough one might think that this reinterpretation was motivated by ideology,[149] it seems better explained on literary grounds. Specifically, the editor has reframed the Nadab and Abihu narrative in order to emphasize the danger involved with approaching God's abode, thereby showing the necessity for the precautions that accompany the blood rite in the adytum described in vv. 3–4.[150] This message is particularly salient when we compare the first two verses of Lev 16:

v. 1	v. 2
וידבר ה' אל משה אחרי מות שני בני אהרן **בקרבתם** לפני ה' **וימתו**	ויאמר ה' אל משה דבר אל אהרן אחיך **ואל יבא** בכל עת אל הקדש מבית לפרכת אל פני הכפרת אשר על הארן **ולא ימות** כי בענן אראה על הכפרת
YHWH spoke to Moses after the death of the two sons of Aaron when **they approached** YHWH **and died.**	YHWH said to Moses: Tell Aaron, your brother, that **he must not enter** at will into the holy precinct...so that **he will not die**, for by means of a cloud I will appear on the the *kapporet*.

From a source-critical perspective, it seems that the author has devised a midrashic reinterpretation that creates a thematic link between the narrative and the pre-existing rite, which involves the entrance of the high priest into the

---

148. An aggadic midrash compares this verse to a doctor who seeks to concretize to his patient the imminent danger of ignoring a particular course of therapy by referring to a former case in which a patient forewent the treatment and died promptly thereafter as a result (see Rashi on v. 1).

149. For example, by the view that God's harsh retribution against Aaron's sons was unjustified.

150. Cf. also Watts, *Ritual and Rhetoric in Leviticus*, 124–25.

adytum. More specifically, the author modeled v. 1 after v. 2 in order to connect the instructions for the rite in the adytum with the narrative of Lev 10:1–7.[151]

But the reinterpretation of the Nadab and Abihu episode seems to have affected more than just the literary form of Lev 16. Verses 1 and 2 seem to imply that Aaron's sons were struck dead while approaching the adytum—that is to say, inside the sanctuary. In light of the laws of corpse impurity outlined in Num 19, such an event would surely defile the sanctuary's appurtenances. But this obvious implication is not spelled out by the text, a conspicuous absence that left quite a few rabbinic authorities and commentators at a loss to explain why the contents of the Tabernacle were *not* defiled.[152] This silence can be easily resolved by assuming that the editor of Lev 16 who composed v. 1 sought to avoid a direct conflict with Lev 10, since the latter leaves no hint that defilement has taken place (because the deaths occurred outside according to its account).

Despite the subtlety of the reference, the editor proceeds to exploit the significance of the episode to the fullest by connecting it with the subsequent ritual instructions of Lev 16. As stated poignantly by Milgrom: "Nadab and Abihu had polluted the sanctuary doubly, in life by their sin and in death by their corpses."[153] Consequently, according to Stratum 2, which deals with an emergency rite, the Nadab and Abihu episode epitomizes the type of event that can threaten the very core of the Israelite cult.

A distinction between Strata 1 and 2 can also be discerned in reference to the Deity's command in v. 2 to burn incense "for by means of the cloud I shall appear over the *kapporet*" (כי בענן אראה על הכפרת) and in the fulfillment of this requirement in vv. 12–13. Several considerations indicate that these references to incense are an addition, stemming from the Stratum 2 redaction. For instance, this condition appears outside the list of preparations, which begin with the expression "With this Aaron shall enter..." in v. 3. Furthermore, the verses that describe the execution of the incense burning (vv. 12–13) disturb the sequence of the rite in the adytum, appearing between the slaughter of the bull (11b) and the sprinkling of its blood (14).[154] The text implies that, in addition to carrying incense and burning coals into the adytum, Aaron must take along a vessel

---

151. Of course, an alternative explanation—in my view, less convincing—is that a redactor composed both versus in light of the stratum 1 adytum rite.

152. See, e.g., the opinions cited in the article "טמאת אהלים," *Enṣiqlopedia Talmudit* (vol. 20; Jerusalem, 1991), col. 196 (Hebrew); Ehrlich, *Randglossen zur hebräischen Bibel*, on Lev 10:2. For a critique of the latter's proposal, see Milgrom, *Leviticus*, 607–8.

153. Milgrom, *Leviticus*, 1011.

154. While noting that these verses disturb the procedural sequence, Noth nevertheless entertains the possibility that the incense was original to the ritual (*Leviticus: A Commentary*, 122–23).

filled with blood, a feat bordering on superhuman.[155] Thus, these references to incense should be ascribed to the Statum 2 editor's efforts to associate the ritual with the Nadab and Abihu episode. Whereas Aaron's sons were struck dead for bringing an unauthorized fire before the Deity (10:1), Aaron is provided with a divinely mandated means of burning incense, which will enable him to approach the divine presence.

It is possible that the blood rite in the adytum and live goat rite were originally independent but have been woven together by the Stratum 2 redactor. The primary evidence for this contention is the verbatim resumptive repetition of v. 6 in 11a, which brackets out the preparations for the goat rite in vv. 7–10. If so, the reference to the two goats in v. 5 must also be interpreted as an addition that is dependent on vv. 7–10. Its secondary nature might be inferred from its position in the text. If the goats were original to the text, it may be argued, we would expect them after the reference to the bull in v. 3, not after a description of the high priest's clothing in v. 4.[156] According to this suggestion, the editor preferred to add the goats at the end in order to preserve the integrity of the original list. Based on these considerations, it would follow that the original blood rite (Ritual A) involved only a bull for the priesthood and the goat rite (Ritual B) involved only two goats.

However, these arguments are not conclusive. In the present form of the text, the two rites are mutually interdependent, such that one cannot separate the texts without damaging their coherence. For example, the priests' bull, designated "his own sin offering bull" (vv. 6, 11), implies the existence of a corresponding offering for the nation (15).[157] Likewise, the parallelism between Lev 16's goat rite and Lev 14's bird rite would indicate that the goat for Azazel was originally associated with another goat used in a blood rite, as we find in the present text.

---

155. The Rabbis resolved this difficulty by assuming that the high priest brought the incense and blood into the adytum separately (*m. Yoma* 5:1, 3). This interpretation assumes that חקלו ("he shall take") in v. 14 implies an additional exit and entry into the adytum.

156. Cf. Exod 29 and Lev 8. Though these chapters follow different sequences, both separate the categories of clothing and offerings. One may also note the syntax of v. 5 in which the verb precedes the object, deviating from the other clauses in the section (vv. 3–4) in which the object is given precedence, constituting items on a list.

157. This difficulty could be resolved in various ways. One could assume that vv. 1, 6 have been glossed to reflect the integration of Rituals A and B. Alternatively, Wefing suggests that the expression simply refers to the fact that the sin offering is performed for the benefit of the high priest, not to differentiate this offering from another (*Atonement*, 49–50). It is also possible that Ritual A originally involved an offering for the nation, but that it was omitted when Ritual B was integrated into the text.

Since any attempt to separate these rites leads to serious gaps, it seems preferable to view the Stratum 1 rites as a functional unity.[158]

In the following description of the procedure of the blood rite (vv. 14—20), one cannot easily establish which sections derive from the original instructions. For example, though the sprinkling of the bull's blood in the adytum (v. 14) was surely present in the original version, v. 14b shows signs that it has been reworked, particularly its chiastic form and the seven-fold sprinkling, which appears elsewhere in demonstrably later texts.[159] In any case, it seems that the original rationale for these rites has been preserved in vv. 6, 11aβ. Specifically, the rites are described as making expiation for the priests, though the expanded form of these formulas in v. 17b, which includes the entire congregation of Israel, probably stems from the H redactor. The role of the sin offering—specifically a bull—as a primary means of making expiation for the priesthood is demonstrated by other rituals, specifically Exod 29, 10–14, Lev 4, 3–12 and 9, 7–11. In comparison, the goal of purging the sanctuary (vv. 16, 19b, 20a) should be viewed as secondary.[160] As shown in our analysis of the ordination ritual described in Exod 29 and Lev 8, the priests' sin offering in the ordination ritual has also been secondarily reinterpreted as effecting purgation of the altar.[161] Thus, the Stratum 2 redaction of Lev 16 corresponds to a more comprehensive editorial agenda evident in Exod 29 and Lev 8.

V. 16b might be original, but its laconic formulation raises questions regarding its intent. Some scholars[162] interpret this command in light of the reference in Exod 30, 10 to the yearly purification of the incense altar:

וכפר אהרן על קרנתיו אחת בשנה מדם חטאת הכפרים אחת בשנה יכפר עליו לדרתיכם קדש
קדשים הוא לה'

Once a year Aaron will make expiation upon its horns with the blood of the sin offering of expiation; purification will be made for it once a year for all time. It is most holy to YHWH.

---

158. Accordingly, the resumptive repetition in v. 11a must be viewed as merely a stylistic (but not redactional) device. So Milgrom, *Leviticus*, 1024.

159. See above pp. 46–48 and 64–67.

160. So already Elliger (*Leviticus*, 205) and Wefing ("*Entsühnungsritual am grossen Versöhnungstag*," 100–119).

161. See above pp. 48–50.

162. Although Exod 30:10 refers only to the incense altar, Milgrom (*Leviticus*, 1034–39) and Gane (*Cult and Character*, 72–80), interpret this verse as implying a two part purification rite inside the Tent involving the daubing of the incense altar and the sprinkling of the veil, analogous to the rites of Lev 4, 3–21. Aside from the question of the authenticity of Exod 30:10's interpretation, their attempt to attribute significance to the numerical pattern of aspersions strains the textual evidence, which limits its description of the Tent rite to a laconic וכן.

We should ascertain from this verse that the purgation of the Tent described in Lev 16:16b is effected by means of the daubing of blood on the golden incense altar. However, the absence of an explicit reference to this altar in Lev 16 raises the suspicion that Exod 30:10 is a late reinterpretation.[163] The lateness of Exod 30:10 is confirmed by the reference to the rite taking place "once a year," a view that is consistent with H's fixing the date of the Day of Expiation (see below).[164] It seems more appropriate to reconstruct the required procedure in light of the sin offering rites of Lev 4:6–7, 17–18, which deal with the sin offering performed inside the Tent for the sin of the high priest or the entire congregation. In particular, one might infer that Lev 16:16b implies a sprinkling of blood against the veil of the shrine, as described in Lev 4:6, 17.[165]

One can only speculate about the original context of these traditions,[166] and, as noted above, a further uncertainty pertains to whether the adytum and goat rites were originally connected. Regarding the adytum rite, the danger that is incumbent on the high priest upon performance of this rite is a clear indication of the severity of the situation that would require the taking of such a risk. The most likely motivation for this rite would then be to rectify a cultic desecration. As for the goat rite, typological parallels might suggest a different type of occasion. As argued by Aartun, the strong similarity between this rite and that of the two birds that purify a patient from skin disease in Lev 14 may provide a hint that the goat rite may have been intended originally to remove a rampant plague from a community.[167] Indeed, the use of animals to carry away sickness is well attested in both Mesopotamian and Hittite sources.[168] Be the original circumstances as they may, subsequent redactions of the ritual transformed these instructions for an emergency situation into a pre-emptive procedure to purify the sanctuary and make expiation for the nation in order to prevent such dire situations.

Stratum 2. We will now attempt to distinguish between Strata 2 and 3, paying special attention to the terminology used to describe the effects of the

---

163. See p. 37 above.

164. Lev 16:29; 23:27. See Knohl, *Sanctuary of Silence*, 29.

165. However, we are not justified in assuming that Lev 16:16b is inferring to the same two part blood rite described in Lev 4:6–7, 17–18, which involves the incense altar.

166. Cf. Noth, *Leviticus: A Commentary*, 119; Aartun, *Studien zum Gesetz*, 84–86.

167. "Studien zum Gesetz," 84–86. Nevertheless, one should not overlook the differences between the two rituals. See Wright, *Disposal of Impurity*, 78–80; Gane, *Cult and Character*, 255.

168. For examples, see Wright, *Disposal of Impurity*, 45–57, 65–69. At the same time, many scholars raise the possibility that the goat originally served as an appeasement offering, in line with the interpretation of Azazel as the name of a demonic figure (see n. 130 above and Wright, *Day of Atonement*, 76).

rites. The function of the blood rites performed in the adytum and Tent are described as follows:

¹⁶וכפר על הקדש מטמאת בני ישראל ומפשעיהם לכל חטאתם וכן יעשה לאהל מועד השכן
אתם בתוך טמאתם
¹⁷וכל אדם לא יהיה באהל מועד בבאו לכפר בקדש עד צאתו וכפר בעדו ובעד ביתו ובעד כל
קהל ישראל

¹⁶Thus he will purge the adytum from the impurities of the Israelites and from the (defiant) transgressions of all their sins, and thus he will do to the Tent of Meeting that dwells among them in their impurities. ¹⁷No one shall be in the Tent of Meeting when he comes to make expiation in the holy domain until he leaves, and he shall make expiation on the behalf of himself, his household and the entire congregation of Israel.

According to v. 16, the blood rite purges the adytum and shrine of the impurities and transgressions of the nation that had accumulated in the sanctuary. Verse 16a's rationale for the blood rites—to purge the adytum of the impurities of the Israelites—reflects the adaptation of the original ritual to the present context, linking it to the defilement of the sanctuary caused by the death of Nadab and Abihu.

The effects of the courtyard rite are depicted as follows:

¹⁸ויצא אל המזבח אשר לפני ה' וכפר עליו ולקח מדם הפר ומדם השעיר ונתן על קרנות המזבח
סביב
¹⁹והזה עליו מן הדם באצבעו שבע פעמים וטהרו וקדשו מטמאת בני ישראל
²⁰וכלה מכפר את הקדש ואת אהל מועד ואת המזבח והקריב את השעיר החי

¹⁸He shall go out to the altar that is before YHWH and make expiation upon it. He shall take some of the blood of the bull and some of the blood of the goat and apply it to the horns around the altar. ¹⁹He shall then sprinkle on it some of the blood with his finger seven times and purify it and sanctify it from the impurities of the Israelites. ²⁰When he finishes purging the adytum, the Tent of Meeting and the altar, he shall bring forward the live goat.

This text uses two verbs "purifies and sanctifies" (וטהרו וקדשו) to describe the goal of these rites. Some scholars understand these two verbs as corresponding respectively to the blood application (ונתן), which purifies, and the sprinkling (והזה), which sanctifies.[169] In this vein, the sprinkling rite is interpreted as a rite of consecration, and this interpretation could be applied to the rites in the adytum and Tent as well. However, a closer examination of the expression "and sanctify

---

169. So Milgrom, *Leviticus*, 1037.

it *from the impurities of the Israelites"* renders such an understanding untenable. The sanctification is nothing other than removal of the final layer of defilement. Thus, the ritual effect accrued to the sprinkling is essentially the same as the daubing, namely purification. Likewise, the formula that expresses the purpose of the blood rites in the adytum and the Tent (v. 16) does not refer to sanctification, only purgation.[170]

Nevertheless, the terminology employed here is significant. The purgation (כִּפֶּר\חִטֵּא) → sanctification (קדשׁ) sequence is evident in the accounts of consecrating the altar (Exod 29:36–37; Lev 8:15), although those verses seem to attribute the latter effect to anointment with oil. The terminology of sanctification in Lev 16:19 conveys the idea that the ritual has successfully accomplished its goal of undoing the negative consequences of Nadab and Abihu's sin and restoring the cultic institution to the original sanctity achieved in Lev 8–9.[171] This parallelism was not lost on the Stratum 3 (H) redactor who viewed this process as a prototype for the ultimate national restoration ritual that would take place on the Day of Expiation. The summary of the tri-partite purging of the sancturary in 20a can be attributed to H in light of its strong similarity to v. 33a, part of the H appendix to the chapter.

In summary, according to the Stratum 2 form, this blood ritual is accomplished in three stages, as the high priest moves from the innermost sanctum outwards. The procedure operates according to the logic of everyday housecleaning, in which one extracts the filth systematically from the innermost domain towards the exit. In this way, the blood rites purge the sancta of impurity and sin and restore them to their pristine state.

Stratum 3 (H). The Stratum 3 reinterpretation of the chapter reveals a clear focus on defiant transgression (פשׁע). This term, which is not attested elsewhere in the cultic law codes, is used frequently in the Bible in reference to acts of rebellion, whether against an earthly overlord (e.g., 1 Kgs 12:19; 2 Kgs 1:1; 3:5, 7; 8:20, 22) or against God (e.g., Isa 48:8; 59:13; Jer 2:8).[172] It appears in Lev

---

170. Once it is recognized that the sprinkling purifies, one must dismiss Milgrom's analogy (ibid.) with the consecration of the priests, which is effected by the sprinkling of anointing oil (Lev 8:30).

171. Sticking to the rationale given by the text, the single daubing and seven-fold aspersions should be understood in terms of purification. Nevertheless, at the risk of over-interpretation, it may be possible to distinguish between these two acts in the following manner. Whereas the daubing results in the purification of the sancta to which the blood is applied, i.e., the *kapporet* and the incense altar, the seven-fold sprinkling, which takes place in the air, may serve to purge the entire corresponding precinct, i.e., the adytum and the Tent respectively. This explanation is consistent with the summarizing statement in the text, according to which the blood rites purge the adytum and the Tent of Meeting (v. 16). Cf. Milgrom, *Leviticus*, 1034.

172. H. Seebass, "פשׁע," *TDOT* 12:135–51; R. Knierim, "פשׁע," *TLOT* 2:1033–37.

16, vv. 16 and 21, to describe the effects of the adytum blood rites and goat rite, respectively. From an analysis of these verses, one can determine the secondary nature of this term. Let us reexamine v. 16:

וכפר על הקדש **מטמאת בני ישראל ומפשעיהם לכל חטאתם** וכן יעשה לאהל מועד השכן אתם בתוך טמאתם

> Thus he will purge the adytum **from the impurities of the Israelites and from the (defiant) transgressions of all their sins,** and thus he will do to the Tent of Meeting that dwells among them in their impurities.

The relationship between impurities and (defiant) transgressions in this verse has caused considerable confusion for commentators. Indeed, the reference to purging transgressions from the adytum in v. 16a is difficult on several accounts. First of all, it contradicts other statements in this chapter that mention only impurities in relation to the purgation of the Tent (v. 16b) and sacrificial altar (19). To remove this tension, some scholars suggest that the transgressions (פשעים) in 16a are subsumed in the category "impurities," thereby assuming that the author has blurred the distinction between sin and impurity.[173]

This interpretation cannot be reconciled with a close reading of the verse. As is readily apparent by the parallelism of verses 16a and 21, the usage of terminology is precise and deliberate.[174] Furthermore, close attention to the syntax of v. 16a shows that care has been taken to distinguish the category of transgressions from impurities. First, the view that "transgressions" is a type of defilement rests on the mistaken assumption that the *waw* in ומפשעיהם serves an explicative function,[175] but this view cannot be maintained. Had the text intended to convey the idea of the "impurities [caused by] their transgressions," it should have used the construct טמאת פשעיהם.[176] Rather, the *waw* is a simple conjunction, joining two distinct types of evil. Second, against the tendency to interpret the phrase לכל חטאתם as denoting a third type of evil that must be eliminated from the adytum,[177] we should recognize that this phrase modifies only פשע ("transgression"). As a result, the import of the verse is as follows: From the wide spectrum

---

173. From this passage, Milgrom draws the following general conclusion: "[T]he result of Israel's wrongdoing is the creation of impurity, which then attaches itself to the Sanctuary and pollutes it" (*Leviticus*, 1033). Milgrom's theory will be examined in more depth below.

174. See above, p. 79.

175. Cf., e.g., Levine, *In the Presence of the Lord*, 76–77.

176. For additional arguments, see Schwartz, "Bearing of Sin," 6–7, 17; Gane, *Cult and Character*, 288.

177. Cf. the following translations: "including all their sins" (Milgrom); "as well as all their sins" (Gane, *Cult and Character*, 290).

of sins (לכל חטאתם), only the defiant transgressions (פשעים) defile the adytum.[178] In other words, unlike ordinary sins, which are personal matters to be addressed by their perpetrators, extreme transgressions have a defiling effect, analogous to impurity, on the adytum.

Turning back to our diachronic analysis, we must ask: To which source should we ascribe this notion of the defiling effects of transgression? This view sharply contradicts P's clear distinction between the effects of sin and impurity. P's sin offering ritual texts are careful to state with precision whether it is sin or impurity that is removed. In reference to the expiation of sins, the standard formula is "the priest shall make expiation on his behalf for his sin and he will be forgiven" (וכפר עליו הכהן מחטאתו ונסלח לו).[179] On the other hand, the goal formulas for purification rituals deal explicitly with defilement. For example, the purification of the parturient is accompanied by the following statement: "[the priest] shall make expiation on her behalf and she will be cleansed from the source of her blood" (וכפר עליה ותהרה ממקר דמיה [Lev 12:7]).[180] Thus, the formulas distinguish clearly between the effects of the two types of rituals: the former results in forgiveness (ונסלח לו), the latter in purity (וטהרה). Thus, P is careful not to conflate the notions of sin and impurity.

H is less rigid in this regard. Though in one case it attributes a defiling effect to sin (Lev 20:3), it more commonly refers to the *sin of neglecting to purify*. In general, H's laws are characterized by an overriding concern with the enduring purity of the Israelite camp in which the Deity dwells. In this context, negligence regarding bodily purity is a sin of immeasurable proportions. For example, the instructions for purification from corpse impurity warn that laxity in observance will result in the defilement of the sanctuary (Num 19:13; cf. also v. 20):

> Anyone who touches a corpse, the body of a person who has died, and does not undergo sprinkling, defiles YHWH's sanctuary; that individual will be cut off from Israel. Since the waters of sprinkling were not dashed upon him, he remains impure; his impurity is still upon him.

Similarly, the corpus of laws dealing with bodily impurities (Lev 12–15) conclude with a a similar admonition (15:31):

---

178. An identical use of לכל is found in Lev 11:42. Cf. Schwartz, "Bearing of Sin," 18, n. 59, who understands the *lamed* as genitival and translates לכל חטאתם "of all their sins"; see also Gane, *Cult and Character*, 288–90.

179. E.g., Lev 4:26; 5:10, 13.

180. For some further examples, see, e.g., Lev 14:19; 15:15, 30; Num 8:21. See Milgrom, *Leviticus*, 256, 857; Schwartz, "Bearing of Sin," 6; Gane, *Cult and Character*, 112–24. The exceptional source is Lev 16:30, which depicts the purification of sin. However, even in this case (stemming from H), the text refers to the purification of people, not sancta.

> You shall set apart the Israelites from their impurities lest they die in their impurities by defiling my Tabernacle that is among them.

These statements have been interpreted variously. The rabbis understood these cases as implying that the defilement of sancta is caused by some sort of subsequent direct contact, such as touching or eating. However, this assumption finds no support in the text.[181] Wenham interprets Num 19:13, 20 as meaning that "the death of someone in the camp could pollute all those in it, and this would defile the Tabernacle of YHWH unless preventative measures are taken."[182] Apparently, Wenham is proposing that the contamination would inevitably spread by direct contact until someone would unknowingly defile the sanctuary, but this suggestion also involves reading quite a bit into the text. In comparison, Milgrom suggests that all forms of severe impurity cause an *automatic* indirect defilement to the sanctuary, and for this reason, the impurity bearers must perform a sin offering to purify the sancta.[183] According to this view, the failure to purify causes a severe defilement that even penetrates the adytum.[184]

Though Milgrom's view is basically correct, it should be modified in light of the recognition that these passages are all attributable to H. These passages must be understood in light of H's stricture whereby all of the most severe impurity bearer's must be exiled from the camp:

> [1]YHWH spoke to Moses, saying: [2]"Command the Israelites to remove from the camp anyone with a skin eruption or a genital discharge and anyone defiled by a corpse. [3]Remove male and female alike; put them outside the camp so that they will not defile the camp of those in whose midst I dwell." (Num 5:1–3).

The implication of this law is that the continued presence of an impurity bearer inside the camp automatically defiles the Sanctuary.[185] According to P, only the person with leprosy is excluded from the camp, as evidenced by Lev 15,

---

181. See, e.g., Rashi and Ramban on Num 19:13. See also Broyer, "איסור טומאה בתורה," 45–53.

182. Wenham, *Numbers*, 145.

183. Milgrom, *Leviticus*, 257; "Impurity Is Miasma," 729–33.

184. See also Gane, *Cult and Character*, 144–62, who accepts Milgrom's interpretation only for cases in which the perpetrator brazenly neglects to purify himself.

185. Similar interpretations were already offered by Büchler (*Sin and Atonement in the First Century*, 265) and Maccoby (*Ritual and Morality*, 186) without recognition of the H stratum and its unique ideology. While Knohl properly emphasizes H's unique ideology regarding the purity of the camp, he uses this observation to support his view of H as a populist movement, seeing this level of holiness as applying to all Israelites settlements (*Sanctuary of Silence*, 185–86). However, Knohl ignores the emphasis of all of these passages on the presence of the Tabernacle in the camp, which serves as the source of the camp's holiness.

which assumes that impurity bearers suffering from a genital discharge can remain within the camp. Since P and H are in disagreement over this critical issue, we must interpret the H sources on their own terms.[186] Nevertheless, we may acknowledge Milgrom's observation that the severity of the impurity has been compounded by the defiance involved in the refusal to purify.[187] Indeed, H's attitude towards impurity in these texts parallels this source's treatment of sin in Num 15:22–31 (see below). These passages emphasize the fundamental distinction between accidental misdeeds and rebellious acts, thereby moving the focus from physical acts (sins) and metaphysical states (impurity) to the underlying intentions of the perpetrator.[188] The types of sin and impurity that are truly abhorrent to the Deity and cause defilement to the Temple stem from flagrant disobedience.[189]

Thus, the reference to defiant transgressions (ומפשעיהם לכל חטאתם) should be attributed to an H redactor.[190] This conclusion is further supported by comparison to the similar expression מכל חטאתם in the H appendix to the chapter (v. 34a). By adding reference to transgressions to Lev 16:16a, the H redactor effectively redefined the type of inpurities that have defiled the sanctuary, identifying them as those resulting from criminal negligence. Apparently, the Stratum 2 form of the text referred only to purging impurity, such as that caused by the corpses of Nadab and Abihu, from the various precincts of the sanctuary (vv. 16, 19). As stated above, the reframing of the Nadab and Abihu incident in vv. 1–2 as a sin of approaching the Deity leads to the inescapable conclusion that they defiled the Tabernacle when they were struck dead inside the Tent. However, such a situation was overly specific and thus unsatisfactory for the H redactor who sought to incorporate the ritual of Lev 16 into a yearly system of expiation.

---

186. Hence, one cannot accept Milgrom's hypothesis that the pollution referred to in Lev 16 stems from the sins committed throughout the year that accumulate in the sanctuary, despite the fact that they have been addressed by the prescribed sin offering ritual at the appropriate time (Milgrom, *Leviticus*, 1033).

187. Milgrom, "Impurity Is Miasma," 730–31.

188. Although H does in at one place seem to conflate the notions of impurity and sin, attributing defilement to sin in Lev 20:3 (see below), this isolated passage should not distract us from H's systematic and explicit message as described here. In general, we should focus on the rhetorical aims of each passage, rather than assume they are engaging in a systematic attempt to define Israelite categories of sin and impurity.

189. In fact, the Tannaitic sages treated the "impurities" described here as a form of sin, concluding that "the goat whose rite is performed inside the adytum and Day of Atonement make expiation for the deliberate defilement of the Temple and its sancta (על זדון טומאת מקדש וקדשיו)" (*m. Shavuot* 1:6), thereby requiring the blood rite on account of the *sin* of defilement.

190. For the view that ומפשעיהם לכל חטאתם is a later addition, see Löhr, *Das Ritual von Lev 16*, 3–4; Elliger, *Leviticus*, 206; Wright, *Disposal of Impurity*, 18–20.

Most important for understanding Lev 16, the concern with defiant trans-gressors is central to H's sin offering laws in Num 15. While sins that were committed inadvertently, or at least without defiant intent, can be expiated by means of the individual sin offerings as described in Lev 4–5, no such possibil-ity is open to the brazen transgressor. This idea, implicit in Lev 4–5, is stated explicitly in Num 15:

> [27]If an individual does wrong inadvertently, he shall offer a she-goat in its first year as a sin offering. [28]The priest shall make expiation on behalf of the person who erred by doing wrong inadvertently before YHWH, to make expiation on his behalf that he may be forgiven. [29]For the citizen among the Israelites and the stranger that resides among them—you shall have one ritual for anyone who acts inadvertently. [30]But the individual, be he a citizen or a stranger, who acts brazenly (ביד רמה) reviles YHWH; that person shall be cut off from his people. [31]For he has despised YHWH's word and violated his commandment, that person will surely be cut off—he bears his guilt.

This passage, which reflects numerous linguistic and ideological character-istics of H,[191] exhibits this source's concern with emphasizing the difference between minor disobediences and flagrant violations of God's sovereignty.[192] The expression ביד רמה, literally "with an upraised hand," signifies a sin com-mitted shamelessly and in the open.[193] This idiom parallels the term פשע in Lev 16, which fulfills an emphatic function to distinguish "(defiant) transgressions" from ordinary everyday sins. Indeed, H stresses elsewhere that the most abomi-nable transgressions against the Deity, e.g., the practice of dedicated children to Molekh (Lev 20:2–3), contaminate the Sanctuary.[194]

---

191. See Knohl, "Sin-Offering Law," 197–98 with references.

192. As noted by Schenker and Gane, Num 15:30 refers to an action that is in open defi-ance of God's sovereignty and law (Schenker, *Recent Interpretation*, 65, 69; Gane, *Cult and Character*, 202–13), framed within the context of a covenantal master–servant relationship between God and Israel (see also Levine, *In the Presence of the Lord*, 103).

193. This expression is used to describe the Israelites departure from Egypt before the eyes of their former Egyptian overlords (Exod 14:8; Num 33:3). On the basis of other combinations of the verb רו"ם with יד, as well as ancient Near Eastern glyptic evidence, C. J. Labuschagne describes this idiom as "a military, or semi-military, expression, signifying readi-ness to fight and the will to prevail. The origin of the expression is without any doubt the physical gesture of the raised hand, with or without a weapon in it, which indicates that one is triumphantly determined to fight and to win" ("The Meaning of *beyād rāmā*," 146).

194. In light of Ezek 23:38–39, Milgrom raises the possibility that the defilement caused by Molekh worship can be attributed to this cult taking place near the temple (Milgrom, *Leviti-cus 2*:1734–35), but there is no hint of such a limitation in the exhortations of Lev 20. See Gane, *Cult and Character*, 156–57.

H's reinterpretation of the purpose of the blood rites in the Sanctuary on the Day of Expiation carefully preserves earlier traditions but reframes them with a dramatic change of focus. On one hand, H's addition of the expression "(defiant) transgressions of all their sins" (ומפשעיהם לכל חטאתם) preserves P's distinction between impurity and sin. As noted above, aside from the use of a conjunctive *waw,* which maintains a distinction between impurity and sin, the expression לכל חטאתם unambiguously defines these transgressions as a type of sin, not impurity. Had H dissolved the distinction between sin and impurity, that is, if טמאת in v. 16 referred to the defilement caused by sin as argued by some modern commentators, the implication would be that *only* sin defiles the sanctuary, not impurity. Thus, H's careful formulation adds a layer of interpretation without undermining the Stratum 2 rationale of the ritual to remove impurity.[195] At the same time, by adding the term פשע, H incorporated an important new dimension to the ritual, namely that extreme acts of rebellion against the Deity also result in the defilement of the Sanctuary and must be purged on the Day of Expiation.[196] This day's rites would then complement the other expiatory offerings that are performed throughout the year, thus forming a comprehensive system for rectifying the relationship between Israel and God.

SUMMARY

In summary, the rites described in Lev 16 appear to have passed through three distinct phases of literary development, each of which provides a distinct interpretation of the ritual acts. Despite the mult-staged developmental process that this ritual has undergone before reaching its current state, Gorman has argued that we may find "a conceptual framework ... operative in the ritual that is capable of holding together in a meaningful way disparate traditions," justifying an analysis of Lev 16 as a "self-contained unit of meaning."[197] Indeed, the present diachronic analysis of the text concurs with this assessment, having revealed a clear thematic continuity that has accompanied the literary development of the text from 1) emergency rituals to address national crises, to 2) a ritual for undoing the effects of Nadab and Abihu's catastrophic sin, to 3) an annual purgation ritual for temple and congregation.

---

195. The conservatism of H has been noted above, 53, n. 54.

196. Outside Lev 16, H takes more liberty to expand the notion of Sanctuary defilement, attributing it to rebellions against divine authority (e.g., Lev 20).

197. Gorman, *Ideology of Ritual,* 67.

Sin Offering Rituals as an Integrated System

In contrast to the fragmentary picture that is available from the biblical sources regarding the sin offering in early traditions, the canonical form of the Torah presents the diverse rituals as an integrated system. Corresponding to the three major partitions of the Tabernacle's structure, the courtyard (החצר), the shrine (הקדש), and the adytum (קדש הקדשים), the Torah presents three types of חטאת rituals, each fulfilling a distinct function, and complementing one another in an integrated and coherent system.[198]

The sin offering rituals for the inadvertent sins of individuals as well as for severe bodily impurities[199] take place at the sacrificial altar in the courtyard. These are the most frequently occurring types of evil as well as the least serious.[200] It is thus fitting that the ritual takes place in the courtyard, which is accessible to any ritually pure Israelite, and that it can be performed throughout the year by any priest. Thus, the courtyard sin offering provides individuals with an accessible means to restore their cultic status vis-à-vis the Deity.

In comparison, the sin offering of the shrine addresses an inadvertent sin of the entire Israelite congregation or that of its cultic representative, the high priest. Although this sin is also inadvertent, it is obviously of a more serious degree. Besides the fact that it implicates the entire nation, that is a quantitative increase in severity, it may also be symptomatic of a more serious social ill by which either the whole congregation or its cultic representative could come to sin. Correspondingly, the ritual must be carried out by the high priest himself and takes place in a realm of greater sanctity, the shrine, to which only priests have access.

The Day of Expiation ritual of Lev 16 deals with the most severe types of evil, those that cannot be addressed by the sin offering rituals throughout the year. As shown above, two types of evil are removed from the adytum, impuri-

---

198. The general approach outlined here is largely derivative of Milgrom's theory (see, e.g., Milgrom, *Leviticus*, 253–61). It should be noted, however, that the rabbis were quite aware of the complementary relationship that exists between the sin offering rituals, which take place throughout the year, and those that take place on the Day of Expiation (e.g., *m. Shavuot* 1:2–6), but the coherence of their understanding is marred by their interpretation of the altar referred to in Lev 16:18 as the incense altar inside the shrine.

199. E,g, those caused by birth (Lev 12:6–8), leprosy (14:13, 19), or irregular genital flows (15:14–15, 29–30).

200. Although these texts refer to the sin offering rites in a shorthand that emphasizes the exceptional elements only, namely, the types of offering brought, leaving out the details of the rite, it seems safe to assume that the rites for the bodily impurities are analogous to those of minor individual sins and not to the rites for expiating communal transgressions, which are performed inside the sanctuary.

ties (טמאת) and transgressions (פשעים). The impurities are caused by a negligent refusal of impurity bearers to undergo the prescribed ritual, thereby contaminating the adytum. The latter term, "transgressions," refers to brazen acts. Thus, both types of evil that defile the most holy realm of the sanctuary are intentional defiant sins, those whose perpetrators are condemned to destruction. The concretized evil caused by these deeds is transferred to the sanctuary, where it defiles the sancta and thereby threatens to incapacitate the primary apparatus by which the nation achieves expiation. This potentially catastrophic situation can be remedied by the blood ritual of the Day of Expiation. On this occasion, the sanctuary is purged of the *depersonalized evil* that affects the corporate personality of Israel; hence, it is appropriate that the ritual omits the usual forgiveness formula (ונסלח להם).[201]

The live goat rite fulfills a similar function, but instead of purging the evils of the sanctuary, the goat carries away the "iniquities" (עונות) of the entire settlement. As argued above, this term seems to refer to an additional form of intentional sin which, since it has been left unexpiated, has fallen on the shoulders of the community. In addition, the transgressions (פשעים) that were removed from the sanctuary are also carried off to Azazel. The implication of these statements is that the sin offering blood rituals, including that of the Day of Expiation, can eradicate only unintentional sin and impurity, but not intentional sin, which must be sent off to the wilderness.

In summary, the sin offering addresses a situation in which the varying degrees of sin and impurity are projected onto the structure of the Tabernacle, whereby the defilement of the Sanctuary mirrors the level of deterioration in the status of the Israelite community vis-à-vis the Deity. In this scheme, the severity of the violation of the relationship between the Israelite nation and God is expressed by the interiority of the penetration of evil in the sanctuary. Since the sanctity of the location is defined by the level of restrictions imposed on entry, the more pervasive the form of evil, the more difficult is the cultic process of purgation.

THE TERM חטאת: ETYMOLOGY AND ETIOLOGY

There is a fundamental disagreement among scholars regarding how to translate the term חַטָּאת. The dominant translation "sin offering," derived from the identical Hebrew term that denotes sin, is found already in the LXX's gloss ἁμαρτία. However, many modern scholars argue for the translation "purification offering,"[202] which is in their view connected with the *piel* verbal form

---

201. Rendtorff, *Leviticus*, 217–18.
202. See already Kennedy and Barr, "Sacrifice and Offering," 874. Of the various schol-

חָטֵא (*ḥiṭṭe*), usually translated "purify." In fact, some interpret the *dagesh* on the second radical of the nominal form as indicating that it is a derivative of the *piel*.[203] The main advantage of this argument is that it addresses the fact that the חטאת is sometimes employed to purify bodily impurities. The most outstanding example is the parturient, since it is inconceivable to associate the act of giving birth with sin.[204] As should already be clear, we are not dealing with a peripheral question of translation but with illuminating the origin and purpose of this ritual.

We will address these arguments one by one, starting with the morphology of חטאת. As noted long ago by Barth, a *dagesh* on the second radical does not necessarily reflect a transitive meaning.[205] Indeed, the identical term חטאת, which denotes "sin," also has a geminated second radical, despite the fact that it is associated with the intransitive *qal* form "to sin." The only solution to this conundrum would have us to conclude, with Levine, that the latter term reflects a mistaken punctuation.[206] However, it seems paradoxical to base one's argument on the Massorites' punctuation while at the same time to discredit their tradition.

But since the verbal forms of חט"א appear in connection with the חטאת offering as well as in similar rites, we should not be hasty to dismiss their relevance. The question is: What can be learned from these forms? To begin with, the *piel* and *hitpael* verbal forms of the root חט"א appear exclusively in cultic contexts,[207] primarily those related to the חטאת offering, indicating that these terms were well-defined elements of the priestly jargon. If so, we must inquire what distinguished these terms from the variants of the roots כפ"ר and טה"ר that appear in similar contexts. A second issue is no less perplexing. Although scholars are nearly unanimous in understanding the *piel* form as a privative usage of the denominative *piel*, which literally means "to de-sin,"[208] a survey of the

---

ars who advocate this view, Milgrom is the most adamant. See J. Milgrom, "Sin-Offering or Purification-Offering," *VT* 21 (1971), 237–39; *Leviticus*, 253–54. See also Wenham, *Book of Leviticus*, 88–89; Kiuchi, *Purification Offering*, 161; Gilders, *Blood Ritual in the Hebrew Bible*, 29–32; Dennis, "The Function of the חטאת Sacrifice," 112–14; Gane, *Cult and Character*, 50–51.

203. Bauer and Leander, *Historische Grammatik der Hebräischen*, §61yß, 476; Milgrom, "Sin Offering or Purification Offering," 1, n. 2; Levine, *In the Presence of the Lord*, 102. Levine (*Leviticus*, 20) views the noun as a derivative of the *piel* verbal form and translates "an offering to remove an offense, purify."

204. For a response to this argument, see below, p. 142.

205. Barth, *Nominalbildung in den Semitischen Sprachen*, §93, 145–46. Cf. Fox, *Semitic Noun Patterns*, 246–47. The relationship between the noun and the *piel* verbal form will be elucidated below.

206. Levine, *In the Presence of the Lord*, 102.

207. That is, excluding the much debated term אחטנה (Gen 31:39), which may or may not derive from the root חט"א.

208. See GKC §52h; Joüon, GBH §52d; Jenni, *Das hebräische Pi'el*, 274; Waltke and

evidence shows that the verb can only indirectly, if ever, be associated with sin. Rather, the preponderance of evidence connects the verb with purification.

For example, the *piel* and *hitpael* verbal forms apply to the removal of impurities such as leprosy[209] and corpse impurity,[210] as well as in the ordination rituals, which do not seem to imply any prior sin (e.g., Exod 29:36; Lev 8:15; 9:15; Num 8:21).[211] Based on this evidence and the premise that lexical meaning can only be determined by actual usage, many would translate the verb "to purify" and dismiss the etymologically derived translation "de-sin" as being completely invalid. But this brings us back to the question: what distinguishes חט"א from כפ"ר and טה"ר?

It would seem that much of the confusion over these terms stems from the conventional way of interpreting the lexical evidence. The following tables present the *piel* and *hitpael* usages of the root חט"א:

PIEL OF חט"א

	Source	Expression	Rite
1	Lev 6:19	הכהן המחטא אתה יאכלנה	Sin offering
2	Lev 9:15	ויקרב את קרבן העם ויקח את שעיר החטאת אשר לעם וישחטהו ויחטאהו כראשון	Sin offering
3	2 Chr 29:24	וישחטום הכהנים ויחטאו את דמם המזבחה	Sin offering
4	Lev 14:49	ולקח לחטא את הבית שתי צפרים ועץ ארז ושני תולעת ואזב	Purification of house from leprosy
5	Lev 14:52	וחטא את הבית בדם הצפור ובמים החיים ובצפר החיה ובעץ הארז ובאזב ובשני התולעת	Purification of house from leprosy
6	Num 19:19	והזה הטהר על הטמא ביום השלישי וביום השביעי	Red cow ritual
7	Ps 51:9	תחטאני באזוב ואטהר תכבסני ומשלג אלבין	Figurative?
8	Exod 29:36	ופר חטאת תעשה ליום על הכפרים וחטאת על המזבח	Sin offering

---

O'Connor, *Introduction to Biblical Hebrew Syntax*, 412. In reference to ויחטא את המזבח (Lev 8:15), Levine understands חט"א as "to remove an offense" (*Leviticus*, 52).

209. *Piel:* Lev 14:49, 52.

210. *Piel:* Num 19:19. *Hitpael:* Num 19:12, 13, 20; 31:19, 20, 23.

211. Ezekiel's deep consciousness of sin would make it advisable not to include his ritual of purifying the altar here (43:18–26). See also vv. 4–11 of that chapter.

9	Lev 8:15	ויחטא את המזבח	Sin offering
10	Ezek 43:20	ולקחת מדמו ונתתה על ארבע קרנתיו ואל ארבע פנות העזרה ואל הגבול סביב וחטאת אותו וכפרתהו	Sin offering
11	Ezek 43:22	וביום השני תקריב שעיר עזים תמים לחטאת וחטאו את המזבח כאשר חטאו בפר	Sin offering
12	Ezek 43:23	בכלותך מחטא תקריב פר בן בקר תמים ואיל מן הצאן תמים	Sin offering
13	Ezek 45:18	תקח פר בן בקר תמים וחטאת את המקדש	Sin offering

Hɪᴛᴘᴀᴇʟ ᴏғ חט"א

	Source	**Expression**	**Rite**
1	Num 8:21	ויתחטאו הלוים ויכבסו בגדיהם	Installation of the Levites
2	Num 19:12	הוא יתחטא בו ביום השלישי וביום השביעי יטהר ואם לא יתחטא ביום השלישי וביום השביעי לא יטהר	Red cow ritual
3	Num 19:13	כל הנגע במת בנפש האדם אשר ימות ולא יתחטא את משכן ה' טמא	Red cow ritual
4	Num 19:20	ואיש אשר יטמא ולא יתחטא ונכרתה הנפש ההוא מתוך הקהל	Red cow ritual
5	Num 31:19	ואתם חנו מחוץ למחנה שבעת ימים כל הרג נפש וכל נגע בחלל תתחטאו ביום השלישי וביום השביעי אתם ושביכם	Red cow ritual
6	Num 31:20	וכל בגד וכל כלי עור וכל מעשה עזים וכל כלי עץ תתחטאו	Red cow ritual
7	Num 31:23	כל דבר אשר יבא באש תעבירו באש וטהר אך במי נדה יתחטא וכל אשר לא יבא באש תעבירו במים	Red cow ritual

The *piel* data are generally divided by the lexicons into at least two groups.[212] Sources 1–3 indicate a translation "to offer/make a sin offering." In these texts,

---

212. These two groups consist of the senses "to offer a sin offering" and "to purify" (see BDB and DCH). In particular, BDB translates the *piel* as "to make a sin offering," "purify from sin," and "purify from uncleanness"; the *hitpael* as "to purify oneself from uncleanness." DCH

the offering or part of the offering serves as the direct object. Accordingly, they refer to the "performing of a sin offering rite" by the priests. Sources 4–7, however, whose association with חטאת offering is tangential at best, are interpreted as expressing a generalized meaning "purify."[213] The remaining sources 8–13 could allow for either translation, but their use of the direct object in many of these cases makes the translation "purify" more attractive.[214]

However, the evidence for the meaning "purify" is exceedingly weak. First of all, this translation would seem to coincide with the *piel* of טה"ר, leading to the insurmountable problem of why a specialized term would be invented to express the same meaning as an already existing conventional term.[215] Secondly, a survey of the *hitpael* evidence is instructive. From all of the contexts listed above, it is clear that the *hitpael* form refers to a defined act of purification, specifically the act of sprinkling, and should be glossed "be cleansed."

Turning back to the *piel* evidence, we should realize that the investigation of the term's sense will only lead to ambiguous results, since several significantly different translations can be plausibly offered for most of the cases. A more productive line of inquiry is to focus on the referent to which the expressions employing חָטָא refer. In nearly all of the cases, the verb is uncontrovertibly referring to a defined physical act such as sprinkling or daubing—not to the effects of the act.[216] Interestingly, this semantic nuance is impossible to capture in translations, so that we have no recourse but to use verbs such as "cleanse" or "purify." This untranslatability is the clearest indication that we are on the right track of understanding this element of the priests' specialized terminology. From this recognition, it becomes apparent that there is only a small step from "perform a sin

---

defines the *piel* as follows: "purify, cleanse from sin" or "offer as a sin offering"; the *hitpael* as "purify oneself, be purified (from sin)." In contrast, HALOT provides only one meaning for the *piel* form "to cleanse from sin, purify" but agrees with the other lexicons as to the *hitpael* "to purify oneself."

213. Ps 51 has no explicit connection to the sin offering. The house purification rites of Lev 14 involve the blood of a slaughtered bird, which is not called a חטאת. While the red cow ritual of Num 19 is referred to as a חטאת rite, one must not overlook the fact that the waters are referred to as מי נדה, not מי חטאת as in Num 8:7. This fact further strengthens Milgrom's argument that the red cow ritual is only secondarily adapted to being a חטאת (see *Leviticus*, 270–78).

214. The converse reason, namely the use of the indirect object, has led BDB and CDH to place Exod 29:36 in this first group.

215. Sklar overlooks this problem when he concludes that these terms are virtually synonymous (*Sin, Impurity, Sacrifice, Atonement*, 111–12).

216. Num.19:19 is a particularly elusive case. At first glance, one may be tempted to view וחטאו as parallel to יטהר ("he shall be pure") in v. 12. However, it is followed in v. 19 by רחץ במים וטהר בערב ("he shall bathe in water and be pure in the evening"), which would seem to indicate a distinction between חט"א and טה"ר.

offering" to "perform an act of ritual cleansing," and the diachronic development of this term's usage becomes readily apparent. Thus, it becomes clear that חִטֵּא is a denominative of the term חטאת ("sin offering"), and that the unattested privative meaning "to de-sin" proposed by the grammarians was misguided. This verb originally denoted the actions associated with the חטאת offering, but later developed a general sense "to perform a purification rite."[217]

In light of this proposed meaning, we can understand how this term differs from other similar cultic terms. The *piel* of טה"ר is of significantly different usage in cultic contexts. It may describe the effect of an act of purification (e.g., Lev 16:19; Ezek 43:26) or refer to the execution of a purification procedure in a general sense (e.g., Lev 14:11). In addition, this form is used to depict the priest's proclamation that a person is pure of leprosy (e.g., Lev 13:6). But it does not describe a specific act of purification; the term חִטֵּא was designated for that purpose.

The usage of the term חִטֵּא is equally distinct from that of כִּפֶּר. The former is used to describe the physical action that is used to purify a house, altar or temple, while the latter generally describes the effects such actions have on their human beneficiaries. Only in four cases does cultic כִּפֶּר receive a direct object: Lev 16:20, 33 (H) and Ezek 43:20; 45:20, but these examples reflect a late semantic development of כִּפֶּר.[218] Furthermore, whereas כִּפֶּר is used to describe the expiation of sin, חִטֵּא is never used explicitly in association with sin. Here too, we come to a similar conclusion: whereas כִּפֶּר refers to a change in a person's standing vis-à-vis the Deity, חִטֵּא refers only to the physical act of cleansing.

A recognition of the first stage of this diachronic development, in which חט"א referred exclusively to performing a חטאת rite, was obscured by the existence of sources in which the connection between them is either tenuous or non-existent. Nevertheless, a source-critical survey of these sources indicates that they are, in fact, relatively late. For example, there are two instances of חִטֵּא that appear in connection with the use of bird's blood to purify a house from leprosy (Lev 14:49, 52), a rite which, despite its similarities, is not termed a חטאת. In this case, Fishbane and Milgrom have demonstrated conclusively that the entire pericope on house purification is a late addition to the laws of "leprosy."[219] Another unique instance of these forms pertains to its usage in relation to the sprinkling rites of the red cow to effect purification from corpse impurity. Although this

---

217. A similar view was already advanced by Kaddari (though without argumentation), who posited that the meaning "to purify" is a secondary generalized development of the primary meaning to "offer a sin offering" (*Dictionary of Biblical Hebrew*, 289). However, whether any of the attestations denotes purification in a general sense is highly questionable.

218. Cf. above pp. 48–50, 53, 57, 58–60, 88, 90–91.

219. See Fishbane, "Biblical Colophons," 438–42; Milgrom, *Leviticus*, 863–87.

rite is termed a חטאת (Num 19:9, 17) and its usage of the verbal forms of חט"א in relation to the waters of sprinkling might, at first glance, be attributed to this association, it can hardly be considered a conventional חטאה. As argued by Milgrom, it is more likely that the present red cow ritual is a secondary adaptation of an ancient exorcistic ritual to the חטאת model.[220] It seems to be more than a coincidence that all of the instances of the *hitpael* form pertain to the sprinkling of the red cow's ash water (as well as one case of the *piel*). All of these sources (including Num 8:21) have been attributed justifiably by Knohl to the redaction of H.[221] The remaining case is that of Ps 51, which seems to have originated in the late pre-exilic period.[222]

As a result, there is reason to believe that the *piel* form of חט"א was originally a term that corresponded specifically to the specific acts associated with the חטאת rite, most specifically the dabbing of blood on the altar. In contradistinction to the early pre-exilic emergence of the חטאת rite, the generalized sense of the *piel* verbal form "to perform a cleansing rite" and the coining of the *hitpael* form seem to have emerged at a later period.

In summary, a comprehensive survey of the *piel* and *hitpael* usages of the root חט"א reveals that they refer to a specific act of purification, not to purification in general. Furthermore, a survey of the *piel* evidence seems to indicate that it was originally associated with the חטאת offering, specifically to describe the blood rite, but thereafter was used to describe comparable acts (dabbing or sprinkling) in similar rites (e.g., purification of a house from "leprosy," the red cow rite for corpse impurity). Similarly, the *hitpael* form emerged to describe the reflexive sense "be cleansed."

Thus, the translation "purification offering" for the חטאת offering by relating it to the verbal form חִטֵּא translated "purify" is ill-advised for two reasons. First, it appears that the verbal form was devised expressly to describe the actions involved in the already existing חטאת rite. Second, the generalized sense "perform an act of purification" seems to be a later semantic development. At the same time, we must acknowledge an important point as reflected by the semantic development of the verbal form, namely that the חטאת offering was understood by the priesthood as purging evil, whether sin or impurity, from the object of the rite (i.e., the altar).

---

220. *Leviticus*, 270–78.

221. Knohl, *Sanctuary of Silence*, 93 and n. 115.

222. Its pre-exilic provenance can be inferred by the recognition that vv. 20–21 are an exilic addition which are in tension with vv. 18–19 (cf. already Ibn Ezra on v. 20). Nevertheless, the preponderance of linguistic parallels from Jeremiah, Ezekiel and Deutero-Isaiah point towards a period close to the exile (see Dalglish, *Psalm Fifty-One*, 223–25).

Accordingly, the term חטאת should be understood in relation to sin, as implied by Lev 4:

אם הכהן המשיח **יחטא** לאשמת העם והקריב על **חטאתו** אשר **חטא** פר בן בקר תמים לה' **לחטאת**

If it is the anointed priest who so **does wrong** to incriminate the people, he shall offer for **the wrong he has done** a bull of the herd without blemish as **a sin offering** to YHWH (4:3).

The clear association between the offering and transgression, appearing in numerous passages, renders the alternative translation "purification offering" highly unlikely.[223] Rather, we should take our cue from the analogous case of the guilt offering (אשם). Just as the אשם is an offering that seeks to remove guilt, so too we should understand the חטאת as an offering to remove sin.

This understanding is reinforced by frequent references to guilt in Lev 4 and elsewhere, as expressed by variants of the verb אש"ם. This verb generally means "incur guilt" or "be condemned." In these contexts, it implies an objective wrong committed that will bring about punishment. In numerous texts, this direct causal relationship is abundantly clear, whereby the verb signifies the condemnation that is a precursor to punishment.[224] A few examples will suffice:[225]

תאשם שמרון כי מרתה באלהיה בחרב יפלו עלליהם ירטשו והריותיו יבקעו

Samaria will bear her guilt, for she has defied her God. They will fall by the sword, their children will be dashed to death, their pregnant women torn open (Hos 14:1).

האשימם אלהים יפלו ממעצותיהם ברב פשעיהם הדיחמו כי מרו בך

Condemn them, O God, let them fall by their own devices. Cast them out for their transgressions, because they have defied you (Ps 5:11).

A particularly instructive case is the narrative in 1 Sam 5:1–7:1, which describes the Philistines ill-fated appropriation of the ark. In response to plagues of hemorrhoids and mice,[226] the Philistine leadership decides to return the ark to the Israelites along with golden images of mice and hemorrhoids as a propitiatory gift (אשם). This account sheds light on the sin offering in several ways. First of

---

223. See M. Melzer's response to Milgrom's view (Milgrom, *"Ḥaṭṭat* Offering," 135); Rendtorff, *Leviticus*, 221.

224. See R. Knierim, "אשם," *TLOT* 1:192.

225. See also Hos 10:12; 13:1; Jer 2:3; 50:7; Ezek 22:4; 25:12; Prov 30:10; Ps 34:23.

226. The latter is based on the reading of the LXX.

all, the Philistines discover their guilt in response to the misfortunes that have struck them. It is only the dire ramifications that bring the Philistines to recognize that they have committed sacrilege. Second, the Philistine offering to the Israelite deity seems to fulfill a double function of appeasement and removing the plagues.[227] Just as the guilt and punishment are two sides of the same coin, so too, the redress of the liability can be expected to remove the punitive sanctions. It seems that this latter conception is expressed in the verbal forms אש״ם in Lev 4–5. In such sources, אש״ם refers to a state of guilt or liability that invokes punishment. Thus, it implies a situation in which the existence of sin can be inferred retroactively from suffering.[228]

Now let us turn to the introduction to the sin offering instructions in Lev 4 (vv. 1–2):

> YHWH spoke to Moses, saying: "Relate to the Israelites as follows: A person who does wrong by violating any of YHWH's prohibitive commandments inadvertently, violating one of them..."

This introduction introduces the ensuing cases as accidental violations of a divine code of conduct, implying that the latter serves as an *objective basis for determining guilt*. Accordingly, the transgression of this law requires rectification, despite the violator's lack of malicious intent.[229]

But what about the cases of bodily impurities, for which "sin offering" seems less appropriate? We must begin by recognizing that the usage of the term תאטח often blurs the line between the "guilt" incurred by a wrongful act and its consequences. Indeed, Koch has pointed out that the biblical sources frequently refer to retribution as a semi-autonomous dynamic whereby a wrongful act will automatically bring calamity upon the sinner.[230] An adherent to this worldview would tend to interpret any form of serious misfortune as stemming from an offense against the Deity. This broad notion may provide us with an understanding of the rationale underlying the use of the sin offering in cases seemingly unrelated to sin.

The sin offering is required for the "purification" of several types of bodily impurity, namely those caused by leprosy (צרעת), genital flux (זוב), and birth.[231] From the textual evidence, leprosy seems be an archetypical divine punish-

---

227. Levine, *In the Presence of the Lord*, 92–94.

228. See also Sklar, *Sin, Impurity, Sacrifice, Atonement*, 39–41.

229. See, Ricoeur, *Symbolism of Evil*, 82–83. R. Knierim, "שגג," *TLOT* 3:1303.

230. K. Koch, "חטא," *TDOT* 4:312; Feder, "Mechanics of Retribution."

231. Lev 12–15. I will not discuss the red cow rite which is performed for corpse impurity, since it departs significantly from the conventional sin offering and seems to be only nominally a חטאת.

ment.[232] Likewise, David's curse on Joab implies that the latter's progeny will suffer from leprosy and genital flux as a consequence of the bloodguilt of Avner:

> When David heard afterwards, he said, "I and my kingdom will be forever clean before YHWH of the blood of Avner the son of Ner. May it fall on the head of Joab and all of his kinsman. May there never cease to be in the house of Joab a gonorheac (זב), leper (מצרע), a holder of the spindle, a victim of the sword or a person lacking bread (2 Sam 3:28–29).[233]

In light of these sources, it is clear that these diseases were attributed to misdeeds. Thus, there is reason to believe that the sin-offering in such cases was intended to address the suspected sin. The unique case of the parturient will be discussed in more detail in the following chapter.

As a result, the lexical examination of the term חטאת has led us to a deeper understanding of the worldview that underlies this ritual. In this world, the distinction between notions such as sin, impurity, curse, and illness is ambiguous because they all boil down to a common denominator—human suffering. This suffering is likewise attributable to a common cause (at least as a possibility)—a transgression against God.

Although the P documents draw a relatively clear distinction between the notions of sin and impurity, terms such as חטאת preserve hints of an earlier conception. However, by the time of the canonical redaction of these texts, the ritual was probably conceived as functioning on a prototypical principle, whereby the offering that removes sins can also remove impurities. Furthermore, as noted by Schenker, the חטאת is brought primarily for involuntary sins, which are not so different from impurities. Though both must be removed, neither are flagrant offences against the Deity.[234] As shown in the diachronic analyses above, the formulas that employ חָטָא and כִּפֶּר with sancta as the direct object represent a late development in which the sin offering was conceived as purging them of evil. Perhaps at this phase of the ritual's development one could correctly refer to a "purification offering," but not at the cost of forgetting its origins as a "sin offering."

Synthesis: The Function of the Sin Offering

None of the sin offering texts offers a comprehensive understanding of the process by which the sin offering serves to expiate sin. In order to arrive at any

---

232. Num 12:10; 2 Kgs 5:27; 2 Chr 26:18–21.

233. On this passage, see Malul, "David's Curse of Joab," 49–67.

234. See Schenker, *Recht und Kult*, 14–15.

sort of systematic scheme, one must integrate information gleaned from various sources into a unified understanding. Such an endeavor is harmonistic from its inception and can only hope to reflect the perspective of the final redactor(s) of the text. At the same time, there is reason to believe that some of the dynamics can be traced back to the earliest documented stages of the ritual.

As a point of departure in his classic studies of the sin offering, Milgrom pointed out that the blood of the sin offering is never applied to a person, only to sancta.[235] This aspect of its procedure is paralleled by the expiatory formulas describing the effect of the offering, in which human beings never appear as the direct object of the verb *kipper*. In comparison, sancta are depicted in several cases as the direct object, which seem to convey the idea of purging evil cathartically from these objects and places.[236] Though these sources are relatively late, even the earlier sources describe the expiatory effect as being indirect, literally "on behalf of" the person or congregation, as expressed by the formula כִּפֶּר עַל. Hence, Milgrom has shown convincingly that the critical stage for the removal of evil takes place at the altar.

A further deduction that can be made from the sources, taken holistically, is that sin or impurity is transferred to the offering's flesh. Lev 16:28 requires that the person who burns the flesh to wash and launder his clothes, just like the person who escorts the sin-bearing goat (v. 26).[237] More explicit is the Moses' statement in Lev 10:17 that the eating of the sin offering serves to bear the sin of the community. Consequently, the burning and the eating of the sin offering flesh are portrayed as means of disposal corresponding to the sanctuary and courtyard rites, respectively.

Several questions cannot be resolved easily. How are the sancta defiled? Is the evil transferred to it by means of the sin offering, or is it automatically contaminated when a person sins or contracts impurity? These possibilities correlate with the question: Is the evil transferred from the offerer to the sin offering by means of the hand-leaning rite at the beginning of the ritual, or is it transferred from the sancta to the flesh when they are purged? In order to answer these questions, the reader must fill significant gaps in the text. In particular, the following alternative schemes offer resolutions:

- *Scheme A*—Transferral by Contact (Zohar, Gane): Sin and impurity are transferred to the sin offering by means of the hand-leaning rite. The blood rite passes the impurity to the sancta, to God, where it apparently

---

235. See *Leviticus*, 253–61 with references to earlier studies.
236. See above pp. 48–50, 53, 57, 58–60, 88, 90–91.
237. Wright, *Disposal of Impurity*, 130–31.

disappears, but the contaminated flesh must be disposed of by either burning or eating.[238]

- *Scheme B*—Transferral at a Distance (Milgrom): Sin and impurity automatically defile the sancta. When they are purged from the sancta, they are transferred to the animal's flesh, which is then disposed of by fire or priestly consumption.[239]

Scheme A poses several difficulties. First, the hand-leaning rite in sacrificial contexts seems to fulfill the sole function of indicating ownership of the offering, not transferral.[240] Second, the notion that the offerer transfers his impurity to the offering would presumably also defile the suet, which is burned as an offering for God. Third, the notion that blood transfers impurity contradicts those sources that indicate that the blood purges the sancta.[241]

Scheme B is less problematic. This theory depicts the role of the blood as a purificatory agent, and is thereby consistent with the sources cited above. Furthermore, numerous H sources refer to the contamination of the sanctuary in cases of deliberate neglect to undergo purification as well as in cases of "(defiant) transgressions" (פשעים).[242] In such cases, since no offering is brought, there would be no means by which the evil would be transferred to the sanctuary.

Though this notion of automatic pollution might strike us as strange at first glance, the Hittite evidence provides us with a striking parallel to this concep-

---

238. See Zohar, "Repentance and Purification," 609–18; Gane, *Cult and Character*, 106–97. According to Gane, the sin offerings brought throughout the year remove evil from their offerers. However, the yearly purgation of the Temple on the Day of Expiation operates according to Milgrom's theory (Scheme B).

239. Milgrom, *Leviticus*, 257–64.

240. See Wright, "Gesture of Hand Placement," 437–46; Gane, *Cult and Character*, 53–56, 63–64 and n. 73 with references.

241. E.g., Lev 8:15; 16:20, 33; Ezek 43:20, 22, 26; 45:18, 20. For Milgrom's critique of Zohar's view, see: "Modus Operandi of the 'Ḥaṭṭa'th'," 111–13. Gane has raised additional points in support of Scheme A, whereby the sin offering removes evil from the offerer, not sancta. First of all, he argues that the preposition מן in the formulas וכפר עליו הכהן מטמאתו\ מחטאתו has the privative meaning of "from" and signifies that the offerer is separated *from* the impurity or sin (*Cult*, 106–29). In response, Milgrom has called attention to the parallel expression וכפר עליו הכהן על חטאתו (Lev 4:35; 5:17; 19:22) in which על takes the place of מן, implying that they are synonymous. Thus, one should translate the preposition מן in the causative sense, meaning: "for, on account of, because of" (See, e.g., Gen 16:10; 1 Kgs 8:5; Jer 24:2; Prov 20:4; GKC §119z). For additional arguments, see Milgrom, "Preposition מן in the חטאת Pericopes," 161–63. In addition, Gane claims that Lev 6:20 attests to the notion that the blood of the sin offering carries the sin or impurity of the offerer to the altar (ibid., 163–75). However, the context implies that the blood, like the flesh, is sanctified. Indeed, Gane's argument cannot be reconciled with the explicit statements that the blood purifies sancta (e.g., Lev 8:15; 16:20).

242. See Lev 16:16; 20:3; Num 19:13, 20. See above, pp. 91–97.

tion. As described above (p. 8), Hittite oracle and ritual texts make frequent reference to various forms of depersonalized evil such as curse (*ḫurta*), bloodshed (*ešḫar*), oaths (*linga*) and impurity (*papratar*). These forces are described as residing in places and objects, threatening to provoke divine retribution against their owners. Through a dynamic of metonymy, akin to Milgrom's automatic defilement, expiatory rituals provide one of the dominant means of avoiding such punishment. Thus, even before embarking on the discussion of a possible historical relationship, we may recognize that the Hurro-Hittite rite provides a typological analogy that lends support to Milgrom's textual analysis.

SYNTHESIS: RECONSTRUCTING THE SIN OFFERING'S HISTORICAL DEVELOPMENT

A broad consensus exists among Bible critics regarding the major stages of development of the sin-offering ritual.[243] They tend to view the book of Ezekiel as the earliest source documenting the sin offering. In Ezekiel's account, there is mention only of blood manipulations, not of burning the suet as an offering to the Deity or of the consumption of the flesh by the priesthood. According to this view, the rite has not yet become an offering at this stage; it is merely a symbolic gesture serving to consecrate the sanctuary.

A slightly later phase is represented by the ordination ritual of Lev 8, which is considered by these scholars to be earlier than Exod 29. This ritual also focuses on the consecration of the Tabernacle, but we find here references to the offering of the suet to God (v. 16) and the burning of the remaining flesh (v. 17). Though some may argue that the reference to the suet is a later addition,[244] the existing text testifies to the sacrificial element of the sin offering. At the same time, there is not yet any distinction between the simple ritual that takes place at the court-yard altar and the expanded ritual that takes place inside the Tent.

In the original blood ritual of Lev 16 as well as the sin offering rites of Lev 4:22–35 we find a similar procedure. However, these sources cite the purpose of achieving expiation for sin. There is some disagreement between scholars over whether this function was already implicit in the prior stages of the rite or a later development.[245] In any case, we still find no distinction between the two types

---

243. I am here referring to the opinions of Rendtorff (*Geschichte des Opfers*, 222–26, 233–34, 249), Gese (*Atonement*, 102, 110–13), and Janowski (*Sühne als Heilsgeschehen*, 232–41).

244. E.g., Gese, *Atonement*, 111.

245. Whereas Rendtorff (*Geschichte des Opfers*, 220) views expiation as a later development, Gese (*Atonement*, 110–11) and Janowski (*Sühne als Heilsgeschehen*, 240) perceive an essential connection between expiation and the blood rite.

of blood rite and no reference to the priestly consumption of the flesh. These two elements appear for the first time in the ritual instructions Lev 4:3–21 and the administrative laws of 6:18–23. Some scholars view the final phase as the theological rationale attributed to the eating of the flesh provided in Lev 10:17.[246]

According to this scheme, we have no knowledge of a pre-exilic sin offering, and the latest stages of its development (e.g., priestly consumption of this flesh) appear only in post-exilic times.

From a methodological standpoint, the late dating for the sin offering advocated by most scholars seems to rest primarily on the supposed priority of Ezek 40–48. The absence of any associated rites such as suet burning is taken to represent a more primitive form of the sin offering, which is construed as support for the general assumption that these chapters are earlier than P. This "correspondence" was taken as sufficient evidence to justifiably ignore external pre-exilic references to the sin offering in Hos 4:8 and 2 Kgs 12:17.[247] In contrast, the present analysis has shown that the sin offering passages of Ezek 40–48 reflect a clear literary dependency on the corresponding laws in P. Moreover, the rationale given for the sin offering in Ezek 40–48 corresponds to the later literary strata of P, as indicated in the diachronic analysis of Exod 29, Lev 8 and Lev 16. As a result, we are forced to recognize that the laconic treatment of the sin offering in Ezek 40–48 does not preserve a primitive form of the ritual. On the contrary, it takes P's treatments for granted.

Accordingly, the diachronic analysis advanced in the present study warrants the rejection of several central premises of the dominant view. In particular, there is no basis for denying the existence of the suet offering in the earliest phases of the rite (e.g., Exod 29:13; Lev 4:8a, 19; Lev 8:16). Furthermore, the conclusion that the allocation of the flesh for priestly consumption is a late development must be questioned. Although this rite seems to appear only in the later literary strata, the reference to eating the sin offering in Hos 4:8 in conjunction with the rationale of "bearing sin," paralleling Lev 10:17, indicates that the latter source either pertains to an earlier period than is generally acknowledged or at least preserves relatively early traditions.

Furthermore, our diachronic analysis seems to indicate that the notion of purging sancta of impurity is a relatively late development. Indeed, references such as Exod 29:36–37, Lev 8:15, Lev 16:16, 19b, 20a, and 33 should be attributed to later literary strata of their respective chapters. In comparison, the

---

246. See Rendtorff, *Geschichte des Opfers*, 222–26; Wefing, *"Entsühnungsritual am grossen Versöhnungstag,"* 141.

247. de Vaux's analysis is much more balanced in this regard (*Old Testament Sacrifice*, 102–6). See also below, p. 249, n. 21

notion of "personal" expiation already appears in the earliest literary strata of Lev 4 and 16.

The present analysis concurs with the consensus opinion regarding the relatively late emergence of the complex blood rite. Though it agrees with these scholars regarding the relative chronology, their post-exilic dating of this phase is questionable. Several considerations would indicate that the sin-offering ritual was already well-developed in pre-exilic times. Aside from the allusion to the sin offering in the words of the eighth-century prophet Hosea, 2 Kgs 12:17 attributes the following command to King Joash (end of the ninth century B.C.E.):

כסף אשם וכסף חטאות לא יובא בית ה' לכהנים יהיו

The silver of the guilt (offerings) and the silver of the sin (offerings) will not be brought to the Temple of YHWH. They will go to the priests.

The historicity of this account need not be questioned, since it was apparently based on the "Annals of the Kings of Judah" (v. 20).[248] Such references correspond well with the analysis of Lev 4:22–35 and the term נשיא above, which found numerous grounds to relate these passages to the institutions that existed in the pre- or early monarchic period.

Thus far, our conclusions have been based exclusively on a literary and ideological analysis of the biblical texts themselves. In the following chapter, we will engage in a detailed comparison between the Hurro-Hittite and biblical blood rites. As will be shown, the Hittite evidence reveals a striking similarity to the early phase of the sin offering as determined by the diachronic analysis presented here.

---

248. See Milgrom, *Leviticus*, 287.

3

THE QUESTION OF A HISTORICAL CONNECTION

Having analyzed the Hittite and biblical evidence independently, we will now address the question of whether or not a historical connection exists between the Hurro-Hittite blood rite and its biblical counterpart. At first glance, such a proposition seems problematic. Two serious considerations undermining such a possibility, or at least the prospect of *proving* such a connection, are: a) the absence of evidence showing a direct exchange of ritual traditions between the Hittites and Israel and b) the chronological gap that exists between the sources. Under these circumstances, a proper assessment must be based primarily on a comparison of the content of the rituals. Though any determination on such grounds would appear, at first glance, to be condemned to subjectivity, it will be shown that the situation is not as futile as it seems.

CRITERIA FOR EVALUATION

In his monograph dedicated to establishing methodological guidelines for comparisons between ancient Near Eastern literature and the Bible, Malul has outlined two basic criteria for evaluating the possibility of a given historical connection, namely, the test for coincidence versus uniqueness,[1] and corroboration to prove the flow of ideas between the two cultures.[2]

The first of these refers to the question: "Are the similarities and/or differences discovered between the sources/phenomena the result of parallel developments, independent of each other and, therefore, coincidental, or do they point to an original phenomenon unique to the sources under comparison?" The second of these criteria pertains to the question: "is it possible to prove the existence of the right conditions for the creation of a historical connection between

---

1. Malul, *Comparative Method*, 93–97. See also Miller, *Kizzuwatna Rituals*, 458–61 regarding the question of "structural or transmitted similarity."

2. *The Comparative Method*, 99–112.

the two cultures under comparison?"[3] These considerations will serve as a useful framework for the following discussion.

THE CASE FOR UNIQUENESS

In the present section, I will examine the fundamental parallelism between the Hittite and biblical evidence, pertaining to the procedure, dynamic, and circumstances of the blood rites. It will be argued that this basic similarity, which extends to all essential aspects of the blood rite in both cultures, can only be plausibly explained on the basis of a common tradition.

PROCEDURE

In both textual corpora, the application of blood to an object, usually cultic, serves as a means of removing a metaphysical form of evil (impurity, sin, etc.) from the ritual patron(s). Furthermore, just as the Hurro-Hittite *zurki* rite is regularity accompanied by the *uzi* rite, in which fat is cooked as an offering to the gods,[4] so too, the suet of the Israelite sin offering is burnt on the altar, producing a "pleasant aroma for YHWH" (Lev 4:31). In fact, several texts make clear that the *uzi* and *zurki* rites were a functional unity, often coming from the same animal;[5] thus, they parallel the suet burning and blood rite of the Israelite sin offering. In addition, both Hittite and biblical texts indicate that the rite was frequently accompanied by a sacrificial meal. In the case of the Hittite-Hurrian ritual, the offerer seems to participate in the meal, although it is not clear if the offerer eats part of the *uzi* offering.[6] In the Israelite sin offering, the officiating priest and his family consume the flesh, except in sin offerings for major communal transgressions.

DYNAMIC

In both cultures, the underlying dynamic by which the evil is removed is identical. The evil is viewed as clinging to a physical object that is associated metonymically with the ritual patrons. By performing the blood rite on the object, the ritual patron is indirectly cleansed/expiated. Though scholars have

---

3. Quotations from 93, 99, respectively.

4. On the regularity of the *uzi-zurki* sequence, see Strauß, *Reinigungsrituale aus Kizzuwatna*, 92–98.

5. See, e.g., pp. 11–12, 17–18 above.

6. This question depends in part on the meaning of the rare verb *arnamitti-*. See above, p. 17, n. 39.

typically recognized the purificatory function of the blood in the Hittite and biblical evidence, most have failed to appreciate the metonymic character of this process. The main exception is Milgrom, whose systematic analysis of the sin offering has given proper emphasis to the action-at-a-distance dynamic through which the Israelites are indirectly purified/expiated by means of the blood rites performed on the sancta.[7] His view finds confirmation in the Hurro-Hittite conception of expiating evil, especially as expressed in the *zurki* rite. The metonymic character of this dynamic caused it to be misunderstood by the ancients as well as moderns (see above, pp. 108–11), and consequently, the preservation of this unique dynamic in both Hittite and biblical evidence provides strong evidence for a historical relationship between these traditions.

CIRCUMSTANCES

The situations that require the performance of the blood rite in both cultures can be assigned to the following categories: expiation, purification, and sanctification, granting that the distinction between them is sometimes ambiguous. As noted above, a primary function of both the *zurki* rite and the sin offering is to expiate sin. Whereas the Hittite texts state explicitly that these rites are aimed to appease the relevant gods and remove the threat of divine retribution, this purpose is tacitly implied by the biblical sources. Strikingly, the texts from both cultures place particular emphasis on expiation for unintentional sins.[8] Furthermore, the blood rite is used in conjunction with the purification of a defiled temple. We find such a case in the Ritual of Ammihatna, Tulbi, and Mati, which is typologically similar to temple purification ritual of Lev 16.[9] Finally, the blood rite was employed in both cultures to consecrate sancta upon the initiation of a new cult structure. Such an application can be found in the Cult Expansion Ritual of the Night Goddess as well as in the altar sanctification rites that appear in Exod 29:36–37, Lev 8:15, and Ezek 43:18–26.[10]

---

7. Milgrom does not employ the term "metonymic," but rather refers to a "miasma" that acts as a "noxious ray" that emanates from the source of defilement and pollutes the sanctuary ("Impurity Is Miasma," 729). Since the dynamics of how this defilement takes place are not immediately clear from the text, the more neutral term "metonymy" is preferable.

8. Regarding the *zurki* rite, see pp. 19–20. above; for the sin offering, see Lev 4; Num 15:22–31.

9. For the Hittite ritual, see pp. 20–23. above; for Lev 16, see pp. 77–97.

10. For the Hittite Cult Expansion Ritual, see pp. 31–32; for the biblical consecration rituals, see pp. 43–53; for Ezek 43 and 45, see pp. 53–60. Although in all of these cases, there is significant evidence to indicate that the "consecratory" use of blood is a secondary development in each culture that emerged from the primary expiatory use of blood, the fact that such a usage developed in both cultures is noteworthy, albeit not surprising in light of the expiatory/

The basic similarities between the rites of the two cultures are summarized in the following table:

FORMAL CHARACTERISTICS OF THE HURRO-HITTITE
AND BIBLICAL BLOOD RITES

	Hurro-Hittite Blood Rite	Biblical Sin Offering
1. Procedure	• *zurki*: blood smearing • *uzi:* fat cooked as offering • Frequently appears in conjunction with sacrificial meal	• Blood daubing/sprinkling • Suet burned on altar as offering • Flesh given to priests
2. Locus of Blood Rite	• Cult statues • Cult appurtenances • Birth stools	• Horns of burnt-offering altar • Curtain of shrine • Cover (*kapporet)* of holy ark
3. Circumstances	• Inadvertent sin/divine anger • Birth rituals • Portentious omens • Desecration of temple • Initiation of new cult equipment	• Inadvertent sin • Severe bodily impurities (incl. birth) • Desecration of temple • Initiation of new cult equipment

THE CASE AGAINST COINCIDENCE

Despite these striking similarities, one must recognize that the scholarly community has become justifiably more wary in reaction to the onslaught of purported parallels between ancient Near Eastern texts and the Bible that have been proposed in the past century and a half of scholarship. In order to restore a proper perspective, it is necessary to juxtapose our findings with the ritual use of blood in other cultures of the ancient Near East and Mediterranean worlds.

In a pair of articles published in 1969 and 1973, McCarthy compared the use of blood in biblical ritual to its use in ancient Mesopotamian, Greek, Ugaritic, Hittite, and pre-Islamic Arabic ritual and reached the conclusion that the positive

---

purificatory function. For the basis of this diachronic argument regarding the biblical evidence, see pp. 48–53 above; for the Hittite evidence, see pp. 228–35 below.

value attributed to blood in Israel was unique among its surrounding cultures.[11] Unfortunately, McCarthy's analysis is undermined by several serious methodological drawbacks. Some of these are immediately apparent in the following formulation of his conclusions:

> Hebrew ritual is much concerned with blood. It must be reserved to God, and it is a purifying agent. This is explained by the fact that "in the blood is life"; so blood belongs to the divine sphere. The explicit statement of this doctrine comes in deuteronomic and priestly documents, but they are explaining a ritual much older than they.[12]

Two of the most serious methodological problems reflected in this passage are the conflation of sacrificial, purificatory and other uses of blood under a common rationale and the use of a secondary verbal interpretation of the ritual activity as a criterion for distinguishing the Israeli view of blood from that of other cultures.

A more sound approach requires a preliminary distinction between various types of ritual action (sacrificial, purificatory, etc.), as implied by the action itself and not verbalized interpretations such as "blood is life."[13] Each of these types would then serve as the basis of an independent comparison. The following survey will apply such an approach to the purificatory/expiatory use of blood.

An additional serious drawback of McCarthy's research is revealed by his treatment of the Hittite evidence:

> The typical purificatory rite in Mesopotamian practice was washing or rubbing with water or oil or milk or the like, not with blood as in Israel. In fact, the Hittite ritual of Papanikri is unusual in cuneiform literature because it uses blood to purify.[14]

This observation should have alerted this author of the possibility of a common tradition. However, he dismisses the evidence in his subsequent description:

> Blood was smeared on a building contaminated by bloodshed, and the removal of the new blood took away the contamination of the old. This is simple imi-

---

11. "Symbolism of Blood," 175–76; "Further Notes, " 210

12. McCarthy, "Symbolism of Blood," 175.

13. For example, when describing the Greek depictions of blood libations to chthonic deities, whose craving for blood is also related to an association of blood with life, McCarthy is led to observe: "Blood is associated not with *true life*, but with its pale and ghostly counterpart" (ibid. 175 [italics added]). Had McCarthy focused on the action itself, propitiatory gifts to chthonic deities, which is not found in biblical ritual, rather than the supposedly unique rational "blood is life," he could have avoided such sophistry.

14. Ibid., 169.

tative magic. Blood is blood, and removing the new takes away the old. It is specific for problems related to blood, not something specially and generally powerful in its own right.[15]

Here McCarthy seems to be confusing the Papanikri Ritual, which involves the smearing of a birth stool with blood to remove divine anger, with an entirely different ritual—one for removing bloodshed (and other evils) from a building![16] This glaring mistake reveals the embarrassing fact that McCarthy, despite his correct citation, did not bother to read the Papanikri Ritual firsthand. Not only is McCarthy's prompt rejection completely unfounded, he fails to realize that the Papanikri Ritual is not the only Hittite source in which such a blood rite appears.

In the following brief survey, the methodological guidelines advocated above will be applied to the ancient Mesopotamian and Greek evidence. These sources support an important conclusion overlooked by McCarthy: The unique tradition regarding purificatory/expiatory use of blood found in biblical sources is also attested in the Hittite sources of Kizzuwatnean origin.

MESOPOTAMIA

Scholarly treatments of blood in Mesopotamian ritual reflects a basic consensus that it has little in common with the expiatory use of blood in the Bible.[17] In Mesopotamian rites, blood is usually associated with chthonic deities. In numerous cases, blood is applied to the door posts as a prophylactic means of repelling demons. The blood is intended to satisfy their blood lust so that they will not attack the ritual patron. Similarly, foundation rituals required the smearing of the foundation stones with blood in order to appease the infernal deities for the invasion of their territory.[18] These apotropaic and propitiatory uses must be distinguished from the use of blood to remove metaphysical evil (impurity, sin, etc.) in the Hittite and biblical evidence.[19] In other Mesopotamian rituals, blood is also applied to a patient's body in order to heal epilepsy and other illnesses.[20] In contrast, the Kizzuwatnean and biblical rites require the application

---

15. Ibid.

16. This text (CTH 446) will be analyzed in ch. 6.

17. Unfortunately, the Hittite evidence is frequently neglected. For references and discussion of the use of blood in Mesopotamian rituals, see: Moraldi, *Espiazione sacrificale*, 227–28; McCarthy, "Symbolism of Blood," 166–68; Janowski, *Sühne als Heilsgeschehen*, 60, n. 166; Abusch, "Blood in Israel and Mesopotamia," 675–84.

18. See above, p. 26.

19. Although a few Hittite sources do associate this blood rite with chthonic deities, this rationale seems to reflect a secondary interpretation (see the detailed analysis on pp. 229–35).

20. See Stol, *Epilepsy in Babylonia*, 105–6, who also refers to some apotropaic uses of

of blood to the object being purified.[21] In light of these fundamental differences, one recalls Oppenheim's succinct distinction between Mesopotamia and the "'blood consciousness' of the West."[22] One wonders if he also had the Hittite evidence in mind.

The closest example to the Hittite and biblical rites appears in the *zukru* festival from Emar. After a festive meal by the "gate of the upright stones (*sikkānu*)," they anoint these stones with oil and blood:

ki-i-me-e KÚ NAG NA₄MEŠ *gáb-bá iš-tu* ÌMEŠ *ù* ÚŠMEŠ *i-ṭar-ru-u*

After eating and drinking, they rub all of the stones with oil and blood.[23]

In light of the fact that these stelae were of great cultic significance and were associated with the divine presence of a particular god,[24] one can hardly overlook the external resemblance between this rite and the sin offering rites that appear in conjunction with the initiation of the altar in Exod 29 and Lev 8. In each of these rites, a central cult object is anointed with oil and daubed with blood as part of a process that aims to endow the object with a level of sanctity. However, for the sake of precision, we should note that since the Emar blood rite repeats itself over the course of the festival, Fleming does not interpret it as a consecration of these stones but as a preparation for the passage of Dagan between the stones.[25]

The fact that the closest parallel from all the Mesopotamian evidence appears in a Late Bronze Age source from Emar further creates the impression that the blood rite reflects a unique southern Anatolian/northern Syrian phenomenon. As such, the blood rite of the *zukru* festival should be understood as one of the many indigenous Syrian traditions preserved by the ritual corpus of Emar. These topics will be discussed in further detail below.[26]

---

blood.

21. Cf., however, the exceptional rite of the leper in Lev 14, but this blood does not derive from the sin offering. A rite that has captured the attention of many scholars appears in the Babylonian New Year Ritual where the purification of a temple is described by the verb *ukappar*. However, this rite involves the absorption and disposal of the impurity by means of the carcass of a sheep, not blood. See McCarthy, "Symbolism of Blood," 169.

22. Oppenheim, *Ancient Mesopotamia*, 192.

23. Emar 373, Msk 7429[2a]+ l. 34. Text and translation: Fleming, *Time at Emar*, 238–39. This rite is repeated in lines 60 and 167.

24. These stones seem to be comparable to the Hittite *huwaši* stones and the biblical מצבות. See ibid., 83, n. 142 with references to earlier research.

25. Ibid., 83.

26. See below for a discussion of the possibility of an etymological connection between *zurki* and *zukru* (pp. 244–47).

ANCIENT GREECE

Numerous references are made in the ancient Greek literature to purification rites employing blood. Unfortunately, the anecdotal nature of many of the references precludes a clear understanding of many of these rites.

One of the earliest references to a blood rite is found in Heraclitus' (late-sixth–early-fifth century B.C.E.) criticism of a practice of washing away bloodguilt with blood. This theme finds abundant expression in the tragedies, in which a murderer washes his hands in blood, usually that of a pig, to cleanse himself from guilt.[27]

As in Mesopotamia, blood was also applied to the body as a means of healing the patient from epilepsy, madness or other sickness.[28] In many of these cases, the blood may be intended to exorcize the demonic Erinyes from the patient's body by appealing to their bloodthirst.[29]

Some of the rituals for the purification of temples and cities incorporated blood rites. These rites involved the encircling of the area with a pig in order to absorb the impurity followed by the sprinkling of its blood. The body of the pig was either burned or disposed of at a crossroads.[30] Unfortunately, the details of these blood rites are not sufficiently clear, both in terms of their procedure and their rationale.[31]

In summary, the Greeks used blood in various purificatory functions, including the cleansing of bloodguilt and healing from illness. These differ from the Hurro-Hittite *zurki* rite and the biblical sin offering in that blood is applied to the body of the person being purified. The scarcity of detail regarding the Greek temple purification rites, particularly regarding the question of whether the blood

---

27. See Parker, *Miasma*, 370–74. See also Vickers, *Towards Greek Tragedy*, 138–56; Burkert, *Orientalizing Revolution*, 56–57; Collins, "Pigs at the Gate," 176–77.

28. See Parker, *Miasma*, 207–22, 230–34.

29. See Burkert, *Orientalizing Revolution*, 57–59. For the connection between blood and chthonic deities in Greek religion, see McCarthy, "Symbolism of Blood," 273; *Further Notes*, 206–10.

30. See Parker, *Miasma*, 30–31; Stowers, "Blood in Greek and Israelite Ritual," 185–86; Collins, "Pigs at the Gate," 178, n. 61. Many of the temple purifications mentioned in the Greek sources do not seem to have involved particular blood rites. Stowers (ibid., 186) assumes the existence of blood rites even in several texts where they are not mentioned, but an examination of these sources raises doubts regarding this assertion.

31. Pausanias (second century C.E.) relates a story from Sparta in which the pollution (and perhaps sacrilege) caused by bloodshed in the Spartan temple to Artemis was purged by staining the altar with human blood (*Description of Greece* III, 16). Unfortunately, we cannot extrapolate to what extent this account reflects a regular practice and whether such a rite continues earlier precedents.

served a propitiatory, purificatory or apotropaic function, does not permit an assessment.

SUMMARY

The textual sources from Mesopotamia and ancient Greece preserve various types of blood rites. One can find little resemblance between any of these rites and their Hurro-Hittite and biblical counterparts in procedure, dynamic, or circumstance. The one possible exception is the *zukru* festival from Emar, but this case merely reinforces the assumed geographical provenance of the blood rite traditions. Consequently, this survey of alternative uses of blood in ancient Near Eastern and Mediterranean ritual serves to emphasize the uniqueness of the parallel between the biblical and Hittite sources.

CORROBORATION: A CONTEXT FOR THE EXCHANGE OF RITUAL TRADITIONS

By recognizing the Kizzuwatnean provenance of the Hittite rituals in question, there remains little doubt that the tradition of the blood rite was introduced to the Hittites by the Hurrian priests of southern Anatolia or northern Syria.[32] As a matter of fact, the blood rite is one of several striking parallels between Hittite rituals and the Bible, many of which are related to Hurrian-influenced Syrian traditions.[33] The following parallels are some of the more likely to be based on a common tradition:

1. "Scapegoat" rites: The transfer of sins and impurity to a goat, found in Lev 16 and Greek rituals, has been traced to an ancient Anatolian tradition.[34]

2. The *azuzhi* offering: Janowski and Wilhelm have connected the ritual involving the goat for Azazel in Lev 16 to an Akkadian oath ritual from Alalaḫ in Northwestern Syria (AlT 126) that mentions the Hurrian

---

32. Hoffner, "Syrian Cultural Influence in Hatti," 104.

33. However, one cannot definitively identify the rites themselves as Hurrian per se. See Trémouille, "La religion des Hourrites," 283–86. Cf. the papers published in Janowski, Koch, and Wilhelm, *Religionsgeschichtliche Beziehungen*.

34. Though the basic idea of transferring evil to an animal should be viewed as a typological parallel (cf. Wright, *Disposal of Impurity*), the prominence of goats in this role in the Mediterranean region is noteworthy. See Bremmer, "Scapegoat between Hittites, Greeks, Israelites and Christians," 175–86; Haas, "Traditionsgeschichte hethitischer Rituale," 131–41. For further references, see Singer, *Hittites and the Bible*, 748–49, n. 157.

offering term *azuz/sḫi* (derived from Akkadian *ezēzu*, "to be angry"), which served the function of placating divine anger.[35]

3. Hand placement: Wright has identified a hand-placement rite in Hittite rituals that serves a similar function to the biblical one-handed leaning rite, namely, to attribute the offering to the person who performs the rite, though Wright refrains from positing a historical connection.[36]

4. The double ritual: Schwemer has amassed persuasive evidence for a common origin for the "double-ritual," comprised of burnt and well-being offerings, found in Syrian ritual texts and the Bible, represented by Hurrian *ambašši* and *keldi,* Ugaritic *šrp* and *šlmm,* and Hebrew עלה and שלמים.[37]

Though a full discussion of these and other parallels and their historical significance cannot be provided here,[38] suffice it to say that the blood rite is not alone in indicating a relationship between the biblical cult and Syrian and Anatolian traditions.

The identification of the Syrian provenance of the Hittite traditions provides us with a solution to the additional problem of finding a plausible cultural context for the exchange of ritual traditions between the diverse ethnic groups of the region. The textual discoveries from Ugarit provide us with a vivid picture of the cultural milieu in which ritual traditions were exchanged between the Semitic inhabitants and the Hurrians. Indeed, the ritual texts from Ugarit reflect a synthesis between these different religious traditions, as characterized by the proliferation of Hurrian gods, offering terms and incantations in the Ugaritic texts.[39] These texts also reflect varying degrees of bilingualism among the ritual practitioners, which obviously facilitated the sharing of ritual traditions.[40] The impression conveyed by this high level of integration is that ritual knowledge was a technology that was sought after and shared.

In summary, the textual evidence from Late Bronze Age Syria demonstrates unequivocally the existence of a context in which ritual traditions were actively

---

35. See Janowski and Wilhelm, "Religionsgeschichte des Azazel-Ritus." Cf. Dietrich and Loretz, "Der biblische Azazel," 99–117 (with new collation of the text).

36. Wright, "Gesture of Hand Placement," 433–46.

37. Schwemer, "Das alttestamentliche Doppelritual," 81–116.

38. Earlier attempts at this task have been either overly cautious (Moyer, "Hittite and Israelite Cultic Practices") or overly daring (Weinfeld, *"Social and Cultic Institutions"*; "Traces of Hittite Cult"). For a critique of Weinfeld's studies, see Hoffner, "Israel's Literary Heritage," 185–88.

39. See Dietrich and Mayer, "Sprache und Kultur der Hurriter in Ugarit," 7–42; Mayer, "Hurrian Cult at Ugarit," 205–11.

40. See Pardee, "L'ougaritique et le Hourrite," 65–80.

exchanged between Semitics and Hurrians. The latter were responsible for transferring these traditions to Anatolia. Further questions regarding the transmission of this tradition to Israel will be discussed in ch. 7.

PARALLEL RITUALS IN THE HITTITE TEXTS AND THE BIBLE

In the previous sections, evidence was presented demonstrating the probability of a common historical origin to the Hittite and biblical expiatory blood rites. We may now consider a few possible parallels in which the similarities extend beyond the blood rite itself, pertaining to complex ritual sequences and the use of additional ritual techniques. Although not all of the examples are equally convincing, such parallels can provide further substantiation for the assumption of a shared body of ritual tradition.

THE BIRTH RITUAL KUB 9.22+ AND THE PURIFICATION RITUAL OF LEV 14

One of the closest parallels is between the Hittite birth ritual KUB 9.22+[41] and the biblical rite for the purification of leprosy in Lev 14, analyzed above. Although KUB 9.22+ has been preserved fragmentarily, it contains a fairly clear description of the blood manipulation and the rites that take place immediately before and after it, which apparently serve to prepare the site where the birth will take place.

The relevant part of the ritual text depicts the activity which takes place inside the inner chamber of the parturient's house:

Ha II
12   *nu ŠA* MUNUS [(^{GIŠ}ŠÚ.A ^{GIŠ}BANŠUR *ša-aš-)d]u¹-uš*
13   ^{GIŠ}GA-*AN-NU-U*[*M* (*ḫar-na-ú-un* MUNUS-*ia*) ^{LÚ}p]*a-a-ti-li-iš*
14   *IŠ-TU* MUŠEN [(*ḪUR-RI wa-aḫ-nu*)-*uz-zi*]

The *patili* priest waves a partridge (over) the chair, the table, the bed, the potstand, and the birth stool of the woman—and the woman.

15   *nu-za-kán* [(MUNUS É.)Š(À *an-da zu-*)]*úr-ki-ia*
16   *ši-pa-an-t*[(*i nu-za-*)*kán* (ŠU^{MEŠ}-*ŠU*)] *a-ar-ri*
17   *na-an* [(*ḫar-na-ú-i pí-ra-an*)] *an-da pé-ḫu-da-an-zi*

And the woman performs the blood rite for herself in the inner chamber. She washes her hands. Then (the *patili* priest)[42] takes her in before the birth stool.

---

41. In Beckman's edition, Text H (*Hittite Birth Rituals*, 86–115).
42. Although Text Ha uses the impersonal plural form, Hb II 12 states explicitly: ^{LÚ}pa-

18   *nu* 1 MUŠEN.[(GAL *ḫa-a-ri-ia ši-pa-an-t*)]*i* 1 MUŠEN.GAL-*ma*
19   *ḫa-a-pí-*[(*ia it-kal-zi-ia k*)]*u-la-mu-ši-ia*
20   *ši-pa-a*[(*n-ti nu ḫar-*)]*na-a-i-in* GIŠGAGḪI.A-*ia*
21   *iš-ḫ*[*ar-nu-ma-a*]*n-zi*[43]

She offers one large bird to the path, and one large bird she offers to *ḫabi, itkalzi*
and *kulamu(r)ši*. Then they s[mear blood][43] on the birth stool and the pegs.

22   *nu* GIŠERIN GIŠ*pa-i-ni* GIŠ*ZÉ-ER-TUM IŠ-TU* SÍG SA₅
23   *an-da iš-ḫi-ia-an na-at* LÚ*pa-ti-li-iš*
24   *da-a-i na-at-kán A-NA* MUNUS[44] *i-pu-ul-li-ia-aš*
25   *an-da da-a-i* Ì.DÙG.GA-*ia-aš-ši-iš-ša-an*
26   SAG.DU-*ŠU la-ḫu-i A-NA QA-TI-ŠU-ia-aš-ši-iš-ša-an*
27   SÍG SA₅ *ḫa-ma-an-ki*

Then a cedar (stick) is tied together with tamarisk and olive (sticks), using
red wool. The *patili* priest takes them and places them on the *garments* of the
woman.[45] (Then) he pours fine oil on her head, and he binds red wool to her
hand.

27   *nam-ma-kán* LÚ*pa-ti-li-iš ḫar-na-a-i-in IŠ-TU* DUGDÍLI.GAL
28   *IŠ-TU* {GIŠ} GIŠERIN GIŠ*pa-i-ni* GIŠ*ZÉ-ER-TUM da-a-i*
29   *nu* MUNUS KAxU-*ŠU šu-up-pí-ia-aḫ-ḫi*

Then the *patili* priest takes *ḫarnai* from the bowl and purifies the mouth of the
woman with cedar, tamarisk and olive (sticks).[46]

The rituals that take place in the inner chamber begin with the swinging of a
partridge (MUŠEN *ḪURRI*).[47] over the furniture. The waving rite should be

---

ti-li-iš.

43. Haas' reconstruction ("Ein hurritischer Blutritus," 73) *iš-ḫ*[*ar-nu-ma-a*]*n-zi* (= "they
smear blood") should be adopted in place of Beckman's *iš-ḫ*[*i-ya-a*]*n-zi* (= "they bind"), since
the the traces of the ḪAR sign can be clearly discerned in the photo of KUB 9.22. Furthermore,
a comparison with the bloodying of the birth stool and pegs in the Papanikri Ritual makes this
reconstruction very secure.

44. The parallel in ABoT 17 II 17 contains the genitival phonetic complement MUNUS-
TI.

45. Like Beckman, I understand *ipulli* as referring to an article of the woman's clothing
(*Hittite Birth Rituals*, 104–6), here in the d-l pl. Cf. Puhvel (*HED* E–I, 379–80), who tentatively
offers the following glosses: "wrap, encasement, chasuble, surplice. Puhvel's interpretation of
the present passage, acc. to which *i*. refers to the sticks' wrapping, is unlikely. For a further
attestation in our text, see III 11–15.

46. Text: Beckman, *Hittite Birth Rituals*, 90.

47. For this identity, see above, p. 21, n. 54.

understood as a means of absorbing the impurity from the objects under the animal being waved.[48] At first glance, the sequence of lines 15–21 is confusing. Although the statement that the woman performs the blood rite in line 15 might at first glance be interpreted as referring to the slaughter of the previously mentioned partridge, it is better understood as a general introduction for the following series of activities, whose focus is the blood rite. First of all, in accordance with the standard Hittite custom, the hand washing should *precede* the sacrificial acts.[49] Secondly, the smearing of blood is not mentioned until lines 20–21. It seems reasonable that the blood for this rite comes from the large bird slaughtered to *ḫabi*, *itkalzi*, and *kulamu(r)ši* described in lines 18–19.

Thus, the series should be understood as follows. The woman first washes her hands in preparation for the rites, which will take place by the birth stool. After a first "big bird"[50] is consecrated to "the path," a second bird is sacrificed next to the birth stool, providing the blood for the smearing of the birth apparatus. Despite the obscurity of the ritual terms *ḫabi* and *kulamu(r)ši*,[51] the presence of the term *itkalzi* (= "purity") seems to indicate that the rite is intended to be purificatory.[52] In the fragmentary lines 20–21, the smearing of the birth stool and pegs is described. From duplicates of the text, it may be inferred that the first bird will be slaughtered the following night at a crossroads to the male gods[53]—

---

48. See Strauß, *Reinigungsrituale aus Kizzuwatna*, 108–11.

49. See Kühne, "Vor-Opfer im alten Anatolien," 254–58.

50. On this designation, see above p. 21, n. 56.

51. Based on the limited attestations of these terms, scholars have proposed that they refer to cult locations. See Laroche, *GLH*, 88, 151–52, Haas and Wilhelm, *Riten aus Kizzuwatna*, 88, and Haas, *Die hurritischen Ritualtermini*, 217. However, these suggestions do not seem to fit the present context.

52. Laroche relates it to the root *itki* (= "*sacré*") and translates *itkalzi* as "*sanctification*" (*GLH*, 128–29). At the same time, Laroche notes that the expression *itkalziaš widar* (= "holy/pure water") appears in KBo 20.129+ I 1. Moreover, in the colophons of a few tablets SÍSKUR *itkalziaš* appears as a gloss on *aiš šuppiaḫḫuaš* (= "mouth washing"). See KUB 29.8 IV 36–37; KBo 20.126+ IV 34–35; cf. also KBo 23.6 Rev. 8'. Subsequently, many scholars have translated *itkalzi* as "purity". See Haas and Wilhelm, *Riten aus Kizzuwatna*, 83–84, Beckman, *Hittite Birth Rituals*, 104, Tischler, *HEG* 3, 447, Haas, *Die hurritischen Ritualtermini*, 225; Giorgieri, "Schizzo grammaticale," 196.

53. ABoT 17 III 13'–15' and KBo 17.64 7'–11'. Although these are duplicates of the end of Ha and not parallel to the present section, the similarity of content seems to justify the inference advocated here. KBo 17.64 7'–10' reads: [(*na-aš-ta* ^LÚ *pa-*)]*a-ti-li-iš* MUŠEN.GAL KASKAL-*ši* [(*ḫa-at-ta-r*)]*i-ša-na-aš pa-ra-a pí-e-t*[*a-i*] [(*na-an*)] *A-NA* DINGER.LÚ^MEŠ *ši-pa-an-*[*ti*]. Translation: "And the *patili*-priest tak[es] forth a big bird to the path, at the crossroads. And he offer[s] it to the male gods" (ibid. p. 115). The continuation of Ha (KUB 9.22) itself refers to the offering at a crossroads of two young goats, one for the male gods of the *šinapši* and the other to the male gods of the city (III 20–23 [see ibid., 94–95]), but makes no further reference to the bird. On the equivalence of the Hurrian term *ḫari* and the Sumerian

who are most likely chthonic deities.[54] Thus, the function of the two birds can be seen as complementary; the first serves to uproot the evil from the birth stool and the second to transport it to the underworld where its threat will be neutralized.

After the parturient purifies the birth stool from contamination, the priest executes a series of rites to purify the woman herself. First, he touches the woman with the bundle of cedar, tamarisk, and olive wood wrapped in red wool. Then he purifies the woman by pouring oil on her head. After tying a string of red wool to her hand, the priest performs a "mouth-cleaning" rite on the woman, using the bundle of sticks to apply the *harnai-* substance.[55]

The following table refers back to the analysis of Lev 14 above and summarizes the elements that comprise the two rituals:

KUB 9.22+	Lev 14
1. Bird-swinging rite	**A. Day 1 (vv. 4–8)**
2. Hand washing	1. Slaughter of one bird*
3. One bird offered to path	2. Bundling of sticks with red wool*
4. One bird offered for purification	3. Purified person sprinkled with blood and spring water*
5. Blood-smearing on birth stool	4. One bird freed*
6. Bundling of sticks with red wool	5. Laundering, shaving and washing
7. Oil poured on head	
8. Hand tied with red wool	
9. Mouth purification rite	
	B. Day 7 (v. 9)
	6. Shaving, laundering and washing

---

logogram KASKAL, see Haas and Wilhelm, *Riten aus Kizzuwatna*, 117–18.

54. Based on the fact that the crossroad sacrifice takes place at night, Beckman suggests that these gods are chthonic (*Hittite Birth Rituals*, 113). This view fits well with the view held by many that the *šinapši* structure (see text cited in previous note) served as a place of worshipping chthonic deities and/or the deified ancestors of the locale (see sources cited above, p. 00, n. 14). In the Ritual of Ammihatna (CTH 471), the male and female deities are the recipients of a *nakušši* goat bearing the impurities (KBo 5.2 III, 30–31; Strauß, *Reinigungsrituale aus Kizzuwatna*, 228).

55. On "mouth-washing" rites in the Hittite literature and their possible connection to the Mesopotamian *mīs pî* ritual, see Strauß, *Reinigungsrituale aus Kizzuwatna*, 181–88. A similar rite appears in the birth ritual KBo 17.65 (Text K) Obv. 10–13; Rev. 32–34. See Beckman, *Hittite Birth Rituals*, 132–33; 142–43.

C. Day 8 (vv. 10–20)

7. Elevation rite with sheep and oil
8. Guilt offering sheep slaughtered
9. Blood daubed on extremities of purified person
10. Oil sprinkled towards tent
11. Oil daubed on extremities
12. Oil poured on head*
13. Sin offering (blood smearing on altar's horns)*
14. Burnt offering

As can be seen from the asterisks (*), nearly all of the rites from the Hittite ritual find parallels in Lev 14. In the following discussion, we will examine some of these traditions in their biblical and broader ancient Near Eastern contexts.

PURIFICATION BY MEANS OF STICKS BUNDLED WITH RED THREAD

An intriguing similarity between the two texts is the use of sticks bundled in red wool for use in purification. In the Hittite rite, cedar, tamarisk, and olive woods, which are bundled in red wool, are dipped in a purificatory substance, *ḫarnai*,[56] which is used to purify the expecting mother's mouth. In comparison, the biblical rite uses cedar and hyssop tied with a crimson thread to sprinkle the mixture of blood and spring water on the person being purified.

The use of red wool and threads is an example of the widespread ancient Near Eastern practice to invoke color symbolism by means of threads and fabrics. In Hittite ritual, red is particularly polyvalent in its symbolism and appears in dramatically different contexts, reflecting a wide range of symbolic associations. It was used to attract gods from their hiding places, to appease their anger and also as a sign of impurity or curse, which could be used in elimination rituals.[57]

---

56. The name of this unknown substance, which is used for sprinkling in various rituals, may be related to the verb *ḫarnai-* (="to sprinkle; to drip"). Cf. *HED* Ḫ, 404–5; *HW*[2] Ḫ, 316–17. Beckman's suggestion, accepted by Puhvel and Haas, that it is derived from wood (i.e., sap) requires further substantiation (Beckman, *Hittite Birth Rituals*, 102–4; cf. Haas, *Materia Magica*, 370).

57. See Haas, *Materia Magica*, 640–41, 653–57. The fact that these texts attribute quite different functions to rites that are quite similar in form serves as a reminder of the importance of context for interpretation.

In biblical ritual, crimson thread[58] appears only twice, for the purification of leprosy (Lev 14:6, 49) and corpse impurity (Num 19:6). In both cases, it is used to tie together a stick bundle of cedar and hyssop for a sprinkling rite. In addition, crimson thread appears in two narrative contexts that are remarkably reminiscent of the use of red string in rituals from adjacent cultures. In Gen 38:28, it is related that when twins were born to Judah and Tamar, the mid-wife tied a crimson thread to the finger of the firstborn. One cannot help but be reminded of the widespread use of red wool in Hittite and Mesopotamian birth rituals.[59] In Josh 2:18, the spies advise Rahab, the harlot, to tie a crimson thread outside her window as a sign for Joshua's troops to spare her family. This usage is quite similar to an apotropaic rite,[60] even reminiscent of the daubing of blood on the doorposts in Exod 12:22. Despite the mundane functions that these narratives attribute to them, these customs may well be rooted in ritual practice. Finally, we should mention the rabbinic tradition recorded in the Mishnah regarding the custom on Yom Kippur to send Azazel's goat off a cliff with a scarlet strap tied to its horns. If a corresponding strap tied to a rock (or according to another opinion—on the entrance to the shrine) turns white, then the Israelites would know that their sins have been atoned.[61] Although this custom is not mentioned in Lev 16, it may reflect an earlier tradition, as it parallels the practice of tying colored threads to animals in elimination rites found in numerous Mesopotamian and Hittite rituals.[62]

Turning to the types of wood used, the Hittite ritual uses tamarisk, olive, and cedar. The tamarisk is prescribed for purificatory rites in Akkadian and Hittite

---

58. The Hebrew term, שני תולעת—literally "red of the worm," indicates the source of the red dye. Cf. Akkadian *huruhurattu* (Ebeling, "Färbestoff," 26).

59. For the use of colored wool for birth amulets in Mesopotamia, see Stol, *Birth in Babylonia*, 49. The wool in this context may have fulfilled an apotropaic function to prevent miscarriage. For an example of such a function for red wool, see Scurlock, "Translating Transfers," 215. See also Reiner, *Astral Magic in Babylonia*, 125–26. It should be noted, however, that the use of red wool (as well as other colors) was a common aspect of Mesopotamian ritual practice, not confined to birth.

60. Cf. Haas, *Materia Magica*, 657.

61. *m. Yoma* 4:2; 6:6, 8. Cf. Isa 1:18. Weinfeld oversteps the evidence with his assertion based on the Mishnaic evidence: "Furthermore cultic customs concerning the scapegoat... attested in later traditions of the second Temple period, can be traced back to Hittite ritual" ("Traces of Hittite Cult," 456).

62. See Wright, *Disposal of Impurity*, 45–57, 65–69

ritual texts.[63] Olive wood serves a similar function in several Hittite rituals.[64] Cedar wood and resin from Lebanon had particular cultic and ritual significance throughout the ancient Near East, as already attested in third-millennium Sumerian texts.[65] In Hittite sources, it is used for diverse functions, but it is most commonly used in purification rites.[66] While its use in temple building is no doubt attributable to the superior quality and durability of the wood, its use in purification rites has been explained in reference to its fragrance and red color.[67]

In comparison, the biblical sprinkling rites use hyssop and cedar. Hyssop[68] appears in several biblical rites and was perceived to have purificatory properties (Ps 51:9). In addition to the sprinkling rites of Lev 14 and Num 19:6, hyssop is also used to daub the blood of the Passover sacrifice on the lintels of the Hebrew homes in order to repel the Destroyer in Exod 12:22–23. Thus, the use of hyssop in the biblical rite stems from the strong indigenous tradition regarding its purificatory powers.[69]

Regarding the use of cedar in Lev 14 and Num 19, several experts in biblical botany came to a surprising conclusion. While the identity of the biblical term ארז with cedar is not disputed, they believe that Lev 14 and Num 19 are exceptions that apply the term to a species of juniper or tamarisk. The rationale for this somewhat strange proposal is that cedar ceases to grow at the northern borders of the Land of Israel.[70] Against this view, it is more probable that the Israelite priests used imported cedar than to assume that ארז in these two passages refers to an entirely different species than the other biblical sources. Nevertheless, the

---

63. On the identification of $^{GIŠ}paini$ as tamarisk, see Hoffner, *Alimenta Hethaeorum*, 119. See also *CHD* P, sub *paini*, which addresses some of Hoffner's reservations. For Mesopotamian rites involving the tamarisk (Sum.: $^{GIŠ}SINIG$; Akk. *bīnu*), see *CAD* B, 240–42. For Hittite sources, see Haas, *Materia Magica*, 283–84.

64. See Haas, ibid., 257–58.

65. For Mesopotamian sources pertaining to cedar (Sum.: ERIN; Akk.: *erēnu*), see *CAD* E, 274–79.

66. Cedar, in the form of wood, resin and oil, serves various functions, including: absorbing maledictions, activating holy water and attracting gods by means of its aroma. See Haas, *Materia Magica*, 277–81.

67. See Milgrom, *Leviticus*, 835; Schmitt, *Magie im Alten Testament*, 163–64.

68. Although its botanical identity has been much debated, there is some consensus today that this name can be applied to the Syrian majorum (Origanum syriacum), known in Arabic as *za'tar*. See Löw, "Der Biblische 'ēzōb," 1–30; Moldenke, *Plants of the Bible*, 160–62; Feliks, *Plant World of the Bible*, 177–78; Zohary, *Plants of the Bible*, 96. This identification is supported by the Samaritan custom to use this plant for their Passover blood rite and correlates well with Rabbinic sources. Cf. Schmitt, *Magie im Alten Testament*, 163–64.

69. Although the tamarisk (Heb. אשל) is widespread in the land of Israel, it is notably absent from ritual use. Moldenke, *Plants of the Bible*, 227–28; Zohary, *Plants of the Bible*, 96.

70. See Moldenke, *Plants of the Bible*, 68, 209–10; Zohary, *Plants of the Bible*, 104–5, 115.

view of these scholars lends weight to the possibility that this Israelite practice has originated in a Syrian milieu.

PURIFICATION BY MEANS OF TWO BIRDS

Another striking similarity between the two texts pertains to the use of a pair of birds. According to the understanding suggested above, the Hittite rite requires the slaughter of one bird, whose blood is used for a blood rite, and a second bird, which is offered to infernal deities. As a result, just as the two birds in the biblical rite serve to uproot and banish the impurity, so too, the birds in the Hittite ritual transport the evil to the underworld. A slightly closer parallel to the latter notion can be found in the goat that is sent off to Azazel in Lev 16, especially according to the widespread interpretation that Azazel refers to a demonic entity who receives the sins of Israel.[71] The latter parallel might even hint that the live bird of Lev 14 was also at one point an offering to a demonic entity.

DAUBING BLOOD ON THE BODY

Whereas the Hittite rite includes the application of a purificatory substance *ḫarnai* to the body of the parturient, Lev 14 requires the sprinkling (v. 7) and daubing (v. 14) of blood on the person being purified. The application of blood to the beneficiary's body is found twice in the Bible in a purificatory function (Lev 14 and the ash-water rite of Num 19) as well as in a consecratory function in the ordination ritual (Exod 29; Lev 8).[72] In the sin offering rituals, however, as in the Hittite *zurki* rite, the blood is applied to an object that purifies the person indirectly. In this regard, the blood rite in Lev 14 exhibits similarity to practices in ancient Mesopotamia and Greece, whose sources refer to the use of blood as a salve to cure severe illnesses, especially epilepsy.[73] Even if Lev 14 in its present form deals with purification and not healing per se,[74] one can hardly ignore the similarity between the blood sprinklings in conjunction with leprosy and these traditions regarding the therapeutic use of blood. Consequently, this tradition should be viewed as independent of the use of blood in the Hittite *zurki* rite and the Biblical sin offering.

---

71. For this and other opinions, see above, p. 77, n. 130.

72. In Exod 24:6–8, blood is splashed on the Israelites in the context of concretizing a covenant with God. But cf. Ginsberg, *Israelian Heritage of Judaism*, 45–46, who suggests that the original form of the text focused on the twelve stelae, metonymically representing the Israelite tribes.

73. See Stol, *Epilepsy in Babylonia*, 105; Parker, *Miasma*, 230–33.

74. See above, p. 60.

PURIFICATORY ANOINTMENT

A final commonality between the Hittite and Biblical rites is the pouring of oil on the head as an act of purification. Anointing with oil is well known from the Bible and Hittite literature as a means of elevating status, particularly of priests, kings and brides.[75] However, it is also well-attested in Hittite, Akkadian and Biblical texts from the Late Bronze Age through the Iron Age as a method of purification.[76] Our examples clearly fit this latter tradition.

As argued in the diachronic analysis of Lev 14 above, the seven-fold sprinkling of oil in Lev 14, 10–14 seems to have originated in H's redaction of the chapter. Nevertheless, there is no reason not to assume that the pouring of oil on the head of the leper was an original part of the ritual. This latter assumption is reinforced by the Hittite parallel.

SUMMARY

In summary, a striking correspondence can be found between the ritual sequences found in KUB 9.22+ and Lev 14, including:

- Lustration by means of sticks bundled with red string
- Use of a pair of birds to purge and send away evil
- Blood-smearing rite (birth stool // leper's sin offering)
- Purification by pouring oil on beneficiary's head

Although the differences between these rituals should not be ignored (some were described in detail above), they are readily understandable in light of 1) the significantly different goals of these two rituals and 2) the assumption that the ritual preserved in Lev 14 has passed through several stages of development before arriving at its present state.[77]

As noted by numerous commentators,[78] one can hardly escape the impression that Lev 14 has preserved some ancient traditions that were lost from the broader textual corpus pertaining to the sin offering. Indeed, comparing the bird rite of Lev 14 to the goat rite of Lev 16, Milgrom observes that the former

---

75. See Singer, "Oil in Anatolia according to Hittite Texts," 183–86; Hoffner, "Oil in Hittite Texts," 111; Franz-Szabó, "Öl, Ölbaum, Olive. B. In Anatolie," 35, 37.

76. See Yakubovich, "Were Hittite Kings Divinely Anointed?" 122–35.

77. This assumption is supported by the textual analysis above (pp. 64–67).

78. For instance, Noth views the basic form of Lev 13–14 as "pre-Priestly" (*Leviticus: A Commentary*, 104).

"represents a more pristine 'undoctored' pagan practice than the scapegoat."[79] Leaving aside pejorative terms such as "pagan," the extensive parallels between this chapter and the Hittite birth ritual KUB 9.22+ seem to confirm Milgrom's intuition that Lev 14 has preserved ancient non-Israelite traditions that have been expunged from other, more thoroughly canonized, biblical rituals.

THE BIRTH RITUAL KBO 17.65 AND LEV 12

We now turn to the biblical laws of the parturient described in Lev 12, which shows similarities to some Hittite birth rituals:[80]

> [1]YHWH spoke to Moses, saying: [2]Speak to the Israelites thus: When a woman produces seed and bears a male child, she shall be impure for seven days; she shall be impure like the days of her menstrual infirmity. [3]On the eighth day the foreskin of his member shall be circumcised. [4]Thirty-three days she shall sit in pure blood: She shall not touch any consecrated thing and she shall not enter the sacred precinct until the days of her purification are completed. [5]If she bears a female, she shall be impure for two weeks like her menstruation and for sixty-six days she shall sit in pure blood. [6]Upon the completion of her purificatory period for a son or daughter, she shall bring a yearling lamb as a burnt offering and a pigeon or turtledove as a sin offering to the priest at the entrance of the Tent of Meeting. [7]He shall offer it before YHWH, and he shall make expiation on her behalf and she shall be pure from her source of blood. This is the law of the parturient for a male or female. [8]If her means do not suffice for a sheep, she shall take two turtledoves or two pigeons, one as a burnt offering, the other as a sin offering. And the priest shall make expiation on her behalf and she shall be pure.

These instructions deal with the state of impurity caused by the mother's post-partum release of lochia. According to these laws, the mother of a male child must abstain from sexual relations with her husband for a period of seven days and avoid contact with the sacred realm for an additional thirty-three days. These

---

79. *Leviticus*, 833. Cf. also his comments on pp. 275, 835.

80. Some apparent parallels between Lev 12 and Hittite birth rituals were already noted by Weinfeld ("Social and Cultic Institutions," 100–101; "Traces of Hittite Cult," 456), but the merits of his studies were undermined by methodological shortcomings. More specifically, Weinfeld attempts to identify exact parallels in the details of the rituals of the two cultures, often by removing them from their broader contexts. This approach causes him to overlook the reality that the Hittites left numerous birth rituals (Beckman's edition includes twenty-seven). With such a large database, the selection of a detail in a given ritual for comparison can be taken as arbitrary (cf. Hoffner, "Israel's Literary Heritage," 186). A more sound approach will be proposed and applied below.

time periods are doubled in the event that she bears a female. Following this purificatory term, she is to bring a sheep as a burnt offering and a bird as a sin offering to the sanctuary.

This ritual in its present form poses some interpretive difficulties. Granted, the posssibility of the parturient bringing her own offering to the Sanctuary is conceivable in the context of the Israelite wilderness camp as described in the Priestly Source of the Pentateuch, in which the Tabernacle is easily accessible to the entire population. However, upon settling in the Land of Israel, this require-ment would place a seemingly unbearable obligation on the new mother. Indeed, whether one subscribes to orthodox religious doctrine or the assumptions of clas-sical Bible criticism, the laws of the Tabernacle are understood to anticipate a centralized cult. Thus, Lev 12 would be forcing the parturient, along with the suckling newborn, to travel potentially enormous distances within forty to eighty days after birth![81] One solution to this problem is to assume that this chapter has been secondarily reframed to a context of cultic centralization. In this light, one might note the somewhat awkward repetition of the locative particle אל in the expression אל פתח אהל מועד אל הכהן (literally, "to the entrance of the Tent of Meet-ing, to the priest" [v.6]), which may indicate that the phrase אל פתח אהל מועד is secondary.[82] Alternatively, by appealing to the general theory of Kaufmann, one can offer a solution that does not posit any reworking of the present text. Accord-ing to Kaufmann, who argues that P predates cult centralization,[83] the "Tent of Meeting" should be viewed as a prototype for any and every local sanctuary. Though neither of these solutions is entirely free of difficulties, one can hardly escape the conclusion that Lev 12 was composed with a local altar in mind.

Now let us turn to a possible Hittite parallel: the Kizzuwatnean birth ritual KBo 17.65.[84] This text consists of a set of rituals that are to be performed in the pre- and post- parturition periods. Remarkably, this tablet preserves two distinct

---

81. The possible objection that these rules were aimed at a purely ideal situation and were never intended to be implemented cannot be sustained. On the contrary, it is probable that these ritual laws and procedures have been secondarily adapted from priestly archives to their present literary context (see pp. 249–52).

82. On this verse, Noth writes: "The simple occurrence of 'the priest' in v. 6 (and 8), and the slight and later redaction by a priestly writer evident in the syntactically incomplete addition of 'the Tent of Meeting (v. 6), both point to it as the work of a pre-Priestly writer" (*Leviticus: A Commentary*, 97). See also Elliger, *Leviticus*, 156–57. Similar expressions appear in the following passages: Lev 14:23; 15:29; 17:5; Num 6:10. It should be noted, however, that the application of this explanation to Lev 17:5 raises considerable difficulties, where the phrase appears as part of an exhortation to slaughter at the Tabernacle. In this case, the deletion of אל פתח אהל מועד would render the verse meaningless.

83. Kaufmann, *Religion of Israel*, 180–84. Interestingly, to my knowledge, neither Kaufmann nor his students have cited Lev 12 as support for their view.

84. In Beckman's edition, Text K, 132–47.

versions of the same ritual on its two sides, and this unusual occurrence allows for confident reconstructions of many broken passages. Aside from the fact that it refers to a blood rite to be carried out in the seventh month of pregnancy (Obv. 8; cf. Rev. 32), it contains an additional passage that is even more intriguing:

Obv.

27 [MUNUS-*an-z(a-ma-za ḫa-)*]*a-*[(*ši nu ku-i*)]*t-ma-an* UD.7.KAM *pa-iz-zi na-aš-ta ḫa-aš-ša-an-t*[(*a-aš*)]

28 [(*ma-a-la*) x-x-x-x-x-x-x-x][85] x [(*a-pí-e-d*)*a-ni* U]D.7.KAM *an-da ši-pa-an-da-an-zi nam-ma* [(*m*)]*a-a-*[(*an*)]

29 [DUMU.NITA *mi-i-ya-r*]*i* [*na-aš mi-i-y*]*a-ri*[!] [(*ku-*)]*e-da-ni* ITU.KAM *nu-kán ma-a-a*[*n*]

30 [UD.1.KAM *na-aš-ma* UD.]3.KAM [x-x-x-x-x-x-x][86] *a-aš-ša-an-za* [( )]

But (when) [the woman] gives birth, and while the seventh day is passing, then they perform the *mala* offering […] of the newborn on th[at] seventh day. Further, i[f a male child is bor]n, whatever month [he is bo]rn, whether [one day or] three [d]ays […] remain—

31 [*na-aš-ta a-pí-e-*]*ez* ITU-[(*az ar-ḫa kap-p*)]*u-u-uš-kán-du nu ma-aḫ-ḫa-an* [ITU.3.KAM *ti-ya-az-zi*]

32 [*na-aš-ta* DUMU.(NITA[!] *ku-u*)]*n-zi-*[(*ga-an-na-ḫi-ta-az*)] *ša-an-ḫa-an-zi ku-un-zi-ga-an-*[(*na-ḫi-ta-ma-az*)]

33 [LÚ.MEŠAZU (*še-*)*i*]*k-ká*[(*n-zi*) *na-at* A-NA   *a-p*]*í-e ši-pa-an-da-an-zi* [( )]

[then from tha]t month let them count off. And when [the third month arrives,] then the male [child] they purify with *kunzigannaḫit.* [For the seers] are expert[87] with *kunzigannaḫit.* [And to …] they offer it.

34 [*ma-a-an-(na* DUMU.MUNUS-*ma*)] *mi-*[(*i-ya-ri*) *na-aš-ta* (*a-*)]*pé-e-ez* ITU-*az ar-ḫa kap-pu-*[*u*]*š-kán-*[(*zi*)]

35 [(*ma-aḫ-ḫa-an)-ma*] IT[(U).4.KAM *ti-ya-a*]*z-zi na-aš-ta* DUMU.MUNUS *ku-un-zi-ga-an-na*!-*ḫi-ti*

36 [(*ša-*)*an-ḫa-an-*]*zi*

_____

85. Beckman estimates that a space of approximately eight more signs exists in this copy than the *ma-a-la a-pé-e-da-ni,* which appears in the parallel section of the reverse side and in copy Kb (KBo 44.49). He suggests that perhaps an additional Hurrian offering term appeared here (*Hittite Birth Rituals,* 157).

86. Regarding this textual gap, see ibid., 158.

87. For *šak(k)-/šekk-* in the sense "to be expert, skilled, or proficient in," see Beckman, ibid., 159–60; *CHD* Š, 31.

But [if] a female child is born, [then] from that month they count off. When the [fourth] month [arriv]es, then they pu[ri]fy the female child with *kunzigannaḫit.*

37 [*ḫa-aš-š(a-an-na-aš-ma ma-)*]*aḫ-ḫa-an* EZEN *ḫa-aš-ši-za ku-wa-pí nu*
     EZEN *ma-aḫ-ḫa-an i-en-zi*
38 [(*n*)*a-aš* ^{GIŠ}*kur-ta-aš i-y*]*a-an-za na-aš* ^{URU}*Ki-iz-zu-wa-at-na nu-mu-kán*
     EZEN KAxU-*it*
39 [*Ú-UL kar-ta n*]*a-an a-pí-e-ez up-pa-aḫ-ḫi*

But when (it is time for) the [bi]rth celebration— (that is) when she gives birth—how they perform the festival [is writ]ten [on a *kurta*] tablet. It is in Kizzuwatna. I do not (know) the festival orally [by heart], [b]ut I will send it from there.[88]

This passage deals with rites that follow birth. On the seventh day, they perform a *mala* offering. Regarding the purification rites for the newborn, the text then makes a gender distinction according to which a male must wait two to three months but a female three to four.[89] After this waiting period, the child is purified with *kunzigannaḫit.* This term seems to refer to some substance that is then used as an offering (line 32).[90] These procedures are then followed by the birth celebration (EZEN *ḫaššannaš).*[91]

The large similarity between this passage and Lev 12 in both structure and content is readily apparent in the following table:

KBo 17.65	Lev 12
Opening: "When the woman gives birth..."	Opening: "When a woman produces seed and bears..."
	If child is male, mother must abstain from sexual relations with husband for seven days
Performance of *mala* offering	Performance of circumcision (*m-w?-l*)

---

88. Text and translation (adapted): Beckman, *Hittite Birth Rituals,* 134–37.

89. The apparent meaning of Obv. 30 and Rev. 39 is that the three month waiting period begins with the month in which the baby is born, regardless of the possibility that only a few days remain in that month. Cf. ibid., 158.

90. For more on *kunz-* and its morphological variants, see ibid., 130–31; Giorgieri, "Schizzo grammaticale," 203, 207.

91. The genitival form *ḫaššannaš* appears also in Rev. 45, but in Obv. 52 we find the variant *ḫa-aš-an-ta-ar-al-li-aš.* For further discussion, see *HW*² H, 410–11.

If child is male, a cleansing rite is performed on child after a two to three month purificatory period	For male child, forty day purificatory period after which mother can be in contact with sancta
	If female child, then mother must abstain from sexual relations with husband for fourteen days
If child is female, a cleansing rite is performed on child after a three to four month purificatory period	For female child, eighty day purificatory period after which mother can be in contact with sancta
Performance of birth celebration	Performance of burnt offering and sin offering

One notes the similar chronological scheme characterized by the following common elements: a special rite within seven to eight days after birth, distinct waiting periods for male and female offspring, a purification rite and a sacrificial regimen.

The most substantial parallel between these texts is the requirement for a longer purificatory period after the birth of a female child. We must note that this distinction between male and female children appears in an additional Kizzuwatna birth ritual KBo 27.67 (Rev. 1–7),[92] which may indicate that this practice was a fixed part of the Kizzuwatnean ritual tradition. If we were to conjecture literary dependency, it would not be a major stretch of the imagination to assume that Lev 12 has substituted its own typological numerical scheme built on multiples of seven and forty.[93] However, we must acknowledge the possibility that the similarity between the texts may be fortuitous. First of all, we must note the fundamental difference between these texts: whereas the Hittite text ascribes impurity to the child, Lev 12 attributes the defilement to the parturient. Secondly, numerous cultures make a distinction based on gender regarding post-natal purification practices, some extending the purificatory period in the case of females and some the opposite.[94] Thus, the similarity between the Hittite and biblical texts may be coincidental.

---

92. In Beckman's edition, Text U, 218–19. It varies somewhat from KBo 17.65, but unfortunately, the fragmentary nature of the text prevents a coherent interpretation.

93. See Meier, "Sabbath and Purification Cycles," 3–11; Pinker, "The Number 40 in the Biblical World," 163–72.

94. See Beckman, *Hittite Birth Rituals*, 160–61 and n. 383; Milgrom, *Leviticus*, 763–65. In several Greek sources, the impurity of the parturient is longer in the case of female offspring. See Parker, *Miasma*, 48–55; S. Stowers, "Greeks Who Sacrifice," 315–16.

Likewise, the comparison of the *mala* rite to the Israelite circumcision is provocative yet problematic.[95] From the outset, we must rule out that the Hittite term refers to circumcision, since a "*mala* of pregnancy" (*armaḫḫuaš mala*) takes place in the seventh month (Obv. l. 6).[96] Furthermore, in the above quoted passage, the *mala* rite appears before the text makes a distinction between a male and female child, so one must infer that it was performed for both, making it highly unlikely that *mala* consisted of circumcision. Nevertheless, before dismissing the comparison altogether, it is worth exploring the meaning of this rare term. It appears to be a derivative of the noun *mal*, which is described in *CHD* (in lieu of a precise definition) as: "(a quality desirable for men in combat, such as boldness, ferocity, skill)."[97] This meaning is most evident in KBo 2.9 I 25–27 where it appears in an appeal to Ištar to remove *mal-* and other qualities from the enemy before the ensuing battle. This meaning seems also to be applicable to the Hurrian form *mali*, which appears in KBo 8.88 Obv. 21 along with other terms for manliness and authority.[98] Its appearance in Hurrian contexts strengthens the possibility that this is in fact the meaning of the term *mala* in our text, which appears among other Hurrian offering terms. Thus, it seems that the *mala* rite was intended to endow the baby with a desirable quality such as vitality or strength. In this light, we may raise the possibility that the Israelites adopted this term and applied it to their native practice of circumcision. While such a hypothesis seems far-fetched, a connection between circumcision and virility would be

---

95. The predominant biblical term is the verbal forms of the root מו"ל, according to the assumption of a triconsonantal root. The only possible candidate for a nominal form is the obscure למולת in Exod 4:26, which has been explained variously by commentators. See Houtman, "Exodus 4:24–26 and Its Interpretation," 81–103; Propp, "That Bloody Bridegroom," 495–518. Only from Mishnaic Hebrew onward do we find the term מילה. Cf. G. Mayer, "מול," *TDOT* 8:158–59.

96. On the reverse, the corresponding rite is called the "*mala* of (the goddess) Apritta" (*mala ŠA* ᵈAprittaya [l. 6]). This rarely attested goddess of Kizzuwatean provenance is referred to elsewhere as "the queen of the gods" (MUNUS.LUGAL ᴰDINGIRᴹᴱˢ¹). See Beckman, *Hittite Birth Rituals*, 168; Miller, *Kizzuwatna Rituals*, 141. A Hittite adjective for "circumcised" may be *paššari-* (see *CHD* P, 204).

97. *CHD* L–N, 124 with references. A similar meaning is probable for the form *malant*; see *CHD* L–N, 128. Similarly, *HEG* M, 100 translates: "Mut, Körperkraft." In contrast, Puhvel translates *mal* as: "brains, wits, wisdom, mindset, disposition" (*HED* M, 20–21; Hoffner and Melchert, *Grammar of the Hittite Language* §§ 9.57, 10.10; cf. *CHD* M, 128 s.v. *mālī*).

98. See Haas and Wilhelm, *Riten aus Kizzuwatna*, 260–63; *ChS* I/9 n. 101, 115. These terms and Laroche's translation of them are as follows (*GLH*, ad loc.): *ḫanumašši* ("fécondité; héroïsme"); *uštašši* ("héroïsme"); and *šarašši* ("royauté"). Giorgieri translates these terms, respectively: "fecondità"; "eroicità, eroismo"; and "pertinente/appartenente alla regalità" ("Schizzo grammaticale," 203, 207). Regarding the proposed etymological connection between *mala* and Hurrian *mali*, see Haas and Wilhelm, *Riten aus Kizzuwatna*, 67; Beckman, *Hittite Birth Rituals*, 153. Cf. *CHD* M, 125 s.v. *māla* for dissenting arguments.

apt. Interestingly, although the practice of circumcision is undoubtedly ancient among the peoples of Egypt, Syria, Canaan, and Transjordan[99] there is no known Semitic cognate for the Hebrew term.[100]

Aside from the aforementioned difficulties, the comparison of these two rituals, especially the attention placed on the structural similarities between them, raises a number of issues about the channels of transmission implied by such a comparison. In particular, by shifting the focus from practices to texts, we are tacitly raising the possibility that the ritual was either translated from Hurrian or Hittite into a Syro-Canaanite Semitic language or the converse. While such a possibility may seem at first glance unlikely, the existence of bilingual Ugaritic-Hurrian ritual texts from Ras Shamra proves that such intercultural interactions were a reality in Late Bronze Age Syria (see above). In passing, we must note that even the transmission of nonverbal ritual practices between these cultures could only take place on the basis of some level of bilingual interaction.

In summary, in light of the other examples that indicate a stream of tradition that connects the Kizzuwatna corpus with the Israelite cult, one should not dismiss a hypothetical connection between KBo 17.65 and Lev 12 out of hand. At the same time, one must acknowledge the possibility that these parallels may be merely coincidental.

THE KIZZUWATNEAN BIRTH RITUALS AND LEV 12

More definitive conclusions can be drawn by comparing Lev 12 with the sub-genre of Kizzuwatnean birth rituals as a whole. Such an approach avoids the danger of overemphasizing any particular text and gives expression to the fact that the dominant ritual techniques could be combined in a variety of forms and with variations among the details. As a result, the discovery of a "perfect match" between rituals of the two cultures, though hypothetically possible, is not the only criterion for identifying a continuum of ritual traditions spanning from Anatolia to Israel.

The blood rite appears in five distinct birth rituals of the Kizzuwatna corpus, appearing either with the Hurrian term *zurki* or with the Hittite verb *išḫarnuma-*. This high propensity within a limited corpus exhibits clearly that this rite was

---

99. See Sasson, "Circumcision in the Ancient Near East," 473–76; Mayer, *TDOT* 8:159–60. In Egypt, circumcision may have been restricted to priests. The widespread observance of this custom throughout the Levantine region finds further support in the appellation "the uncircumcised" (ערלים) used in relation to the Philistines in the early historiographic sources (e.g., Judg 14:3; 15:18; 1 Sam 14:6; 17:26, 36), implying that this characteristic was exceptional. See Faust, *Israel's Ethnogenesis*, 85–91.

100. See Mayer, *TDOT* 8:159.

very common in the southern Anatolian–northern Syrian milieu. In most cases, the blood rite seems to have taken place before birth,[101] but there are cases where it took place afterwards.[102] In all of these cases, the birth stool and pegs are the locus of the blood smearing. Strikingly, the source of blood in all cases, like the biblical rite, comes from a bird.

Regarding the sacrificial animals involved, the closest parallel to the biblical ritual is that of Papanikri. In comparison to the biblical rite, which involves the slaughter of one bird for the blood rite and the burning of a sheep as a burnt offering, the Papanikri ritual involves the slaughtering of two birds for the blood rite and the cooking of a sheep as a sacrificial offering.[103]

While the fragmentary nature of most of the ritual texts precludes an understanding of the circumstances that motivated their performance, the Papanikri text gives us one answer. As observed above,[104] this ritual was performed in a case when the birth apparatus broke, which was interpreted as a manifestation of divine anger. In order to pacify the gods, a new set of birth apparatus is constructed, which is then smeared with blood. The other birth rituals in which the blood rite appears are less informative as to the nature of the dangerous forces, but since most of these rituals take place before delivery, they seem to address the dangers associated with labor. Such a rationale would hardly be surprising: If many women are apprehensive of giving birth in the modern age, one can hardly imagine the fear that accompanied this event in the ancient world (or in developing countries today), considering the high rate of mortality for both child and mother. This understanding is supported by the birth ritual Bo 4951+, which deals explicitly with the possibility of a stillbirth.[105] Although the *uzi* and *zurki* rites appear in this ritual, the fragmentary nature of this text precludes a clear understanding of their role.

Turning back to Lev 12, the parturient's requirement to bring a sin offering has puzzled ancient and modern commentators. Unwilling to entertain the thought that the act of conception was sinful, the Tannaitic sage R. Simeon explained that the parturient vows impetuously at childbirth to cease marital rela-

---

101. KBo 5.1 (Papanikri): I 25–27; KUB 9.22+ (Text H): Ha II 15–20; KBo 17.65+ (Text K): Obv. 8; Rev. 32.

102. KBo 5.1 (Papanikri): III 41; Bo 4951 (Text J): Rev. 10'–12'. The place of the blood rite in the sequence of KBo 21.45 (Text O) is not clear due to its fragmentary condition (II 2').

103. Cf. Weinfeld, "Traces of Hittite Cult," 456 who draws a parallel between a different Hittite birth ritual and the biblical rite. KBo 21.45 (Text O) I 10'–11' mentions a bird and a sheep as *uzi*- offerings. It is not clear which animal is used for the blood rite (II 2'), but based on the other examples, we must assume that it was a bird.

104. See pp. 9–13.

105. See Beckman, *Hittite Birth Rituals*, 124–27 (Text J),

tions with her husband.[106] Among modern commentators, Lev 12 has come to the foreground of the controversy over whether the purpose of the חטאת is to remove sin or impurity. As noted above, Milgrom views this case as a conclusive proof that the חטאת offering is a "purification offering," not a "sin offering," since we have no reason to attribute sin to the parturient.[107]

However, a different conclusion emerges from our comparison of Lev 12 with the Kizzuwatnean birth rituals. Just as in the Hittite texts, where the purpose of the blood rite is to address the dangers associated with birth, one may postulate that such was originally the case with the Israelite parturient's sin offering. As in the Papanikri ritual, this purpose may have involved appeasing the Deity for prior offenses. Of course, we must not confuse the *original* function of the rite with the purpose of the rite as described in Lev 12. According to Lev 12, the rite is intended to "make expiation on her behalf from the source of her blood" (וכפר עליה וטהרה ממקר דמיה [v. 7]). This rationale, which relates the offering to her discharge of lochia, pertains to the concern with impurity, not sin. In other words, the historical explanation offered here need not preclude the exegetical interpretations of Lev 12, which understand the chapter in light of the priestly system of impurity laws.[108] At the same time, it allows us to understand the original context in which the parturient was expected to bring a sin offering.[109]

In fact, Lev 12's emphasis on ritual impurity may be representative of a broader tendency in Priestly ritual. In the previous chapter, I found evidence indicating that the use of the sin offering in cases of bodily afflictions, such as leprosy and abnormal genital flux, may stem from the fundamental belief that these abnormalities are the result of a divine punishment.[110] However, the relevant chapters in their present form (Lev 12–15) show little trace of any such suspicion, creating the impression that impurity is a morally neutral category, completely distinct from sin. This transition may imply a corresponding ideological transformation that sought to free such bodily conditions of the stigma of divine wrath.

---

106. *b. Nidda* 31b. This explanation should probably be viewed as facetious, as many further objections could be added to those of the Amora R. Joseph (ad. loc.).

107. Milgrom, "Sin Offering or Purification Offering," 237–39; *Leviticus*, 253. Cf. above p. 99–108.

108. For some recent theories, see Milgrom, *Leviticus*, 766–68; Whitekettle, "Leviticus 12 and the Israelite Woman," 393–408; idem., "Levitical Thought and the Female Reproductive Cycle," 376–91 with references.

109. Douglas' anthropological intuitions bring her to a similar understanding of the origins of Lev 12, but she maintains, correctly, that the present text has been adapted to the priestly worldview (*Leviticus as Literature*, 181–82).

110. See pp. 107–8.

It is remarkable that the closest parallels to biblical texts are found in the Hittite birth rituals. Can this observation provide insight into the context of transmission of these rites to Israel? Since the Bible does not mention any birth rituals aside from Lev 12 nor designates a cultic role for women, this line of inquiry seems to lead to a dead end.[111] However, if we turn our attention to the fact that the closest parallels, Lev 12 and 14, are found in the collection of laws dealing with bodily impurities (Lev 12–15), we can suggest a more plausible direction. Specifically, if our etiology of the sin offering is correct (pp. 99–108), we may propose that these impurity laws were originally employed in "medical" contexts such as sickness and childbirth. Accordingly, we can tentatively infer that the need for expiation was most acutely felt in situations of danger. Though the actual origin of this tradition remains to be determined (see below, pp. 243–47), it is clear that these contexts often involved the sharing of ritual expertise between cultures.

Summary

This section has examined some texts that exhibit close parallels between the Hittite rituals in which the *zurki* rite appears and specific biblical rituals that feature the sin offering. In particular, numerous similarities were identified between the Kizzuwatnean birth ritual KUB 9.22+ and Lev 14, which might plausibly point towards a common source. While a historical connection between KBo 17.65 and Lev 12 remains debatable, one cannot dissociate the parturient's sin offering from the widespread practice of the *zurki* rite in the Kizzuwatnean birth rituals. Consequently, the comparison of specific ritual texts supports the assumption of a common tradition as argued earlier in this chapter. Before examining further questions pertaining to the historical background of the transmission of this practice, I will first delve into the symbolism of the blood rite in order to determine the sociocultural context in which the expiatory use of blood originated.

---

111. It is likely, however, that birth rituals were much more common than is reflected by the biblical evidence (see above, p. 130).

PART II

4

RITUALS, SIGNS AND MEANING:
THEORETICAL FOUNDATIONS

Our examination of Hittite and biblical texts has focused on use of blood in blood rites for expiation, purification, and consecration. The immediate question raised by these functions of blood, particularly in light of the uniqueness of this practice compared to other cultures, is: Why did the Hittites and Israelites attribute this kind of capability to blood? In approaching this question, we will consider both ancient and modern interpretations of these rites. In the case of the Bible, this body of exegetical tradition is formidable. In order to reexamine this question anew and to appreciate fully the new Hittite evidence, it is necessary to clear away some entrenched misconceptions.

Jewish and Christian exegetes have traditionally interpreted the expiatory power of blood in the biblical offerings, including the sin offering, in light of the statement in Lev 17:11 that the נפש (*nepeš*)—usually translated "life"—is in the blood. As will be shown later in some detail, the import of this verse has been both misunderstood and exaggerated. For the moment, let us briefly mention a few basic problems, exegetical and methodological. First, Lev 17:11 can be understood as dealing with all of the offerings or a certain subgroup of offerings, but it cannot be construed as focusing specifically on the sin offering. Accordingly, it is not clear that this verse's programmatic statement regarding sacrificial blood is relevant to understanding the unique sprinkling and smearing rites of the sin offering. Second, since this source is attributable to the late Priestly layer H, we cannot assume automatically that this source's understanding is consistent with earlier Priestly conceptions. Third, we must face an even more basic question: Since ritual signs are generally recognized as permitting multiple interpretations, can any single explanation of a ritual activity be taken as authoritative?[1]

---

1. See Gilders, *Blood Ritual in the Hebrew Bible*, 1–13.

This last point is sufficiently serious so as to demand a full consideration of our basic assumptions in confronting the question of the *meaning* of ritual acts. This task is not easy. It requires facing some of the most hotly contested issues in the social sciences, not to mention philosophy, psychology, and literary theory. As I hope to show, the discipline of modern ritual studies has offered several approaches to dealing with the question of ritual meaning but has by no means exhausted the possibilities. Here I will offer my own approach to applying the notion of "meaning" to ritual symbolism, one that will provide the basis for our subsequent inquiry into the origins of the symbolism of the Hittite and Israelite blood rites.

Ritual Interpretation and the Question of Meaning

Since the establishment of anthropology as an academic field at the turn of the twentieth century, much controversy has surrounded the methodological premises underlying the interpretation of ritual. In order to understand the reasons for the increasing skepticism as to the prospect of determining the "meaning" of a particular ritual, it is worthwhile to review some of the major trends in ritual interpretation and their approaches to the question of "meaning." The comparison of varying methods of ritual interpretation is complicated by the divergent uses of the term "meaning" by different scholars, who do not necessarily explicitly state the theoretical tradition to which they subscribe in employing this term. In order to evaluate these different methods properly, one must first probe the analyis to discern whether the author is employing the term "meaning" in relation to conscious intention, purpose, or something else. Frequently, the application of "meaning" to the field of ritual involves an inconsistent combination of these uses. In the following brief survey, I will not be able to give adequate attention to these intricate problems. My focus will be upon providing the necessary background for the current state of research in ritual studies.

Until the mid-twentieth century, the dominant approach to ritual interpretation focused on the perspective of the participants (the "emic" approach). By employing an analogy to linguistic discourse, anthropologists sought to "decode" the symbolism of the ritual.[2] Since the metaphor of "decoding" implies univalent meaning (understood as the intention of participants), this approach was ill-equipped to account for the plurality of interpretations of ritual acts that exist within the society, including the issue of "public" (shared) versus "private"

---

2. For a critique of this approach, see Sperber, *Rethinking Symbolism*, 4–33; Lawson and McCauley, *Rethinking Religion*, 138–39.

(individual) explanations of rituals.[3] This problem was compounded by the recognition that the understandings of ritual activity invariably change over time.
One solution to this conundrum, proposed by Victor Turner, was to distinguish
between different types of meaning attributed to ritual signs within a given culture and to analyze the relationship between them. However, the viability of this
approach is undermined by its reliance on a vague notion of "meaning."[4]

A radical departure from the participant-centered approach was that of structural anthropology. Applying the fundamentals of Saussurian linguistics to the
study of cultures, Lévi-Strauss and his students sought to uncover the underlying
conceptual system reflected in symbolic behavior. As a basic principle, advocates
of this approach deemphasized the participants' perspective, assuming that an
outsider's perspective allows identification of cognitive structures that underly
cultural phenomena.[5] They view the pursuit of these structures as superseding
questions of meaning.[6]

One of the most devastating challenges to the classical notion of ritual meaning came with Staal's provocative article "The Meaninglessness of Ritual."[7]
Among his arguments, Staal pointed out that the practitioners of rituals often
show little interest in the meaning of ritual and focus almost exclusively on the
technical details of correct performance. If the participants themselves attach no
significance to the interpretation of rituals, how can the anthropologist justify
exegetical pursuits? Arguing that ritual is activity for its own sake, Staal rejects
the application of any possible sense of the term "meaning" to ritual, whether
understood as intention, function, or goal.

Finally, post-structuralist literary theory's critique of the conventional identification of "meaning" with authorial intent could be viewed as discrediting the
"emic" approach to ritual interpretation entirely. Indeed, Bell has applied the
deconstructionist notion of *différance*—described as "the endless deferral of

---

3. For extensive discussion of such issues, see Firth, *Symbols: Public and Private*, esp.
170–214.

4. Turner employs a trichotomous classification of meaning: "exegetical" (native interpretation), "operational" (observed usage), and "positional" (relation to other symbols taken as
a system). See *Forest of Symbols*, 43–54. For a critique of Turner's terminological laxity, see
Sperber, *Rethinking Symbolism*, 13, 29.

5. This approach parallels the mentalism implicit in Saussure's two-fold division of the
sign into sound image and concept. By excluding any relation to an external referent, Saussure
could isolate language from historical (diachronic) factors, yielding a static synchronic system.
See Hodge and Kress, *Social Semiotics*, 16–17. A similar result is achieved by structuralists in
regard to cultural phenomena in general.

6. Or perhaps that Levi-Strauss understood "meaning" as reference, such that myths and
rituals refer to the structures of the mind. See Penner, "Language, Ritual and Meaning," 4–5.

7. "Meaninglessness of Ritual," 2–22. For a critique, see Penner, "Language, Ritual and
Meaning."

meaning both within the text and within the act of interpreting"[8]—to the domain of ritual. Though some of these methodological developments lead to rather dubious conclusions,[9] it is nevertheless clear that much of the naiveté surrounding the idea of "revealing" a ritual's (unified) meaning has been dispersed.

Accordingly, scholars in recent decades have shifted their attention from what rituals *mean* to what rituals *do* and explore the effects of rituals on participants and society as a whole.[10] While this approach may place ritual studies onto a more sturdy methodological footing, it tends to deemphasize the understanding and motivations of participants. As with structuralism, the context for ritual interpretation is moved from its native setting to the university.

Until recent decades, the philological study of ancient Near Eastern and Biblical rituals has generally ignored these developments. Not only do these studies assume the unambiguous meaning of ritual signs, they express a naïve conviction in their ability to uncover this meaning. This approach will be apparent in some of the views regarding the symbolic meaning of blood mentioned below. At first glance, this attitude can be justified by the fact that the ritual text can be taken as an authoritative source by which to determine ritual meaning. However, the vast majority of texts deal exclusively with the details of performance, thus falling under the purview of Staal's critique. Most ritual signs are left explained, and even the interpretations which are provided in a particular ritual are not necessarily applicable in other contexts. Only recently have scholars begun to incorporate the refined theoretical approaches to ritual studies offered by the social sciences.[11] The new body of research has sought to come to terms with the growing skepticism regarding ritual meaning.[12]

Most relevant to the present discussion is Gilders' recent study *Blood Ritual in the Hebrew Bible*. Gilders raises numerous questions pertinent to the use of blood in Israelite cult and shows the failure of earlier studies to confront the serious methodological issues which pertain to ritual symbolism.[13] Using Peircian terminology, Gilders focuses on the manner in which blood acts as an *index* to

---

8. Bell, *Ritual Theory, Ritual Practice*, 113; cf. also 105–6.

9. For instance, Bell remarks, "People do not take a social [i.e., societal Y.F] problem to a ritual for a solution. People generate a ritualized environment that acts to shift the very status and nature of the problem into terms that are endlessly retranslated in strings of deferred schemes" (ibid., 106). One finds difficulty in squaring mystifying claims such as these with the very real-world circumstances and goals of ancient Near Eastern rituals (e.g., sickness, plague, warfare).

10. For examples of research in this direction, see Bell, *Ritual Theory, Ritual Practice*, 88–93, 197–223; Kapferer, "Ritual Dynamics and Virtual Practice," 35–52 with references.

11. For a discussion of these developments, see Klingbeil, *Ritual and Ritual Texts*, 45–69.

12. See Gane, *Cult and Character*, 3–24.

13. Gilders, *Blood Ritual in the Hebrew Bible*, 2–6.

focus attention and establish status.[14] For example, the ritual texts make clear that only the priests have the privilege of performing the blood manipulations; thus, the blood rites serve not only to express but also to establish the status of the priests. Similarly, following Bell's concept of "ritualization," he examines how blood serves to create distinctions, such as between the sacred and profane.[15] By focusing on what blood rites do, Gilders manages to circumvent the perilous questions that pertain to "meaning."

Without dismissing the methodological advances of the new criticisms of ritual meaning, there remains a suspicion that the grounds for their skepticism have been exaggerated. The criticisms of the participant-centered approach are often based on a simplistic notion of "meaning" that ignores the fact that even a theory of linguistic meaning must account for polysemy, diachrony, and interpersonal/individual dimensions. Furthermore, on the pretense of methodological stringency, these skeptical approaches leave unexplored fundamental questions. How do ritual acts attain their world-transforming capability? And more to the point here, why did the Hurrians, Hittites, and Israelites use blood in their expiatory rituals? But before we can address these questions, we need to establish some of our methodological premises.

THE POTENCY OF SIGNS

At the outset of this study, I stated my view that ancient Near Eastern rituals are primarily intended to address concrete societal and personal concerns. In ch. 1, I noted that many of these problems are attributable to metaphysical causes. Rituals provide the opportunity to breach the veil of purely physical causality and allow the ritual participants to interact with these unseen forces. Let us now examine some of the dynamics by which ritual signs attain their ability to be viewed as a viable means to alter the state of the world.

It is commonly understood that the belief in ritual efficacy is based on the perception that signs are inherently potent. In providing an explanation for speech taboos and word magic, Benveniste writes, "For the speaker there is a complete equivalence between language and reality. The sign overlies and commands reality; even better, it *is* that reality."[16] Leaving aside speculative theories about why people come to believe in an inherent connection between signs and things, we may at least try to understand why such a connection is perceived as indispen-

---

14. Ibid., 7–8. For this approach, he credits Jay, *Throughout Your Generations Forever*, 6–7. For more on the notion of "index," see below, p. 162.

15. See Bell, *Ritual Theory, Ritual Practice*, 72, 169–238.

16. *Problems in General Linguistics*, 46.

sible for a ritual's success. The following remark of Wittgenstein on Frazer's *The Golden Bough* can point us in the right direction:

> In magical healing one *indicates* to an illness that it should leave the patient. After the description of any such magical cure we'd like to add: If the illness doesn't understand *that,* then I don't know how one ought to say it.[17]

In this statement, ritual is viewed as an attempt to communicate—more accurately, to signal—to an inanimate force (the illness) to leave. But this point raises the obvious question, How is one to talk to an illness? One must find a language that *even* an illness can understand.

The importance of this insight can be shown with a simple example.[18] A sorcerer gains a specimen of hair from a potential victim and burns the hair to inflict harm on him. By using the hair of the victim, the sorcerer is establishing a channel of influence with the victim. By burning the hair, the sorcerer expects that a similar act of destruction will befall the victim. From an analytical standpoint, we may say that, through an analogical act (metaphor), the sorcerer articulates the message of what he desires to happen to the object of his ritual act—the victim. Through a relation of contiguity (metonymy), the sorcerer establishes an indexical relation with the victim.[19] In a manner analogous to language, the sorcerer establishes through these nonverbal gestures both the *message* (burning-destruction) and its *reference* (the victim so-and-so).

Applying Wittgenstein's statement to a case such as this, we may draw the following conclusion: In establishing a language by which one can interact with impersonal forces, the fundamental requirement is the creation of a univocal message free of ambiguity.[20] Conversely, a ritual act will most likely not be effective if it is ambiguous (permitting more than one interpretation) or obscure (defying interpretation). These points lead to the important conclusion: Notwithstanding the modern tendency to emphasize the multivalency of ritual signs, it seems that univalency is a basic requirement for ritual efficacy.

In the following sections, I will elucidate several issues pertaining to the motivation of signs, but I must first clarify my terminology.

---

17. Wittgenstein, *Remarks on Frazer's Golden Bough*, 6e–7e.

18. This example adapted from Leach, *Culture and Communication*, 31 (with several refinements).

19. Cf. Rhees, "Wittgenstein on Language and Ritual," 78–79.

20. In certain ways, this requirement is similar to that of adults attempting to communicate with a preverbal child in that they are highly dependent on concrete objects and indexical cues (such as pointing) to convey their intentions.

BASIC DEFINITIONS

In this study, I will view rites as being comprised of *signs*.[21] It is important to emphasize that my use of this term here departs from common usage due to my exclusive interest in the ritual use of signs. As a corollary to my view of ritual as goal-oriented activity, signs do not necessarily need to represent something else.[22] Contrary to the typical semiotic view that a *sign* "stands for" something else—a view that construes the role of signs in predominantly mentalistic terms, in my use of the term, it refers to a type of stimulus that elicits a response, whether that of a live interlocutor or a metaphysical mechanism embedded in the world. Thus, sign use involves the expectation that it can be used to directly effect changes in the world.[23] In Turner's words: "It must not be forgotten that ritual symbols are not merely signs representing known things; they are felt to possess ritual efficacy, to be charged with power from unknown sources."[24]

Incidentally, this emphasis on the goal-oriented practical effects of the sign can also be applied to verbal language. In general, people are not busy contemplating internal representations of the words they speak or hear. As remarked by Zipf, "Man talks in order to get something."[25] Voloshinov employs a similar premise as a foundation for his linguistic analysis. According to his account, the basic reality of language is the speech act, in which the speaker adapts the generic verbal sign to express the speaker's contextually situated intentions. He writes, "In actuality, we never say or hear *words*, we say or hear what is true or false, good or bad, important or unimportant, pleasant or unpleasant, and so on."[26]

As a further clarification, I should point out that the term "sign" designates an *analytical* category, and it should not be misconstrued as implying that people usually perceive signs to be a discrete category of objects in their everyday activities. Generally, people are not aware of objects or gestures acting as signs any

---

21. Following C. S. Peirce, I will use "sign" as a general category. Some specific types of signs—e.g., icons, indexes, symbols—will be described below.

22. Cf. A. J. Greimas' attempt to outline a semiotics of gesturality, encompassing both "practical" and "mythical" gesturality (the latter including ritual). Since these aim to transform the world, they do not seek to communicate. See "Towards a Semiotics of the Natural World," 31.

23. This characterization has affinities to behavioristic notions of semiotics, such as that of Charles Morris. However, unlike Morris, I do not require that the sign must serve as a substitute stimulus, e.g., the buzzer, in causing salivation in Pavlov's dog, is acting as a substitute for meat. See *Signs, Language and Behavior*, 5–7.

24. *Forest of Symbols*, 54.

25. *Human Behavior and the Principle of Least Effort*, 19.

26. *Philosophy of Language*, 70, emphasis in original. Cf. pp. 65–71.

more than they view a doorknob as a *tool* when opening the door. Nor is a sign a particular kind of object. For example, a mop placed across a doorway might be a sign that the floor is wet. For the purposes of this study, *sign* will be defined as an object that serves to function, whether by the intent of a sign user or as a consequence of an act of interpretation, to cause a response or convey information not immediately entailed in its practical function as a tool.

We may now tackle some thorny issues dealing with the "meaning" of ritual activity.[27] The most widespread approach views the meaning of signs as the idea evoked by the sign.[28] This prominent tradition, rooted in Cartesian mind/body dualism and adopted by Saussurian linguistics, asserts that "meaning" refers to the concept or idea represented by a sign. According to this definition, the "meaning" of a ritual would be the conscious intention of a participant in a ritual, the set of ideas that accompanies the physical act. Several weaknesses can be found with this approach. First of all, common sense dictates—and ethnography confirms—that participants do not necessarily have any fixed set of ideas when they carry out a ritual. Second, like verbal language, the meaning of a nonverbal sign must be shareable. When questioned about the meaning of a particular word, I may either provide an alternative expression (one that fulfills a similar function) or offer a set of contexts in which one can properly use the term, but I cannot refer to ideas in my mind. *A fortiori*, an anthropologist or philologist studying a foreign culture cannot hope to penetrate the minds of members of a foreign culture.

A more viable notion of "meaning," inspired by the writings of Wittgenstein, emphasizes the *use* of the sign.[29] Comparing language to games such as chess, Wittgenstein pointed out common fallacies in mentalistic notions of "meaning." Just as the rules that govern the movement of the chess pieces cannot be viewed as a mental content, since players usually do not think about the rules while playing, so too, the use of words can be more accurately viewed as an application of a set of rules, which define their correct use and function. Wittgenstein writes, "An intention is embedded in its situation, in human customs and institutions. If the technique of the game of chess did not exist, I could not intend to play a game of chess. In so far as I do intend the construction of a sentence in advance, that is made possible by the fact that I speak the language in

---

27. See Hobart, "Meaning or Moaning?," 39–64.

28. E.g., Geertz's influential view of signs as "vehicles for conception" (*Interpretation of Cultures*, 91). For an overview of different approaches to "meaning" in semiotics, see Nöth, *Handbook of Semiotics*, 92–102. For an elaborate discussion of its application to cultural phenomena in general, see Strauss and Quinn, *Cognitive Theory of Cultural Meaning*, 12–88.

29. For a useful overview, see Hacker, "Meaning and Use," 26–44.

question."[30] In this light, we may state that the meaning of a rite is its purpose as determined by social practice, regardless of how it is interpreted by individual participants. Accordingly, we may define "meaning" as *the function of a sign or sign system, including the expected responses that will be elicited by its use.* By defining "meaning" such that it is not identified with intention, whether that of an author or of a participant, it does not fall victim to the critiques of Staal or the post-structuralists presented above.[31]

By mentioning the critical role of social practices, we must discuss an additional analytic concept, namely that of context. Despite decades of asserting that the *meaning* of a statement or activity must be determined by its *context*—that is, that a statement or act must not be taken "out of context"—linguists and anthropologists have only begun to recognize the problems involved in delineating the latter concept. Though participants in an interaction usually sense intuitively which aspects of the situation are relevant to understanding a given act's meaning, it is often exceedingly difficult for the outsider to identify these elements. Contrary to the naïve assumption, one cannot posit the "context" as a given by which to understand the "meaning," since the determination of the relevant context itself requires interpretation. In this respect, context is meaning-dependent just as much as meaning is context-dependent.[32] However, by focusing on the functional aspect of ritual acts, perhaps we may avoid this ambiguity. If "meaning" denotes the function of the ritual, then we may define "context" as the background conditions and social practices that enable the ritual act to be potentially effective. An important application of this definition, which will be pivotal for our analysis of the blood rite, is that the context can be reconstructed through an analsis of the ritual act's meaning.

LIFE IN A MEANINGFUL WORLD

As noted above, any object or gesture can potentially be interpreted as a sign, even when people responding to them do not recognize them as such. Though this phenomenon, in which signs are everywhere yet tend to remain invisible, may seem strange at first, it is an unavoidable consequence of our everyday absorbed manner of dealing with reality. In order to overcome the common tendency to exaggerate the role of consciousness and intentionality in human behavior, we can make use of Heidegger's view of "significance" (*Bedeutung*),

---

30. *Philosophical Investigations* §337, cited in Hallett, *Meaning as Use*, 117.

31. As Norris points out in light of Wittgenstein's approach, the skepticism of deconstructionists is "a misplaced scruple produced by a false epistemology" (*Deconstruction: Theory and Practice*, 129).

32. See Holy, "Contextualization and Paradigm Shifts," 50.

which is quite similar to the notion of meaning advanced here. Heidegger provides a non-mentalistic account of the manner in which one's surroundings have significance in purposeful activity. When a person is absorbed in everyday coping, that person does not pay attention to the fact that a given object is a tool, sign or whatever. But if, for whatever reason, one's attention is drawn to the object, one may then be led to *interpret* its significance. Regarding the latter, he writes:

> In interpreting, we do not, so to speak, throw a "signification" over some naked thing which is present-at-hand, we do not stick a value on it; but when something within the world is encountered as such, the thing in question already has an involvement which is disclosed in our understanding of the world, and this involvement is one which gets laid out by the interpretation.[33]

In the manner in which the world is experienced, humans do not give significance to brute objects. Rather, when people are engaged in their purposeful activities, they encounter objects as already significant in the manner determined by their context. According to this description, we may assert that the significance of a sign is derivative of its function in a particular real-world context.[34]

As an illustration of this view, Heidegger notes that one may hear a chirping bird or a motorcycle, but one never hears meaningless complexes of sound. To perceive the latter would require extensive training as a sound engineer. In contrast with the Searle's characterization of verbal language as "acoustic blasts" to which people give meaning, Heidegger stresses the fact that our experience of language always takes for granted the fact that speech is inherently meaningful: "Even in cases where speech is indistinct or in a foreign language, what we proximally hear is *unintelligible* words, and not a multiplicity of tone-data."[35] In other words, everday experience involves meaningful coping; only through a secondary, reflective analysis can this data be viewed in abstract or meaningless terms.

Heidegger's phenomenological description can be complemented with a developmental account, based on similar principles, taken from cultural psychology and anthropology. Although the Soviet psychologist L. S. Vygotsky (1896–1934) is most famous for his contributions to developmental psychology, he used his developmental research as a springboard for broader theorizing and experimentation regarding the role of sign systems in the development of

---

33. *Being and Time*, 190–91.
34. See Dreyfus, *Being-in-the-World*, 97.
35. Heidegger, *Being and Time*, 207 (his italics); See Dreyfus, *Being-in-the-World*, 218–19; idem., "Phenomenological Description Versus Rational Reconstruction," 189.

cultures (cultural-historical psychology).[36] In particular, he argued that sign systems, foremost among them language, serve as tools that fundamentally change the nature of mental processing. By inheriting this "spiritual culture," the individual inherits an orderly system for dealing with the world, comprised of bodily practices, linguistic forms, norms of logical reasoning, moral conventions, laws, etc.[37] In light of this developmental account, we may refer again to the misleading yet popular notion that humans give significance to the brute facts of the world. The developmental process is precisely the opposite. Through exposure to the objectified products of culture, children are initiated into a meaningful world in a gradual process that begins with their emergence from the womb, if not earlier.[38]

Since the topic of the present work is ritual, we will focus on the nonverbal aspects of culture. Following Mauss, Bourdieu has discussed in detail the profound role played by "practice"—patterns of bodily activity such as gait, facial expressions, tone of speech and ways of sitting and using implements—in shaping individuals' experience of the world. These allow the transmission and perpetuation of societal values without them ever needing to be expressed in verbal discourse.[39] In fact, by virtue of the fact that these attitudes are transmitted implicitly rather than explicitly, they are more likely to become part of the uncontested and seemingly objective reality of a particular culture.[40] Even the material artifacts produced by a society are endowed with a socially determined function that serves to objectify cultural knowledge and values. In this account, the collective understandings that comprise a particular culture are objectified in the material world, so that consciousness both shapes and is in turn shaped by cultural objects.

To sum up this point, in the context of everyday activities in which people engage in purposeful action, a dialectical process of embodiment and internaliza-

---

36. Vygotsky's view was not a simple comparison of "primitives" with children, but a nuanced recognition of the existence of certain common principles influencing human and cultural development, such as the processes involved in the use of language and other sign systems (see Wertsch, *Vygotsky and the Social Formation of Mind*, 40–41).

37. The term "spiritual culture" is borrowed from the Soviet philosopher Ilyenkov (1924–1979), whose views were met with enthusiasm by Vygotsky's former collegues and students. See Bakhurst, *Consciousness and Revolution*, 192–200.

38. For a general account of the cultural dimension in a developmental context, see Shweder et al., "The Cultural Psychology of Development," 865–937.

39. See Mauss, "Les techniques du corps," 364–86; Bourdieu, *Outline of a Theory of Practice*, 87–95.

40. According to Bourdieu, such dispositions lie outside the "universe of discourse," which is divided into orthodox and heterodox opinions. In contrast, these pertain to the taken-for-granted "universe of the undiscussed"—what he calls the *doxa*, (*Outline of a Theory of Practice*, 164–71).

tion takes place. By transforming material substances into tools and signs, they represent cultural knowledge that in turn serves to enculturate individuals. This dialectical process can be depicted as follows:

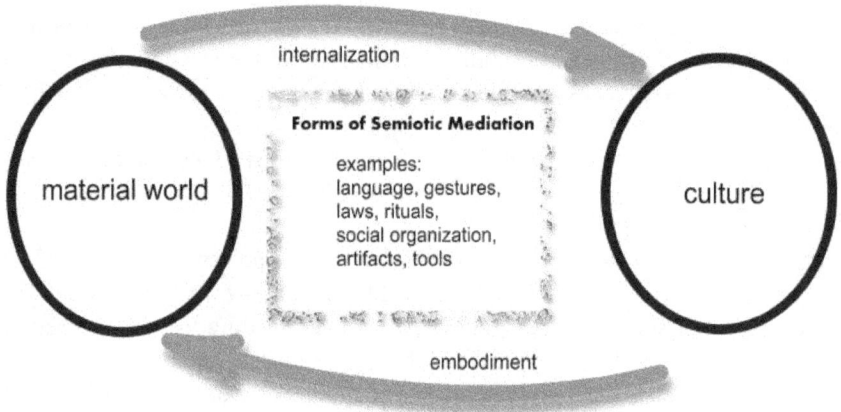

In this process, intellectual activity is objectified in the form of social practices and artifacts. In turn, these social products shape the experience of each individual. The net result of this process is that all things become signs in potential. In many cases, this significance (of material objects, gestures, etc.) can be exploited by ritual.

FROM CONCRETE TO ABSTRACT

A further insight of Vygotsky that can contribute to our present discussion is his account of a child's acquisition of word meaning, as this process can be used as an analogy for the use of signs within a culture over the course of history. Vygotsky argued that the acquisition of word meaning in children is a gradual process that begins by learning the association between the word and an object in the immediate extralinguistic context (word reference). The child does not initially share the conceptual categories of the adults with whom it communicates. Rather, communication is based on indexical word references. Wertsch summarizes this approach as follows: "The indicatory or indexical function of speech makes it possible for adults to draw children into social interaction because it allows intersubjectivity on perceptually present objects even though complete agreement on the interpretation or categorization of these objects is lacking."[41] Based on accumulating experience, the individual gradually becomes progressively less dependent on contextual cues in understanding the word meanings and conceptual categories shared by members of the same culture.[42]

An analogical process can be found in the role of concrete signs in cultural discourse. The basic principle for sign formation is the collective recognition of the significance pertaining to the sign vehicle. This requirement underlies the general tendency characteristic of both linguistic and non-linguistic sign use: the progression from the concrete to the abstract. The concrete image provides a ground for a shared understanding that can then be expanded to more abstract usages. The following discussion, incorporating insights from diverse fields in the human sciences, will demonstrate the broad applicability of this model.

A conventional wisdom espoused by anthropologists is that primitive cultures use concrete signs in order to express abstract ideas. Beattie articulates this idea as follows:

> Sociologically this is the most important thing about symbols; they provide people with a means of representing abstract ideas, often ideas of great practical importance to themselves, indirectly, ideas which it would be difficult or even impossible for them to represent to themselves directly. We sometimes forget that the capacity for systematic analytical thinking about concepts is a product of several millennia of education and constant philosophizing.[43]

In his sophisticated investigation of the symbolism of the Papua New Guinean Baktaman tribe, Barth comes to a similar conclusion, "Through metaphor something familiar or distinctive is used as a model or analogy for something less familiar or less obvious, something less clearly conceptualized but now illuminated by the analogy."[44]

Similarly, Turner's analysis of the symbolism employed by the Ndembu tribe of Central Africa led him to discern two poles of a sign's meaning, the "sensory pole" and the "ideological pole." By "sensory pole," Turner is referring to native interpretations related to the outward form of the sign that invoke natural and physiological phenomena.[45] In contrast, the "ideological pole" refers

---

41. "Semiotic Mediation," 57.

42. See Lee, "Origins of Vygotsky's Semiotic Analysis," 82–89; Wertsch, "Semiotic Mediation," 53–62. For some refinements to this view, see Williams, "Vygotsky's Social Theory of Mind," 273–81.

43. Beattie, *Other Cultures*, 70.

44. Barth, *Ritual and Knowledge*, 199.

45. Turner, *Forest of Symbols*, 28.

to native interpretations related to principles of social organization. For example, he depicts the symbolism of the milk tree (*mudyi*) as follows:

> The semantic structure of the *mudyi* may itself be likened to a tree. At the root is the primary sense of "breast milk" and from this proceeds by logical steps series of further senses. The general direction is from the concrete to the increasingly abstract, but there are several different branches along which abstraction proceeds.[46]

Though Turner is here discussing the multiplicity of meanings that converge on a ritual sign in the synchronic plane, it appears that the concrete → abstract progression that he discerns represents the diachronic evolution of the sign's meaning. In other words, the sensory impressions and concrete analogies evoked by a sign provide the raw materials from which more abstract and complex notions can be expressed.

These observations correspond with one of the central thrusts in recent cognitive linguistic research, namely, the recognition of the pervasive degree to which bodily experience serves as a conceptual source domain for various forms of linguistic expression.[47] One of the most prominent examples of this tendency can be found in metaphorical language, whereby intangible ideas are expressed by means of analogies taken from physical experience. For example, expressions such as "I'm feeling up today" and "My spirits rose" stem from the orientational metaphor HAPPY IS UP, itself based on bodily postures associated with a positive emotional state.[48] Similarly, expressions such as "I was fuming" and "I nearly exploded" stem from the ANGER IS HEAT metaphor, which is based in the biochemical reactions that take place in an angry person.[49] These linguistic idioms are not mere "figures of speech" but reflections of the process by which bodily experience serves as the basis for mental conceptualization and interpersonal communication.[50]

---

46. Ibid., 53–54.

47. Cognitive scientists often use the concept of the "image schema" to describe fundamental bodily experiences such as containment, center/periphery, source-path-goal, etc. These fundamental experiences frequently serve as source domains for other less concrete notions (e.g., LIFE IS A JOURNEY). For recent discussion of this term and its applications, see the various contributions to B. Hampe, ed., *From Perception to Meaning.*

48. Lakoff and Johnson, *Metaphors We Live By,* 14–21.

49. See Lakoff and Kövecses, "Cognitive Model for Anger," 195–221. The use of similar metaphorical pathways to express a particular set of ideas in diverse language groups can be taken to reflect universal cognitive processes. See Blank, "Words and Concepts in Time," 43; Kövecses, *Metaphor in Culture,* 35–64.

50. See further Lakoff, "Contemporary Theory of Metaphor," 202–51; Sweetser, *From Etymology to Pragmatics*; Traugott and Dasher, *Regularity in Semantic Change,* 34–40.

In these diverse domains, a basic dynamic is at work in which a concrete object or common bodily experience serves as a basis for the interpersonal communication of less tangible notions. This use of signs (including metaphorical speech) exemplifies the Vygotskian concept of semiotic tools described above in which signs serve as shared mental technologies to facilitate communication and thought within a culture.[51] These semiotic tools can be viewed as collective property that the individual can appropriate when needed.[52] Accordingly, they can be viewed as a form of thinking "outside the mind."[53]

Through the dialectic of internalization and embodiment, described above, objects and gestures become eligible to act as signs in interpersonal discourse. As noted above, the use of a given material entity or gesture as a sign implies an expressive capacity, a significance recognized between members of the society. Voloshinov describes the social essence of sign use as follows: "Every sign, as we know, is a construct between socially organized persons in the process of their interaction."[54] This social significance, invested in objects and activities, lays the foundations for the culture's capacity for abstract discourse.

These observations lead to a more accurate understanding of the type of logic by which rituals operate. It also reveals the fallacy of attempting to understand rituals by discursive verbalized logic. Bourdieu writes,

> Rites, more than any other type of practice, serve to underline the mistake of enclosing in concepts a logic made to dispense with concepts; of treating movements of the body and practical manipulations as purely logical operations; of speaking of analogies and homologies (as one sometimes has to, in order to understand and convey that understanding) when all that is involved is the practical transference of incorporated, quasi-postural schemes.[55]

Indeed, as we shall see below, ritual owes its effectiveness to its ability to harness the meaning embedded in social practice.

Accordingly, metaphor and metonymy can be identified as important explanatory principles underlying the diachronic development of polysemous words. See Gibbs, *Embodiment and Cognitive Science*, 174–80.

51. See Wertsch, *Vygotsky and the Social Formation of Mind*, 17–57.

52. For analysis of the process of appropriation in the individual's use of conventional linguistic forms and genres, see Bakhtin, *Speech Genres and Other Late Essays*, 71–87; Wertsch, *Mind as Action*, 73–78.

53. See Gibbs, "Taking Metaphor out of Our Heads," 145–66.

54. *Philosophy of Language*, 21; see also 9–22 and Bakhtin and Medvedev, *Formal Method in Literary Scholarship*, 7.

55. *Outline of a Theory of Practice*, 116. See also Voloshinov, *Philosophy of Language*,

The Motivation of the Sign

One of the theoretical premises that underlies the modern view that ritual is meaningless stems from the widespread analogy between language and ritual and the Saussurian emphasis on the *arbitrariness* of the linguistic sign. This premise entails that the sign is *unmotivated*, that is, that there is no intelligible connection between the signifier (the sign) and the signified concept, just as there is no inherent relationship between the concept "dog" and the sound /dog/. Although few scholars would dispute the fact that ritual signs are generally less arbitrary than linguistic ones, the linguistic analogy has nevertheless remained a pervasive influence on modern research on ritual symbolism.[56] Perhaps one reason is that the motivation for ritual signs tends to be forgotten over the course of time, resulting in the perception that they, too, are arbitrary. Consequently, in order to avoid exaggerating the arbitrariness of ritual signs, an understanding of their life cycle is of central importance.

Let us begin by examining a few specific types of signs, so as to gain an appreciation for the dynamics that motivate their use. A useful starting point is C. S. Peirce's trichotomous categorization of signs: *index*, *icon*, and *symbol*. The first of these, the *index* is "really affected" by its referential object and focuses the interpreter's attention on the object.[57] A weathercock indicates the direction of the wind. Smoke indicates fire. Since an index is physically connected with its object, it does not require an interpreting mind to establish the connection. For example, Peirce cites the case of a bullet hole as a sign of a shot "whether anyone has the sense to attribute it to a shot or not."[58] An *icon* is defined as "a sign which stands for something merely because it resembles it."[59] Some examples are paintings, pictographic writing, and literary metaphors. The third type of sign, the *symbol,* is related to its object by means of convention. Peirce characterizes the *symbol* as "a Sign which is constituted a sign merely or mainly by the fact that it is used and understood as such…without regard to the motives which originally governed its selection."[60] We may view this categorization as reflecting three types of relations by which objects acquire their symbolic use: causality (index), similarity (icon), and convention (symbol).

Comparable processes take place on a larger scale in the formation of rituals. Frazer distinguished between magic based on the "law of similarity" (homeo-

---

56. See Sperber, *Rethinking Symbolism*, 23–33.

57. Peirce, *Collected Papers*, §2.248; cf. §§2.283–290, 305–306. See also Nöth, *Handbook of Semiotics*, 113–14; Rappaport, *Ritual and Religion*, 54–68.

58. §2.304. See also §2. 299.

59. *Collected Papers*, §3.362. See Nöth, *Handbook of Semiotics*, 121–23.

60. Peirce, *Collected Papers*, §2.307. See also §§2.292–298.

pathic magic) and magic based on the "law of contact" (contagious magic). Both of these dynamics are based on concrete paradigms of causation derived from everyday practical experience. These are employed metaphorically to affect intangible entities and forces.[61] Processes such as these constitute the inner logic of ritual activity.

Within Peirce's trichotomy of signs, only the category of *symbols* is arbitrary. Indexes are existentially connected to the objects that they represent, and icons possess similar characteristics to their referents. Peirce was fully aware that the use of signs in society often outlasts the situation in which they originated, as can be inferred from his formulation used to describe a *symbol*, namely, that it is used as a sign "without regard to the motives that *originally* governed its selection" (emphasis added). This tendency results in the preservation of signs in cultural discourse, fossilized by convention. When the historical factors underlying the emergence of an *icon* or *index* have disappeared, their usage may continue in the form of conventional *symbols*.[62] At this point, one may characterize the relation between a sign and its use as arbitrary.[63]

An example of this process is pictographic writing in ancient Mesopotamia.[64] In the earliest texts, an iconic relationship existed between most signs and their meaning.[65] However, after the system gained acceptance, two major transformations erased any connection between sign and object. First of all, the form of the logograms was conventionalized, removing much of the iconic quality of the signs. Secondly, the signs were employed to represent phonetic values which, unlike the words signified by logograms, bear no connection to the visual form of the sign. If we were to analyze this system on the basis of its final form,

---

61. Cf. Lakoff and Johnson, *Metaphors We Live By*, 69–76.

62. Peirce, *Collected Papers*, §§2.90, 92. Peirce's subtle references to this process were noted by Chandler (*Semiotics: The Basics*, 44–45).

63. In the Saussurian account, this is described as the arbitrary relationship between the signifier and signified.

64. For the origin and development of the cuneiform system, see the contributions of P. Michalowski and J. C. Cooper in Daniels and Bright, *The World's Writing Systems*, 33–36, 37–48, respectively; and also Durand, "Cuneiform Script," 20–32.

65. The evolutionary scheme presented here is in essence the scheme advocated by Gelb in *A Study of Writing*, though anticipated by Peirce (*Collected Papers*, §2.280). Contrary to the impression conveyed by some recent works, this view has not been refuted by the arguments of Schmandt-Besserat, many of which are themselves subject to question. For these, see Schmandt-Besserat, *Before Writing*; idem., *How Writing Came About*. Indeed, R. K. Englund, one of the leading experts in the archaic texts, has recently written: "I have stated above [pp. 53–55 Y.F.] my conviction that with few exceptions all proto-cuneiform signs are pictographic representations of real things" ("Texts from the Late Uruk Period," 71). It should also be mentioned that iconicity does not obviate the role of convention (see Eco, *A Theory of Semiotics*, 201–17).

we would conclude that the relationship between sign and object is arbitrary. But this approach would preclude any understanding regarding the diachronic process by which the system emerged![66]

We may describe this phenomenon as follows: To the extent that a sign's meaning is apprehensible from its immediate context, it does not require a conventional rule to determine its meaning. Stated differently, to the extent that a sign use is spontaneous and independent of convention, it must rely on contextual cues.[67] Thus, a sign's reliance on convention is proportionate to its opaqueness, that is, its lack of transparency.

In light of the preceding, we may suggest the following distinct stages in the life cycle of a ritual. In the "formation" phase, the ritual is devised to address a real need in a specific context. The motivation of the ritual symbolism is transparent, having originated by processes such as those described above. In the "codification" phase, the rules of performance are made explicit and binding. In certain cultures, this process involves very detailed legislation. A nearly inevitable result of this process is that the ritual will be transmitted in its fossilized form into a new sociohistorical context in which the original motivation may be no longer applicable. The final phase, "reinterpretation," involves filling this vacuum. Confronted with a canonical ritual with unclear motivation, a new interpretation must be provided. These new interpretations frequently seek to incorporate the symbolism of the ritual into the larger cosmological and ideological framework of the culture. As the arbitrariness of the connection between sign and meaning rises, so does the sign's flexibility, allowing multiple uses and interpretations. Only at this point can one rightfully find an analogy with the linguistic sign.[68]

In summary, historical developments tend to obscure the original motivation of signs. Accordingly, the use of the sign becomes progressively more dependent on convention. Discussing this tendency as it pertains to various forms of symbolism and social codes, Guirard comments: "Like languages, therefore, such semiological systems have a double frame of reference according to whether they are considered diachronically from the point of view of their history and

---

66. See also Searle's similar discussion of the origin of paper money in *Construction of Social Reality*, 38–43.

67. Hallett attributes a similar observation to Wittgenstein (in reference to unconventional uses of a word): "No language-game too bizarre, no word-use too far-fetched, *provided* the new use was duly explained, its connection with the rest of life duly indicated" (*Meaning as Use*, 110).

68. This scheme owes much of its inspiration to the description of Berger and Luckmann's discussion of verbal signs and societal institutions (*Social Construction of Reality*, 33–38 and 51–57 respectively). The complexities raised by such processes for structuralist analysis are discussed by Levi-Strauss, *The Savage Mind*, 154–60, esp. 156–57.

origin, or synchronically from the perspective of their functioning in a given culture."[69] Viewed within a historical framework, these systems are motivated, but viewed synchronically (after the system has been codified), they may appear arbitrary. In the following chapters, I will employ a diachronic frame of reference in order to pursue an understanding of the blood rite in its original historical context.

The non-arbitrary origin of the sign provides the key to the methodology for understanding the original correspondence between action and function, which we have defined as the motivation of a ritual. The assumption of an inherent connection between a sign and its use requires that we examine material contexts, natural and social, which may bear upon its ritual use. A similar methodology has been suggested by Bourdieu for understanding ritual practice by "relating it to the real conditions of its genesis." This goal can be achieved by logically reconstructing "the significance and the functions that agents in a determinate social formation can (and must) confer on a determinate practice or experience, given the practical taxonomies which organize their perception."[70] In other words, when an interpretation of a ritual sign not only corresponds to its ritual use but can also be traced back to social situations in the material existence of the culture that would lend this significance to the ritual sign, we may have confidence that we have understood the original motivation of the ritual.[71]

The point of this endeavor is not merely to discover the original intent of a given ritual practice. Rather, on the basis of the interdependence of meaning and context, we will use the significance attributed to the ritual act as a window through which we can better apprehend the conceptual world of the culture. Once we realize that cultural discourse is dependent on codes, both verbal and nonverbal, it becomes increasingly important to recognize the dynamics at work in the emergence and transformation of these codes.

I will now apply these guidelines in seeking the original motivation of the Hittite and Israelite blood rites. Having previously defined the terms, I can now articulate my objective as follows: In light of the meaning (i.e., the function) of the blood rite as reflected in the textual evidence—expiation, purification and consecration—I will now seek to understand the context in which blood acquired this significance.

---

69. *Semiology*, 27.

70. *Outline of a Theory of Practice*, 114.

71. In this manner, we can overcome the skeptical attitudes of certain scholars toward the prospect of recovering the "lost origins" of signs (e.g., Culler, *The Pursuit of Signs*, 113–14; cf. Sperber, *Rethinking Symbolism*, 17).

5

THE BLOOD OF THE SIN OFFERING:
ORIGINS, CONTEXT, AND MEANING

THE BLOOD RITE AND THE SEMANTICS OF כִּפֶּר

The centrality of the blood rite for achieving expiation emerges clearly from the goal formulas describing the sin offering's effects.[1] In particular, Milgrom has pointed out the fundamental correspondence between the grammatical form of כִּפֶּר (*kipper*) formulas and the blood rites. Just as the sin offering's blood is never applied directly to a person, so a person never appears as the direct object of a כִּפֶּר formula. In comparison, sancta *do* appear as the direct object of כִּפֶּר formulas because blood is applied to them. These observations led Milgrom to the conclusion that the blood rites purge sancta, not people.[2] Moreover, the direct connection between the blood manipulations and expiation is clearly expressed in several passages (e.g., Lev 16:16; Ezek 43:20). Finally, the criterion for distinguishing between different types of sin offering ritual is the location of the blood rite (Lev 6:23; 10:18; 16:27). This intimate connection between blood and expiation was duly recognized by early Christian and Jewish tradents. Indeed, the assertion in the epistle to the Hebrews "Without shedding of blood there is no forgiveness"[3] finds affirmation in the Rabbinic dictum "There is no expiation except by blood (אין כפרה אלא בדם)"[4]

---

1. Regarding the importance of goal formulas for ritual interpretation, see Gane, *Cult and Character*, 6–24.

2. See Milgrom, *Leviticus*, 255–26.

3. Hebrews 9:22 (NASB).

4. E.g., *Sipra,* Dibora Dindava, Pereq 4:10 (ed. Weiss, p. 6a); *b. Zevahim* 6a; b. Menahoth 93b. See de Vaux, *Old Testament Sacrifice*, 93. At the same time, one must concede that the blood rite is not a *sine qua non* for expiation, as is clear from the ability to substitute flour in the case of an indigent (Lev 5:11). See Brichto, "On Slaughter and Sacrifice," 30; Eberhart, *Bedeutung der Opfer im Alten Testament*, 135–36, 169–70, 262.

A much-discussed topic in modern research is the meaning of the root כפ״ר,
and, in particular, the use of the *piel* form כִּפֶּר in reference to cult rituals.[5] Fortunately, Janowski's comprehensive survey of the relevant data, including Semitic
cognates, epigraphic evidence, related nouns, syntax, and usage provides a solid
basis for any further discussion.[6] Nevertheless, despite the abundant research,[7]
much ambiguity still surrounds כִּפֶּר and its relationship to the blood rites.

Research on the meaning of כִּפֶּר has tended to focus on etymology, proceeding from the assumption that the abstract usages of this verb can be traced back
to a more concrete precursor. In implementing this methodology, scholars have
made extensive use of Semitic cognates to the Hebrew term. Until the nineteenth
century, scholars tended to point to the Arabic *kafara,* "to cover," which is also
used in the religious sense "to absolve." Proponents of this view note that the
expression אל תכס ("do not cover up") in Neh 3:37 parallels אל תכפר in Jer 18:23.
However, even if we assume that Nehemiah is expressing his understanding of
the Hebrew term, a questionable supposition in itself, one can hardly rely on this
late evidence for the verb's etymology.[8]

Since the decipherment of Akkadian, scholars have turned to the verb
kupurru for guidance, whose various meanings include "to smear" and "to wipe
(off)." The latter sense is also evident in later Aramaic dialects. Most importantly, this verb is used to describe a cultic act of purification and appears in
ritual contexts which are strikingly similar to the cultic use of כִּפֶּר in the Bible.
However, this comparison is not without its difficulties. Whereas כִּפֶּר refers to the
results of a ritual, *kupurru* denotes a particular wiping rite.[9] Indeed, one cannot
find any unequivocal source where any כפ״ר derivative means "to wipe," even
outside the Priestly corpus.[10]

It seems that many scholars have fallen victim to the fallacy of using etymology as an indication of meaning. Against this tendency, Barr warns: "Etymology
is not, and does not profess to be, a guide to the semantic value of words in their
current usage, and such a value has to be determined from the current usage and

---

5. Although the traditional notions of "root-meaning" have generally been rejected by
linguists in recent decades, there are still ample grounds to attribute semantic content, albeit
indeterminate, to Hebrew roots. See most recently: M. Arad, *Roots and Patterns. Hebrew Mor-
pho-syntax* (Dordrecht, Netherlands: Springer, 2005), 53–105.

6. Janowski, *Sühne als Heilsgeschehen.*

7. For a history of research, see ibid., 15–26.

8. See also Levine, *In the Presence of the Lord*, 58; Janowski, *Sühne als Heilsgeschehen*,
99–100.

9. See ibid., 46–47, 58; Wright, *Disposal of Impurity*, 291–99. For further discussion, see
Feder, "*kuppuru, kippēr* and Etymological Sins."

10. The alleged attestation in Gen 32:21 will be discussed below.

not the derivation."[11] As a result, the only reliable approach is to examine the biblical evidence itself to understand how the ancient Hebrew speech community used this term.

Even if the use of cognate evidence could be justified on methodological grounds, the practical implementation of this research strategy would be frought with insurmountable difficulties. First of all, it is quite possible that most of the attested meanings for *kpr* in Semitic languages, such as "to cover," "to smear" and "to wipe" are etymologically connected.[12] Such polysemy all but precludes any potential value to comparison. Secondly, since the biblical sources do not employ כִּפֶּר in a concrete sense (see below), there is little basis for relating its abstract usages to any of these possible meanings. In other words, there is no reason to assume that any of these potential "original meanings" were known to Hebrew speakers.[13]

A more promising approach, one that focuses on the intralinguistic evidence of biblical Hebrew, has been to focus on the nominal form כֹּפֶר (*koper*). In sharp contrast to the ambiguity surrounding verbal forms of כפ"ר, the usages of the noun כֹּפֶר allow a fairly precise understanding. The כֹּפֶר is a propitiatory gift or payment given in situations when the giver is at risk, usually in mortal danger, and placed at the mercy of another. Under these circumstances, the כֹּפֶר was expected to mitigate the latter's punitive actions. The biblical usages reflect several semantic nuances for this term, including "bribe,"[14] "ransom," and "compensatory payment."[15] Since the *piel* verbal form כִּפֶּר appears in conjunction with the giving of a כֹּפֶר,[16] some scholars have interpreted this evidence as indicative that the verb is a denominative verbal derivative of כֹּפֶר, which could be translated accordingly "to ransom" and/or "to make compensation."[17]

---

11. *Semantics of Biblical Language*, 107. See also Hill, *Greek Words*, 30–31.

12. See Landsberger, *Date Palm and Its By-Products*, 31–32 and n. 95; Lang, *TDOT* 7:289.

13. See also Morris, *Apostolic Preaching*, 148; Janowski, *Sühne als Heilsgeschehen*, 100–102.

14. E.g., 1 Sam 12:3; Amos 5:12; Prov 6:35; Job 36:18.

15. It is debatable to what extent which of the latter two glosses better captures the essence of כֹּפֶר (see below). See, e.g., Exod 21:30; Num 35:12; Ps 49:8; Job 33:24. Cf. Sklar, *Sin, Impurity, Sacrifice, Atonement*, 60–79. Two possible cognates for the term כֹּפֶר are: 1) the West Semitic term *kub(b)uru*, attested in legal sources from Emar as an additional payment accompanying transactions (Pentiuc, *West Semitic Vocabulary*, 96–97, with other possible readings) and 2) Akkadian **takpurtu/takpūru*, attested in NB and Seleucid legal documents as an equalizing payment (*CAD* T, 86–87). Unfortunately, these terms do not contribute much to our inquiry aside from providing more grounds for etymological speculation.

16. E.g., Exod 30:15–16; Num 31:50. The verb may also appear in conjunction with a bribe or appeasement gift not explicitly called a כֹּפֶר (e.g., Gen 32:21).

17. E.g., Morris, *Apostolic Preaching*, 143–51; Brichto, "On Slaughter and Sacrifice," 26–28, 34–35.

However, this approach also poses difficulties. Many of the verbal usages of
כִּפֶּר do not necessarily involve a gift in any form, including some of the sources
deal with appeasing anger (e.g., Num 17:11–12; 25:13; Prov 16:14). In fact, such
sources seem to indicate that *appeasement* is more fundamental to the sense of
the verbal form than the act of gift giving. Furthermore, verbal forms of כפ"ר are
employed in the sense of compensating bloodguilt in contexts where monetary
compensation or ransom are strictly forbidden.[18] Consequently, a denominative
derivation from כֹּפֶר seems highly doubtful.

From the foregoing, it may appear that the pursuit of a more preceise understanding of כפ"ר is a futile task. Nevertheless, this impasse can be overcome by
means of a reexamination of the social contexts in which these forms were used.
Many earlier studies were led to unnecessary confusion by taking the lexico-
graphic data as a homogenous mass, irrespective of social context, to be arranged
according to the logical intuitions of the lexicographer.[19] By examining the
sociolinguistic contexts in which these forms were used, we can attain a clearer
picture of the factors leading to semantic transitions. In particular, the following
concrete social situations can be identified: A) appeasing a person of authority to
avert a harsh punitive action; B) removal of culpability for bloodguilt.

In reality, A is merely a specific case of B, a recognition of key importance
for reconstructing the diachronic semantic development of כפ"ר derivatives. The
following analysis will attempt to trace the transformation in the semantics of
כפ"ר as a function of its social context. Specifically, it will be argued that the
original attested sense of כִּפֶּר is "to appease," a meaning that corresponds to
כֹּפֶר in the sense of "propitiatory gift" or "bribe." However, in the context of the
blood feud, these forms were employed in the sense of "compensation," particularly כֹּפֶר in the sense "ransom" and כִּפֶּר in the senses "to compensate" or "to
expiate (guilt)." In light of these observations, I will presently argue that cultic

---

18. E.g., Num 35:33; Deut 21:8; 32:43.

19. In several recent studies, the failure to make clear distinctions regarding the genre
and social context of sources has resulted in very confused results (e.g., Milgrom, *Leviticus*,
1079–84; Sklar, *Sin, Impurity, Sacrifice, Atonement*, 80–159. The studies of Schenker and
Janowski are noteworthy advances in this regard, though they overemphasize semantic properties in their analysis (cf. Lakoff, *What Categories Reveal*, 16–22), leading them to merge the
separate categories of "appeasement" and "expiation" in seeking an analytically determined
common denominator—at the expense of a more sociolinguistic approach to the data. Nevertheless, I agree with them in viewing the earliest usage of כפ"ר derivatives as relating to
appeasement. Specifically, Schenker includes all of the evidence of כֹּפֶר under the translation
"le prix l'accommodement," and then uses this definition as a basis to interpret the Priestly
notion of expiation as a whole (Schenker, "kōper et expiation," 32–46). Janowski identifies the
original *Sitz im Leben* of כפ"ר as the appeasing of an angry adversary (*Sühne als Heilsgeschehen*, 177).

usages of כִּפֶּר and its appearances in abstract contexts that employ terms for sin as objects should be understood as originating in the usage of כִּפֶּר in these concrete social contexts.

Genesis 32:21 exemplifies Situation A. Since it is the only non-cultic text with a seemingly concrete direct object for כִּפֶּר, it has been used in numerous attempts to discover the original concrete sense of this verb.[20] In anticipation of a potentially violent clash with Esau, Jacob sends an appeasement offering with the following accompanying message (Gen 32:21):

ואמרתם גם הנה עבדך יעקב אחרינו כי אמר אכפרה פניו במנחה ההלכת לפני ואחרי כן אראה
פניו אולי ישא פני

And you shall say: "Behold, Jacob is also behind us, for he has said: 'I will propitiate his anger with this gift that goes before me. Then I will behold his countenance, perhaps he will show me favor.'"

The idiom אכפרה פניו has been interpreted variously by scholars. By advocates of the meaning "to cover," it is translated: "I will cover his face."[21] Other scholars interpret the expression in light of the Aramaic and Akkadian meanings "to wipe off," and understand the statement elliptically as: "I will wipe (the wrath off of) his countenance."[22]

The weakness of all of these interpretations is their insistence on a literal translation of פניו, ignoring the insight of traditional Jewish commentators that פנים ("countenance") is a common idiom for anger (e.g., Lev 20:5; 1 Sam 1:18; Jer 3:20).[23] Indeed, a more convincing understanding of this expression is read-

---

20. See Janowski, *Sühne als Heilsgeschehen*, 95–100 with references.

21. Stamm, who connects Hebrew כפ"ר with Arabic *kafara* ("to cover"), translates this idiom: "das Antlitz mit dem Geschenk bedecken," and makes referrence to the expression "eye-covering" (כסות עינים) mentioned in the gifts given to Abraham and Sarah in Gen 20:16 (Stamm, *Erlösen und Vergeben*, 62). Cf. Ibn Ezra, who understands כפ"ר in this verse as "to cover, to conceal," but recognizes the idiomatic use of פניו here (see below).

22. So Rashi, citing the Aramaic. The Akkadian takes precedence in the arguments of Levine (*In the Presence of the Lord*, 60) and Milgrom (*Leviticus*, 1084), who cite the expression *šumma pānīšu ukappir* ("If he wipes his face") from Mesopotamian omen literature. Regarding this source, Levine writes: "It was considered ominous if a new-born infant rubbed his hand over one or the other side of his face, as babies are wont to do" (*In the Presence of the Lord*, 60–61). Since this reference is a prosaic description of a physical act, one wonders how Levine (and others) can refer to this phrase as an "idiom" in Akkadian (60), let alone connect it with Gen 32:21! For further discussion, see Feder, "*kuppuru, kippēr* and Etymological Sins."

23. So Onqelos, Rashi, and Ibn Ezra. Clearly, this idiom is based on the principle of metonymy, whereby the facial expression is taken as synonymous with the emotion expressed. Compare also Gen 31:2: "Jacob saw Laban's countenance, and it was no longer with him as it had been in the past" (וירא יעקב את פני לבן והנה איננו עמו כתמול שלשום).

ily apparent once we recognize the wordplay present in this verse. The word "face" (פנים) appears four times in four distinct expressions. The first and third of these pertain to Esau's "face," whereas the second and fourth pertain to Jacob's face, creating a parallelism:

> I will propitiate his anger (פניו) with this gift that goes before me (לפני),

> Then I will behold his countenance (פניו), perhaps he will show me favor (ישא פני).

Jacob hopes that the gift will bring Esau to show him favor, ישא פני (literally: "lift my face"), using an idiom most frequently attested in the context of bribery (e.g., Lev 19:15; Deut 10:17).

Since פנים in the expression אכפרה פניו is a metonymic figure of speech, this verse does not contribute to the search for a concrete sense of כפ"ר. In essence, the usage is identical to that of Prov 16:14, which asserts that an appeasement gift can spare a person from the king's wrath:

> חמת מלך מלאכי מות ואיש חכם יכפרנה

> The king's anger is a messenger of death, but the wise man can assuage it.

In these non-Priestly texts, anger is the direct object of כִּפֶּר, implying that כִּפֶּר signifies a means of assuaging anger, generally to avoid a life threatening danger.[24] Neither of the main candidates for a concrete meaning, "to cover up" or "to wipe off," is applicable to this usage. Unfortunately, the preoccupation with Semitic cognates has distracted many scholars from the true relevance of these passages. Although these sources do not indicate a concrete meaning for כִּפֶּר, they do exemplify a *concrete social situation*, namely that of appeasing a rival.[25]

A similar meaning for כִּפֶּר can also be found in several Priestly texts. For example, when the Deity becomes infuriated with the persistent complaints of the Israelites and sends forth a plague to obliterate them, Aaron must intercede on their behalf (Num 17:11–13):

> [11]Moses spoke to Aaron: Take the fire pan and place on it coals from upon the altar and add incense. Go quickly to the congregation and make appeasement for them (וכפר עליהם) because wrath has come forth from YHWH and the plague has begun! [12]Aaron took it as Moses had commanded and he ran into the midst of the congregation, and, behold, the plague had begun among the people. He

---

24. See Janowski, *Sühne als Heilsgeschehen*, 110–15.
25. So Ramban on Gen 32:21. Schenker, "kōper et expiation," 34–37.

put on the incense and made appeasement for the people (ויכפר על העם). [13]He stood between the dead and the living and the plague ceased.

In this passage, the burning of incense quells God's anger and brings him to spare the rest of the congregation. Similarly, when God's fury is aroused by the Israelite's licentiousness and participation in the Midianite cult, the resulting plague is only stopped by Phineas' zealous act of impaling the offenders (Num 25:11–13). In these sources, Aaron's and Phineas' acts of pacifying the Deity on behalf of the people are expressed by the form כָּפֶּר עַל. The Priestly use of כָּפֶּר in the context of assuaging God's anger parallels the appeasement of an angry superior described in Gen 32:21 and Prov 16:14.

For reasons that I will present below, the semantic category of "appeasement" should be viewed as historically primary. This could be expressed alternatively as the priority of "propitiation" to "expiation."[26] The distinction between these terms has been articulated as follows:

> In propitiation the action is directed towards God or some other offended person. The underlying purpose is to change God's attitude from one of wrath to one of good-will and favour. In the case of expiation, on the other hand, the action is directed towards that which has caused the breakdown in the relationship. It is sometimes held that, while God is not personally angry with the sinner, the act of sin has initiated a train of events which can only be broken by some compensatory rite or act of reparation for the offence. In short, propitiation is directed towards the offended person, whereas expiation is concerned with nullifying the offensive act.[27]

In the ensuing discussion, I will attempt to show the transformations that occurred in the usage of כפ"ר in the context of blood retribution, corresponding to a transition from "propitiation" to "expiation." This line of inquiry will also shed light on the expiatory function of blood in ancient Israelite society.

THE ISRAELITE VIEW OF BLOODSHED

In light of the theoretical premises outlined at the beginning of this chapter, an investigation of the symbolic value of blood (דם/*dam*) in the Israelite cult requires an understanding of blood's relevance in ancient Israelite society. In this case, the results are obvious and unambiguous: the vast majority of idiom-

---

26. See Barr, "Expiation," 281.

27. C. Brown, "Reconcilliation," *NIDNTT* 3:151. For further discussion of these concepts, see below, pp. 229–36, 252–60.

atic references to blood (דם\דמים) point towards the context of murder.[28] At first glance, this may seem as a rather odd place to seek an understanding of the expiatory power of blood in the cult, a context that attributes a positive significance to blood. Nevertheless, by examining the numerous references to bloodshed in the Bible, an elaborate and coherent conceptual scheme can be disclosed.[29]

A fundamental aspect of this scheme is the animistic view of blood, which entails the belief that blood shed by a premeditated and unjustifiable murder will remain in a state of seething hostility with a single-minded demand for vengeance. The idiom "innocent blood" (דם נקי), which implies that a person's life fluid contains an index of his moral character, is ample testimony to the centrality of the context of homicide in understanding the symbolic significance of blood in ancient Israel.[30] A well-known example of this idea appears in God's reproach of Cain after the murder of Abel (Gen 4:10–12):

> [10]He said: What did you do? Listen, your brother's blood cries out to me from the ground. [11]Now you are cursed by the land that opened its mouth to accept your brother's blood from your hand. [12]When you work the land, it will not continue to give its produce to you. You will be a wanderer and fugitive in the land.

The threat of unappeased blood was a central concern to Israelite society as a whole due to the threat of famine and other forms of collective retribution.[31]

This danger could be averted only by satisfying the blood's claim for revenge through retaliation against the perpetrator. In this context, vengeance was not only a right of the victim's kin, but their obligation to the community.[32] In this capacity, "the redeemer of blood" (גאל הדם)[33] was expected to emancipate the victim's blood from its state of discord, which it is itself powerless to rectify.[34]

---

28. See B. Kedar-Kopstein, "דם," *TDOT* 3:240–45.

29. For a systematic treatment of the notion of bloodguilt in ancient Israel, see also Feder, "Mechanics of Retribution."

30. This expression appears no fewer than eighteen times: Deut 19:10, 13; 21:8, 9; 27:25; 1 Sam 19:5; 2 Kgs 21:16; 24:4 (twice); Isa 59:7; Jer 7:6; 19:4; 22:3; 26:15; Ps 94:21; 106:38; Prov 6:17. Cf.: Prov 1:17.

31. Cf., e.g., 2 Sam 21:1–9; Deut 21:1–9. For discussion of these passages, see below. For cross-cultural parallels, see Frazer and Gaster, *Myth, Legend and Custom*, 65–69.

32. For a recent discussion of the blood feud in ancient Israel, see Barmash, *Homicide in the Biblical World*, 20–52.

33. E.g., Num 35:19–27; Deut 19:6, 12; Josh 20:3–9; 2 Sam 14:11.

34. So, e.g., Merz, *Blutrache bei den Israeliten*, 46–49; Koch, "Die israelitische Auffassung vom vergossenen Blut," 448–49. Cf. Christ, *Blutvergiessen im Alten Testament*, 126–27, who argues unconvincingly that גאל הדם means "relative of the killed."

Not surprisingly, God himself was also involved in ensuring the appeasement of the spilled blood. In cases of individual accountability, he is portrayed as the choreographer of earthly action (e.g., Gen 9:5). But in cases of blood retribution on a national scale, he could assume the role of avenger (e.g., Deut 32:43). Various idioms are employed to describe the Deity's role in orchestrating vengeance. In these contexts, he is described as "demanding the blood" of the victim (דם ש"דר\ש"בק)[35] and as "avenging blood" (דם נק"ם).[36]

The state of bloodguilt and the obligation for retribution it entails are not described in abstract terms but in various graphic idioms depicting the state of blood. For example, the image of a bloodstain that clings to the murderer serves to illustrate the belief that guilt exists as an objective reality, bringing negative consequences until it is addressed.[37] Conversely, regarding a person who committed a crime that incurs capital punishment, it is stated: "his blood is with him" (בו דמיו), signifying that his executioner incurs no guilt.[38]

Biblical legal sources forbid the acceptance of ransom to protect a premeditated murderer from revenge (Num 35:31; cf. Exod 21:12–14; Deut 19:11–13). This restriction has been taken as evidence of the Bible's high regard for human life, whereby the death of a person is not treated as an economic loss that can be compensated monetarily, in distinction from other ancient Near Eastern law codes.[39] Although this observation is valid, it is probable that this notion of "justice" is not biblical in origin but originates from pre-biblical conceptions of spilled blood.[40] Evidence for the latter can be found in the refusal of the Gibeonites, pre-Israelite inhabitants of Canaan, to accept monetary compensation for their murdered ancestors (2 Sam 21:4; see below). Furthermore, several passages convey in semi-mythological terms that the forces of destruction and death cannot be bribed.[41] One must assume that a person tainted with bloodguilt would

---

35. E.g., Gen 9:5; 42:22; Ezek 33:6; Ps 9:13.

36. Deut 32:43; 2 Kgs 9:7; Ps 79:10.

37. E.g., 2 Sam 3:28–29; 1 Kgs 2:5, 33.

38. See Lev 20:9–16, 27. So too the expression "your blood is on your head" (ראשך על דמך [2 Sam 1:16]). For discussion of these expressions, see Reventlow, "Sein Blut Komme," 421–30; Koch, "Die israelitische Auffassung vom vergossenen Blut," 442–43; Christ, *Blutvergiessen im Alten Testament*, 105–18.

39. For references and a critical evaluation, see Barmash, *Homicide in the Biblical World*, 142–47.

40. McKeating also traces the rejection of monetary compensation to the Canaanite's belief in blood taint ("Development of the Law of Homicide," 61–68). However, he views the delegitimization of compensatory payments in Israel as a later development, thus overlooking the unanimity of biblical sources in their rejection of compensation payment. As a result, McKeating fails to recognize the continuity between the pre-biblical and biblical conceptions.

41. Isa 47:11 (reading שחדה). Ps 49:8–10 (cited below) expresses the futility of bribing God, here portrayed as a blood avenger. Cf. also Isa 28:15. On the other hand, God can

be placed at the mercy of such forces. Moreover, according to Num 35:33, a community that accepts a ransom on behalf of an intentional murderer casts guilt upon the land:

33וְלֹא תַחֲנִיפוּ אֶת הָאָרֶץ אֲשֶׁר אַתֶּם בָּהּ כִּי הַדָּם הוּא יַחֲנִיף אֶת הָאָרֶץ וְלָאָרֶץ לֹא יְכֻפַּר לַדָּם
אֲשֶׁר שֻׁפַּךְ בָּהּ כִּי אִם בְּדַם שֹׁפְכוֹ
34וְלֹא תְטַמֵּא אֶת הָאָרֶץ אֲשֶׁר אַתֶּם יֹשְׁבִים בָּהּ אֲשֶׁר אֲנִי שֹׁכֵן בְּתוֹכָהּ כִּי אֲנִי ה' שֹׁכֵן בְּתוֹךְ בְּנֵי
יִשְׂרָאֵל

33You shall not incriminate the land in which you live, for blood incriminates the land and no expiation can be made for the land for the blood that was shed on it except by means of the blood of him who shed it. 34You shall not pollute the land in which you live, in which I myself dwell, for I, YHWH, dwell among the Israelites.

The unatoned blood is described here as defiling the land in which YHWH dwells, a taint that can only be removed by the death of the perpetrator.[42] Although the personified depiction of blood has been partially interred beneath the terminology of defilement, one may still hear the distinct echo of screaming blood.

In summary, the biblical sources clearly depict premeditated murder as a crux where social institutions and religious beliefs are inextricably intertwined. Although the Israelite belief system underwent certain transformations, the threat of unatoned blood maintained its potency.

HOMICIDE AND BLOOD COMPENSATION

Having discussed pervasive Israelite notions of bloodguilt, we can better understand how this social context bears on the usage of כפ"ר. Three of the earliest biblical attestations of the root כפ"ר appear in the context of homicide (2 Sam 21:3; Exod 21:30; Deut 21:8b). In this section, we will examine these passages and explore their possible relevance for the semantics of כפ"ר.

In 2 Sam 21, a source that can be dated with a high level of probability to the tenth century B.C.E.,[43] David discovers that the enduring famine that has ravaged the land stems from the bloodguilt left by his predecessor Saul (vv. 1–6):

"redeem" a person from the grave (Hos 13:14; Ps 49:16; 103:4; Job 33:23–30).

42. Regarding the sense of חנ"ף in this passage, see K. Seybold, "חנף," *TDOT* 5:42–43; Licht, *Commentary on the Book of Numbers*, 198–99. For the translation "incriminate," see already *Onqelos*; cf. Ps 106:38.

43. It is likely that this story was intended to fulfill an apologetic function in justifying David's murder of Saul's progeny, originating in Davidic or Solomonic times. See Halpern,

[1]There was a famine in the time of David, year after year, for three years, and David sought an audience with YHWH. YHWH said: Blood is on Saul and his house[44] because he killed the Gibeonites. [2]The king summoned the Gibeonites and spoke with them. (Now the Gibeonites were not of Israelite stock, but rather a remnant of the Amorites, to whom the Israelites had given an oath, but Saul sought to wipe them out in his zeal for the people of Israel and Judah.) [3]David said to the Gibeonites: What can I do for you and with what can I make amends (ובמה אכפר) so that you will bless the allotment of YHWH? [4]The Gibeonites answered: We have no claim of silver or gold against Saul and his household, and we have no claim on the life of any man in Israel. And [the king] responded: Whatever you say I will do for you. [5]They said to the king: The man who eradicated us and decimated us, destroying us so that we would not survive throughout the territory of Israel—May seven of his male offspring be handed over to us so that we will impale them before YHWH in Gibeah of Saul, chosen of YHWH.[45] And the king said: I will do so.

When David inquires of God, apparently through an oracle, he is informed that the blight stems from the guilt incurred by Saul when he murdered the Gibeonites. David must therefore make restitution with their descendents.[46]

His subsequent appeal to the Gibeonites: "With what can I make amends?" (ובמה אכפר) raises two potential means of compensation: money and blood. Under the present circumstances, only the latter is legitimate. Specifically, revenge must be exacted from Saul's lineage. As noted above,[47] the view that deliberate homicide cannot be compensated monetarily, finds expression in bibli-

---

David's Secret Demons, 84–87. Cf. P. Kyle McCarter, "The Apology of David," *JBL* 99 (1980), 489–504; idem., *II Samuel* (AB), New York 1984, 555.

44. This translation accords with the Septuagint, requiring merely a change in word division from the MT: אל שאול ואל ביתה דמים.

45. For MT's reading בחיר ה', cf.: 1 Sam 10:24. Many scholars, following the Septuagint, read: בגבעון בהר ה'. According to this reading, the verse might refer to the high place mentioned in 1 Kgs 3.

46. Although Malamat and Fensham have correctly pointed to the centrality of treaty-breaking in the punishment that fell on the Israelites (Josh 9:15), the punishment of famine cannot be dissociated from the specific sin of bloodshed, which is known in biblical sources and elsewhere to incite the land to withhold its produce. See Malamat, "Doctrines of Causality," 8–12; Fensham, "Treaty between Israel and the Gibeonites," 96–100. Rather, we should view the aspect of treaty breaking as explaining that the Gibeonite blood was spilled unjustifiably, since otherwise their death would be justifiable in light of the divine command to exterpate the Canaanite population. As Greenberg writes, bloodguilt "was incurred only through slaying a man who did not deserve to die," referring to the biblical notion of "innocent blood" (see above). See M. Greenberg, "Bloodguilt," *IDB* 1:449.

47. See above, pp. 175–76.

cal legislation[48] and reveals a degree of continuity between the Israelites and the indigenous inhabitants of Canaan.

The continuation of David's question in v. 3, which continues "that you will bless the allotment of YHWH," leaves no doubt that אכפר refers to the placation of the Gibeonites.[49] Despite the fact that David's question maintains the primary sense of כֻּפַּר in reference to the *appeasement* of the Gibeonites, their response makes clear that the real source of the calamity facing Israel is the bloodguilt that requires *compensation*.[50] This ambiguity hints at the blurring of the distinction between the notions of appeasement and compensation. Whereas the former addresses the angered parties, the latter focuses on correcting the wrong committed, treated objectively. Thus, this passage anticipates a transition that will take place in the usage of the verbal forms of כפ"ר in the context of bloodguilt, from appeasement to compensation.[51]

The second relevant source, from the Covenant Code, seeks to set limitations on the normative practice of blood revenge by making distinctions between direct versus indirect causation of death. In the case of a habitually goring ox, an exceptional leniency is made to allow the owner to escape blood retribution (Exod 21:29–30):

[29]ואם שור נגח הוא מתמל שלשם והועד בבעליו ולא ישמרנו והמית איש או אשה או השור יסקל
וגם בעליו יומת
[30]אם כפר יושת עליו ונתן פדין נפשו ככל אשר יושת עליו

[29]If the ox has been a habitual gorer, and the owner had been informed yet he did not guard it, and it kills a man or woman—the ox will be stoned and also

---

48. Gen 9:6; Num 35:33. However, in contrast with the Gibeonites' revenge on Saul's progeny, Deuteronomic law prohibits revenge on family members (Deut 24:16).

49. This request for a blessing implies that the bloodguilt was conceived as a curse upon the land. This curse is only removed by the quasi-cultic killing of Saul's progeny "before YHWH" in v. 5. Cf. also Samuel's execution of Agag, king of Amalek "before YHWH" (1 Sam 15:33).

50. Levine suggests that אכפר in our verse may be an attestation of a denominative *piel* form of כֻּפַּר in the sense "to ransom," writing: "The implication of the denominative usage may be present in 2 Sam 21, where David inquires of the offended Gibeonites: 'What shall I do for you, and with what shall I pay ransom?'" (*In the Presence of the Lord*, 67, n. 36). Although the continuation of the verse (omitted from Levine's citation) leaves no question that this usage of כֻּפַּר preserves the primary sense "to appease," he has correctly pointed out the ambiguity underlying the idea of expiation depicted in this passage.

51. Sources that indicate the primary sense of כֻּפַּר include: Gen 32:21; Exod 32:30; Num 17:11–12; 25, 13; Isa 47:11, amending שחדה; Prov 16:14. This usage is evident is some sources that pertain to bloodguilt as well, e.g., Deut 32:43; 2 Sam 21:3. The relative earliness of "propitiation" to "expiation" was already suggested by Barr ("Expiation," 281).

the owner will be killed. [30]If a ransom is laid upon him, he shall pay for the redemption of his life in accordance with what has been laid upon him.

Although intentional killing can only be requited by the death of the perpetrator, this case of criminal negligence allows a possibility for a monetary compensation (כֹּפֶר).

The debate stirred by the sense of כֹּפֶר in this passage is instructive. While most commentators and translators understand it as a "ransom" as explicated by the adjacent term פדין נפשו ("redemption of his life"), Schenker has argued that these terms are not necessarily synonymous. In fact, it is equally likely, he argues, that פדין נפשו was employed to emphasize a quality not automatically inferable from כֹּפֶר.[52] Accordingly, since the other concrete usages of both כֹּפֶר and verbal forms of כפ"ר involve appeasement, Schenker translates כֹּפֶר here as "somme d'apaisement."[53] In response, Janowski has countered this argument with the observation that unlike other attestations of כפ"ר derivatives, our passage explicitly states that the payment is to serve as a substitution for the life of the incriminated party.[54]

These opposing claims are not beyond resolution. Although Schenker is correct in identifying the primary sense of כֹּפֶר as "bribe" or "propitiatory gift,"[55] we should agree with Janowski that the expression פדין נפשו is intended to define this particular usage of כֹּפֶר as a substitutionary payment.

But we must ask: Why is it incumbent to state that the payment serves a substitutionary function? Would it not be sufficient if it succeeded in appeasing the potential blood avengers and persuading them to relinquish their claim? In light of Israelite notions of bloodguilt, we may be able to provide an explanation.[56] Since the community as a whole will face repercussions if the victim's blood is left unavenged, it was necessary that the blood debt be satisfied—either by the life of the perpetrator, or at the very least, by a substitutionary payment. This unique requirement specific to the circumstances of bloodguilt seems to have provided the social context for כֹּפֶר to acquire the particular nuance of "ransom." It is worth noting that "ransom" is expressed in the later homicide law of Num 35:31 (H) as כֹּפֶר לנפש, showing that the substitutionary character of כֹּפֶר in this

---

52. Schenker, "kōper et expiation," 43.

53. Ibid., 37.

54. Janowski, *Sühne als Heilsgeschehen*, 157–58 and esp. n. 268.

55. Most cases imply a context of judgment; see: 1 Sam 12:3; Amos 5:12; Job 36:18.

56. The topic of bloodguilt resurfaces a few verses later in Exod 22:1–2. Specifically, the question of bloodguilt in a case of killing a burglar is dependent on whether the event took place at night or in the daytime, determining whether or not "blood" is on the property owner (דמים לו\אין לו דמים). The implication of these verses is that if he has unjustifiably killed the burglar, he is stained with the latter's blood and must be killed himself.

context was already self-understood and did not require an additional explanatory idiom such as פדין נפש. From the *Sitz im Leben* of homicide compensation,
the "ransom" usage of כֹּפֶר was adapted to other metaphorical contexts.[57] Consequently, Exod 21:30 signals a transition in the sense of כֹּפֶר, which pertains
specifically to the circumstances of bloodguilt.

The third case is found in Deut 21:1–9, which addresses a situation of bloodguilt that cannot be resolved by the normal process of blood retribution because
the murderer is unknown:

> [1]If you find a corpse on the ground that YHWH your God gave to you to inherit,
> fallen in the field, and it is not known who killed him, [2]your elders and judges
> shall go out and measure (the distance) to the cities surrounding the corpse.
> [3]And it will be that the city closest to the corpse, the elders of the city shall take
> a female cow of the herd that has not been used for labor and has not pulled a
> yoke. [4]The elders of that city shall take the cow down to a perennial stream
> that has not been cultivated and has not been sown, and they shall break the
> cow's neck there in the stream. [5]The priests, the sons of Levi shall approach,
> for YHWH, your God, has chosen them to serve him and bless in the name of
> YHWH, and according to their command shall be every dispute and injury. [6]All
> of the elders of that city that is closest to the corpse shall wash their hands in the
> stream over the broken-neck cow. [7]They shall recite, saying: 'Our hands have
> not spilled this blood and our eyes have not seen it. [8]Expiate (כַּפֵּר) for your
> people, Israel, that you have redeemed, and do not place innocent blood amidst
> your people, Israel,' and the blood shall be expiated (ונכפר להם הדם). [9]Thus shall
> you purge the innocent blood from your midst when you act properly in the
> eyes of YHWH.

This text, in which legal and cultic perspectives converge, offers clear testimony as to the profound anxiety associated with bloodguilt in Israelite society.
The prescribed procedure addresses both moral and metaphysical aspects of the
unatoned bloodguilt.[58] In order to interpret the usage of the כפ"ר forms in this

---

57. E.g., Isa 43:3; Ps 49:8; Job 33:24. See Janowski, *Sühne als Heilsgeschehen*, 169–74.
The only other concrete situation in which the "ransom" usage is employed is Exod 30:12, in
the enigmatic context of a census.

58. Much has been written about the purpose and the dynamics involved in the ritual. See
Wright, "Deuteronomy 21:1–9," 388–93 for a survey and critique of these views. The interpretation of the ritual advocated here generally concurs with Wright's understanding that it is
a reenactment of the murder to eliminate the impurity (389–90, 393–94). Numerous attempts
have been made to interpret the ritual by means of a reconstruction of its pre-canonical stages
(e.g., Zevit, "'eglâ ritual"; Dion, "Deutéronome 21, 1–9," 13–22). Due to the speculative nature
of these theories, I have preferred to interpret the ritual in its present textual form, without
denying the possibility of editorial expansions.

passage, we must first attempt to understand the underlying dynamics of this peculiar ritual.

The first step of the ritual involves measuring the distance to the settlements surrounding the corpse in order to determine which city has been incriminated by its proximity to the murder. Since the bloodstain is assumed to bring infertility, one of the functions of the ritual is to transfer the "blood" to an uncultivated area. From there, it will be eliminated by means of a perennial stream.[59]

But this transfer is only one aspect of the ritual. On a more moralistic plane, the blood of the victim is expunged from the land and the inhabitants of the nearest town are exonerated from guilt by means of a ritual reenactment of the murder.[60] This dimension, overlooked by many commentators, can explain several of idiosyncratic features of the ceremony, particularly the means of killing the cow and the location of this act. The basic requirement is that, unlike the original murder, the reenactment is to be bloodless. Thus we can understand that the unusual means of death by which the cow is killed, the breaking of its neck, is required to minimize the possibility of blood loss.[61] Likewise, the performance of the killing in a perennial stream ensures that any small amounts of blood that may unintentionally be caused by the neck-breaking will immediately be washed away. This unique procedure underscores the tremendous significance attached to spilled blood.

The elders' declaration of innocence is a fascinating use of ambiguity to invoke two discrete levels of meaning. After washing their hands over the dead cow, they announce: "Our hands have not spilled this blood and our eyes have not seen it" (v. 7). The ambiguity of the expression "this blood" has led to unnecessary confusion regarding whether the words are referring to that of the dead man or the cow.[62] Adherence to the former possibility would make the breaking of the cow's neck superfluous and make the whole rite incoherent. The latter possibility is equally difficult. If the point of the ritual killing was to be bloodless, then how can they refer to "this blood"? The fallacy of these arguments lies in attempting to understand the words on one level of meaning when the purpose of the declaration is, by use of ambiguity, to create an analogy between

---

59. See Patai, "'Egla 'Arufa," 64–66; Rofé, "עגלה ערופה," 119, 140–41; Wright, "Deuteronomy 21:1–9," 393–98.

60. Scholars who recognize that the ritual is a reenactment tend to understand it merely as a means of relocating the blood to more benign place (for references, see ibid., 389, n. 9). The interpretation offered here diverges significantly from that view.

61. So, e.g., McKeating, "Development of the Law of Homicide," 63, n. 22; Carmichael, "A Common Element," 133.

62. Note Patai's confused explanation: Since "*this* blood" must refer to that of the cow, the elders' denial of guilt is in effect placing the blame on the murderer for bringing about the death of the cow (*"Egla Arufa,"* 67).

the broken-necked cow and the murdered person. In its immediate local context, the announcement refers to the fact that no blood has been spilled in the killing of the cow. However, since the allusion to "this blood" is at tension with the immediate context—any of the cow's blood that may have been spilled has already been washed away—an alternate referent comes to mind, namely the dead person. In other words, the out-of-place expression "this blood" serves a double function, evoking the context of the murdered person without undermining the truth-value of the statement in reference to the bloodless killing of the cow, as if they were claiming: "we have not spilled *any* blood."[63] Thus, the analogy serves to assert that no blood has been spilled whatsoever, as expressed explicitly in the declaration: "Our eyes have not seen [the blood]" (v. 7b). In this manner, the reenactment of the killing serves retroactively to erase the bloodguilt of the original victim.

Based on these considerations, it becomes clear that this passage depicts a highly mechanical notion of bloodguilt. Accordingly, one should not be surprised that the city can be exhonerated by the elders' declaration that no blood has been spilled—a claim that is patently false![64] Once we recognize that the city has been automatically implicated with the guilt of the unknown killer by default, it should not surprise us that this guilt can be exculpated by means of a dramatic performance. Likewise, the use of the passive form of כפ"ר in the expiatory formula "and the blood will be expiated for them" (ונכפר להם הדם [v. 8b]) indicates a mechanistic notion of bloodguilt. Thus, this ritual depicts the dynamic of bloodguilt and retribution as an impersonal process that can be rectified by a formal means of expiation.

In comparison to the passive formulation of v. 8b, which seems to have concluded the original ritual instructions, I concur with most modern commentators in viewing the divine intervention insinuated by v. 8a as a Deuteronomic addition intended to emphasize the role of God in the expiatory process. Interestingly, even according to this addition, God's role is that of Israel's agent who intervenes to avert the otherwise inevitable ramifications of bloodguilt.[65] This semi-autonomous dynamic of bloodshed retribution is likewise insinuated by the Deuteronomic exhortation that closes the passage: "Thus shall you purge the innocent blood from your midst…" (ואתה תבער הדם הנקי מקרבך [v. 9]).[66]

---

63. Although Wright identifies the double-meaning active in this declaration ("Deuteronomy 21:1–9," 394), he mistakenly infers that some blood must have been spilled (n. 22), thereby overlooking the bloodless killing and its significance.

64. See Loewenstamm, "עגלה ערופה‏," 77–79.

65. von Rad, *Old Testament Theology,* 1:270; Christ, *Blutvergiessen im Alten Testament,* 90.

66. A similar formula appears in connection with the requirement to hand over the inten-

This ostensibly mechanistic conception of bloodguilt is pervasive in the Deuteronomic legislation. For instance, this idea is implied by the conclusion to the laws of the cities of refuge for unintentional killers (Deut 19:10):

ולא ישפך דם נקי בקרב ארצך אשר ה' אלהיך נתן לך נחלה והיה עליך דמים

Lest innocent blood be shed in the land which YHWH your God gives you as an inheritance and blood will be upon you.

Likewise, the requirement to erect parapets on the roof is that "you will not place blood on your house" (ולא תשים דמים בביתך [22, 8]). These references to the seemingly automatic consequences of bloodshed has it corollary in Deuteronomy's formula "so you shall purge the evil from your midst" (ובערת הרע מקרבך), which follows the requirement for capital punishment in the cases of the most serious transgressions.[67] The latter formula requires communal action to avoid the otherwise inevitable destruction that would ensue by allowing the continued existence of the wrongdoer amidst the community.[68]

This Deuteronomic notion of bloodguilt is an example of a literary tendency to depict cosmic retribution as a depersonalized automatic process. Though such sources have often been taken as evidence for a primitive pre-theistic worldview, I have shown in a detailed study of this phenomenon that these mechanistic depictions of retribution are in many cases secondary developments emerging within the framework of a theistic worldview.[69] For the purpose of the present discussion, we may compare this phenomenon to Berger and Luckmann's notion of *reification*, whereby social phenomena "are treated as if they were something else than human products—such as facts of nature, results of cosmic laws, or manifestations of divine will."[70] In our case, we find a similar process of depersonalization, in which an earlier personalized notion of reward and punishment, governed by either mythological beings or deities, was ultimately treated as a self-contained autonomous dynamic. In other words, a dynamic that was once understood as the expression of the wills of personalized supernatural actors was ultimately treated as an embedded law of nature.

---

tional murderer to the blood avenger (Deut 19:13; cf. also 2 Sam 4:11).

67. Deut 13:6; 17:7; 19:19; 21:21; 22:21, 24; 24:7. Regarding these formulas, see L'Hour, "Une législation criminelle dans le Deutéronome," 1–27.

68. Gammie, "Theology of Retribution," 6–7. Cf. Koch, "Die israelitische Auffassung vom vergossenen Blut," 410–14.

69. See Feder, "Mechanics of Retribution."

70. *Social Construction of Reality*, 89. This usage is a nuanced appropriation of the Marxist concept of *Verdinglichung*.

The concept of bloodguilt provides an excellent example of such a process. According to the ancient mythological conception, it is the blood itself that must be placated (e.g., Gen 4:10). Although the Israelite notion of bloodguilt became demythologized, the belief in the dangers of unatoned blood remained unabated. In a process akin to reification, the idea of punishment, which was once attributed to personified blood's desire for revenge, became perceived as an autonomous dynamic in which adverse ramifications automatically result from uncompensated bloodshed. More importantly for our discussion, the expiation of bloodguilt, as represented in Deut 21:1–9 could avert the otherwise inevitable retribution.

Turning back to the semantics of כפ״ר, this notion of reification can also explain the semantic transition of כפ״ר forms from their use in the sense of "appeasement" to their use in the sense of "expiation" or "compensation." These latter two terms reflect a change in focus from placating one's adversary to rectifying the wrong itself. This transition corresponds to the difference between *appeasing* angry blood (e.g., Gen 4) or kinsmen (e.g., 2 Sam. 21) to *making compensation* for a blood debt (e.g., Deut 21). In other words, the focus of כִּפֶּר is no longer the murderer's adversary, whether the blood or the victim's kin, but the objectified guilt caused by the murder.

Several factors can explain the semantic transition of כֹּפֶר from "bribe" to "substitutionary payment" as represented by its usage in the context of bloodguilt (Exod 21:30; Num 35:31–32). The כֹּפֶר in the context of the blood feud may originally have served the function of *appeasing* the victim's kin. However, since the basic premise of blood compensation requires that the murderer forfeit his own life, the כֹּפֶר payment was viewed as a substitution for his life. Furthermore, unlike propitiatory payments and bribes in other situations, the payment of a כֹּפֶר in the context of bloodguilt assumes a judicial framework, or at the least, societal norms, which impose an objective state of guilt to which the murderer must comply. Accordingly, the כֹּפֶר was considered more of a ransom than an arbitrarily determined payment. Moreover, due to related beliefs pertaining to the dangers of unatoned blood, the substitutionary character of the payment takes on significance for the community at large. These considerations served to distinguish the usage of כֹּפֶר in the context of bloodguilt from other situations.

Now let us turn to the verbal form כִּפֶּר and its semantic transition from "appease" to "compensate." Reflecting the former sense, Deut 32:43 depicts God as the blood avenger of Israel who appeases the land for Israel's spilt blood:

הרנינו גוים עמו כי דם עבדיו יקום ונקם ישיב לצריו וכפר אדמתו עמו[71]

---

71. הרנינו שמים עמו והשתחוו לו כל אלהים כי דם בניו יקום ונקם ישיב לצריו ולמשנאיו 4QDtn reads: ישלם ויכפר אדמת עמו. Although many scholars amend אדמתו עמו to אדמת עמו in line with the

Acclaim his people, O nations, for He will avenge the blood of his people
and pay his enemies back with vengeance, and he will appease the land of his
people.

כֻּפֶּר refers here to the appeasement of the land, an idiom which parallels that of
appeasing the blood. The *personification* of the land in this verse can be juxtaposed with the *objectification* of bloodguilt expressed in Num 35:33:

ולא תחניפו את הארץ אשר אתם בה כי הדם הוא יחניף את הארץ ולארץ לא יְכֻפַּר לדם אשר³³

שפך בה כי אם בדם שפכו

ולא תטמא את הארץ אשר אתם ישבים בה אשר אני שכן בתוכה כי אני 'ה שכן בתוך בני³⁴

ישראל

³³You shall not incriminate the land in which you live, for blood incriminates
the land and no expiation can be made for the land for the blood that was shed
on it except by means of the blood of him who shed it. ³⁴You shall not pollute
the land in which you live, in which I myself dwell, for I, YHWH, dwell among
the Israelites.

As noted above, this verse also hints at the folkloric notion of appeasing the
blood, and by extension, the land. However, the passage deliberately uses
the terminology of incrimination (חנ"ף) and pollution (טמ"א) to distance itself
from this idea. Correspondingly, it employs the passive form יְכֻפַּר to shift the
emphasis from the protagonists to the guilt objectified. Strikingly, this transition
finds expression in the impersonal construct with the passive form יְכֻפַּר.[72] This
unusual syntax conveys the impression that the expiation is a mechanical process, focussing attention on the objective state of the bloodguilt, which can only
be compensated by means of the blood of the murderer (cf. Gen 9:6). This meta-
morphosis represents a semantic transition in the usage of כפ"ר derivatives by
which they acquired a sense of "compensation." This Priestly usage was anticipated in the ambiguous notion of bloodguilt as portrayed in 2 Sam 21:3 and the
mechanistic dynamic of expiation implied by the ritual of Deut 21:8a.

In fact, this mechanistic conception finds pervasive expression in the
Priestly sources' depiction of bloodguilt, especially in their use of the verbal
forms of כפ"ר in the sense of "making compensation/ransom."[73] It also underlies

Qumran, Greek, and Latin versions, yielding "the land of his people," the same result can be
achieved by interpreting MT as a construct chain. Cf. חיתו ארץ (Gen 1:24); בנו צפר (Num 23:18).
See GKC §90o.

72. Neither "land" nor "blood" can be the subject of this verb. Aside from the fact that
"land" is feminine, both terms are preceded by the preposition -ל, designating them as indirect
objects.

73. A possible connection between blood vengeance and cultic expiation was already

the Priestly tenet: "The one who spills the blood of man, by man his blood will be spilled" (שֹׁפֵךְ דַּם הָאָדָם בָּאָדָם דָּמוֹ יִשָּׁפֵךְ [Gen 9:6a]), that treats blood vengeance as part of the divinely orchestrated world order, in which spilled blood must be repaid by that of the perpetrator. The substitutionary value of blood appears twice in conjunction with כפ"ר in H (Lev 17:11; Num 35:33), which demonstrates that an awareness of the original *Sitz im Leben* for the expiatory usage of כפ"ר was preserved even by later tradents of the Priestly tradition.[74] Finally, a few late Priestly sources that employ כִּפֶּר in the sense "to ransom"[75] are clearly influenced by the usage of כִּפֶּר in the sense "substitutionary payment."[76] Consequently, etymology in this case is not only a matter of history, since it might also elucidate an aspect of meaning.[77]

In summary, the context of bloodguilt has emerged as an important semantic frame determining the usage of כפ"ר. Such a method allows the identification of usages in the sense of expiation that emerged from the original sense of appeasement. This semantic transition affected the nominal form כֹּפֶר as well as verbal forms, such as כִּפֶּר. The Priestly tradition, building on an awareness of the *Sitz im Leben* in which the expiatory sense of כפ"ר emerged, applied this terminology to the cult. This awareness is most evident in relation to the sin offering, in which כִּפֶּר is associated with the expiatory character of blood.

---

suggested in general terms by Tullock (*Blood-Vengeance,* 257–63). For uses of כפ"ר in the context of bloodguilt: Lev 17:11 (which assumes bloodguilt imputed in v. 4) and Num 35:33. Both of these passages will be analyzed below. For כפ"ר in the sense of ransom, outside the context of bloodguilt, see Exod 30:15–16; Num 31:50.

74. I disagree with Schwartz's view that the usage of כִּפֶּר in Lev 17:11 is "almost midrashic in nature" ("Prohibitions Concerning 'Eating' the Blood," 71; accepted by Gilders, *Blood Ritual in the Hebrew Bible,* 173). Although the specific application may be unique in Lev 17:11, the present analysis indicates that the substitutionary role of blood signified by כִּפֶּר attests to the preservation of the original concept of expiation in Priestly tradition.

75. Exod 30:15–16; Lev 17:11; Num 31:50; 35:33. Num 8:19 should probably also be included; see Milgrom, *Book of Numbers,* 369–70. Excluding Exod 30:15–16, Knohl attributes all of these sources to H (*Sanctuary of Silence,* 104–6).

76. Levine views these sources as a separate category of כִּפֶּר, which is a denominative of כֹּפֶר (*In the Presence of the Lord,* 67–73). But since these attestations seem to reflect the influence of כֹּפֶר on the already existing form כִּפֶּר, it seems that the label "denominative" is misleading. Cf. Janowski's view that the verbal and nominal forms were originally independent derivatives of the root כפ"ר, which semantically influenced each other (*Sühne als Heilsgeschehen,* 174). Cf. also Stamm, *Erlösen und Vergeben,* 62, 65–66.

77. Cf. Barr, *Semantics of Biblical Language,* 107–9.

Payment in Blood

In parallel to these semantic developments pertaining to כפ"ר, the social context of the blood feud endowed blood with a particular symbolic significance. The role of blood in this instution can best be elucidated by reference to Marx's comparison of the use and exchange values of a commodity. In any market economy, a given commodity itself is divorced, or abstracted, from its inherent purpose and traded for other goods in accordance with its value in the market.[78] In the same way, blood retaliation results in an abstraction of the value of the murdered party's life. By turning the victim's blood into an exchange value, it becomes a debt that can be "repaid" by the death of the murderer, which, needless to say, would otherwise have no value to the injured party. The abstraction is more clearly evidenced by the opening of a possibility for monetary compensation for the murder. From the analogy of commodities, we begin to see that even talionic עין תחת עין punishment—literally "an eye *in the place* of an eye"—involves an abstract notion of exchange. Through this process of substitution, even an act whose results are otherwise irreversible could be rectified.[79]

This principle allows for the development of a system of monetary compensation for bodily injuries and even homicide. Although the Bible explicitly forbids monetary payment under circumstances of premeditated murder, it is clear that monetary compensation was perceived as an option (e.g., Exod 21:29–30), albeit illegitimate in many cases. This impression is verified by the cuneiform literature.

Within the context of the blood feud, blood was viewed in monetary terms. For example, God's protection of the meek is described as follows (Ps 72:14):

מתוך ומחמס יגאל נפשם וייקר דמם בעיניו

He will redeem their lives from oppression and violence; their blood is precious
in His eyes.

This monetary construal of blood, implied by the expression "is precious" (וייקר), is not some spontaneous figure of speech invented by the author, but rather reflects the association of blood and money that originated in the context of blood retribution. It is not accidental that the parallelism of "their blood" (דמם)

---

78. See Marx, *Das Kapital*, 39–76.

79. Although Daube (*Law*, 114–47) correctly emphasizes the notion of substitution implied by the talion formula, he mistakenly infers the existence of a primitive belief that "if you deprive a man of a certain power or faculty, this power or faculty becomes yours" (p. 121). Daube's implausible conclusion stems from a misunderstanding of the underlying abstraction, i.e., the distinction between use and exchange values.

and "their lives" (נפשם), appears in the context of pursuit by violent adversaries, as can be seen also from the following passage (Ps 49:8–10):

8אח80 לא פדה יפדה איש לא יתן לאלהים כפרו
9ויקר פדיון נפשם וחדל לעולם
10ויחי עוד לנצח לא יראה השחת

8A man cannot redeem (his) brother, nor give God his ransom.
9The price of their lives is too high, that He would desist (from him) forever
10So he would live for eternity, never seeing the grave.

Using similar terminology, this passage scoffs at the prospect of bribing God to avoid death, asserting that the redemption fee would be too expensive (ויקר פדיון נפשם). Like Ps 72:14, the imagery is clearly rooted in the social institution of paying off blood avengers. Thus, these Psalms provide further evidence for the notion of a monetary substitution for life that is equated conceptually with blood.[81]

In these passages, we find the terms "blood" (דם) and "life" (נפש) used virtually interchangeably in conjunction with redemption from life-threatening danger. This correspondence is not surprising. In situations of bloodguilt, it is the *blood* of the perpetrator that is demanded to pay back that of the victim. As noted above, in cases of talionic punishment, we find the formula "life for a life" (נפש תחת נפש\נפש בנפש).[82] Thus, the terms "blood" and "life" are central to formulas that deal with the notion of substitution.

As a result, it is not surprising that "blood" became linguistically associated with payment, generating the idiom "blood money." This semantic transfer is evident in the use of the Akkadian cognate *dāmu* ("blood"), which is used as an idiom for "blood money" already from the early-second millennium B.C.E.[83] A parallel expression is not found in the Bible, probably because monetary compensation for bloodguilt was eschewed in most cases. Nevertheless, the notion of blood money did ultimately find its way into the Hebrew lexicon during the late Second Temple period, most likely through exposure to the surrounding cultures. In particular, the term דמים/דמי appears commonly in Mishnaic Hebrew and the Jewish Aramaic of Israel and Babylonia, in the senses "payment," "price," or

---

80. Several MT manuscripts read אך.

81. From the expression ויקר פדיון נפשם, it is a small step to refer to one's life (נפש) as being "valuable" (יק"ר). See 2 Kgs 1:13 and Prov 6:26.

82. נפש תחת נפש: Exod 21:23; Lev 24:18. נפש בנפש: Deut 19:21.

83. *CAD* D, 79.

"value" in reference to damages[84] as well as in more general contexts.[85] While this lexical data from the post-biblical period provides an important confirmation for the close association between blood and payment in the context of the blood feud, one must not overlook the following crucial insight regarding the biblical period itself. Unlike Mesopotamia, where monetary compensation for homicide was accepted and "blood" (*dāmu*) became a term for blood money, the shunning of monetary compensation in Israel caused blood itself to be treated as a means of restitution, since the blood debt could only be repaid by means of blood itself.

In summary, by appealing to the social context of homicide compensation, we can understand the semantic development of the term דמים: "blood" → "blood money" → "payment"/"value." This semantic transfer is indicative of the process by which blood—the substance—came to be viewed as a medium of ransom and payment.

DEBT, PAYMENT, AND THE SEMANTIC DEVELOPMENT OF כפ"ר

In order to appreciate fully the relevance of the association of blood with payment, we must consider its relation to the metaphoric scheme, dominant in ancient Israelite discourse, which viewed transgression and its punishment in commercial terms.[86] The metaphoric notion of "payment" served as a dominant notion for divine recompense in the context of both reward[87] and punishment.[88] For example, the *hiphil* form of שו"ב in the sense of "paying back" is used to describe divine retribution for various wrongs, including bloodshed.[89] Furthermore, the *piel* form of של"ם ("to pay") refers to divine retribution for transgressions in numerous texts,.[90]

---

84. E.g., *m. Ketubot* 12, 1–2; *m. Bava Qamma* 5, 4; 8, 1–2. See Sokoloff, *Dictionary of Jewish Palestinian Aramaic*, 152, sub. דמין (= "price, payment"); idem., *A Dictionary of Jewish Babylonian Aramaic* (Ramat Gan: Bar-Ilan University, 2002), 343, sub. דמי (= "price, value, payment"). Sokoloff compares this semantic development with that of Akkadian *dāmu*.

85. E.g., *m. Terumot* 5:1; *m. Pesahim* 2:4; 9:8.

86. For the role of metaphors in cultural models, and the question of the interrelationship between metaphor conceptions, see Lakoff and Johnson, *Metaphors We Live By*, 97–105; Holland and Quinn, *Cultural Models*, 6–13; Cole, *Cultural Psychology*, 122–24.

87. 1 Sam 24:20; Prov 13:21; 19:17; Ruth 2:12.

88. E.g., Deut 7:10; 32:35, 41; Judg 1:7; 2 Sam 3:39; 2 Kgs 9:26; Ps 31:24.

89. In cases of homicide, see, e.g., 2 Sam 16:8; 1 Kgs 2:32. Other examples: 1 Sam 25:39; 1 Kgs 2:44; Hos 4:9; 12:15. See Christ, *Blutvergiessen im Alten Testament*, 97–101.

90. In order to defend his notion of the "schicksalwirkenden Tatsphäre," Koch makes an ingenious attempt to divorce these idioms from their commercial connotations. He understands השיב with God as the subject as to "turn (the effects of) an action back towards the person who did something" ("Vergeltungsdogma im AT," 139–40; "Doctrine of Retribution," 63–64). He

A survey of the occurrences of שִׁלֵּם (*šillem*) reveals a pervasive notion of returning a situation to balance.[91] Apparently, this connection originated on the background of the predominant practice of weighing commodities on scales in ancient commerce. This concrete image served as a potent metaphor for conceptualizing the balance of costs and benefits for transactions in general. In the application of שִׁלֵּם to the social sphere, an unbalanced social situation (e.g., an unpaid debt, an unavenged murder) requires a counter action to restore the balance. This balance can be returned in one of two ways: either the indebted party will fulfill his obligation, or else the other side can take punitive action. The flexibility of this notion proved extremely apt as a metaphor for the notion of retribution, as is apparent in the expression "pay back 'bad' for 'good'" (שִׁלֵּם רעה תחת טובה),[92] which implies that there are two forms of currency, good and bad. A good action calls for a good action in exchange. A bad action can be rectified either by a compensatory act by the wrongdoer (the good thereby negates the bad) or the other party is entitled to punish the bad action in order to settle the balance.

A salient example of this conception is the promise to Abraham, which employs the verbal adjectival form of של"ם: "They shall return here in the fourth generation, for the sin of the Amorites is not yet complete" (כי לא שָׁלֵם עון האמרי עד הנה [Gen 15:16]). The metaphor of retribution as an equitable transaction dictates that the crime must fit the punishment; thus, the expulsion of the Amorites must wait for the accumulation of their iniquity. As noted above,[93] this underlying notion of an objective balance between an action and its consequences is a fundamental aspect of the notion of divine retribution as depicted in numerous biblical sources, which seem to imply an automatic and almost mechanistic dynamic.

---

understands שִׁלֵּם with God as the subject as expressing the idea that the Deity "completes" the action that the person set in motion ("Vergeltungsdogma im AT," 134–35; "Doctrine of Retribution," 60–61). See also the critical evaluation of Christ, *Blutvergiessen im Alten Testament*, 97–101.

91. It is quite likely that the *piel* usage of שִׁלֵּם as an expression for payment is based on a metaphorical conception of the transaction as an entity that must be "completed." This derivation would thus be similar to Akkadian *mullu*, which involves the conceptualization of transactions as a container that should be "filled" (see *CAD* M/1, 181–83), parallel to the English idiom "fulfill" an obligation. This hypothesis assumes a basic "root-meaning" of של"ם, which pertains to "wholeness" and "well-being" This basic sense of the various של"ם derivatives is well-supported by the biblical evidenced as well as that of cognates. See Eisenbeis, *Die Wurzel šlm* im *Alten Testament*, 8–51, 355–56; idem., *HALOT* 4:1506–10, 1532–36; K.-J. Illman, "שלם," *TDOT* 15:97–105. Cf. Gerleman, "Die Wurzel šlm im Alten Testament," 1–14; idem.,"שלם," *TLOT* 3:1337–48.

92. E.g., Gen 44:4; Jer 18:20; Ps 35:12. Cf. also משיב רעה תחת טובה (Prov 17:13).

93. See above, pp. 107–8 and pp. 182–84.

This broad notion of retribution as exchange sheds light on the general conceptual framework in which כפ"ר in the sense of compensation was progressively divorced from its original social context. For instance, several sources convey the idea that sin can be expiated by means of pain or destruction. In Isaiah's temple vision, the scorching of the prophet's lips with a blazing coal is given expiatory value (6:7):

ויגע על פי ויאמר הנה נגע זה על שפתיך וסר עונך וחטאתך תְּכֻפָּר

He touched my mouth and said: Now that this has touched your lips, your iniquity has been removed and your sin has been expiated.

The same dynamic, expressed in nearly identical terminology, applies to the nation as a whole (27:9):

לכן בזאת יְכֻפַּר עון יעקב וזה כל פרי הסר חטאתו בשומו כל אבני מזבח כאבני גר מנפצות לא
יקמו אשרים וחמנים

Thus with this Jacob's iniquity will be expiated and this is the only price for removing his sin—by placing all of the stones of his altar like crushed blocks of chalk, with no sacred posts or incense altars left standing.

These passages assert that expiation of sin is conditional on negative experience. Such a notion assumes a dynamic of equitable exchange in which the suffering of punishment allows the guilt debt to be cancelled. The following verse expresses the converse message:

בחסד ואמת יְכֻפַּר עון וביראת יקוק סור מרע

By kindness and truth iniquity will be expiated, and with fear of YHWH he will turn from evil (Prov 16:6).

Here a positive action serves to compensate for an earlier wrong.[94] These usages of כפ"ר are based on the metaphorical notion of retribution as commerce, implying both positive and negative ways of compensating for a wrong committed in order to restore a favorable action-consequence balance.[95] These references to "expiating sin" (כפ"ר עון) in the prophetic, wisdom and psalmodic literature rep-

---

94. 1 Sam 3:14 seems to express a similar idea but in a cultic context.

95. For the metaphoric conception of sin as debt in Second Temple Judaism, particularly the theme that the debt can be repaid by suffering, see Anderson, "From Israel's Burden," 1–30; idem., *Sin: A History*, 43–74; and p. 260 below.

resent a semantic extension of the use of כפ"ר in the context of blood vengeance and the cultic literature.

A final stage of semantic development can be identified in which terms for sin (חטאת\עון) appear as the direct object of כִּפֶּר without any connection to a compensatory act. The most prominent examples are those where God appears as the subject of כִּפֶּר, where it is usually translated "forgive."[96] Even these more "generic" usages of כִּפֶּר, which refer to expiation or forgiveness in general terms can be traced back to the notion of compensation by means of their syntax in which sin appears as the direct object.

Blood on the Altars' Horns. In light of the preceding discussion of the sin offering's symbolism and terminology, let us now examine the significance of the altars' horns, which serve as the primary locus of the sin offering's blood manipulation. As noted above, the horns of the burnt offering and incense altars play a central role in the sin offering's blood manipulations. Continuing our method of inquiry, which assumes that ritual use is an extention of the sign vehicle's concrete role within the culture, it is remarkable that we are drawn yet again to the context of homicide.

Before the establishment of cities of refuge, a murderer would seek to avoid his demise at the hands of the blood avenger by fleeing to the nearest cult place (i.e., "sanctuary"), due to the view that killing in a cult place was considered sacrilegious.[97] However, the textual sources indicate that this protection was conditional on the level of culpability of the killer. If he was guilty of premeditated homicide, the avenger was authorized to remove the murderer from the sanctuary and execute him, as stated in the Covenant Code (Exod 21:14):

> If a person acts maliciously against his fellow to kill him with guile, you shall take him away from my altar to die.

Such a case is related in 1 Kgs 2:28–34 where Joab attempts to escape execution by clinging to the horns of the altar, but to no avail. Solomon is unrelenting (vv. 31–33).

The sin offering blood rite has adapted the symbolism and terminology of murder compensation and transformed them into a cultic means of expiating sin. Just as in the context of homicide expiation, כִּפֶּר is used in reference to the repayment of a blood debt, the sin offering rituals employ this verb in reference to the use of blood as a means of making restitution for guilt, conceptualized as

---

96. E.g., Jer 18:23; Ezek 16:63; Ps 65:4; 78:38; 79:9; 2 Chr 30:18.

97. For a similar institution in ancient Greek culture, see Parker, *Miasma,* 182–83. Interestingly for the present discussion, the Greeks considered the existence of murder pollution to be conditional on the circumstances of the killing (p. 112).

a debt vis-à-vis the Deity. Hence, it is striking that the blood manipulations are performed in most cases on the altars' horns, considering their institutionalized function in the context of the blood feud. These observations raise the following provocative question: In recognition that altar asylum was only effective for murder that lacked criminal intent, is it coincidental that the primary circumstance for performing the sin offering is for unintentional sin?[98]

The proposed interpretation of the role of the altars' horns in the sin offering by reference to the social context of the blood feud finds support in Jer 17:1:

חטאת יהודה כתובה בעט ברזל בצפרן שמיר חרושה על לוח לבם ולקרנות מזבחותיכם

The sin of Judah is inscribed with a stylus of iron, engraved with an adamant point on the tablet of their hearts and on the horns of your altars.[99]

In this exhortation, Jeremiah emphasizes the indelibility of Judah's sin. The reference to "tablets of their hearts" in connection with the horns of the altars is not arbitrary. The prophet seems to be referring to amulets worn for apotropaic purposes,[100] which are thus similar to the horns of the altar, which can provide asylum for a fugitive against capital punishment. Such tactics will be of no use in evoking God's mercy at the moment of reckoning.[101] On the contrary, since Judah's sin is inscribed upon them, they will only remind the Deity of the punishment they deserve.

It is difficult to assess whether Jeremiah's words reflect an original idea or if they reveal a theological conception that was current among the priesthood, to which even the priests Anathoth were privy. Since the sancta serve as the primary interface in which Israel can approach its God, it is quite fitting that such a site would also serve as an index of Israel's conduct vis-à-vis the Deity. In any case, it is remarkable that Jeremiah's words—which involve a play on the offering term חטאת—articulate the metonymic scheme that underlies the dynamics of the sin offering (see pp. 108–11 above).[102]

---

98. Lev 4:2, 13, 22, 27; Num 15:22–31. See Gane, *Cult and Character*, 198–213.

99. In some MT manuscripts and versions: "their altars."

100. See Haran's comments in Milgrom, "*Ḥaṭṭat* Offering," 134. For לוח לב, see also Prov 3:3; 7:3. Cf. also Miller, "Apotropaic Imagery in Proverbs 6, 20–22," 129–30.

101. Jeremiah employs similar arguments in his famous Temple sermon (see 7:4, 11).

102. Milgrom seems to overlook the significance of this verse for his own theory. He views Jeremiah's words as an ironic play on the term חטאת: "Judahites want to believe that their 'purification offering,' namely, its blood, is daubed on the altar, thereby effecting their expiation; but in truth, the prophet tells us, it is their 'sin' condemning them before God" (*Leviticus*, 288). While the latter half of Milgrom's statement surely captures the gist of the prophet's exhortation, that the sins on the altar incriminate Israel, he misses the fact that Jeremiah's words are explicitly stating the dynamic which underlies his own "Dorian Gray" theory regard-

In fact, this verse in Jeremiah can provide crucial insight into the function of the כפרת, the site of the innermost blood manipulation of the Day of Expiation ritual of Lev 16.[103] Though many scholars have focused on the role of the כפרת include as the ark's cover or as the site of divine presence, the preponderance of evidence indicates that the primary function of the כפרת is its role in expiation.[104] As described above, the sin offering system as a whole should be seen as a means by which Israelites can seek expiation from their sins and thereby avoid punishment. This understanding coincides with Jeremiah's comparison of the altar's horns to an amulet, whereby both are perceived as a means of protection against misfortune. Accordingly, the blood sprinkling and daubing on the כפרת described in Lev 16 are not some incidental use of this appurtenance. Rather, they represent its main purpose, namely to provide the Israelites with a means to expiate (כִּפֶּר) their most severe transgressions.

SUMMARY

In this chapter, we have ventured to understand the expiatory power attributed to blood in biblical sources by examining the dominant concepts associated with blood in ancient Israelite society and their relation to the verb כִּפֶּר. The theoretical basis for this methodology is the assumption that the ritual significance attached to a ritual sign is an outgrowth of the significance of the sign in material existence. A survey of biblical references to blood across literary genres indicates that the dominant meaning attached to blood is "bloodguilt."

An examination of the biblical sources shows clearly that blood has distinct conceptual relevance due to the belief that the vital force of a creature resides in the blood (see following section). This belief finds distinct expression in situations of homicide where the spilled blood demands vengeance. Whereas certain societies in the ancient Near East seemed more open to the possibility of monetary compensation for spilled blood, the ancient Israelites, apparently continuing a pre-existing custom in Syria and Canaan, required the death of the perpetrator in the absence of ameliorating circumstances. The failure to execute this strict justice was assumed to implicate the entire community in the vengeance demanded by the blood.

The talionic practice of compensating for blood spilled with the blood of the perpetrator caused blood to be viewed in terms of its exchange value. This aspect

---

ing the projection of Israel's sins on the sancta.

103. For an extensive discussion of the כפרת and the various opinions regarding its function, see Janowski, *Sühne als Heilsgeschehen*, 277–354.

104. This understanding concurs with the Septuagint's translation *hilastērion* ("place of expiation").

finds it most obvious expression in the practice of substitutionary payments that absolve a murderer of bloodguilt. It is not surprising that in this social context blood became conceptually associated with payment, giving rise to idioms such as "their blood is precious" (וייקר דמם [Ps 72:14]). This development is further attested linguistically by the fact that "blood" became a term for blood money in Akkadian, and that ultimately, דמים became a term for payment in later Hebrew and Aramaic dialects. Further analysis of this conceptual scheme has revealed that blood represents not only the "debt" incurred by the murderer, but also the currency by which it must be paid back. Indeed, in cases of premeditated murder, the only acceptable form of payment is the blood of the perpetrator.

A corresponding conceptual development is evident in the study of derivatives of the root כפ"ר. Isolating the usage of כפ"ר terms in concrete social contexts, two basic situations were identified: 1) appeasing a superior in a moment of anger or judgment and 2) compensating bloodguilt. These contexts are characterized by distinct semantic nuances, which can be summarized as follows:

Social Situation	Sense of כֹּפֶר	Sense of כִּפֶּר
1) Appeasing superior	"propitiatory gift"	"appease" (judge/adversary)
2) Blood revenge	"substitutionary payment"	"compensate"/"expiate" (bloodguilt)

The use of כִּפֶּר in the context of expiating bloodguilt was adapted to the cultic realm and applied to expiatory offerings. Finally, כִּפֶּר was used more generally by the prophets and in the Psalms. These stages of semantic development can be depicted linearly as follows:

appeasement ⇒ expiation for ⇒ cultic expiation ⇒ expiation for sin in
              bloodguilt   prophetic, wisdom, and
                                                     psalmodic literature

A crux of this investigation has been that the semantic field of compensation, which is rooted in the institution of the blood feud is the basis of the cultic usage of כִּפֶּר. As opposed to the distinct semantic field of "appeasement," which refers to the placation of anger, the כפ"ר derivatives, which pertain to "compensation," refer to the removal of sin, namely bloodguilt. This reconstruction finds striking corroboration in the Greek translation of כִּפֶּר, *hilaskomai*. Whereas the earliest inscriptional evidence of this verb reflects the sense "propitiate," its use in the Septuagint indicates a transition to "expiate" (see below, pp. 254–55)

The awareness of the social context and meaning of the blood–כפ"ר nexus was preserved by the Priestly traditions. Whereas H articulates this meaning verbally, referring explicitly to the substitutionary role of blood in the context of expiating bloodguilt (Lev 17:11; Num 35:33), P foregoes verbal explanations, noting only the function of the ritual: By daubing the blood of the sin offering on the horns of the altar, the priest makes expiation on behalf of the offerer (וכפר עליו הכהן), removing his liability to the Deity. For reasons that will be outlined below (pp. 257–60), P's depiction of ritual is still rooted in a worldview where ritual actions speak louder than words.

EXCURSES: BLOOD AND SPIRIT (נפש)

In order to fully assess the theoretical ramifications of this study, we must now compare the conclusions of the foregoing analysis to a few of the dominant theories that seek to explain the expiatory power of blood. Almost all commentators, medieval and modern, attribute the expiatory power of blood to the belief that the נפש, translated "life," is in the blood. This alleged equation of life and blood appears in three separate passages in the Torah as rationales for the prohibition of ingesting blood, in Gen 9:4; Lev 17:11, 14 and Deut 12:23.[105] Since these passages focus on the prohibition of ingesting blood in all three of these cases, one may doubt their relevance to the symbolic value of blood in the cult. However, since Lev 17:11 explicitly connects the prohibition of consuming blood with its expiatory function, theories based on the "blood is life" equation seem to be on firm ground.

Nevertheless, the methodology of such scholars is highly problematic. נפש is an extraordinarily polysemous term, and its sense in any given case can only be determined, if at all, by means of a careful examination of the context. It can refer to the vital force or spirit that sustains a human or animal,[106] or to an individual "person" or "being,"[107] but it never refers to "life" as an abstract concept, a sense reserved for חיים.[108] Hence, the common modern translations "life" and "soul" create a seemingly irresistible tendency to read foreign concepts into the biblical text.

I will now examine the sources that assert an inherent connection between blood and נפש in order to determine the sense of the latter term in these contexts. Only then may we attempt to extrapolate the relevance of these statements, if

---

105. See also Gilders' lucid discussion (*Blood Ritual in the Hebrew Bible*, 14–24).

106. E.g., Ps 19:8; 23:3; Ruth 4:15; Lam 1:11, 16. See Westermann, "נפש," 748; Seebass, "נפש," 510.

107. Westermann, "נפש," 755–56; Seebass, "נפש," 512–14.

108. Westermann, "נפש," 754; Seebass, "נפש," 510.

any, for the symbolism of blood in expiatory rituals. The first of these sources, attributable to P, relates God's blessing to Noah after the flood (Gen 9:1–7):

> [1]God blessed Noah and his sons and said to them: Be fertile and increase, and fill the land. [2]Fear and dread of you shall be upon all the beasts of the land and upon all the birds of the sky—all that moves on the land—and all the fish of the sea. They have been given into your hand. [3]Every moving thing that lives shall be yours for consumption. Like the green grass, I have given you everything. [4]However, you may not eat flesh with its life, that is, its blood (אך בשר בנפשו דמו לא תאכלו). [5]But for your lifeblood I will demand a reckoning; I will demand a reckoning from the hand of every creature, and from the hand of man. From the hand of the man's brother, I will demand the life of the man. [6]The one who spills the blood of man, by man his blood will be spilled, for He made man in the image of God. [7]So be fertile and increase, abound on the earth and increase upon it.

The restoration of life after the flood as described in this passage is modeled after the account of the creation of life in Gen 1:26–30. However, the deluge has left an indelible imprint on history, forever changing the rights and obligations of humans. Until now mankind has been confined to a vegetarian diet (as implied by Gen 1:29), but now he is permitted to partake of meat. His one restriction is that he must not eat the "flesh with its *nepeš*, that is, its blood" (בשר בנפשו דמו).[109]

There are persuasive reasons for adopting the translation "spirit" in this context, understood as the animating force that sustains the creature. First of all, despite its apparent ambiguity, v. 4 like other verses that state the prohibition of ingesting blood seems to assume that the association of blood with the *nepeš* is a self-evident reason for the prohibition. The self-sufficiency of this rationale is understandable if we assume that the text is referring to consuming the spirit of the animal.[110] On the other hand, if we are to understand *nepeš* as "life" or "life

---

109. This rendering takes the *bêth* of בנפשו as signifying "with" (thereby paralleling עם in Deut 12:23) and assumes that דמו is in apposition to נפשו (Ibn Ezra). See further Rendtorff, "Another Prolegomenon to Leviticus 17:11," 25; idem., *Leviticus*, 166–67. Regarding the relationship between this passage and Gen 1:26–29, see Fishbane, *Biblical Interpretation in Ancient Israel*, 318–21. He views the two restrictive clauses marked by אך (vv. 4–6a) as additions from an independent legal source with 6b as an editorial gloss.

110. See Ramban on Lev 17:11; Elliger, *Leviticus*, 228. Some other views include: 1) Drinking the blood was part of pagan religious rites (Maimonides, *Guide to the Perplexed*, 3, 46). This explanation is more fitting for the expression eating "on the blood" (Lev 19:26, 1 Sam 14:32–35), which apparently refers to divination by means of evoking chthonic deities. See Grintz, "Do not Eat on the Blood," 78–105; Milgrom, *Leviticus* 2:1490–93. 2) God will avenge the spilled blood of the animal (Jub 6:7). Although this interpretation gives due weight to context (vv. 5–6), it cannot be sustained. A serious weakness with this interpretation is that in vv. 5–6 the Deity declares explicitly that he will exact blood vengeance since mankind was cre-

force," we might think that ingesting blood could have positive effects.[111]

Further support for this view can be found in the subsequent verses, which promise divine retribution for the killing of humans (vv. 5–6). In v. 5, as reflected in the three-fold repetition of the idiom דר״ש דם, God is depicted as the blood avenger who will exact revenge on behalf of mankind: "But for your lifeblood I will demand a reckoning" (דמכם לנפשתיכם אדרש). This theme is continued in v. 6 where it is stated that spilled blood can only be expiated by the blood of the perpetrator, evoking the ancient concept of appeasing blood. Assuming that this passage is thematically coherent, we must understand the sequence of vv. 4–6 as implying that the spirit that is contained in animal blood and forbids its consumption is analogous to the animating force in the blood of humans, which demands vengeance in cases of murder.[112]

Additional sources that equate blood with נפש are found in Lev 17. We will begin with the first section (vv. 1–7):

> [1]YHWH spoke to Moses, saying: [2]Speak to Aaron, his sons and all of the Isra-
> elites and say to them: This is what YHWH has commanded, saying: [3]Any
> man from the House of Israel who slaughters an ox, sheep or goat in the camp
> or slaughters outside the camp [4]and does not bring it to the Tent of Meeting
> to offer as an offering to YHWH before the Tabernacle of YHWH, blood will
> be imputed to that man—he has spilled blood—and that man will be cut off
> from his people. [5]So that the Israelites will bring their sacrifices that they are
> offering in the open field and bring them to YHWH to the opening of the Tent
> of Meeting to the priest, and they shall slaughter them as well-being offer-
> ings to YHWH; [6]that the priest shall toss the blood on the altar of YHWH at
> the entrance to the Tent of Meeting and turn the suet into smoke as a pleasing

---

ated in the image of God, implying that *only* the killing of humans entails punishment. 3) The prohibition serves as a reminder of the inviolability of life, so that man will not come to treat bloodshed lightly. For example, Cassuto writes that the blood prohibition serves "as a reminder that in truth all flesh should have been forbidden, and hence it behooves us to avoid eating one part of it in order to remember the former prohibition" (*Commentary on the Book of Genesis*, 126). Similarly, Delitzsch, Dillman, Jacob and Westermann view the blood prohibition as a preventative measure against the trait of brutality (see C. Westermann, *Genesis 1–11* [trans. J. J. Scullion; Minneapolis: Fortress, 1994], 465 with references). Since this view assumes that נפש can be equated with "life" (some of these commentators translate "Seele" but then treat the latter as synonymous with "Leben"), it must be rejected (see below). 5) All life belongs to God; hence, it must be returned to him. For references and discussion, see below.

111. Gilders, *Blood Ritual in the Hebrew Bible*, 16–17.

112. Brichto proposes that the passage is asserting that "[man's] license to kill is unilat-eral: man may victimize animals, not animals man nor man his fellowman" ("On Slaughter and Sacrifice," 20–21, n. 2). A similar view was already expressed by medieval Jewish commenta-tors, e.g., Ibn Ezra, Sporno. These views fail to account for the significance attributed to the blood in these verses.

aroma for YHWH. [7]They will no longer slaughter their sacrifices to the satyrs after whom they stray —this will be for them an everlasting statute throughout their generations.

This law requires that the slaughter of every animal eligible for sacrifice take place inside the precincts of the Tent of Meeting. More specifically, an Israelite who seeks to partake of one of them for food must offer it first as a well-being offering in the Tabernacle.[113] The text continues to state emphatically that anyone who fails to comply with this requirement and slaughters outside of the Tabernacle will be held accountable for the blood of the animal. To this effect, v. 4 employs two judicial formulas: 1) "Blood will be imputed to that man" (דם יחשב לאיש ההוא) and 2) "He has spilled blood" (דם שפך).[114] The subsequent verses elaborate on this rationale by claiming that anyone who performs ritual slaughter outside the precinct of the Tabernacle is suspected of sacrificing to desert satyrs (שעירים [v.7]).[115] In addition to the weighty accusation of cultic infidelity, the perpetrator is guilty of the unjustified killing of the animal. Thus the argument of vv. 4, 7, which will be further explicated in v. 11, is that the dichotomy legitimate/illegitimate slaughter of the animal is comparable to the justified/unjustified killing of a human, the latter of which falls under the category of spilling "innocent blood" (דם נקי) and invokes punishment.[116]

We will return to vv. 10–12 momentarily. Verses 13–14 present the law for hunting game:

13ואיש איש מבני ישראל ומן הגר הגר בתוכם אשר יצוד ציד חיה או עוף אשר יאכל ושפך את דמו וכסהו בעפר

14כי נפש כל בשר דמו בנפשו הוא ואמר לבני ישראל דם כל בשר לא תאכלו כי נפש כל בשר דמו הוא כל אכליו יכרת

[13]Any man from the Israelites or the proselytes that dwell among them that hunts down a beast or bird that may be eaten shall spill out its blood and cover it with earth. [14]Since the spirit of all flesh—its blood—is with its spirit,[117] I

---

113. Milgrom, "Prolegomenon to Leviticus," 152–53; Milgrom, *Leviticus*, 708–13; Schwartz, *Holiness Legislation*, 66–77.

114. Milgrom, *Leviticus* 2:1457.

115. See B. Janowski, "Satyrs," *DDD*, 1381–84.

116. Cf. Gilders, *Blood Ritual in the Hebrew Bible*, 163–66.

117. Some possible solutions for understanding this difficult expression include: 1. Deleting בנפשו; 2. Interpreting the *beth* of בנפשו as a *beth essentiae:* "blood is its spirit"; 3. Interpreting the *beth* as signifying "with": "its blood is with its spirit." To avoid textual emendation and due to the dubiousness of the *beth essentiae* (cf. Brichto, "On Slaughter and Sacrifice," 26, n. 18), we may opt for the third solution, which corresponds with the understanding of the *beth* in the formula אך בשר בנפשו דמו ("but flesh *with* its spirit, that is, its blood"

said to the Israelites: You must not eat the blood of any flesh, because the spirit of all flesh is its blood, anyone who eats it will be cut off.

According to this law, even in cases of hunting game, where the draining of the blood is not part of the killing process, the hunter must pour out the blood on the ground and cover it with earth. Interestingly, this type of killing is not labeled "murder" as was non-sacral slaughter (v. 4). This reinforces the interpretation offered above that it is the illegitimacy of non-sacral slaughter, suspected as being an offering to satyrs (v. 7), that incurs the bloodguilt, not the taking of the animal's life in of itself.

Nevertheless, even the blood of game should not be taken lightly. The requirement to cover the blood stems from an ancient belief that uncovered blood will invoke vengeance.[118] The threat implied by such a situation is abundantly attested in biblical sources where the failure to appease spilled blood is depicted in terms of its exposure. According to Ezek 24:7–8, the unatoned (= exposed) blood in Jerusalem's midst calls for its destruction:

> [7]For her blood is still within her. She set it on the surface of a rock. She did not pour it out on the land to cover it with earth. [8]To stir up rage, to arouse vengeance I placed her blood on the surface of a rock to remain uncovered.

Conversely, the ceremonial covering of the blood with dirt is tantamount to its appeasement, an idea expressed clearly in Job 16:18:

> Earth, do not cover my blood; let there not be a resting place for my outcry![119]

These sources and others imply a folkloric view whereby spilled blood will call for vengeance unless it is properly buried and thereby placated.[120] As a result, we may assume that the requirement to cover the blood of game originated from

---

[Gen 9, 4]) advocated above. See also Milgrom, *Leviticus* 2:1483–84. See also above, p. 197, n. 109.

118. See, e.g., Bertholet, *Leviticus*, 60; Ehrlich, *Randglossen zur hebräischen Bibel*, 60. Milgrom originally advocated this opinion (see "Prolegomenon to Leviticus," 152; *Leviticus*, 709), but subsequently changed his mind (*Leviticus 2*, 1482–84). His preferred explanations (which he views to be non-contradictory) are that the rite is intended 1) to prevent the blood from being used in chthonic rites and 2) so that the blood "be returned to God." Ironically, if such beliefs were attributed to the practice, they would likely achieve the opposite effect, implying that the Israelites worship a chthonic deity by offering blood libations to the ground! See further below.

119. NJPS translation. See also Isa 26:21.

120. See also: Gen 4:10; 37:26; Isa 26:21.

this conception. This notion fits the context of Lev 17, which asserts that the blood of illegitimately sacrificed animals demands a reckoning (v. 4).[121]

The third source that equates blood with נפש appears in a similar context in Deut 12. While granting Israel permission to engage in non-sacrificial slaughter, the law reiterates the prohibition of ingesting blood (vv. 23–24; cf. vv. 15–16):

²³רק חזק לבלתי אכל הדם כי הדם הוא הנפש ולא תאכל הנפש עם הבשר
²⁴לא תאכלנו על הארץ תשפכנו כמים

²³Just be careful not to consume the blood, because the blood is the spirit, and you must not eat the spirit with the flesh. ²⁴You shall not consume it; you shall pour it out like water.

Once again, ingesting blood is eschewed on the grounds that "the blood is the *nepeš*" (הדם הוא הנפש). However, Deut 12 does not require the covering of the blood, which can be poured out "like water." This expression denies blood any supernatural or sacred qualities, and seems to be a deliberate rejection of any concern with adverse ramifications caused by the spilled blood of animals.[122]

A dominant misconception that appears throughout commentaries dealing with Gen 9:1–7, Lev 17 and Deut 12:23–24 is the notion that life belongs to God. This theory is largely attributable to the uncritical translation of נפש as "life." This alleged doctrine is used by scholars to explain the prohibitions of murder and consuming blood as well as the requirement to pour out the blood of game on the ground.[123] From the outset, let us recognize that in none of the aforementioned sources can we find even a hint of the idea that life belongs to God.[124]

---

121. Based on the structure of v. 14 and its reference to the prohibition of ingesting blood, Schwartz argues that the requirement to cover the blood is intended as a protective measure against the possibility of ingesting it ("Prohibitions Concerning 'Eating' the Blood," 62; *Holiness Legislation*, 122–25). But this is an inadequate explanation for the "ritualized activity" of covering the blood (Gilders, *Blood Ritual in the Hebrew Bible*, 23–24). More likely, the intent of v. 14 is that the rationale for covering the blood is the same as that which motivates the ban on its consumption (as well as its severe penalty of כרת). Namely, just as the animating spirit that resides in the blood precludes its consumption, so too, it is the reason for the blood-covering requirement.

122. See M. Weinfeld, *Deuteronomy and the Deuteronomic School* (Oxford: Clarendon, 1972), 214.

123. E.g., Reventlow, "Sein Blut Komme," 414; von Rad, *Genesis: A Commentary*, 128; Noth, *Leviticus: A Commentary*, 132; Füglister, "Sühne durch Blut," 150–54; Brichto, "On Slaughter and Sacrifice," 22; Sarna, *Genesis*, 61.

124. A more solid argument for such a claim could be made from Lev 3:16–17, which deals with the prohibition of eating suet and blood. Although we find an explicit statement that "All suet is God's" (כל חלב לה'), there is no corresponding statement regarding blood, implying that the latter is not included in this rationale. Likewise, Lev 7:23–27 treats the prohibitions

Nor should we expect such a notion, having recognized that נפש in these texts refers to the animating force in blood, a concept that is somewhat less congenial to theological speculation than "life" or "soul."[125] Particularly startling is the common assertion that pouring out the blood on the ground is returning life to its Creator.[126] According to the biblical canon, the Deity can dwell in the heavens, Tabernacle or Temple, and he may even occasionally grant a cameo revelation elsewhere, but he is never described as living in the ground. Moreover, there is reason to believe that the Israelite God would take offense at being grouped with chthonic deities that dwell in the earth and receive blood libations![127]

In summary, our survey of the blood prohibition formulas that assert an intimate connection between blood and נפש indicates that the latter term denotes the animating soul that was believed to reside in the blood. Two pieces of evidence support this conclusion. First, the equation of blood with *nepeš* is offered as a self-explanatory rationale for forbidding the ingestion of blood. Second, the blood prohibition as it appears in Gen 9 is juxtaposed with the topic of avenging spilled blood, implying that we are dealing with some form of the animated conception of blood which cries out for vengeance, albeit in a less personified form.

The latter impression is reinforced by the references in Lev 17 to the blood prohibition, which associate blood with *nepeš*. In this chapter, we find explicit reference to the notion of accountability for the spilled blood of animals as well as the requirement to cover the spilled blood of game, a practice whose origin is attributable to the notion that uncovered blood invokes revenge.

As a result, the various theories based on a principle that blood is "life" or contains "life" must be rejected because they remove these statements from their literary contexts.

---

of eating suet and blood as distinct rules. We should mention that these sources do not refer to the idea that the נפש is in the blood. Only in Ezek 44:7, 15 are suet and blood depicted jointly as God's portion of the sacrifice, which he calls "my food" (לחמי), but even here there is no hint at the idea of returning life to God. See also Gilders, *Blood Ritual in the Hebrew Bible*, 20–24. Finally, the statement in Lev 17:11 that God gives the blood to Israel does not imply his "ownership" of blood. Rather, as argued by Gane, the entire animal is transferred to the Deity's possession by means of the hand-leaning rite (*Cult and Character*, 53–56, 63–64 and n. 73).

125. If we were to relate these sources to the narrative describing the creation of man in Gen 2:7, it would be preferable to associate the blood with Adam's earthly composition than with the "breath of life" (נשמת חיים) that the Deity blows in his nostrils. Accordingly, the pouring out of blood on the ground corresponds to the fate of Adam, whose earthly composition will return to the ground when he dies (3:19).

126. See, e.g., Dillmann, *Exodus und Leviticus*, 589; Driver, *Deuteronomy*, 148; Milgrom, *Leviticus 2:*1476.

127. Cf. Ps 16:4; 50:13. Remarkably, Levine understands the requirement to pour blood out on the altar as a "blood libation" that placates the God's rage, a remnant from the worship of chthonic deities (*In the Presence of the Lord*, 69).

Now we may address the source in which the association of blood with נפש is given cultic significance, namely Lev 17:10–12:

¹⁰ואיש איש מבית ישראל ומן הגר הגר בתוכם אשר יאכל כל דם ונתתי פני בנפש האכלת את
הדם והכרתי אתה מקרב עמה

¹¹כי נפש הבשר בדם הוא ואני נתתיו לכם על המזבח לכפר על נפשתיכם כי הדם הוא בנפש
יכפר

¹²על כן אמרתי לבני ישראל כל נפש מכם לא תאכל דם והגר הגר בתוככם לא יאכל דם

¹⁰Any man from the House of Israel or from the proselytes that dwell among them who ingests any blood, I will set my countenance against that man, and I will cut him off from the midst of his people. ¹¹For the spirit of the flesh is in the blood, and I myself have assigned it to you on the altar to make ransom for your lives, for it is the blood that ransoms by means of the life. ¹²Thus I commanded the Israelites: None of you may consume blood, and the proselyte among you shall not consume blood.

Verse 11 provides a rationale for the prohibition of consuming blood (vv. 10, 12), while simultaneously explaining why bloodguilt is not incurred for legitimate slaughter. This verse is divided into three clauses:

For the spirit of the flesh is in the blood,	כי נפש הבשר בדם הוא
and I myself have assigned it to you on the altar to make ransom for your lives,	ואני נתתיו לכם על המזבח לכפר על נפשתיכם
for it is the blood that ransoms by means of the life.	כי הדם הוא בנפש יכפר

The first of these cites the underlying premise that the animating spirit is in the blood. The following clause lends this notion relevance to the use of blood in the cult, stating that God has given the blood to the Israelites to make ransom for their lives.¹²⁸ The third clause provides a synthesis of the previous two. Since

---

128. See Schwartz, "Prohibitions Concerning 'Eating' the Blood," 50–51; *Holiness Legislation*, 111. The expression כפ"ר על נפש, like the nominal construct כֹּפֶר נפש, refers to ransom payment. See Exod 30:12, 15, 16; Num 31:50; 35:31; Prov 13:8. Cf. Levine, *In the Presence of the Lord*, 67. As pointed out by Schwartz, the expression ואני נתתיו לכם (translated here: "I myself have assigned it to you") seems to have a double-meaning. Since the expression נת"ן על המזבח usually appears with the priests as the subject, describing their performance of the cultic rites, it may also be translated "I myself *have placed* [the blood] on the altar *for you*." According to either translation, the message is the same: the offerer should not view himself as giving the blood to God, but rather the opposite, that God is providing him with the opportunity to ransom his life.

blood contains the spirit (נפש) of the animal, it can be viewed as being of the same currency as the life (נפש) of the offerer, and thus the former can be given as a substitute for the latter.[129]

As many scholars have recognized, Lev 17:11 is a relatively late explanation for the long-established custom of pouring out the blood on the altar.[130] Based on our analysis of the term נפש in the blood prohibition formulas, we may now understand the underlying logic on which Lev 17:11 is based. As we have seen, the basis of the prohibition against ingesting blood is the premise that it contains the "animating soul" (נפש) of the animal. In contrast, the logic of ransom expounded by Lev 17:11 is based on the talionic formula "a life for a life" (נפש תחת נפש\נפש בנפש), in which נפש should be understood as "person" or "being."[131] Thus, the author has midrashically linked two well-known formulas, one pertaining to the blood taboo and the other to talionic punishment, by means of the polysemous term נפש, despite the distinct sense of this term in each context.[132] Thus, the author is providing an artificial *discursive* logic for the rite, which is made possible by the verbalization of the cultic process.[133]

---

129. The *beth* here should be understood as a *beth instrumentii,* as this is only attested meaning in the phrase כִּפֶּר ב- (e.g., Gen 32:21; Exod 29:33; Lev 5:16). The alternative suggestion, that the *beth* is a *beth pretii* (translating "the blood makes a ransom for the cost of [the offerer's] life"), is superfluous after the second clause and bears no connection to the first clause. For references to earlier discussions, see Schwartz, "Prohibitions Concerning 'Eating' the Blood," 47, n. 2 and Milgrom, *Leviticus 2:*1478. See also Gilders, *Blood Ritual in the Hebrew Bible*, 175–76 who warns against confusing this concept of ransom with the idea that the animal is a substitute for the offerer.

130. Bertholet, *Leviticus*, 60; Elliger, *Leviticus*, 228; Christ, *Blutvergiessen im Alten Testament*, 139. The same goes for scholars who date H after P such as Knohl (*Sanctuary of Silence*, 112–13), Milgrom (*Leviticus 2*, 1472–79) and Gilders (*Blood Ritual in the Hebrew Bible*, 12–13).

131. Exod 21:23; Lev 24:18; Deut 19:21. The dependency of this clause on the talionic formula was noted by Elliger (*Leviticus*, 228) and Gerstenberger (*Leviticus*, 60).

132. This distinction is missed by most scholars. Seebass ("נפש," 513–14) includes both the talionic formulas and the blood prohibitions under the meaning "individuated life." DCH (sub. נפש) lists both formulas under the heading "life, lives; soul," translating נפש תחת נפש (Lev 24:18) "a life shall be for a life" and נפש הבשר בדם הוא (Lev 17:11) "the life of the flesh is in the blood." In contrast, Kaddari (*Dictionary of Biblical Hebrew*, sub נפש) correctly distinguishes between נפש in the blood prohibition formulas, which he defines as "the link between the body and the inner force within it" (העירוב שבין הגוף לכוח הפנימי שבו), and נפש in the talionic formulas, understood as "the bodily aspect of the person" (החלק הגופני שבאדם). More specifically, he understands the latter formulas as referring to the monetary value of a person's body or body parts which have been injured (ערך גוף האדם או ערך חלקי הגוף שנפגעו).

133. Although the meaning of כִּפֶּר as well as the symbolism of blood implied by this statement are firmly rooted in tradition, this rationale must be distinguished from the predominately nonverbal logic that underlies the sin offering (see below).

This rationale should be viewed as part of Lev 17's polemic against non-sacrificial slaughter. Though many scholars understand Lev 17:11 as referring to the use of blood in expiatory offerings,[134] this view should be rejected out of hand, as this chapter makes no reference to expiatory offerings. Since the major thrust of the chapter deals with banning the non-sacral slaughter of animals, its topic must be the well-being offering, as it is the only offering of which laymen may partake (v. 5).[135] Indeed, the reference to ransom in v. 11 alludes clearly to the imputation of bloodguilt in v. 4 for non-sacrificial slaughter. Even if the purview of v. 11 includes the wider scope of offerings discussed in vv. 8–9, there is no justification for applying its statement to the unique blood manipulation of the sin offering.

Leaving this fundamental problem aside, let us examine briefly some of the dominant theories regarding the expiatory role of blood that are based on this verse:

- As life, it cancels the effects of sin and impurity, which are equated with death.[136]
- The power of "life-force" grants it a potency as a purifying agent that cleanses the defilement of sin and impurity.[137]
- It represents the life of the offerer, which is symbolically sacrificed or dedicated to God.[138]

The first two of these theories must be rejected simply because they attribute a fallacious sense to נפש: "life" and "life-force" respectively. The rationale provided by Lev 17:11 is quite different: the animal's soul (נפש) contained in the blood can serve as a ransom for the life of the offerer, exonerating him from the guilt of killing the animal. There is no assertion whatsoever that the blood possesses some kind of rejuvenating and vitalizing power or that it represents symbolically the concept of "life." The third view is likewise untenable. According to the midrashic twist of the meaning of נפש in this verse, the life of the

---

134. E.g., Rendtorff, *Leviticus*, 169; Schwartz, *Holiness Legislation*, 117–20. Schwartz argues that these verses pertain to the expiatory sacrifices which may be consumed (i.e., the guilt offering by laymen and the courtyard sin offerings by the priests). However, the blood rite of the sin offering, which requires special acts of daubing and sprinkling (signified by the verbs נת״ן and הז״ה respectively) is distinct from that of the guilt offering, whose blood rite is like that of the burnt and well-being offerings in which blood is tossed around the altar (זר״ק על המזבח סביב...); hence, we should not expect a common rationale joining them. Cf. Lev 1:5, 11 (burnt); 3:2, 8, 13 (well-being); 7:2 (guilt).

135. See also Milgrom, *Leviticus* 2:1474–78.

136. E.g., Milgrom, *Leviticus*, 711–12, 768; cf. 1002–3.

137. Füglister, "Sühne durch Blut," 147–65.

138. Hoffmann, *Das Buch Leviticus, vol. 2* on Lev 17:11–12; Gese, *Atonement*, 106–7; Janowski, *Sühne als Heilsgeschehen*, 240–41.

animal is given *in lieu* of the offerer's life. It does not *represent* the offerer. Furthermore, the ransom serves to permit the slaughter of the animal itself, but it does not expiate other types of guilt. As a result, the attempts to explain the expiatory power of blood on the basis of the connection between blood and the נפש cannot be reconciled with a contextually based understanding of Lev 17:11.

The findings of this investigation regarding the symbolic significance of blood contrast markedly from those of previous research. The disparity in results can be best understood by comparing the methodology applied in the present study to that of previous studies.

Most scholars will agree that the association of blood with life derives from the recognition that loss of blood leads to death. For the same reason, the dominant idiom for murder in biblical Hebrew as in many languages is to "spill blood" (שפ"ך דם). In Peircian terminology, we may thus state that blood is an *index* of life. In this light, the association of blood with vitality is by no means arbitrary. At the same time, the use of blood as a means of expiation cannot immediately be inferred from its association with this association. In fact, as noted above, scholars have offered quite divergent explanations of how the power of blood, as life, can effect expiation.

Leaving aside the weaknesses of these various theories, the multiplicity of theories in itself demonstrates that even the equation "blood is life" does not fully explain the expiatory power of blood. Furthermore, if, hypothetically, we were not aware of the use of blood in the Israelite cult from other sources, and we knew only of the association of blood with "life" (according to the common translation), we might not assume that blood has an expiatory function whatsoever. Since the Deity may have just as easily assigned another substance for the purpose of expiatory rites, we may say that the choice of blood depends on an essentially arbitrary act of divine designation. Thus we should view the expiatory use of blood according to these theories as a *symbol*, as it is dependent on an external code to grant it meaning.[139]

In contrast, the expiatory power of blood as proposed here is not arbitrary but has emerged out of the significance lent to blood in the context of expiating bloodguilt. This explanation corresponds well with Voloshinov's understanding of the social foundations of signs:

> Individual choice under these circumstances, of course, can have no meaning at all. The sign is a creation between individuals, a creation within a social milieu.

---

139. Cf. Elliger, *Leviticus*, 228 and Schenker, "Das Zeichen das Blutes," 199–201, who ascribe this function to divine decree. This opinion was anticipated by the Tanna R. Yohanan b. Zakhai's view towards the efficacy of the red cow ritual (see *Pesiqta d'Rav Kahana* 4, 7).

Therefore the item in question must first acquire interindividual significance, and only then can it become an object for sign formation.[140]

Thus, the use of the motivated sign by the ritual practitioner is viewed as inherently meaningful action. Taken in this light, ritual action can be perceived as implicitly more powerful than verbal magic. Whereas the latter involves a deliberate act of attributing functions to objects and activities, ritual action operates on the assumption of embedded meaning. Rituals are not an arbitrary set of gestures seeking to impose one's will on the world from "outside," but the use of actions whose function has originated and been determined by the world to affect it from the "inside."[141]

---

140. Voloshinov, *Philosophy of Language*, 22.
141. See below, pp. 258–60, for a more detailed discussion of ritual efficacy.

6

The *Zurki* Rite: Origins, Context, and Meaning

I will now apply the same methodology to understand the expiatory use of blood in Hittite ritual, proceeding with the assumption that the ritual use of a sign is merely an extension of its significance in the material existence of the culture. However, in the case of the Hittite textual evidence, we must also accommodate the fact that the texts demonstrate, explicitly or implicitly, four distinct understandings of blood's expiatory value. In these sources, blood is presented as a propitiatory gift or bribe to chthonic deities, a currency of compensation, an agent of purification, and an agent of consecration.

These categories are provisional, serving as a convenient means to arrange the data, but they will be reevaluated below. For the moment, I will explore the evidence for each of them. By seeking to understand the conceptual role of blood in each of these schemes taken by itself, we can then attempt to determine their interrelationship.

Bribing Chthonic Deities

A seemingly universal notion that can be found in Anatolian, Mesopotamian, ancient Greek, and ethnographic sources is the belief that the dwellers of the underworld crave blood.[1] This bloodthirstiness is attributed to the dead and chthonic deities. Most likely, this conception stems from the assumption that the dwellers of the underworld seek to replenish the life fluid that they are so direly lacking.[2] This belief finds expression in two distinct uses of blood in ritual. First, in conjunction with the belief that such entities are charged with the dirty work (in which they revel) of punishing man for his misdeeds, blood is used as a prophylactic measure to bribe these agents.[3] By satisfying their bloodthirst,

---

1. See, e.g., Turner, *Forest of Symbols*, 10; Collins, "Pigs at the Gate," 173, 181–82.

2. This conception is described explicitly in Greek sources. See Onians, *Origins of European Thought*, 255, 271–72; Linke, "Blood as Metaphor," 338–39.

3. In Greek mythology, this role is played by the Erinyes. See Grintz, "Do not Eat on the

they will be dissuaded, it is hoped, from carrying out their retributory mission. Second, blood is used to attract underworld entities so that they will come and take away a threat to the ritual patron (sin, impurity, etc.) and bring it back to the underworld. We find variations of both of these themes in the Hittite ritual corpus in general, and in the context of the Kizzuwatnean blood rite in particular.

An example of the prophylactic use of blood can be found in the foundation ritual KBo 15.24+ described above (pp. 23–26). In this text, the officiating priest appeals to the earth to block the passage of malicious deities from the underworld. At a later stage in the ritual, statues are smeared with blood before being deposited in the foundations of the new structure. As argued above, this ritual seems to combine the Kizzuwatnean blood rite with the Mesopotamian tradition of smearing foundation stones with blood as a preemptive means of appeasing the chthonic deities for intruding upon their dwelling.

Similar themes can be detected in the fragmentary text KBo 13.101.[4] Besides the ritual of Papanikri, this is the only text known to me that depicts blood smearing with an accompanying declaration. In this fascinating fragment, the ritual officiant, whose words are related in the first person, attempts to appease chthonic deities in reaction to a foreboding omen that has appeared. Despite the fragmentary nature of the text, we can discern that the ritual entailed numerous offerings, including that of a male sheep and a goat. Various parts of the animals' bodies are offered into a pit (*pattešar*) and the blood of at least the sheep is smeared on the place where the omen appeared. The latter act is reminiscent of the blood-smearing rite in the Papanikri Ritual. In the latter case, in order to counteract the threat portended by the breaking of the birth stool, new birth stools are made that are smeared with blood. In addition, he offers sweet breads and libates *tawal* and *walhi* drinks.

He then addresses the otherwise unknown Sun Deity of the Sign (^{d}UTU IŠKIM):

Obv.
26' [*ki-i-i*]*š-ša-an me-ma-ah-hi zi-ik* ^{d}UTU IŠ.KIM [...]
27' [*ku-e*]-*da-ni pé-di* ISKIM-*in i-ia-at-ten ki-nu-un-na-a*[*t*...]
28' [*a-p*]*a-at AŠ-RU iš-har-nu-um-ma-u-en na-at*-[x] *ma$^{?}$-ah$^{?}$-h*[*a?-an*...]
29' [*an*]-*da ta-wa-li-it wa-al-hi-it ni-*⌈*in-ga*⌉-*nu-*[*me-en*...]
30' [*ku-i*]*n* ⌈IS⌉KIM-*in* GE$_{6}$-*iš* KI-*aš an-da* [*pašta*]
31' [*na-an*] x[x] *pé-e-da-az le-e ni-ni-*⌈*ik*⌉-[*te-ni*...][5]

Blood"; Parker, *Miasma*, 104–5.

4. Duplicate: KUB 57.61.

5. Cf. the textual reconstruction in *CHD* Š, 34b. I thank Prof. Jared L. Miller for providing me with photos of this tablet.

I speak [th]us: "You, Sun-Deity of the Sign [...] [I]n that place that you (pl.) have given a sign, now[...] we have smeared that place with blood. *Ju*[*st as*] we have sat[iated] it [...] with *tawal* and *walhi* (beverages), [...]do not mo[ve] the sign that the Dark Earth [has swallowed] from (its) place!"

Despite the fragmentary state of this text and the tentative nature of this reading, we can nevertheless attain a reasonably secure understanding of the purpose of the blood rite, at least according to this priest: Just like the *walhi* and *tawal* libation, the blood that was applied to the site of the omen is intended to quench the thirst of these infernal deities. This text may also hint at an additional theme. The mention of the Dark Earth in l. 30' and the demand not to move the evil from its place in l. 31 may imply that the blood is serving as bait to attract the infernal deities, so that they will take away the evil to the underworld.

A more explicit and detailed treatment of the latter theme can be found in the Ritual for Purifying a House (CTH 446).[6] Although there is no blood-smearing rite in this text, it does contain a blood libation, providing a vivid illustration of the relationship between blood and the infernal deities.

This ritual is intended to remove evil in one of various forms that has taken up residence in a particular house. The text introduces itself as follows:

I
1   [*ma*]-*a-an* É-*ir e-eš-ḫa-na-aš pa-ap-ra-an-*[*na-aš*]
2   *ku-úr-ku-ri-ma-aš li-in-ki-ia-aš pár-ku-nu-wa-*[*an-zi*]
3   *nu ut-tar-še-et ki-iš-ša-an*

When [they] cleanse a house of blood, impurity, threat (or) perjury, their treatment is as follows:

A fuller description of the circumstances and suspicions that necessitate the performance of the ritual are stated upon the arrival of the exorcist priest ([LÚ]AZU) at the house. In order to facilitate communication with underworld deities, he digs pits inside the house at its four corners and at the place of the hearth. He then addresses the Sun Goddess of the Earth:

9   *nu ki-iš-ša-an me-ma-i ták-na-a-aš* [d]UTU-*i ki-i u*[*t-tar*?]
10   *da-aš-ki-u-wa-ni ki-i* É-*ir ku-wa-at tu-ḫa-it-t*[*a*
11   *ša-ra-a ne-pí-ši ku-wa-at ša-ku-eš-ki-iz*[-*zi*]

---

6. Text edition: Otten, "Beschwörung der Unterirdischen." It has recently been translated by Collins ("Purifying a House: A Ritual for the Infernal Deities," in *COS* 1.68:168–71). Cf. also Haas, *Geschichte der hethitischen Religion*, 282–91.

He speaks as follows: "We are taking this m[atter] to the Sun Goddess of the Earth. Why is this house gasp[ing]? Why is it looking up constantly to the heavens?

12 *na-aš-šu* DUMU.LÚ.U$_{19}$.LU *li-in-kat-ta na-aš-ma e-eš-ḫar i[-ia-at]*
13 *nu-uš-ša-an* TÚG *še-ek-nu-uš-ša-an ki-e-da-aš pár-na-aš [ša-ra-a p(í-ip-pa-a-a-aš)]*
14 *na-aš-ma-kán an-da kur-ku-ri-ia-at ku-iš-ki na-aš-ma [(ḫur-za-aš-ta)]*
15 *ku-iš-ki na-aš-ma-kán e-eš-ḫa-aš-kán-za li-in-kán-za an[(-da ú-it)]*

Either a man perjured, or he s[pilled] blood, and he turned his tunic [up] to these houses, or someone has threatened, or someone has cursed. Or a murderer or a perjurer has entered.

16 *[(n)]a-aš-ma-za a-ni-i-e-et ku-iš-ki na-(aš)-ša-an an-da [pa-it?]*
17 *[(n)]a-aš-ma-kán* É-*ri-pát an-da e-eš-ḫar i-ia-an ki-nu-na [(ka-a-aš pár-na-aš)]*
18 *i-da-a-lu pa-ap-ra-tar* NI-IŠ DINGIR-*LIM e-eš-ḫar ḫu-ur-ta-in [(kur-ku-r) a-in]*
19 *e-eš-ḫa-aḫ-ru wa-aš-ta-in ar-ḫa tar-na-ú ta-ga-a-a[n-zi-pa-a(š)]*
20 *ḫu-im-pa-aš* É.ŠÀ-*na-an-za* GUNNI-*an-za* 4 *ḫal-ḫal-du-um-ma-[ri-a(š)]*
21 É*ḫi-i-la-aš* KÁ^{ḪI.A}-*eš ar-ḫa tar-na-an-[du]*

Or someone has performed (witchcraft?) and [entered], or blood has been spilled in the house itself. May this now release the evil, impurity, perjury, blood, curse, threat, tears and sin of the house. May the floor, the (roof?)-beam, the bedroom, the hearth, the 4 corners, the courtyard, and the gates release!

The text identifies a peculiar occurrence, described as the house "gasping" or "looking to the heavens," as portending calamity for the house's owner and the city. Among the possible causes for this situation, the house may have been contaminated either by the presence of a wrongdoer or blood inside of it or by a threat or curse directed towards it.[7]

The ritual centers on an invocation of the underworld deities, here referred to as the Anunnake, which is accomplished in part by the construction of iconic clay daggers. In addition, the priest combines various materials, including silver, gold, iron, and tin to form a statue of the "God of Blood" (II, 70–73). The priest then performs the following rites:

---

7. According to Otten's understanding of I, 12–13, the turning up of the *šeknu* garment is a magical act by which a person transfers evil to another ("Beschwörung der Unterirdischen," 143). For other opinions, see Melchert, "Pudenda Hethitica," 141–45; *CHD* P, 270–71. Cf. also van den Hout, *Purity of Kingship*, 224–25.

III
1   *nu-za-kán* ŠU^{MEŠ}-*ŠU a-ar-ri nu* ^{TU}₇BA.BA.ZA ^{TU}₇*ga-an-ga-ti* [*(da-a-i)*]
2   *nu wa-a-tar ku-it PÚ-az ú-da-aš nu ú-e-te-ni*
3   BAL-*an-ti* EGIR-*ŠÚ-ma-kán* 1 SÍLA A-*e-te-ni-it* BAL-*ti*
4   *na-an ha-at-ta-an-zi nu-uš-ša-an e-eš-har* IM-*aš*
5   *hu-u-up-ri tar-na-a-i na-at e-eš-ha-na-aš* DINGIR-*LIM-ni pí-ra-an*
    GAM-*ta* ME-*i*
6   *nu kiš-an me-ma-i a-a-li-iš ma-am-ma-aš*
7   ^dA.NUN.NA.GE₄ *ki-e-da-ni-iš-ma-aš ud-da-ni-i hal-zi-hu-un*
8   *nu ke-e-el pár-na-aš* DI-*eš-ša-ar ha-an-na-du-ma-ti*
9   *nu-kán ku-it* ḪUL-*lu e-eš-šar an-da*
10 *na-at šu-me-eš da-at-ten na-at e-eš-ha-na-aš* DINGIR-*LIM-ni pí-eš-ten*
11 *na-at kat-ta-an-ta* GE₆-*i ták-ni-i pí-e-da-a-ú*
12 *na-at a-pí-ia tar-ma-ad-du*

He washes his hands. He takes porridge and *gangati* soup. He libates into the water that he has brought from the spring. Afterwards, he libates on 1 lamb with the water and they slaughter it. He lets the blood flow into a clay basin. He places it down before the God of Blood. He speaks as follows: "*āliš mamnaš!* Anunnake, I have invoked you for the matter. Decide the case of this house! The evil blood that is inside, you take it and give it to the Deity of Blood. Let him carry it to the Dark Earth. Let him nail it down there!"

According to the priest's words, the blood libation that is presented in a clay basin serves as an incentive to lure up the "God of Blood." When he comes up to take this physical blood, he is expected to take away also the "bloodstain" that has tainted the house. Since this blood libation seeks to appease the demonic entities and thereby spare the blood of the ritual patron, it should be regarded as a bribe.

The priest then digs an offering pit before the Anunnake and libates *walhi* and *marnuwan* drinks. Using a legal motif, he implores them to decide the case of the house favorably, but thereafter, in a very different tone, reminds them of their demoted status in the divine hierarchy and even threatens them should they fail to comply with his wishes.

On the following day, the priest makes more food offerings. He addresses a triad of deities, Memešarti, the moon god (EN.ZU) and Išhara, who are here approached in their infernal aspect:

IV
1   EGIR-*an šu-wa-an-du-ma-at nu* GE₆-*iš* KI-*aš* [*(la-ga-aš-mi-it)*]
2   *ar-ha e-ep pár-na-aš* URU-*aš e-eš-har wa-aš-túl pa-ap-ra-tar*
3   *NI-EŠ* DINGIR-*LIM* ḪUL-*lu-un* GÌR-*an pa-an-ga-wa-aš* EME-*an*

4 GAM *pa-a-šu*[8]

Push yourselves back! O Dark Earth, restrain their inclination. May it swallow down the blood, sin, impurity, perjury, evil foot, and common gossip of the house and city.

The priest beseeches the deities to let their blood lust be satisfied and control their sadistic desire to inflict punishment. He then petitions the Dark Earth itself to restrain these deities and swallow the evils of the house.

The priest then continues his efforts to appease the infernal deities:

5   *nu* ^{UZU}NÍG.GIG *za-nu-zi na-at ar-ḫa ku-ir-zi* NINDA.GUR$_4$.RA$^!$-*ia*
6   *pár-ši-ia na-at-kán ḫa-at-te-eš-ni še-er da-a-i A-NA* GUNNI-*ia*
7   *da-a-i* GEŠTIN-*ia* BAL-*an-ti nu-kán* DUG KA.GAG NAG *la-ḫu-wa-i*
8   *nu* ^{GI}A.DA.GUR$^{ḪI.A}$ *tar-na-a-i e-ku-zi-ma Ú-UL ku-iš-ki*

He cooks the liver and cuts it up. He breaks thick bread(s). He places them above the pit and on the hearth. He libates wine. He prepares a jug of *piḫḫu* beer for drinking. He leaves straws, but nobody shall drink.

9   *nu te-ez-zi* ^{d}*Me-me-šar-ti-iš* AN-*aš ták-na-aš-ša* ^{d}EN.ZU-[*a*]*š*
10   ^{d}*Iš-ḫa-ra-aš* NI-EŠ DINGIR-*LIM ḫur-ti-ia-aš* UG$_6$-*aš* DINGIR^{MEŠ}
11   *ku-iš kiš-du-an-za ku-iš ka-ni-ru-wa-an-za* DINGIR-*LIM-iš*
12   *nu-za ú-wa-at-ten iz-za-at-ten e-ku-ut-ten nu-mu-kán ḫa*[*r-pí-*]*ia-at-ten*
13   *na-aš-ta* É-*ir-za* URU-*az* ḪUL-*lu p*[(*a-ap-*)]-*ra-tar e-eš-ḫar*
14   NI-EŠ DINGIR-*LIM wa-aš-túl ḫur-da-a-in ar-ḫa p*[(*ár-ku-nu-*)]*ut-ten na-at* GÌR^{MEŠ}-*ŠÚ*
15   ŠU-*ŠÚ iš-ḫi-ia-at-*<*ten*>^{9} *na-at* GE$_6$-*iš* KI-*aš an-da e-ep-du*

He says: "Memešarti of Heaven and Earth, Moon God, Išhara—gods of perjury, curse and blood—every god that is hungry, that is thirsty, come and eat and drink. Join with me and cleanse the house and city from evil, impurity, blood, perjury, sin and curse. Bind (their) feet and hands! Let the Dark Earth keep them in!

Throughout this ritual text, the underworld deities are portrayed as capricious and subject to an overwhelming carnal desire for blood.[10] The exorcist seeks to turn their bloodlust to his own advantage. He urges them to enjoy their feast, but to take the leftover evils home with them to the underworld.

---

8. Text: Otten, "Beschwörung der Unterirdischen," 134.

9. For emendation, cf. II, 8.

10. Regarding the underworld deities as bloodthirsty agents for punishing transgressions, see Collins, "Necromancy, Fertility," 227–29.

Whereas the themes of bribing and baiting the chthonic deities appear here in the context of a blood libation, these tactics are employed in the aforementioned ritual fragment KBo 13.101 in the context of the blood-smearing rite. There the blood was smeared on the place of a portentous omen in order to quench the thirst of underworld deities. These deities were implored to take away the threat to the Dark Earth.

BLOOD AS COMPENSATION

The connection between blood and chthonic deities is insufficient to explain the symbolism of the Kizzuwatnean blood rite in many instances. In particular, we find the blood rite in the context of numerous rituals that appeal to heavenly gods who head the North Syrian pantheon, namely, Tešub and Hebat. Needless to say, these gods are not characterized with the same bloodthirsty attributes as their infernal counterparts. In fact, it was probably considered disrespectful to invite the heavenly deities to blood feasts and thereby treat them in the same cultic manner as the chthonic deities. Not surprisingly, we find in some of these texts hints of a dramatically different rationale, according to which blood serves as a means of compensating a debt to the gods.

As in biblical sources, the Hittite literature indicates a strong conceptual association between blood (*ešḫar*) and the social practice of homicide retribution. Indeed, if the sources quoted in the available Hittite lexicons (in particular *HED* and *HW²*) may serve as a cross-section of Hittite literature as a whole, we observe that the references to blood that are related to bloodguilt drastically outnumber other references to blood, including those in its literal meaning as a physical substance. In particular, we can identify two common idiomatic usages of the term *ešḫar* that appear repeatedly throughout Hittite historical and legal sources. The first is the expression *ešḫar iya-*, literally "to make blood," which refers to the act of murder. The second is the idiom *ešḫar šanḫ-*, literally "to demand blood," which refers to the seeking of compensation for bloodguilt.[11] Based on the prevalence of such idioms, it is clear that the social institutions associated with homicide and its retribution left their imprint on the use of blood as a sign in Hittite society.

In the following sections, I will demonstrate that the social practice of homicide retribution provided the context in which blood became associated with compensation. The preliminary analysis will be divided into two stages. The first section will focus on the use of a metaphor of compensation to describe homicide retribution in early historical sources. This metaphorical notion of

---

11. For these idioms, see Dardano, "'La main est coupable'," 349–53.

compensation is further developed in the later prayers of the Hittite king and queen, which apply this theme to a much broader scheme of transgression and restitution in the context of mankind's relations with the gods. In the subsequent sections, I will explore the notion of bloodguilt as treated in Hittite ritual texts in order to understand its role in relation to the larger framework of Hurro-Hittite notions of evil and expiation. These parallel investigations will shed light on the references to the metaphor of compensation that appear in conjunction with the Kizzuwatnean blood rite.

COMPENSATING BLOODGUILT

Hittite sources from the end of the empire (late-fourteenth—early-twelfth century B.C.E.) reveal a dominant metaphoric scheme that depicts divine retribution in terms of debt and compensation. In the following section, I will argue that this extended metaphorical use of the punishment-as-payback motif originated in the social context of blood vengeance and was later extended to apply to a broader range of transgressions.

The key term for this discussion is *šarni(n)k-* the usages of which include: "to compensate," "make/pay compensation for," "replace," "make restitution for."[12] Its derivative noun *šarnikzil* can be glossed: "compensation," "compensatory damages," "substitutionary payment."[13] As is readily apparent, the usage of these terms is primarily related to tort law. However, in later texts we find a growing tendency to apply these expressions metaphorically, especially in religious contexts as idioms of making atonement with the gods.

In earlier sources, the metaphorical usage of this terminology is found in relation to blood vengeance and to the implementation of the death penalty in a case of conspiracy to murder the king (see below). Already in one of the earliest documents, the Telipinu Proclamation (CTH 19; late-sixteenth century B.C.E.), the gods are depicted as zealous collectors of this debt. A leitmotif of this text is the attribution of Hatti's ills to bloodguilt caused by usurpers of the royal throne. More critical for our investigation than the many references to bloodshed (§§7, 11, 13, 20, 27, 30, 49) is the depiction of the notion of divine vengeance in this document. In numerous passages, Telipinu asserts that the gods "demand the blood" (*ešhar šanh-*) of the murdered party from the murderer and from the Hittite nation, which is collectively guilty, for example:[14]

na-pa DINGIR^MEŠ *at-ta-aš-ša-aš* ^m*Zi-dan-ta-aš e-eš-ḫar-še-et ša-an-ḫe-er*

---

12. See *CHD* Š, 282–86; Haase, *Beobachtungen zur hethitischen Rechtssatzung*, 21–24.
13. See *CHD* Š, 279–81; Haase, *Beobachtungen zur hethitischen Rechtssatzung*, 24–25.
14. Text: Hoffmann, *Der Erlaß Telipinus*, 24. See also I, 42, 66.

The gods demanded the blood of his father, Ziddanta (I, 69–70).

Since the basic meaning of the verb *šanḫ-* is "to seek," many translators have glossed this idiom "sought (revenge for) the blood."[15] Such renderings, which ignore the fact that "blood" serves as the direct object of the verb, obscure the underlying conception, according to which the gods are "demanding the blood" of the victim from the perpetrator.[16] Hence, this expression parallels, syntactically and conceptually, the biblical idiom דר"ש דמים.[17] In other words, the gods are charged with collecting the blood debt, which must ostensibly be paid back in kind.

This text concludes with a set of decrees. These include a rule for homicide, in which the possibility of compensation, denoted by *šarnink-*, is mentioned:[18]

Rev. IV

27   *iš-ḫa-na-aš-ša ut-tar ki-iš-ša-an ku-iš e-eš-ḫar i-e-ez-zi nu ku-it e-eš-ḫa-na-aš-pát*

28   *iš-ḫa-a-aš te-ez-zi ták-ku te-ez-zi a-ku-wa-ra-aš na-aš a-ku ták-ku te-iz-zi-ma*

29   *šar-ni-ik-du-wa nu šar-ni-ik-du* LUGAL-*i-ma-pa le-e ku-it-ki*[19]

The matter of bloodshed is as follows: Whoever commits bloodshed, that which the "lord of the blood" says (will happen). If he says 'He shall die,' let him die, but if he says 'He shall make compensation,' let him make compensation. For the king (there will be) nothing, however.

This edict explicitly states that the murderer's heir (the "lord of the blood") must decide whether or not compensation will come in the form of the perpetrator's death or as monetary compensation.[20] In this passage, *šarnink-* is applied only to the option of monetary compensation, consistent with the concrete legal sense of the term. At the same time, the juxtaposition of blood retribution with mon-

---

15. So van den Hout, *Purity of Kingship*; Hoffmann translates "die Götter forderten (Vergeltung für) das Blut." Even more idiomatically, *CHD* Š, 167–68 translates "to avenge the death (lit. blood)."

16. This point has been noted already by Melchert ("Three Hittite Etymologies," 269).

17. E.g., Gen 9:5; 42:22; Ezek 33:6; Ps 9:13. See also above, p. 175.

18. I understand this edict as stating a general law for murder whose relevance is not restricted to the royal circle. This impression is strengthened by the subsequent law (§50), which deals with "witchcraft in Hattuša" (URU*Ḫattuši alwanzanaš*).

19. Text: Hoffmann, *Telipinu*, 52. Cf. also the translation of van den Hout, "The Proclamation of Telipinu," in *COS* 1.76:198.

20. The final line of the passage probably means that the king receives no share from the compensation payment (Westbrook, *Biblical and Cuneiform Law*, 49–50). Alternatively, according to Hoffner (*Homicide*, 311), the king will have no role in the decision.

etary compensation provides clear indication of the manner in which the notion of "compensation" could be attributed also to the former. In fact, we find in the Telipinu Proclamation itself the application of *šarnink-* to the administration of the death penalty (§31; see below).

An additional early source that may apply the terminology of compensation (*šarnink-*) to the taking of blood vengeance can be found in the account of Muršili I's (ca. 1620–1590 B.C.E.) military expedition against Aleppo:

Obv. II

10' [*nu ANA* KUR ^{URU} *Ḫal-p*]*a pa-it nu-za ŠA A-BI-ŠU*
11' [*ešḫar* EG]IR *ša-an-aḫ-ta*
12' [*nu-uš-ši* ^{m}*Ḫa-at-tu-š*]*i-* DINGIR-*LIM-iš ku-it*
13' [*waštul ŠA* KUR (?) ^{URU}]^{U} *Ḫa-la-ap a-ni-ia-u-wa-an-zi pa-iš*
14' [*na-at-*(*ši* LUGAL)] KUR ^{URU}*Ḫa-la-ap šar-ni-ik-ta*[21]
15' [*nu* L(Ú^{MEŠ} KUR ^{URU}*Ḫu*)]*r-la-aš-ša*
16' [KUR.KUR^{MEŠ} *ḫu-u-m*]*a-an-da ḫar-ni-ik-ta*

He (Muršili) set out [against Aleppo] to demand his father's [blood]. The [transgression? of] Aleppo that Hatušili gave to him to handle, [22] the king of Aleppo made compensation [for it] to him. [And], he destroyed [a]ll [of the lands] of the Hurrians. (KBo 3.57 + KUB 26.72).

Despite the fragmentary state of the text, it is clear that Muršili's campaign was to execute retribution on Aleppo for a prior insubordination.[23] Since the context is severely damaged and the reconstruction of line 13' uncertain,[24] we cannot rule out the possibility that the sense of *šarnikta* in l. 14' is that the king of Aleppo was forced to pay tribute.[25] However, since the subsequent lines of

---

21. Transcription and reconstruction: S. de Martino, *Annali e Res Gestae antico ittiti* (StMed 12; Pavia: Italian University, 2003), 194–97. Cf. the discussion by Steiner, "Aleppo Vertrag," 16–20. For additional literature, see de Martino, *Annali e Res Gestae*, 189–90.

22. As pointed out by Steiner ("Aleppo Vertrag," 19, n. 37), since l. 14' changes the subject to the king of Aleppo, there is some awkwardness in interpreting *kuit* in a causal sense. Accordingly, he interprets *kuit* as the indefinite pronoun for neutrum accusative, which in his reconstruction anticipates *uttar* in l. 13'. De Martino accepts this reasoning and applies it to his reconstruction *waštul* (*Annali e Res Gestae*, 107, n. 570). The latter approach has been adopted here.

23. This understanding is further supported by the reference to the transgressions of Aleppo against Hattušili I at the beginning of the treaty between Muwattalli II and Talmi-Šarumma of Aleppo (KBo 1.6 Obv. 20).

24. For references to other proposed reconstructions, see de Martino, *Annali e Res Gestae*, 196, n. 565.

25. So Steiner, "Aleppo Vertrag," 19, 24. Cf. de Martino, *Annali e Res Gestae*, 197 and n. 572.

this text, as well as other documents,[26] attest to Muršili's destruction of Aleppo, this interpretation seems unlikely. A more probable interpretation is indicated by the generally accepted reconstruction *ešḫar* in line 11',[27] which implies that the people of Aleppo were responsible for the death of Hatušili.[28] Accordingly, the "compensation" mentioned in line 14' must refer to Muršili collecting his father's blood debt in kind. According to this reconstruction of the passage, we find once again the correspondence between the idiom of "demanding (the victim's) blood" (*ešḫar šanḫ-*) and the verb *šarnink-*.

The metaphorical usage of *šarnink-* and *šarnikzil* was greatly expanded in texts from the end of the Hittite empire. In particular, these terms appear in prayers that seek to persuade the gods that the "debt" incurred by the intrigues and misdeeds of previous rulers has already been "repaid." In these sources, the petitioner, invariably either the king or queen, assumes that the present adversity stems from divine punishment for some transgression, usually that of a preceding generation.[29]

For example, Hattušili III seeks to avoid retribution for the sin of banishing Queen Danuhepa[30] in the following appeal:

II
10   ... *nu-kán ma-a-an* ᵈUTU ᵁᴿᵁ*A-ri-in-na* GAŠAN-*YA*
11   *A-NA* [INIM ᶠ]*Da-nu-ḫé-pa še-er* TUKU.TUKU-*iš-ta ku-it-ki*
12   *nu a-pa-a-at-ta-ia ut-tar ŠA* ᶠ*Da-nu-ḫé-pa i-ia-a*[*t k*]*u*[*-iš*
13   *nu-za a-pa-a-aš-ša* DINGIR-*LIM-iš ka-ru-ú ki-ša-at*[   ]
14   *na-aš-kán* KASKAL-*az ar-ḫa ti-ia-at*
15   *na-at IŠ-TU* SAG.D[U-Š]*Ú ka-ru-ú pa-ra-a šar-ni-ik-ta*
16   *nu* ᵈUTU ᵁᴿᵁ*A-ri-in-*[*n*]*a* GAŠAN-*YA ŠA* ᶠ*Da-nu-ḫé-pa ut-tar*
17   *am-me-el* U₄^{ḪI.A}-*aš am-mu-uk A-NA* KUR ᵁᴿᵁ*Ḫa-at-ti-ia*

---

26. See also Telipinu Proclamation §9 (Hoffmann, *Der Erlaß Telipinus*, 18–19). In KBo 3.27 30'–31', it is reported that Hattušili commanded his son Muršili to destroy Aleppo.

27. For references, see de Martino, *Annali e Res Gestae*, n. 564. Steiner's first objection to this reconstruction, that the preverb *appan* does not appear in conjunction with *ešḫar šanḫ-*, cannot be sustained (cf., e.g., KUB 14.14+ Rev. 21'). His second objection, that we have no clear evidence that Hatušili's was killed in a confrontation with Aleppo, depends on the reconstruction of the present text. See Steiner, "Aleppo Vertrag," 18–19, n. 36.

28. This conclusion was drawn (with varying levels of conviction) by several scholars. See Klengel, *Geschichte Syriens*, 149; Astour, "Hattušiliš, Halab, and Hanigalbat," 107; Wilhelm, *Grundzüge der Geschichte und Kultur der Hurriter*, 31; Kempinski, *Syrien und Paläestina*, 49–52.

29. For Muršili II's First Plague Prayer, which shows continuity with the earlier notion of compensating blood debt, see below.

30. For discussion of this incident, see van den Hout, *Purity of Kingship*, 44–53; Singer, "Danuḫepa and Karunta," 739–52.

18   *me-na-aḫ-ḫa-an-da* EGIR-*pa le-e* [*ḫ*]*u-it-ti-ia-at-*[*ti*]
19   *a-pé-e-ni-iš-šu-wa-an ut-tar am-mu-uk* [*me-n*]*a-aḫ-ḫ*[*a-an-da*]
20   *am-me-el* U₄ᴴᴵ·ᴬ-*aš* EGIR-*pa ḫu-it-ti-ia-u-wa-an-z*[*i*]
21   *Ú-UL a-ra-a-an ŠA* ᶠ*Da-nu-ḫé-pa-ma ut-tar* [*ku-iš*]
22   *pa-ra-a i-ia-at ka-ru-ú a-pa-a-aš-pát šar-ni-ik-t*[*a*]

If the Sun Goddess of Arinna, my lady, became angry in any way over the [matter] of Danuhepa, that one who carried out that matter of Danuhepa has already become a god (i.e., he died). He stepped off of the road and has already paid for it himself. O Sun Goddess of Arinna, my lady, do not drag up again the matter of Danuhepa against me and the land of Hatti in my days. To drag up again such a matter against me in my days is not right. The one who carried out the matter of Danuhepa, that same one has already made compensation himself.[31]

In this prayer, as in others, the death of the perpetrator is portrayed as "making compensation" for the misdeed.

The statement that the perpetrator has "paid for it himself (lit. 'with his head'" (*IŠ-TU* SAG.DU-*ŠÚ para šarnikta*), which appears here and elsewhere is a clear borrowing from earlier legal traditions.[32] This idiom is already found in the Telipinu Proclamation (§31) in reference to a crime demanding the death penalty, apparently conspiracy to murder the king.[33] Thus, the notion of forfeiting one's life as a compensation for sin in later Hittite prayers seems to be a metaphorical extension of earlier legal traditions associated with homicide. This development may be viewed as part of a general Hittite tendency to portray their relationship with the gods in legal terms.[34]

---

31. CTH 383; KUB 21.19+. Text: Sürenhagen, "Zwei Gebete Hattušilis," 92; Translation adapted from Singer, *Hittite Prayers*, 98–99.

32. This translation takes SAG.DU-*ŠU* as serving a reflexive adverbial function, meaning "himself" (see *HW*² H 355; Dardano, "'La main est coupable'," 358–66; cf. R. Westbrook and R. D. Woodard, "The Edict of Tudhaliya IV," *JAOS* 110 [1990], 645). This sense is incontrovertibly demonstrated by Puduhepa's use of this idiom in reference to herself in KUB 21.27+ (quoted below), which could hardly refer to her having "paid with her head."

33. For the text, see Hoffmann, *Der Erlaß Telipinus*, 34. For references to discussion regarding the interpretation of this passage, see van den Hout, *COS* 1.76:197, nn. 54–55.

34. For example, they employed the terminology of presenting an argument before court (*arkuwai-*; *arkuwar*) to refer to their prayers, in which they plead their case before the gods (see *CHD* Š, 286). For this term and the underlying conception of prayer, see Singer, *Hittite Prayers*, 5–11. Incidentally, a parallel metaphorical conception underlies the Hebrew expression for prayer, התפלל. Derived from the root פל״ל whose *piel* usages reflect a sense of judgment, the *hitpael* form in numerous instances preserves a sense of advocating a person in judgment (see, e.g., Gen 20:7; Num 11:2; 1 Sam 2:25; Job 42:8).

In late oracle texts, we find a somewhat different but related notion in which an expiatory offering is called *šarnikzil*:

Rev. III
43 *nu kiš-an* DÙ-*an-zi* EME ᶠᵈIŠTAR-*at-ti A-NA* DINGIR^{MEŠ} [LUGAL-*UT-TI*]
44 *pí-ra-an ar-ḫa a-ni-ia-an-zi* GIDIM-*ia ša-ra-a*
45 *a-še-ša-nu-wa-an-zi šar-ni-ik-ze-el-la* ME-*an-zi*
46 *na-at A-NA* GIDIM SUM-*an-zi*...[35]

They will do as follows: They will remove the curse (lit. "tongue") of Šaušgatti from before the gods [of kingship]. They will set up (icons of) the dead. They will take the compensation and give it to the dead.

In this passage, a ritual is prescribed for removing curse from objects associated with the kingship. Although the nature of this ritual remains obscure,[36] it seems to involve the presentation of gifts or offerings as compensation (*šarnikzil*) to the offended dead (represented by icons). A similar usage is expressed in a prayer of Queen Puduhepa to the Storm God of Zippalanda:

IV
35' ...DINGIR-*LUM-mu* EN-*YA*
36' *ke-e-da-ni me-mi-ni ka-ri ti-ia ḫar-na-a-u-aš-za ku-it* MUNUS-*za*
37' *A-NA* DINGIR-*LUM* EN-*YA še-er* S[AG.D]U-*za šar-ni-in-kán ḫar-mi*
38' *nu-mu-kán* DINGIR-*LUM* EN-*YA A-NA* ᵈ[IŠKUR] *A-BI-KA* Ù *A-NA* ᵈUTU URUTÚL-*na*
39' *u-wa-a-i-nu-ut*...

O God, my lord, accede to this matter. Since I am a woman of the birth stool,[37] and to God, my lord, I have personally made restitution, O God, my lord, intercede on my behalf with [the Storm God], your father, and the Sun Goddess of Arinna![38]

Here the term *šarnikzil* seems to apply to a votive offering intended to propitiate the gods.

---

35. CTH 569; KBo 2.6+KBo 18.51. Text: Hout, *Purity of Kingship*, 210.
36. See van den Hout, ibid., 236–37.
37. For this expression, see Beckman, *Hittite Birth Rituals*, 233–34 and Singer, *Hittite Prayers*, 101.
38. CTH 384; KUB 21.27+. Text: Sürenhagen, "Zwei Gebete Hattušilis," 118; Translation: Singer, *Hittite Prayers*, 105.

Although *šarnink-* and *šarnikzil* are the primary terms expressing compensation, a similar metaphorical usage pertains to other terms as well, such as *maškan-* ("bribe"; "propitiatory gift") and *zankilatar* ("fine"; "penalty"). Regarding *maškan*, the textual evidence draws a clear distinction between its secular legal usage and its application to relations with deities. Its usage in legal contexts is confined to the sense of "bribe" and refers to an illegitimate gift seeking to win the other party's favor. In contrast, its usage in religious contexts bears no pejorative connotation, referring to offerings and propitiatory gifts to the gods. The textual attestations indicate that the metaphorical usage of this term in relation to the religious sphere is later and, by implication, derivative of the legal usage.[39]

In summary, Hittite sources from the end of the empire demonstrate a growing tendency to conceptualize the religious notions of sin and atonement in terms of the legal metaphor of compensation for damages. This tendency is manifested most clearly in the use of *šarnink-, šarnikzil* and related terms in prayers and oracle records.

In the case of *šarnink-/šarnikzil,* the lexical evidence indicates a diachronic development in which the religious metaphorical usage emerged later than its legal usage. This diachronic distinction raises the question whether the debt–compensation scheme for guilt and atonement was a purely intralinguistic semantic development or if it stems from the infiltration of Hurrian ideas (see following section), whose profound religious influence on the royal theology of the Empire period is well-known. Although this metaphor is quite appropriate and might be assumed to be a natural semantic development, intercultural comparison indicates that this notion cannot be simply taken for granted. Indeed, the ubiquitousness of the metaphor in the Hittite prayer and oracle texts must be contrasted with the absence of such a metaphor in the Mesopotamian literature.[40] In this light, the emergence of such a prevalent theological conception among the later monarchs of the empire may in fact indicate Hurrian religious influence.

---

39. Interestingly, the difference between the usage of *maškan* in these text genres finds expression not only in this semantic distinction, but even in orthography. In legal instructions, the lemma appears as *ma-aš-ka-an,* but in religious contexts as *maš-kán.* This difference seems to stem from the relative age of these sources. More precisely, it seems that the shortened form reflects its origin in divinatory texts which tend to employ abbreviated formulas. See *CHD* L–N, 209–10 for the evidence.

40. To my knowledge, the only comparable idiom in Akkadian is *gimilla turru,* literally ("to return the favor"), which is used to describe divine vengeance in some literary texts (*CAD* G, 74–75; T 272). However, this idiom lacks the economic connotations of *šarnink/šarnikzil.* Cf. also the term *mullû* ("compensatory payment") in Neo-Babylonian texts in the usage "to give somebody his full desert," but both cases cited by *CAD* M, 190 refer to a human seeking vengeance, not a god.

BLOODGUILT AND EXPIATION IN THE HURRO-HITTITE RITUAL CORPUS

In the Hittite ritual texts, the term *ešḫar* is used to signify bloodguilt and appears alongside concepts such as impurity (*papratar*) and perjury (*NĪŠ ILIM*). These concepts are depicted as dangerous entities that threaten the well-being of the ritual patron until they are removed. The prominence of these terms in the Kizzuwatnean literature indicates that they reflect a dominant set of concerns held by the Hurrians of southern Anatolia. This impression is further supported by Hurrian incantations that have been integrated into the *itkalzi* Ritual.[41] In these incantations, blood (*zurki*) is listed along with various types of evil, including *arni* ("sin"),[42] *parili* ("crime")[43] and *azuzḫi* ("rage").[44] In these sources, blood is treated as one of several types of depersonalized evil that pose a threat to the ritual patrons.

In the ritual texts, blood is depicted as a type of force that resides in a particular object, which is discernable only by the gods and wields danger in a latent form, reminiscent of the invisible bloodstain on Lady Macbeth's hands. The profound anxiety that these texts express regarding the possibility of bloodguilt is remarkable. It may perhaps stem from a general anxiety that the common procedure of compensating bloodguilt monetarily is insufficient in many cases to remove the stain.[45]

Although bloodguilt appears as one among many types of evil threatening the ritual patron in the ritual texts, there are clear indications that it nevertheless maintained a unique status. A useful illustration can be found in the ritual for purifying a house described above (pp. 211–15). Throughout this ritual text, we find numerous lists of the kinds of evils that the exorcist seeks to banish. Though the items in these lists are more-or-less fixed, there are some variations. The most common items are blood (*ešḫar)*, impurity (*papratar)*, threat (*kurkurimaš)*, perjury *(linkiaš)*, curse *(ḫurtiaš)*, tears (*išḫaḫru*), and sin (*waštul*). These lists vary in length; from one to seven types of evil are mentioned at a given time. A comparison of the items on each list reveals the fact that the sin of bloodshed receives

---

41. See Laroche, "Études de Linguistique Anatolienne," 97–98.

42. A derivation of the Akkadian term *arnu*. See *HW²* A, 328; Giorgieri, "Schizzo grammaticale," 198.

43. See *CHD* P, 154–55. Haas offers the translations "Anstoss, Ärgernis." (*Die hurritischen Ritualtermini*, 237).

44. See KUB 29.8 II 41, IV 13, 20 (=*ChS* I/1 no. 9, p. 93, 99); KBo 8.154 6–7 (= *ChS* I/1 no. 38, p. 38); KUB 32.24+ II,19, II,12' (=*ChS* I/1 no. 20, p. 168). For the derivation of *azuzhi*, see Janowski and Wilhelm, "Religionsgeschichte des Azazel-Ritus," 157–58.

45. An examination of the Hittite laws of homicide is beyond the scope of this discussion. See Hoffner, *Laws of the Hittites*, 165; "Homicide in Hittite Law," 293–314 for references and discussion.

more attention than the others. Blood appears in all of the lists, excluding one ostensible exception where "evil tongue" is singled out.[46] This observation is particularly significant in light of the fact that, in many cases, only two or three evils are mentioned, yet blood is always mentioned. Moreover, in three passages "evil blood" is singled out as the main evil.[47] Thus, this text seems to portray bloodguilt as the prototypical evil. Although several factors may contribute to granting bloodguilt this unique status, the most important of these is probably the profound concern regarding the threat of unplacated blood.

Another factor distinguishing bloodguilt from the other forms of evil described in the ritual text pertains to its manner of expiation. As noted above, the Hittite ritual corpus depicts bloodguilt as a form of depersonalized danger that poses a threat to the ritual patron in a way analogous to curses, black magic, and violated oaths. However, unlike these other forms of evil, bloodguilt was associated with a clearly defined dynamic for restitution, namely, that of blood compensation, in kind or monetarily. It would not be surprising, therefore, to find this dynamic applied by analogy to these other forms of evil. What we would then expect to find would be a transition from the specific notion of *compensating bloodguilt* to a more generalized notion of *expiation*. Such a development would parallel the expanded usage of the metaphor of compensation (*šarnink-*) from the context of blood vengeance in early historical documents to its more generalized usage in the prayers from the later monarchs. This rationale, I submit, is implicit in the depiction of the Kizzuwatnean blood rite as compensation.

THE BLOOD RITE AND COMPENSATION

In his First Plague Prayer, Muršili II (ca. 1321–1295 B.C.E.) refers explicitly to the performance of a "ritual of blood" (*išḫanaš* SISKUR) as a means of atoning for his father Šuppiluliuma's murder of Tudhaliya the Younger.[48] In Muršili's view, it is Tudhaliya's blood that plagues Hatti:

Obv.
33   *... nu-kán ú-wa-at-ten* DINGIR[MEŠ EN^MEŠ-*YA*]
34   *a-pu-un A-WA-AT* ^m*Du-ud-ḫa-li-ia* DUMU-*RI A-NA A-BI-YA ki-nu-un ap-pé-ez-z*[*i*

---

46. The lists are followed in the following sections: §§ 1, 5–6, 8, 9, 13, 15, 21, 25, 30, 38, 40, 42, 44, 45, 46, 48 and 50 (barely preserved). The exceptional case is §46, but even this follows an instance in §45 where blood is singled out. Section numbers (absent in Otten's transcription) follow Collins' translation (*COS* 1.68:168–71).

47. §§ 8, 30, 45.

48. For the background of this episode, see Bryce, *Kingdom of the Hittites*, 168.

35 *an-da ša-an-ḫa-at-ten nu-kán A-BU-YA IŠ-TU ŠA* ᵐ*Du-ud-ḫa-li-ia iš-ḫa-*
   na-[az ak-ta A-NA A-BI-YA-ma]
36 *ku-e-eš* DUMUᴹᴱˢ.LUGAL *BE-LU*ᴹᴱˢ PA LÚᴹᴱˢ *LI-IM* LÚᴹᴱˢ
   DUGUD *an-da ki-ša-an-da-at nu a[-pu-u-uš-ša a-pé-e-ez]*
37 *me-mi-ia-na-az a-kir A-NA* KUR ᵁᴿᵁ*Ḫat-ti-ia-kán a-pa-a-aš-pát*
   me-mi-aš a-ar-aš nu KUR [ᵁᴿᵁ*Ḫat-ti-ia a-pé-e-ez]*
38 *me-mi-ia-na-az ak-ki-iš-ki-u-an ti-i-[ia]-at*

But you came, O gods, [my lords], and have now taken vengeance on my father
for this affair of Tudhaliya the Younger. My father [died (?)] because of the
blood of Tudhaliya, and the princes, the noblemen, the commanders of the thou-
sands, and the officers who went over [to my father], [they] also died because of
[that] affair. This same affair came upon the land of Hatti, and the people of the
land of [Hatti] began to perish because of [that] affair.[49]

Muršili has no doubt that the country is facing divine retribution for the murder
of Tudhaliya. In fact, an oracle inquiry had already confirmed his suspicion that
Tudhaliya's bloodstain evoked the wrath of the gods (Rev. 14'–16').

Lest we take Muršili's words to be a mere figure of speech, the continuation
of the prayer shows that the concept of bloodguilt must be understood literally:

Rev.

8'   …*[n]u A-BI-YA ku-[it*
9' [ᵐ*Du*]*-ud-ha-li-ia-an* [. . . . .] *nu-za A-BI-YA a-pád-da-an* EGIR[*-an-*
   da
10' [*nu*] *iš-ḫa-na-aš* SISKUR [*i-ia-at* ᵁᴿᵁ*Ḫ]a-ad-du-ša-aš-ma-za Ú-UL ku-it-*
   ki [*i-ia-at*]
11' [*ú-w*]*a-nu-un-ma-za* X [*iš-ḫa-na-aš* SISKUR] *am-mu-uq-qa i-ia-nu-un*
   KUR*-e-an-za-ma*
12' [*Ú-UL*] *ku-it-ki i-ia-[at Ú-UL-ma-kán A-NA*] KUR*-TI ku-it-ki še-er i-e-er*

[Because] my father […] Tudhaliya [and…], my father therefore [performed]
afterwards the ritual of blood for himself. But [the land of] Hatti did not [per-
form] anything for itself. I [ca]me along and performed [the ritual of the blood],
but the land did [not] perform anything. They did nothing [on behalf] of the
land.

---

49. CTH 378.1; KUB 14.14+. Text and reconstructions generally follow Goetze, *Klein-*
asiatische Forschungen, 164–77. Translation adapted from Singer, *Hittite Prayers*, 61–64; cf.
also G. Beckman, "Plague Prayers of Muršili II," in *COS* 1.60:156–58; van den Hout, "Muršili
II's 'First' Plague Prayer," 259–63.

Muršili here states that both his father, Šuppiluliuma, and himself performed the blood ritual (*išḫanaš* SISKUR) in order to remove the bloodguilt from the royal line.

In addition to this rite, appeasement needed to be brought on behalf of the nation:

21' DINGIR^MEŠ *BE-LU*^MEŠ-*YA ŠA* ^m*Du-ud-ḫa-li-ia ku-it e-eš-ḫar* EGIR-*an ša-an-ḫa-at*[-*te-ni*]

22' *nu-kán* ^m*Du-ud-ḫa-li-ia-an ku-i-e-eš ku-en-nir nu e-eš-ḫar a-pu-u-uš šar-ni-in*-[*ki-ir*]

23' *nu* KUR ^URU*Ḫa-at-ti-ia a-pa-a-aš iš-ḫa-na-an-za ar-ḫa nam-ma zi-in-ni-e*[*š-ta*]

24' *na-at* KUR ^URU*Ḫat-ti-ia ka-ru-ú šar-ni-ik-ta...*

Because you, O gods, my lords, [have] taken vengeance for the blood of Tud-haliya, those who killed Tudhaliya [have made] restitution for the blood. But this bloodshed is finished in Hatti as well: Hatti too has already made restitution for it.

As in other passages throughout this text, we find here the idiom *ešḫar šanḫ-* in reference to the gods demanding payment for Tudhaliya's spilled blood from Šuppululiliuma's progeny and the land of Hatti as a whole. But we also find *šarnink-* to express the idea that the blood debt has already been repaid, specifi-cally, by the death(s) of the perpetrator(s) and by means of the "ritual of blood."

It is very possible that the expression *išḫanaš* SISKUR refers to the same blood rite that is referred to in the Kizzuwatnean corpus either by the Hurrian term for blood, *zurki,* or by the verb *ešḫarnuma-*.[50] From the mid-fifteenth cen-tury B.C.E. on, the Hittite official religion was increasingly being influenced by Hurrian traditions, including the integration of Hurrian deities into the national pantheon and the use of Hurrian ritual techniques. By the time of Muršili II, this influence was already well-established.

The identification of the "ritual of blood" referred to by Muršili with the procedure described in the Kizzuwatna corpus finds support in the use of similar

---

50. So already Haas, *Geschichte der hethitischen Religion*, 291, who treats the identifica-tion as self-evident. The choice to use the Hittite term can be explained on various grounds. First of all, whereas the Kizzuwatnean texts originated and received their primary form in the strongly Hurrian region of Kizzuwatna, this prayer most probably was composed by either Muršili or the royal scribes of Hattuša. Thus, we might expect a preference for Hittite idioms. Furthermore, the use of the Hittite term serves a powerful rhetorical role in emphasizing the catastrophic effects of violent succession on the country, thereby echoing the Telipinu Procla-mation.

terminology in the Papanikri Ritual. Recall that, after the performance of the blood rite, we find the following declaration:

Obv. I

41 *ma-a-an-wa* AMA-*KA na-aš-ma A-BU-KA ap-pé-ez-zi-az*
41 *ku-it-ki wa-aš-ta-nu-wa-an ḫar-kán-zi na-aš-ma-wa zi-ik*
43 *ka-a pa-ra-a ḫa-an-da-an-ni na-aš-ma za-aš-ḫi-it ku-it-ki*
44 *wa-aš-ta-nu-wa-an ḫar-ta nu ḫar-na-a-uš ḫu-u-ni-ik-ta-at*
45 GIŠGAGḪI.A-*ma-wa du-wa-ar-na-ad-da-at ki-nu-na-wa*
46 *ka-a-ša* DINGIR-*LUM* 2 TÁ.ÀM *šar-ni-ik-ta*[51]

"If your mother or father have committed some sin in the end, or you have just committed some sin as a consequence of divine intervention or in a dream, and the birth stool was damaged or the pegs were broken, O divinity, she has made atonement for her part two times."

Strikingly, the Papanikri Ritual employs the term *šarnink-* to convey the notion of expiating sin. Taking this passage by itself, we might find it puzzling that the gesture of bloodying birth stools could be deemed a form of "compensation." This problem is compounded by the recognition that this ritual, like others, appeals to the storm god Tešub and his consort Hebat. These heavenly deities, unlike those of the underworld, were not conceived as capricious blood hounds, whose anger could be swayed by sating their blood thirst. However, in light of the symbolism of blood debt and compensation as elucidated by the historical texts, there remains no difficulty. Just as transgressions were conceived as debts for which the gods could exact payment in the form of the perpetrator's blood, so too, the symbolic gesture of offering blood could serve as a payment to remove guilt.

BLOOD AS AN AGENT OF PURIFICATION

An additional scheme reflected in the ritual texts involves the purification of an object by means of the blood rite. An example is the blood rite using two birds in the birth ritual KUB 9.22+, analyzed above (ch. 3). The first bird is slaughtered, providing the blood to be smeared on the birth stool. A purificatory function is indicated by the appearance of the Hurrian term *itkalzi*, which signifies "purity," in conjunction with this rite (II, 19). Based on duplicates of the text, it would seem that the second bird is taken to a crossroad, where it is offered to chthonic deities. If this reconstruction is correct, then the ritual dynamic would seem to be

---

51. Text: Strauß, *Reinigungsrituale aus Kizzuwatna*, 288.

as follows: The blood of the first bird serves cathartically to remove the impurity, which is then transferred to the underworld by means of the second bird.

Most of the attestations of the *zurki* rite aim to remove some form of evil, for example, curse, sin, or impurity, from the locus of the blood rite and/or the ritual patron. Since there is no hint in many of these sources indicating the underlying dynamic by which the evil is removed, the term "purification" could be used as a general category to encompass these rituals. At the same time, we must keep in mind the inadequacy of such labels for understanding the Hittites' understanding of the ritual activity, a problem to which we will return below.

BLOOD AS AN AGENT OF CONSECRATION

A unique understanding of the blood rite can be found in Night Goddess' Cult Expansion Ritual, discussed above (p. 32):

IV
38   ...*nu* DINGIR-*LUM* GUŠKIN *ku-ut-ta-an* Ú-*NU-TE*MEŠ
39   ꜥŠAꜣ [DINGIR-*L*]*IM* GIBIL *ḫu-u-ma-an e-eš-ḫar-nu-ma-an-zi*
40   *nu* DINGIR [GIBI]L É DINGIR-*LIM-ia šu-up-pé-eš-zi*...[52]

The golden deity, the wall, and all of the equipment of the new deity they smear with blood. He sanctifies the new deity and the temple.

As noted above, this passage employs the verb *šuppeš-*, which can be glossed "purify" or "sanctify." Unlike the vast majority of examples that refer to the removal of some evil force, this passage seems to imply that blood endows the sancta with a positive quality or force. It seems that this passage in particular has captured the imagination of modern scholars who have sought to interpret the purificatory power of blood in Hittite ritual as stemming from the belief that it carries life force. For example, Haas proposes "Da nach allgemeiner Ansicht im Blut die Lebenskraft ruht, liegt der Gedanke entsühnender oder regenerierender Blutriten nahe. Sie können mithin ubiquitär entstanden sein."[53] In a similar vein, Beckman writes, "On the basis of what we have already rehearsed here about the Hittite conception of blood, I suggest that the ancient Anatolians felt they were imparting a vivifying quality to the objects and locations that they daubed with this liquid."[54] Although these statements fit the above-cited passage, it is doubt-

---

52. Text: Miller, *Kizzuwatna Rituals*, 296–97.

53. Haas, "Ein hurritischer Blutritus," 68.

54. Beckman, "Blood in Hittite Ritual," 101. I thank Prof. Beckman for sharing a draft of this article before its publication. In the earlier part of this article, Beckman cites numerous sources that connect loss of blood with death. Since these sources deal with the negative conse-

ful that they can be used as a unified theory to explain the use of blood in the Kizzuwatnean *zurki* rite.

MAKING SENSE OF THE INTERPRETIVE SCHEMES

In light of the preceding, it seems that modern interpretations of the rite are much more unified than those of the Hittites. In this investigation, we have identified no fewer than four distinct interpretive schemes, according to which blood may serve as a propitiatory gift or bribe to chthonic deities, a currency of compensation, an agent of purification, and an agent of consecration.

An attempt to align the various sources with these different schemes is included as an appendix at the end of this chapter. Of these schemes, the life-force theory proposed by Haas and Beckman fits only the last of these. The first two schemes involve either the propitiation of deities or the expiation of an offense committed against the deities. The third scheme, purification, refers to the removal of evil, not the transference of a positive quality such as "life force."

However, we must not content ourselves merely by recognizing the multiplicity of ancient interpretations for the rite. We may probe further, asking: Is it possible to understand more fundamentally the relationship between these schemes? Can any process of conceptual development be detected that may allow us to determine which of these is primary and which is secondary?

A first step towards addressing these questions involves reexamining the distinction between the concepts of "propitiation" and "expiation,"[55] which can be viewed as alternative perspectives on a given conflict. As explained above, "propitiation" involves approaching the conflict in personalized terms, in which one seeks to appease the anger of the offended party. "Expiation" approaches the problem in a depersonalized manner, viewing the offense as an objectified wrong, whereby guilt can only be removed by redressing the offense.

As stated above (pp. 223–24), the Hittite ritual texts, especially those of southern Anatolian (Kizzuwatnean) origin, tend to address adversity in a variety of depersonalized and seemingly mechanistic forms. As suggested above in reference to the biblical notion of bloodguilt (pp. 183–84), such types of depersonalized and mechanistic forms of evil are the result of a tendency towards "reification." As a result of this tendency, various personalized schemes of sin and punishment are depicted as involving depersonalized and mechanistic

---

quences of blood loss, not its alleged positive metaphysical power, they can hardly provide an explanation for the ritual use of blood as an agent of expiation and purification. See following section for further discussion.

55. See above, p. 173.

process of retribution. As I have shown elsewhere,[56] a similar tendency can be found in the depiction of oaths in Mesopotamian and Hittite texts, reflecting a transition from viewing the gods as guaranteeing compliance with oaths to viewing the oaths as autonomous agents capable of enforcing themselves. As is readily apparent in relation to both bloodguilt and oath violation, one of the main factors contributing to the mechanization of retribution is the belief in the direct cause–effect relationship between a transgression and its punishment.

The upshot of this discussion is that the notions of propitiation and expiation should not be viewed as diametrically opposed. Rather, they coexist along a continuum:

Means of Redressing Evil

Propitiation	Expiation	Purification

◄──►

Personalized   **Objectified**

Conceptualization of Evil

As illustrated by this diagram, the means by which rituals seek to remove evil are directly related to the manner in which the evil is conceptualized. In a case of a transgression against the subjective will of a deity, the ritual patron seeks to propitiate the angry god. In the Hittite texts, this notion is expressed in concrete terms in the form of invitations to the relevant gods (usually chthonic) to eat an offering. Alternatively, if the sin is treated as an objective reality, that is, it not only offends a deity but also assumes some form of real existence, then it must be removed by expiation. As shown above, this conception is expressed by the terminology of "compensation" (*šarnink*). Finally, if the evil is itself an offensive force or substance that must be removed, but does not involve an offense against a god, then the removal may be understood as purification, expressed by terms such as *šuppi* ("clean," "holy") and *parkui* ("pure, clean") with their verbal derivatives. Despite the existence of such conceptual distinctions, their application to a given practice was not always exclusive. Indeed, the Hurro-Hittite blood rite could be interpreted in terms of all three of these schemes—propitiation, expiation, and purification—even in the same text.

At this point it is worth noting that the categories "propitiation," "expiation" and "purification" correspond to distinct phases in the lexical development of the verbal forms of Hebrew כפ״ר. In our investigation of the usages of כפ״ר, it was determined that the primary sense of "propitiation" gave way to the objectified notion of "expiation" in the context of blood retribution. In turn, our diachronic

---

56. See Feder, "Mechanics of Retribution."

analysis of the sin offering texts demonstrated the secondary nature of the notion of purging sancta, expressed by the formula כִּפֶּר אֶת (with a direct object). This latter phase represents the transition from the sense of "expiation" to that of "purification." Interestingly, all of these conceptions that are expressed in the lexical development of כפ"ר can already be found in the varying conceptions of the blood rite in the Hittite evidence. However, in the latter case, the various schemes are not expressed by means of a unified terminology. One might say that all of the interpretive possibilities that were latent in the blood rite found their linguistic fruition in the senses of Hebrew כפ"ר and the corresponding biblical interpretations of the sin offering.

Can any of these schemes be identified as the original motivation for the blood rite? In theory, the three categories (propitiation, expiation, purification) are sufficiently similar to allow any one to develop from any other, thus precluding any definitive determination of originality. Nevertheless, certain considerations militate for regarding the scheme of "blood as compensation" as the original.

First of all, by logical induction, we might assert that the "blood as compensation" scheme would seem less likely to develop from either of the others. As noted above, since blood libations are appropriate only for infernal deities, it is doubtful that the ritual practitioners would extend this practice secondarily to the heavenly gods. On the other hand, if the "blood as compensation" scheme is original, one could easily understand why the rite would be adapted to the notion of bribing the chthonic deities. Similarly, one could understand how an act of expiation performed by smearing blood on an object could be reinterpreted as a cathartic act of purification. However, it is less probable to expect a purificatory use of blood to be reinterpreted in light of the more complex theological scheme of debt and compensation. However, when dealing with the development of ritual traditions, such logical considerations cannot be conclusive taken by themselves.

Second, by classifying the Hittite ritual texts in relation to their place of origin and school of tradition, we may attain some clarity regarding the influences involved in the various rationales. Among the texts whose state of preservation allows such a classification, we may identify at least two distinct groups, namely, texts originating from the priestly circles of Kummanni,[57] and

---

57. The following birth rituals that contain the blood rite can be associated with this group: the Papanikri Ritual (CTH 476), KUB 9.22+ (CTH 477.H), Bo 4951 (CTH 477.J), KBo 17.65+ (CTH 489). Beckman has noted the commonalities between this group of texts (*Hittite Birth Rituals*, 98, 149). To these birth rituals we should add the Ritual of Ammihatna, Tulbi, and Mati (CTH 472).

texts associated with the cult of the Night Goddess of Šamuha[58]

Although these schools shared ritual traditions and are often grouped together as a singular unified "Kizzuwatnean" corpus, distinct traditions can be identified that are peculiar to one or the other of these circles. Most prominently, texts that originated from the Kummanni circle tend to focus on the divine couple Tešub and Hebat, whereas the Šamuha texts generally refer to the Night Goddess and Pirinkir. Furthermore, Strauß has identified several traditions that seem to be more regular in the Šamuha texts.[59]

Further justification for differentiating between these two schools of ritual tradition can be found in the considerable geographic distance between Kummanni and Šamuha, even granting a measure of uncertainty regarding the exact location of both sites. Regarding Šamuha, Müller-Karpe and others have argued for an identification of the city with Kayalıpınar on the upper Kızılırmak (Halys River), near Sivas.[60] Although the city Kummanni has been commonly identified with classical Comana in the Anti-Taurus, identified with the remains in the village of Şar,[61] a new consensus seems to be emerging that locates Kummanni further south, perhaps on the slopes of the Amanus.[62] According to Miller's calculation, the distance from Kummanni to Šamuha would be anywhere from 160 km to 300 km, depending on whether the former or latter location of Kummanni is preferred.[63]

A possible objection to this distinction between the ritual traditions of Kizzuwatna and Šamuha can be raised based on KUB 32.133. According to this text, Tudhaliya I (ca. 1425—1385 B.C.E.) replicated the Kizzuwatnean cult of the Night Goddess in Šamuha, which would imply that the Night Goddess cult of Šamuha is based entirely on Kizzuwatnean traditions. In fact, many scholars have inferred that the Cult Expansion Ritual KUB 29.4+ refers to this very event.

---

58. Regarding the rituals that include the blood rite, this group would include the Šamuha Ritual (CTH 480), the Cult Expansion Ritual (CTH 481), and the Walkui Ritual (CTH 496).

59. Strauß, *Reinigungsrituale aus Kizzuwatna*, 189–97.

60. See Müller-Karpe, "Kayalıpınar in Ostkappadokien," 363–64;Wilhelm, "Noch einmal zu Šamuha," 885–90.

61. See *RGTC* 6/2, 84.

62. The most forceful advocate of the latter opinion is Trémouille ("Kizzuwatna, terre de frontière," 59–78). This view has found further support in two recently discovered documents, RS. 94.2406 and Kp 05/226. For these, see, respectively, Bordreuil and Pardee, "Ougarit-Adana, Ougarit-Damas," 115–25 and Wilhelm, "Die hurritischsprachige Tafel Kp 05/226," 233–36. See also Forlanini, "Geographica Diachronica," 269–70.

63. Miller, *Kizzuwatna Rituals*, 358 and n. 508. Miller notes that these distances would be 220+ km and 320+ km for those who locate Šamuha on the Karasu tributary of the Euphrates.

Thus, one might assume that the ritual traditions of these two locations were virtually identical.

However, this inference is highly problematic. Aside from the questionable identification of Tudhaliya's cult expansion with that of KUB 29.4+,[64] one cannot disparage the influence of local traditions, even assuming that the Night Goddess cult of Šamuha originated in Kizzuwatna. Strikingly, the explicitly stated motivation for composing the ritual text KUB 32.133 is to combat the changes made by the priests of Šamuha to the Night Goddess' cult! This purpose is laid out clearly in its introduction:

1   *UM-MA* ᵈUTU-*ŠI* ᵈ*Mur-ši*-DINGIR-*LIM* LUGAL.GAL DUMU ᵐ*Šu-⸢up⸣-pí-lu-li-um-ma* LUGAL.GAL UR.SAG

2   AB.BA-*YA-za-kán ku-wa-pí* ᵐ*Tù-ut-ḫa-li-ia-aš* LUGAL.GAL DINGIR GE₆ *IŠ-TU* É DINGIR GE₆

3   ᵁᴿᵁ*Ki-iz-zu-wa-at-ni ar-ḫa šar-ri-i-e-et na-an-za-an I-NA* ᵁᴿᵁ*Ša-mu-ḫa*

4   É DINGIR-*LIM ḫa-an-ti-i i-ia-at nu-za ḫa-az-zi-wi₅-ta iš-ḫi-ú-li*ᴴᴵ·ᴬ-*ia ku-e*

5   *I-NA* É DINGIR GE₆ *kat-ta-an ḫa-ma-an-kat-ta ú-e-er-ma-at-kán* LÚ.MEŠDUB.SAR.GIŠ

6   LÚᴹᴱˢ É DINGIR-*LIM -ia wa-aḫ-nu-uš-ke-wa-an da-a-ir na-at* ᵈ*Mur-ši*-DINGIR-*LIM-iš*

7   LUGAL.GAL *tup-pí-ia-az* EGIR-*pa a-ni-ia-nu-un* {erased sign} *zi-la-du-wa ku-wa-pí*

8   *I-NA* É DINGIR GE₆ ᵁᴿᵁ*Ša-mu-ḫa ma-a-an* LUGAL *na-aš-ma* MUNUS. LUGAL *na-aš-šu* DUMU.LUGAL

9   *na-aš-ma* DUMU.MUNUS.LUGAL *I-NA* É DINGIR GE₆ ᵁᴿᵁ*Ša-mu-ḫa ú-iz-zi nu ke-e*

10   *ḫa-az-zi-wi₅-ta e-eš-ša-an-du*

Thus (says) His Majesty, Muršili, Great King, son of Šuppiluliuma, Great King, Hero: When my forefather, Tudhaliya, the Great King, split the Night Goddess from the temple of the Night Goddess in Kizzuwatna and worshipped her separately in a temple in Šamuha, those rituals and obligations that he ordained for the temple of the Night Goddess, the wood tablet scribes and the temple personnel came and began to incessantly alter them. I, Muršili, Great King, have

---

64. For example, Miller has pointed out that the timescale of the latter text, which seems to assume a distance of a one to two day journey between the old and new temples, is incompatible with the large distance between Kizzuwatna and Šamuha (*Kizzuwatna Rituals*, 357, with references to earlier research). This discrepancy raises the possibility that the Cult Expansion Ritual preserves a later adaptation of the *type* of ritual performed under the tutelage of Tudhaliya I, which may have been subject to additional local influences and ritual traditions. For his part, Miller prefers the alternative possibility that the Cult Expansion Ritual is of Kizzuwatnean origin and served as the prototype for Tudhaliya's performance.

reedited them from the tablets. Whenever in the future, in the temple of the Night Goddess of Šamuha, either the king, the queen, prince or princess come to the temple of the Night Goddess of Šamuha, these shall be the rituals.[65]

In light of this testimony, no further evidence is needed to demonstrate that the traditions of Kizzuwatna took on a life of their own when transplanted to Šamuha, placed at the mercy of the local scribes and cult personnel. Indeed, it is doubtful that Muršili's reactionary measures were of avail.

This distinction between the ritual traditions of Kummanni and Šamuha is crucial for determining the relationship between the various rationales for the blood rite. In texts representing the Kummanni circle, we find examples of both the compensation and purification schemes. In comparison, the Šamuha rituals involve the notion of blood as a gift to the chthonic deities, using blood to summon up deities from rivers and ritual pits. At the same time, as noted above, the Cult Expansion Ritual also involves an instance where blood is portrayed as an agent of purification/sanctification. Nevertheless, it is remarkable that, not only within the same text, but even in the same passage, the blood rite appears in conjunction with the digging of a ritual pit.

Consequently, one may infer that the notion of an expiatory/purificatory blood rite caused some confusion among the ritual experts of Šamuha who reinterpreted it in light of their traditional chthonic blood rites. A similar localizing tendency seems to underlie the use of fish for the *zurki* rites in these texts, by which they adapted the Kizzuwatnean tradition to the local custom (see above, p. 16). It seems that the relatively large geographical distance between Šamuha and the North Syrian origin of these traditions had its effect. In this context, it is worth noting that the Šamuha corpus reveals a well-preserved body of Mesopotamian traditions, which may have arrived by way of a channel other than that of North Syria, such as via Mittani.[66] Thus, indigenous traditions possibly in conjunction with Mesopotamian influence seemed to have left their imprint on the understanding of the blood rite in these texts.

---

65. Obv. I 1–10. Text and translation: Miller, *Kizzuwatna Rituals*, 312–13, with adaptations.

66. Miller finds several indications of an accurate written Mesopotamian legacy in the Cult Expansion Ritual. In light of the assumption that the primary channel for such traditions would be North Syria, he views this evidence as reflecting a Kizzuwatnean source for the text (Miller, *Kizzuwatna Rituals*, 367–69). While this may be correct, we should not view Kizzuwatna as an exclusive channel of Mesopotamian influence. Indeed, Strauß has shown that certain Mesopotamian ritual traditions appear unique to, or at least more pronounced in, the Šamuha texts, which lends support to the possibility that Mesopotamian ideas may have also been transmitted through a Mittanian channel (Strauß, *Reinigungsrituale aus Kizzuwatna*, 191–215).

Aside from these two ritual schools, we may refer also to the depiction of the blood rite in the foundation ritual KBo. 15.24+. As noted above, among numerous other themes manifesting clear Mesopotamian influence, the blood rite was reinterpreted in light of the Mesopotamian practice of smearing blood on foundation stones as a means of placating underworld deities for invasion of their territory (see above, p. 26). This text provides clear evidence for the adaptation of the ritual tradition to fit local conceptions.

In light of these considerations, we should ascribe priority to the Kummanni traditions regarding the blood rite. As such, the theme of propitiating chthonic deities should be understood as a secondary development, leaving the compensation and purification schemes as viable options.

At this point, we must address the inadequacy of some of our theoretical distinctions. In theory, we may distinguish between the notions of compensation (= expiation) and purification on the basis of their underlying metaphors. Whereas the former refers to an act of restitution to remove guilt, the latter pertains to an act of washing to remove defilement. In practice, the Hittites conflated these two notions, as they both pertain to the removal of an objectified form of evil. For instance, the Papanikri Ritual, which seems to be based on the rationale of compensation, includes the following statement after the ritual sequence involving the blood rite (I, 47): "Then the ritual patron shall be pure again" (*nu BĒL* SÍSKUR *parkuiš namma ešdu*), thereby employing the terminology of cleanliness. Thus, despite the fact that the Papanikri Ritual explicitly seeks to appease divine anger as caused by a transgression, it does not abstain from using the terminology of purification. Such considerations indicate that the distinction between the schemes of "compensation" and "purification" does not apply to the Hittite conception of the blood rite. Rather, we should include both of these notions in the category of expiation, that is, the removal of an objectified form of evil, including offenses against the gods, by means of a mechanistic process.

In summary, in the foregoing analysis, we have found that the various rationales given to the Hurro-Hittite blood rite essentially boil down to two main traditions: the notion of blood as compensation and the use of blood as a bribe to chthonic deities. The scheme of compensation was found to be more characteristic of the Kizzuwatnean tradition, thus indicating that it is probably more original in its association with the *zurki* rite. As in the analysis of the relation between blood and the terminology of expiation (כִּפֶּר) in the Bible, the association of blood and compensation *(šarnink)* in Hittite literature was traced back to the dynamics of blood retribution in which the gods were viewed as demanding the blood of the perpetrator. In this context, blood serves the function of appeasing divine anger and removing guilt. As embodied in the *zurki* rite, this compensatory function of blood was appropriated for the sake of making expiation for various transgressions and eliminating threats to the patient. This broad application of the notion of compensation finds support in Hittite literary sources that show a growing use of a metaphor of debt and compensation to depict the notions of sin and atonement.

THE COMPENSATION THEME IN HITTITE AND BIBLICAL SOURCES

These converging lines of evidence based on the independent study of the biblical and Hittite sources can now provide the grounds for a more generalized integrated reconstruction, expressed in the following terms: The blood rite apparently emerged in Syria or southern Anatolia at a time no later than the Late Bronze Age. The symbolism of the blood rite is an expression of the unique notion of bloodguilt among the inhabitants of this region. According to this belief, violently spilled blood can only be appeased/compensated by that of the perpetrator. Neglect of the obligation to avenge the blood entailed collective punishment on the society. In light of the mechanistic notion of action and consequence assumed by this notion of bloodguilt, the blood rite emerged as a ritualistic means of expiating a diverse array of similarly mechanistic forms of evil.

The underlying conception on which this reconstruction is based, namely, the belief in profound metaphysical ramifications associated with spilled blood, finds support in an additional unique parallel that connects the Hittite literature and the Bible. As was recognized long ago, the revised version of §6 of the Hittite Laws bears a striking resemblance to the ritual described in Deut 21:1–9. In the older law §6, we find the law regarding the liability of a property owner on whose land a person has been killed:

KBo 6.2 I
7   *ták-ku* LÚ.U₁₉.LU-*aš* LÚ-*aš na-aš-ma* MUNUS-*za ta-ki-i-ia* URU-*ri a-ki ku-e-la-aš ar-ḫi a-ki*
8   1 ME ᴳᴵˢ*gi-pé-eš-šar* A.ŠÀ *kar!-aš-ši-i-e-ez-zi na-an-za da-a-i*[67]

> If a person, man or woman, is killed in another city. (The victim's heir) shall deduct 100 *gipeššar* from the land of the person on whose property the person died and take it for himself.

This law ascribes liability to the owner of the property and requires that he pay to the kin a fixed compensatory payment of 100 *gipeššar* (= 3 acres).[68] Hoffner

---

67. Text edition: Hoffner, *Laws of the Hittites*, 20.

68. If converted to silver, this payment would have an approximate value of 8.25 shekels (Hoffner, ibid., n. 19, based on §183).

suggests that the large payment may be based on the assumption that the victim is a merchant, who bore a very high status in early Hittite society.[69]

The late Hittite recension of this law (IV) contains significant elaborations:

KBo 6.4 I

9   *ták-ku* LÚ-*aš da-me-e-da-ni* A.ŠÀA.GÀR *an-da a-ki ták-ku* LÚ *EL-LAM*

10 A.ŠÀA.GÀR É 1 MA.NA 20 GÍN KÙ.BABBAR-*ia pa-a-i ták-ku* MUNUS-*za-ma* 3 MA.NA KÙ.BABBAR

11 *pa-a-i ták-ku* Ú-*UL-ma* A.ŠÀA.GÀR *dam-me-el pé-e-da-an*

12 *du-wa-an* 3 DANNA *du-wa-an-na* 3 DANNA *nu-kán ku-iš ku-iš* URU-*aš an-da*

13 SIxSÁ-*ri nu a-pu-u-uš-pát da-a-i ták-ku* URU-*aš* NU.GÁL *na-aš-kán ša-me-en-zi*

If a person is killed on another's property, if (the victim) is a free person, (the owner) shall give the property, the house and 1 mina and 20 shekels of silver. If it is a woman, he shall give 3 minas of silver. If it is not (private) property (but) an uncultivated place, 3 *danna*s in each direction (is measured), whatever city is determined, (the heir) takes the same [payments]. If there is no city, he forfeits (his claim).

The first section of the amended law deals with a case where a body is found on someone else's private property. If the victim is a free male, his heirs are entitled to the property and house of the landowner as well as one mina and twenty shekels of silver. If the victim is a woman, they are entitled to three mina. These sums are much higher than those of §§1–4, which deal with killing committed in the heat of anger or by accident. Thus, the high payment in the late recension would seem to imply that it is meant to compensate for intentional murder. More precisely, if we will entertain the possibility that the payment served an expiatory function (an assumption that will be strengthened below), one may suggest that the high fee is intended to make expiation for the *possibility* that the killing was premeditated. We should note in passing, that the responsibility of payment that falls on the property owner does not necessarily imply that he is the prime suspect. More likely, it reflects the belief that unatoned blood will inevitably invoke retribution on the owner of the property on which it is found, akin to the Deuteronomic laws cited above.[70] A similar idea is also expressed in the introduction to the Hurro-Hittite ritual for the purification of a house, cited above, where it

---

69. Hoffner, ibid., 172; idem., "Homicide in Hittite Law," 300 with references.

70. Rofé is on the right track with his recognition that the stringency of these laws is motivated by religious considerations ("עגלה ערופה," 132). However, his view that the Hittites conceived of the sanctity of their land in such a way that ownership was nullified by the blood shed on it is not convincing.

is stated that either the entrance of a murderer to the house or the occurrence of murder inside the house may have left behind the bloodstain that demands retribution (I, 15–17).

The latter half of this prescription addresses a case where a person has been killed in the open country. The law requires that the authorities take a measurement to determine whichever city is the closest to the body. The city that is implicated by this procedure must provide the monetary compensation.[71]

In summary, the Hittite Laws impose a high level of liability on the property owner on whose land a body is found. The primary concern of these rules is not the appeasement of the heirs, as is demonstrated by the case of a body found on uncultivated land, in which revenge is not applicable. Rather, it would seem that the compensatory payments serve to make expiation for the spilled blood and protect the property owner from divine retribution.

Similar considerations seem to find expression in a correspondence between the Babylonian monarch Kadašman-Enlil II and the Hittite king Hattušili III (ca. 1267–1237 B.C.E.). In response to a complaint of the Babylonian ruler that his merchants are being murdered in Hittite territory, a claim that apparently included a demand to impose capital punishment on the perpetrators, Hattušili III responds that the Hittite practice is to extract a monetary compensation instead.[72] The text continues:

> [aš]-ra ša na-pu-ul-tu₄ i-na ŠÀ-šu di-ku ul-la-lu

> They purify the [pl]ace in which the person was killed.

Since the terminology of "purity" is applied to judicial innocence in both Akkadian and Hittite,[73] some commentators have understood the "purification" mentioned here as an accompanying ritual act or exculpatory oath.[74] However, it is equally possible that the compensatory payment serves to exonerate the place

---

71. I understand the expression *nu apuš=pat dai* ("he will take those same ones") as an anaphoric reference to the payments that are stated in the case where the body is found on someone's property. For a survey of translations and discussion, see Hoffner, *Laws of the Hittites*, 174; "Homicide in Hittite Law," 304.

72. CTH 172; KBo 1.10+. Text: Klengel, "Mord und Bußleistung," 190; Hagenbuchner, *Korrespondenz der Hethiter*, 285, 291–92. English translations: Beckman, *Hittite Diplomatic Texts*, 136; H. A. Hoffner Jr., *COS* 3.31:52.

73. Hoffner ("Homicide in Hittite Law," 305) suggests that despite the fact that the D form of *elēlu* employed here refers generally to cleansing rituals (see *CAD* E, 81–82), the Hittite scribes may have had in mind their own *parkunu-* which applies to both ritual and legal contexts (*CHD* P, 172–73). A closer semantic parallel to the latter term is the D of *ebēbu* (see *CAD* E, 5–7).

74. See Hoffner, "Homicide in Hittite Law," 305.

where the murder took place. In any case, we must not be deceived by the Hittite practice of employing monetary means of compensating bloodguilt into thinking that the goal was merely social stability; a central factor underlying the laws is the fear of the supramundane ramifications of unatoned blood.

The similarities between the Hittite law and Deut 21:1–9 in circumstances and procedure are striking. They both address a situation where the conventional remedies for blood retribution are not applicable, threatening the community at large with retribution. At this point, the texts diverge: Whereas the Hittite law prescribes a solution based on its prevailing system of economic compensation, Deut 21 requires expiation by means of a ritual reenactment of the murder, in line with the Bible's rejection of monetary compensation for bloodguilt.

The parallism between these sources may not be coincidental. First of all, we should recognize that there is little evidence for a concern with the danger posed to the community by unatoned blood in Mesopotamian documents.[75] This fact seems to indicate that this phenomenon was particular to the eastern Mediterranean. Second, the additions to the Hittite Laws were composed at a period when the Hittite kingdom was profoundly influenced by the religious traditions of the Hurrians based in southern Anatolia and northern Syria. Although one would need to identify signs of Hurrian influence in other additions to the laws in order to prove this conjecture definitively, the possibility must nevertheless be taken into consideration. Third, these ideas correspond to beliefs regarding bloodguilt that are well-attested in Ugaritic and Hittite sources from the Late Bronze Age and early biblical sources.[76] Among the latter is 2 Sam 21, which attributes these ideas to the pre-Israelite residents of Canaan. As a result, we are well advised in viewing the beliefs associated with expiating bloodguilt as part of a cultural continuum that spanned the Levant from Anatolia through Canaan.[77]

The recognition of a common belief regarding the dynamics of bloodguilt and retribution is an issue of central importance to our investigation of the blood ritual. Indeed, our investigation of the motivation of the blood rite in biblical and Hittite sources leads to the conclusion *that the mechanistic conception of blood retribution and its corresponding expiation is the native context for the expiatory use of blood.* It is this set of beliefs, peculiar to the inhabitants of the Levant in

---

75. Although §24 of the Laws of Hammurabi states that the city must make restitution in a case when the murderer is not apprehended, there is no indication that the concern is anything but financial. See Barmash, *Homicide in the Biblical World*, 106–15

76. See Rofé, "עגלה ערופה," 135–38; Zevit, "'eglâ ritual," 389.

77. The existence of this common belief supports Singer's proposed notion of the "Levantine Crescent" as a distinct cultural sphere encompassing the eastern Mediterranean (see his review of review of *Religionsgeschichtliche Beziehungen* in *JAOS* 117 [1997]: 604).

the Late Bronze Age that was transmitted to both the Hurrian priests of southern Anatolia and to the Israelite priesthood.

APPENDIX: THE RATIONALES OF THE BLOOD RITE ACCORDING TO TEXT

WELL-PRESERVED TEXTS[78]

Text		Deity	Purpose	Scheme
Papanikri	KBo 5.1+	H	Expiate Sin/Appease Divine Anger	C
Mursili's Prayer	KUB 14.14+	H	Expiate Sin/Appease Divine Anger	C
Birth Ritual H	KUB 9.22+	H	Remove impurity/evil	P
Birth Ritual K	KBo 17.65+	H	Remove impurity/evil	P
Ammihatna, Tulbi, and Mati	KBo 23.1+	H	Defilement of Temple	P
Muwalanni Ritual[79]	KBo 11.2+	H	?	P?
Šamuha Ritual	KUB 29.7+	C/H?[80]	Remove curse	P
Walkui's Ritual	KBo 32.176	C/H?	Remove impurity, Expiate sacrilege	P
Foundation Ritual	KBo 15.24+	C	Placate chthonic deities	G
Cult Expansion of Night Goddess	KUB 29.4+	C/H?	Attract deity from underworld	G

78. Bibliographical references are provided here only for sources not discussed previously. The order of items reflects an attempt to group similar texts together, as pertains to the deities involved and rationale

79. R. Lebrun, "Rituels de Muwalanni," 47.

80. Since the Night Goddess seems to dwell in the Earth by day and assume an astral aspect by night, she manifests both chthonic and astral characteristics (cf. Miller, *Kizzuwatna Rituals*, 390–93). Since the *zurki* rites appear in conjunction with drawing her out of a river or pit, the former seems more relevant for interpretation.

" "		C/H?	Consecrate sancta	S
Ritual of Sun God	KBo 13.101+	C	Placate chthonic deities	G

FRAGMENTARY TEXTS[81]

Text	Deity	Function	Scheme
KUB 17.8+[82]	H?	Remove Impurity/Evil	P
IBoT 3.148[83]	H	Remove Impurity/Evil	P
Birth Ritual J[84]	H?	Remove Impurity/Evil	P
CTH 783[85]	C?	Remove sickness	P
KBo 35.151+[86]	H	Remove Impurity/Evil	P
CTH 705[87]	H	Remove Impurity/Evil	P
CTH 701c[88]	H		
KBo 29.3+[89]	H	Remove Impurity/Evil	P

Key:

Deity: H= Heavenly; C= Chthonic

Scheme: C= Compensation; P= Purification; G= Gift to Chthonic Deities; S= Sanctification

---

81. Due to the fragmentary nature of these texts, their classification in these various categories is much less certain than the well-preserved documents.

82. *ChS* I/9, 100–101.

83. Ibid., 108, 110, 116.

84. Beckman, *Hittite Birth Rituals*, 124–27. This text is similar to Birth Ritual K, but is noteworthy for its explicit reference to stillbirth. Ritual O (ibid., 206–7) mentions the *uzi* and *zurki* rites, but does not inform us otherwise regarding its rationale.

85. Ibid., 161.

86. Ibid., 202.

87. *ChS* I/3–2, 247–50.

88. *ChS* I/9, 156–57.

89. Starke, *Die keilschrift-luwischen Texte*, 98–100.

7

TRACKING THE BLOOD RITE TRADITION:
ORIGINS, TRANSLATION, AND TRANSFORMATION

This chapter will attempt to join some of the loose ends left from the foregoing analyses of the historical and semiotic development of the Hurro-Hittite and biblical blood rites. From the historical perspective, it will raise the question of the original ethnic or geographical provenance of these traditions. In addition, it will address the ramifications of this study for understanding the prehistory of the Priestly sources of the Bible. Subsequently, we will investigate the transmission and translation of the biblical sin offering rituals to later Jewish and Christian tradents with a focus on the contribution of this ritual tradition to later metaphoric notions of sin and expiation.

More fundamentally, this chapter will shed new light on the profound role of ritual in the evolving discourse of a culture. Needless to say, ritual is not a static object that is passed from one culture to another, or one generation to the next. Needless to say, even if the ritual activity is more-or-less fixed, it is subject to a process of continual reinterpretation in light of its changing cultural context. But the crux of this chapter's argument is quite different than these rather banal observations. Ritual should not be viewed as being redundant—whether as a posterior enactment or aesthetic adornment—to the pre-existing verbally articulated beliefs of a culture. Rather, ritual plays an active role in the construction and shaping of cultural discourse.

THE SYRIAN ORIGINS OF THE BLOOD RITE

When surveying the scattered pieces of evidence that pertain to the early history of the blood rite, one cannot easily arrive at a clear cultural–ethnic attribution. From the Kizzuwatnean provenance of the Hittite evidence, there is no question that the rite was transmitted to the Hittites by means of Hurrian tradents from southern Anatolia or northern Syria. But did the custom originate among the Hurrians, or was it perhaps adopted from the Semitic inhabitants of Syria?

Based on the existing evidence, it seems that the most promising basis by which this question could be resolved would be linguistic. Recalling the evidence for a similar rite as part of the *zukru* festival from Emar, a possible approach to answering these questions consists of viewing the Hurrian term *zurki* as etymologically related to the Syrian ritual term *zukru(m)*, on the assumption that one of these terms has undergone metathesis. Such a connection finds support in the recognition that the anointment of the *sikkānnu* stones with blood and oil in the Emar ritual could be taken as the climactic moment of the procession, which would justify the naming of the complex ritual after the blood rite.[1] If such a linguistic connection could be determined, the relationship between them could reveal the cultural origin of the blood rite.

In order to evaluate these possibilities, we must also consider pertinent sources from Mari that ostensibly refer to this rite. Several sources from Mari employ the idiom *zukram...nadānum* ("to give/offer...the *zukru*") in the context of offerings that King Zimri-Lim of Mari (eighteenth century B.C.E.) should perform for Addu, the storm god of Aleppo. This formula appears also in the Emar texts, which supports the inference that the latter is a continuation of the same ritual tradition.[2] It is important to note that the *zukrum* is mentioned here as a demand of the Amorite leadership of Yamḥad, relating it to the cult of Addu of Aleppo, which would indicate a provenance in western Syria. Interestingly, these references from Emar and Mari are the only sources for *zukru(m)* in Akkadian.[3]

Scholars have yet to find a convincing explanation for the meaning of the term *zukru* based on its probable Semitic cognates. Basing himself on the Mari evidence alone, Dossin derived the term from the common Semitic root *zkr*, arriving at the translation "un ensemble d'animaux males."[4] However, such an understanding seems to be negated by the detailed offering lists of the Emar rituals that do not identify the sex of the animals and even incorporate ewes for the central *kabadu* offerings.[5] Alternatively, Fleming has argued for a derivation from the root *zkr* 'to name, mention,' suggesting to translate *zukru* as "invocation" or "spoken offering."[6] Although Fleming has found abundant evidence for a relationship between invocation of gods and cultic acts in various cultures of

---

1. Fleming (*Time at Emar*, 76–77) uses the expression "the main event" to refer to the series of activities that takes place at the stones, which includes a feast, the anointment of the stones and the driving of Dagan's statue between the stones.

2. For a survey of these sources, see ibid., 113–21.

3. Cf. *AHw*, 1536; *CAD Z*, 153.

4. See G. Dossin's translation and comments in Lods, "Une tablette inédite de Mari," 104–6; cf. also Lafont, "Les prophètes du dieu Adad," 11.

5. See Fleming, *Time at Emar*, 122–23, n. 321.

6. For arguments to support the latter, see ibid., 121–26

the ancient Near East, he is unable to find reference to any such activity in the *zukru* ritual texts themselves.

At first glance, this etymological gap could be filled by assuming a Hurrian origin for the term, that is, a *zurki* → *zukru* borrowing. In the absence of a satisfying Semitic derivation, we might be justified in appealing to the Hurrian *zurki*. Such a derivation could provide a meaningful sense to the formula *zukram... nadānum,* which could be glossed as "to offer the blood." Such an understanding is more consistent with the sacrificial contexts of these references than an obscure "spoken offering."

However, this proposal also has its weaknesses. Aside from the need to assume a metathesis, the differences in scribal conventions regarding the rendering of Hurrian and Akkadian in the cuneiform script prevent a simple equation of the phonetic values. In particular, there exists significant ambiguity regarding the Hurrian phonetic values reflected by the set of cuneiform signs for sibilants. Regarding the orthographical conventions for rendering Hurrian at Mari and Emar, the Zv signs are understood to reflect /s/ or perhaps allophonic /z/, which would yield a reconstructed /su/ or /zu/.[7] In comparison, Hittite scribes consistently used Zv to represent the affricate /ts/, yielding /tsu/.[8] If the Hittite scribes had intended to render /su/, we would expect them to employ the ŠU sign. Conversely, if the scribes of Mari and Emar had intended to render the affricate /tsu/, we would expect them to use ṢU, not ZU. The final syllable is no less ambiguous. Despite the consistent orthographic rendering *zu-ur/úr-ki,* the final KI sign may reflect the voiced allophone /gi/, yielding /tsurgi/. Due to such ambiguities involved in the relationship between the cuneiform orthography and Hurrian phonology, the argument for a *zurki* → *zukru* loan is quite tenuous. As a result, the assumption that *zukru(m)* is based on the common Semitic root *zkr* seems much more probable.[9]

The arguments for a Semitic origin, that is, a *zukru* → *zurki* borrowing are more substantial. Metathesis of this type is fairly well attested in Hurrian, though most prominently in the Nuzi dialect.[10] This derivation would also find

---

7. See Wegner, *Hurritische: Eine Einführung,* 37, 40; Giorgieri, "Schizzo grammaticale," 185–86, n. 43–44. Wilhelm does not include /z/ in his phonemic inventory of Hurrian ("Hurrian," 98).

8. See Hoffner and Melchert, *Grammar of the Hittite Language,* §1.90–91 (37–38).

9. Fleming views the *zukru* festival as reflecting an indigenous Syrian tradition ("Ritual from Emar," in Chavalas and Hayes, *New Horizons,* 59).

10. Interestingly, the Nuzi dialect of Hurrian frequently inverts the sequence consonant + liquid, especially when the initial consonant is a fricative; e.g., *faġri→farġi, šadna→šanda.* See Wilhelm, "Hurrian," 101; cf. Giorgieri, "Schizzo grammaticale," 195. For the final –i, cf. loans such as *arnu* (Akk.) → *arni* (Hur.) where the Hurrian nominal suffix is used (ibid., 198–99).

support in certain factors that indicate a Semitic origin for the blood rite (see below). However, this suggestion is also problematic, since the Hurrian term also appears elsewhere where it apparently refers to "bloodguilt."[11] In order to sustain the hypothesis of a Hurrian borrowing, one needs to posit a semantic restriction in the latter in which the term *zurki* (from *zukru*) acquired the limited sense of "blood."[12]

At this point, we may turn to some non-linguistic considerations. On one hand, a "Hurrian" attribution of the rite seems problematic. Such a label implies a Pan-Hurrian promulgation of the practice, but there is no evidence for the *zurki* rite outside of the Hittite texts of Kizzuwatna.[13] On the other hand, while the references to *zukru(m)* from Mari and Emar raise the possibility of a Semitic origin, such a conclusion is not inevitable. In particular, one should note that the Mari references are of unclear meaning and that the known ritual texts from Ugarit do not mention this rite.

From the foregoing, it appears that conventional tools of analyis lead to an impasse regarding the origins of the blood rite. Under these circumstances, we may raise the possibility that the solution to this *historical* question may ultimately lie in the analysis of the symbolism of these rites presented above. Specifically, if the reconstruction of the original symbolic motivation of the blood rite is correct, then there may be grounds for asserting that the biblical evidence, despite its later date of composition, demonstrates a clearer awareness of the related conception of bloodguilt. In other words, although Hittite sources also show an awareness of a notion of compensating (*šarnink-*) blood with blood, this conception finds clearer expression in the biblical sources that depict the ancient idea that the land polluted with blood will invoke collective vengeance. As argued above, such a notion seems to underlie the late addition to §6 of the Hittite Laws, whose parallel in Deut 21:1–9 might indicate that the former is a result of growing North Syrian influence on Hittite beliefs. Although such arguments amount to no more than circumstantial evidence, they provide some support for

---

11. KUB 29.8+ (ChS I/1, Nr. 9) Obv. II 41; Rev. IV 12–15, 20–22. See Haas and Wilhelm, *Riten aus Kizzuwatna*, 64; Strauß, *Reinigungsrituale aus Kizzuwatna*, 93 and n. 354.

12. For an alternative derivation, one might also compare two offering terms derived from *sarāqu* ("to scatter, sprinkle"): 1) *surqinnu*, attested in NB and SB (*CAD* S, 408); 2) *sirqu*, attested in OB, Boğazköy, SB, and NB (*CAD* S, 317–18). Although the existence of *sirqu* attestations from Boğazköy might ostensibly strengthen the possibility of a connection, this term seems to refer to an offering of foodstuffs. Furthermore, one could not easily account for vocalic transition from $i \rightarrow u$ in the hypothetical *sirqu* $\rightarrow$ *zurki* borrowing. Since neither of these terms is found in connection with a blood rite, we cannot assume any connection to the *zurki*.

13. Such ambiguity pertains to many, if not most, practices that are attributed to the Hurrians in modern research. See Trémouille, "La religion des Hourrites," 279, 291.

the assumption that the blood rite is indigenous to Syria (and perhaps Canaan), rooted in the indigenous notions of bloodguilt and its expiation.

Regarding the lines of transmission by which the Israelites received this tradition, numerous possibilities present themselves, dependent primarily on how one explains the origins of the Israelites and their arrival/emergence in Canaan. Since Semites and Hurrians occupied both Syria and Canaan in the Late Bronze Age,[14] none of the possible scenarios poses a problem for explaining the transmission of this ritual tradition to the Israelites. Nevertheless, a Syrian context of transmission is more strongly reflected in the evidence. As noted above (p. 124), the ritual texts from Ugarit provide indisputable documentation for the open exchange of ritual traditions between Hurrians and Semites.[15] Furthermore, the blood rite is only one of several biblical rituals that find provocative parallels in the textual evidence from Syria and Anatolia (cf. above, pp. 123–24).

Despite many uncertainties, this evidence may contribute to placing the question of Israel's origins on firmer empirical footing. In particular, the fact that the blood rite traditions can be traced back to Syria may provide some support for the Syrian ancestry of at least some of the early Israelites. Indeed, Fleming has adduced support from common traditions found in the extra-biblical documents from Mari and Emar for the biblical traditions regarding a Syrian origin for the patriarchs.[16] The evidence of the Kizzuwatnean blood rite, among other shared ritual traditions from this region, may also point in this direction.

TOWARDS A PREHISTORY OF P

The results of this study touch upon one of the most hotly contested topics in modern biblical research, namely, the dating of the Priestly literature. Reflecting on the state of research, Levine recently offered the following assessment:

---

14. As revealed by some of the personal names found in the letters from Ta'anakh and El Amarna from the fifteenth and fourteenth centuries, respectively, the Hurrians formed part of the population of Canaan in the Late Bronze Age (see Hoffner, "Hittites and Hurrians," 221–24).

15. In addition, we must not forget the dramatic upheavals and population dispersals that occurred throughout the Mediterranean region during this period, such that the ethnic breakdown of Syria and Canaan underwent dramatic changes. See Na'aman, "The 'Conquest of Canaan'," 239–43 with references. However, it is not clear to what degree these migrations were responsible for the transmission of ritual traditions to Israel. See Collins, *Hittites and Their World*, 85–90, 213–18.

16. See Fleming, "Emar: On the Road from Harran to Hebron," 222–50; "Genesis in History and Tradition," 193–232.

In my view, it is unlikely that inner-Biblical evidence alone, as enlightening as it may be, can enable us to reconstruct the formation of priestly literature, in particular. This is because Torah literature has been variously analyzed in terms of its distinctive language and themes, and the relationship of the *Priesterschrift* to the other sources, and there is no clear way to demonstrate the conclusiveness of any reconstruction over others. Biblical texts provide no colophons, and efforts to date them can only produce a relative chronology, at best. Ultimately, it is on the basis of comparative evidence that we may succeed in locating this material in a more or less definitive historical setting, because such external information, though limited, is available in its original form, and can often be dated, and its provenance identified quite precisely.[17]

The results of the present study should be viewed on the background of these remarks, which demonstrates that the biblical sin offering exhibits continuity with Late Bronze Age Syrian and Anatolian ritual practices. However, one must admit that these results have little bearing on the dating of P in its canonical form; nevertheless they do point out some fundamental problems with the manner in which P is conventionally understood in modern scholarship.

Twentieth-century scholarship of P was dominated by a sharp dichotomy between theories asserting its composition in either the pre-exilic or post-exilic periods. As is known, the prominence of this distinction is largely attributable to Wellhausen's brilliant argumentation in favor of his assumed evolutionary scheme in which ancient Israelite religion, originally spontaneous and connected to nature, was transformed by P into a formal legalistic religion. This assumption led him to view the cultic rules of P as being composed later than the Priestly narrative. The profound influence of this model on subsequent research needs no further elaboration here.[18] The important point for our purposes is that the Wellhausenian challenge has dictated the theoretical framework even for its opponents, with the alternative "solutions" proposed being almost invariably predetermined by "problems" formulated in accordance with the Wellhausenian model. For this reason, despite its temporary productivity, this paradigm has significantly contrained the creativity of subsequent research.[19]

---

17. Levine, "Leviticus: Its Literary History," 12.

18. As far as research in Priestly ritual is concerned, I am referring particularly to the research of Koch, Elliger, and the early studies of Rendtorff, among others. Interestingly, Rendtorff has departed significantly from the Wellhausenian model in his more recent research and even subjected this "paradigm" to a penetrating critique. See Rendtorff, "The Paradigm is Changing," 51–68. Rendtorff points out that even important figures such as Gunkel, von Rad, and Noth failed to recognize the underlying tension between the form-critical approach and the dominant source-critical paradigm.

19. As noted above (p. 35), the viewpoints on both sides of the pre-exilic/post-exilic argument have moderated in the past twenty years. Advocates of a pre-exilic date admit

Indeed, if one evaluates the evidence from "outside" the paradigm, one notices that Wellhausen's assumption regarding the chronology of the priestly material, according to which narrative preceded ritual, was largely counterintuitive. Indeed, a form-critical approach that incorporates the comparative evidence from the ancient Near East would have led to a different assumption, namely, that the genre of "ritual instructions" had priority. In particular, one might assume that the priests had a greater interest in recording ritual procedures than in composing an etiological narrative about the origins of the Israelite cult. More to the point, the abundance of non-canonical (i.e., outside of any centralized corpus) ritual instructions from Mesopotamia, Hatti, and Egypt would confirm this assumption.[20]

These postulates regarding the relative chronology of priestly materials find support in the present study. The diachronic analyses of the sin offering rituals presented here provide clear evidence that earlier literary materials passed through several stages of editing and reinterpretation, especially in the context of adapting these instructions to their present narrative context.

This discussion leads to another important issue, regarding the historical gap that seems to separate the Hittite documentation (up to the early-twelfth century B.C.E.) from the biblical record. Leaving aside for the moment the Priestly material whose dating is disputed, the only datable references to the sin offering are found in 2 Kgs 12:17 and Hos 4:8, which refer to events of the late-ninth and eighth centuries B.C.E., respectively.[21] However, once we recognize the probability that the priestly traditions existed as written professional instructions and perhaps orally before P was ultimately transformed into a literary document, the age of these traditions may be considerably older. In fact, we have found indications that one of the earliest sin offering texts, Lev 4:22–26, might stem from the period when tribal chieftains still wielded authority (pp. 41–43). For this reason,

---

the existence of exilic and/or post-exilic redactions, and proponents of the later dating have acknowledged the existence of pre-exilic traditions (see Carr, *Reading the Fractures of Genesis*, 134). Nevertheless, it seems that the basic assumptions according to which the Priestly materials are dated awaits a more fundamental critique.

20. See Weinfeld, "Towards the Concept of Law," 61–62 (Hebrew); *Social and Cultic Institutions*, 95–129. Incidentally, this case illustrates the error of a "purist" methodology which promotes concentrating exclusively on the biblical evidence at the expense of comparative materials. See also Machinist, "Wellhausen and Assyriology," 469–531.

21. Regarding this source, see above, pp. 112–13. See also Milgrom, *Leviticus*, 286–88. Of course, many scholars dispute the interpretation of these passages, but not infrequently these commentators are adjusting the textual data to fit their *a priori* assumption of P's lateness. See, e.g., Harper, *Amos and Hosea*, 257, who asserts regarding Hos 4:8 that "the sin offering was unknown prior to Ezekiel," and D. Kellermann, "אשם," *TDOT* 1:434, for whom it is clear that 2 Kgs 12:17 is a late addition "reflecting conditions in the postexilic period."

I disagree with the assessment of Milgrom that "the place and the date of the ḫaṭṭā'ʾ's origin may be moot, but it is probably the innovation of a temple and not of an open, countryside altar (bāmâ)."[22] Rather, it seems that the sin offering may well have been originally practiced at local altars,[23] continuing a tradition that reaches back into the pre-biblical period.

A useful analogy can be found in the literary record of ancient Mesopotamia, especially regarding its ritual texts. Although the vast majority of ritual texts are preserved in copies from the Neo-Assyrian period, such as those from Aššurbanipal's library (seventh century B.C.E.), one can hardly dismiss these traditions as late inventions. Indeed, the textual finds of sites such as Emar and Boğazköy (among others) provide evidence in many cases to the existence of these traditions already in the Late Bronze Age, if not earlier.[24] In such cases, we are dealing with a gap in the textual record of no less than five hundred years.

The Mesopotamian evidence demonstrates the danger of drawing far-reaching conclusions based on arguments from silence. In particular, it shows that the continuity of ritual traditions could span centuries in the absence (to our present knowledge) of written records. Scholars may justifiably choose a conservative approach that dates a practice exclusively on the basis of existing evidence, but there is no "problem" posed by the textual gap in cases where the earliness of a practice *is* validated, as in our case.

At the same time, we should recognize that the causes of the textual gap in Mesopotamia and Israel are different. Although the paucity of ritual texts (according to present knowledge) in Babylon and Assyria until the Neo-Assyrian period merits systematic research, we may mention in passing some probable factors. First of all, a strong oral tradition may have obviated the need for writing down ritual procedures. In fact, one may question the extent to which the ritual practitioners were literate in the demanding cuneiform writing system. The enlistment of professional scribes for this purpose may have been perceived as an unnecessary burden, financial and otherwise. Secondly, there is some evi-

---

22. Milgrom, *Leviticus*, 289. To support this position, Milgrom writes: "For this sacrifice predicates not just an altar but a building, a complex of sancta inside a shrine…," overlooking the fact that the earliest sources mention only an altar.

23. See above p. 135 and pp. 111–13.

24. Of course, this is a vast topic and no attempt to attain comprehensiveness can be made here. Regarding the evidence from Boğazköy, see Schwemer, *Akkadische Rituale aus Ḫattuša*, 50–52; Strauß, *Reinigungsrituale aus Kizzuwatna*, 197–215. For Emar, see Dietrich, "Die akkadischen Texte von Emar," 40–48. Similar conclusions can be drawn from findings from Mari, Ugarit, and Ebla. For early forerunners of Eme-sal prayers and rituals, see Black, "Eme-sal Cult Songs and Prayers," 23–36; Gabbay, "Sumero-Akkadian Prayer 'Eršema'," 18–21.

dence that the ritual traditions were considered to be esoteric lore that it was forbidden to publicize.[25]

The situation in Israel was quite different. For starters, the textual evidence supports the assumption that the priests were literate in the much simpler alphabetic script and thus capable of recording and reading the ritual traditions themselves.[26] On the other hand, unlike the clay tablets of Mesopotamia that have survived the millennia, Israelite scribes of the First Temple Period relied primarily on papyrus, which disintegrates in all but the most dry climatic conditions after a relatively short time.[27] Accordingly, even if we assume that the Israelite priests made use of written instructions, the preservation of (some of) these texts is solely attributable to their ultimate inclusion in the biblical canon.

Although some scholars assert that Priestly traditions were kept secret in a way analogous to some Mesopotamian texts,[28] this supposition seems questionable. In particular, this assumption seems to be at odds with the characterization of the priests as teachers of Torah to the masses.[29] It should be noted that proponents of this argument are responding primarily to the Wellhausenian assertion of P's so-called lack of influence on Israelite society. But the latter premise is itself subject to challenge, since it is a) based primarily on an argument from silence and b) fails to recognize that much of the ideological content of P may reflect a relatively late stage of these traditions. On the other hand, if one assumes that P represents a codification of ritual instructions that may have been practiced at local sanctuaries long before their redaction, one need not posit a deliberate policy of concealment. Since these instructions were intended specifically for ritual practitioners, not the wider public, it is not clear what type of influence such traditions could be expected to exhibit upon prophetic or narrative materials.

In the same article, Levine comments that "the argument, based on inner-Biblical considerations, as to whether the *Priesterschrift* is pre-exilic or post-exilic, has become stale."[30] In my opinion, this stagnation is largely attributable to the reluctance of scholars to relinquish the Wellhausenian model of the Priestly composition. Of course, I am not claiming that scholars entirely ignored the relevance

---

25. Ginsberg, *New Trends in the Study of Bible*, 23; Cohen, "Was the P Document Secret?," 39–44. Cf. van der Toorn, *Scribal Culture*, 65–66, 219–21.

26. Carr, *Writing on the Tablet of the Heart*, 152.

27. See Haran, "Book Scrolls in Israel in Pre-Exilic Times," 161–73; Carr, *Writing on the Tablet of the Heart*, 86.

28. For some references to some earlier precursors to this notion of P's pre-history, see Carr, *Reading the Fractures of Genesis*, 135, n. 39. Cf. also the views of Ginsberg and Cohen cited in n. 25 above.

29. See, e.g., Deut 17:9–12; 31:10–13; Hos 4:6; Ezek 7:26; 22:26; Neh 8:8–9; 2 Chr 19:8–11. It appears that this characterization was already applicable in pre-exilic times.

30. "Leviticus: Its Literary History," 12.

of comparative materials for reconstructing the prehistory of Priestly materials.[31] In fact, Levine himself made a substantial contribution to this endeavor many years ago in his attempt to trace biblical ritual texts to archival temple documents.[32] However, it seems that the enduring emphasis on the Jerusalem temple as the locus for ritual activity neglects the possibility for decentralized ritual practice, thus maintaining (wittingly or not) the Wellhausenian bias.[33] The fallacy of this assumption is most evident in light of the Hittite ritual materials, which paint a vivid picture showing how localized cults served to address the daily concerns of the populace. Perhaps these texts can provide a more fitting model for the precanonical stages of the Priesly composition.[34]

TRANSMISSION, TRANSLATION AND TRANSFORMATION: BLOOD AND THE CONCEPT OF "EXPIATION"

In order to analyze the ideas depicted in the ancient Hittite and biblical documents, we often resort, with or without further reflection, to employing modern terms such as "propitiation" and "expiation."[35] The vitality of these notions today is attributable to modern theological discourse, which is itself an outgrowth of earlier generations of biblical translation and interpretation. In this section, we will trace the historical process by which the concept of expiation and its associated terminology developed, from its appearance in the ancient Hittite and biblical sources to the early and later biblical translations.

As argued above, the roots of the Hittite and biblical notions of expiation can be found in the context of bloodguilt and retribution. Whereas the earliest phase of this belief seems to relate to the belief that the blood of the murdered person, bearing his vital spirit, screams out for vengeance from the gods, the later conception described in both the Hittite and biblical evidence depicts "bloodguilt" as a stain that activates a mechanical process of retribution. This

---

31. See n. 18 above.

32. Levine, "Descriptive Tabernacle Texts," 307–18. See also Rainey, "Order of Sacrifices," 485–98.

33. Levine recognized this point, writing: "We are also aware that prescriptive rituals represent a type of text as ancient as temple records and that, historically, it is not necessary to posit that all ritual prescriptions are based on temple records" ("Descriptive Tabernacle Texts," 318). Unfortunately, the significance of such observations for dating Priestly materials has been left largely unexplored.

34. For some recent studies on the textual development of the Hittite rituals, see Miller, *Kizzuwatna Rituals*, 469–537; Christiansen, *Ritualtradition der Ambazzi*, 309–29.

35. As elucidated above (p. 173), these two terms can be distinguished as follows: Whereas "propitiation" refers to the appeasement of the angered party, "expiation" refers to the rectification of the offense that caused the breakdown in the relationship.

mechanical notion was described above as representing a transition from the idea of "propitiating" (the blood, the victim's kin, the gods) to "expiating" (the guilt).

The Hittite and Hebrew scribes employed different strategies to express the latter idea. The Hittites conceptualized the appeasement of blood in terms of "making compensation" (*šarnink-*). In other words, they employed a metaphor by which the removal of bloodguilt was conceptualized as a debt to be repaid. This analogy was clearly facilitated by the fact that in Hittite society restitution for bloodguilt was in many cases achieved monetarily. The biblical sources reveal a different lexical process, whereby the terminology for "placating" or "making amends" (i.e., propitiation), כִּפֶּר was used with a new syntax. Whereas expressions with כִּפֶּר in the sense of propitiation are generally characterized by the lack of a direct object (e.g., 2 Sam 21:3) or a term for anger as the direct object (e.g., Gen 32:21; Prov 16:14), its use in the sense of expiation feature blood or sin as the direct object. As a result, the focus was transferred from appeasing the offended parties to addressing the wrong committed and removing guilt. This syntactical transformation reflects the fundamental transition from the folkloric conception of appeasing blood to the objectified notion of remedying the bloodguilt. This latter use of כִּפֶּר (translated as "expiate") implies a mechanical dynamic of retribution in which sin automatically yields adverse consequences unless some restitutory act is performed.

These observations reveal the intimate relationship between literary expressions and cultural practices and explanatory schemes. As the personalized notion of propitiation gave way to a depersonalized notion of expiating guilt, a new conception emerged that lacked a means for verbal expression, requiring the adaptation of existing terminology (*catachresis*). Indeed, the application of *šarnink-* and כפ"ר to describe the mechanical dynamic of expiation required an innovative use of these verbal forms. In both of these cases, the earlier sense of these terms was adapted to express the unique conception underlying the notion of expiating bloodguilt. In the following brief survey of the translation of כִּפֶּר into Greek, Latin, and English, we find an interesting interplay between changing religious conceptions and terminology, reflecting both innovation and continuity with the ancient notion of expiating bloodguilt. [36]

Interestingly, the strategy employed by the Bible in adapting the usages of כִּפֶּר served as a model for its Greek translators. Throughout the LXX, the

---

36. The following brief survey is far from complete. In particular, it focuses on the use of the terms "expiation"/"expiate" as well as their Greek and Latin precedents as translations for כִּפֶּר in the Hebrew Bible. Accordingly, it does not deal with such terminology in the New Testament and early and Medieval Christian discourse. Furthermore, it does not deal with the history of the English usage of "expiation"/"expiate" outside the Bible, though much relevant information on this topic can be found in the Oxford English Dictionary.

Hebrew term is translated consistently by derivatives of *hilaskomai* ("propiti-ate," "appease"), particularly the intensive form *exilaskomai*. These terms were already used in ancient Greek before the Septuagint in the sense of propitiating an angry deity. However, as recognized by numerous scholars, the LXX departs from earlier usage.[37] Already in 1931, Dodd drew his dramatic conclusion:

> Thus Hellenistic Judaism, as represented by the LXX, does not regard the cultus as a means of pacifying the displeasure of the Deity, but as a means of deliv-ering man from sin ... thus evolving a meaning of *hilaskesthai* strange to non-Biblical Greek.[38]

Though Dodd's study has been subject to much discussion and critique, regard-ing both its methodology and its conclusions,[39] more recent studies tend to support his view that the Greek translators of the Bible employed *hilaskomai* forms unconventionally.[40]

Lang's summary of the data is particularly insightful. Referring to the use of *hilaskomai* derivatives with words for sin in the dative form, he writes:

> The construction of the verb *exiláskomai* carefully imitates that of *kipper*, espe-cially in the use of prepositions ... The usage just described is a semitism; it does not agree with the common Greek idiom, in which a human being is the active subject and God is the object.[41]

---

37. This distinction is particular clear in the usages of *hilaskomai*, where the glosses used by the lexicons of the LXX such as "to be forgiving" and "to be merciful" (with God as subject) are unattested in the early non-biblical evidence. See Lust et al., *A Greek-English Lexicon of the Septuagint*, 214; Muraoka, *Lexicon of the Septuagint*, 269. Surveying the evidence provided in the Lidell-Scott lexicon, one notes the sense "appease" in relation to gods appears already in Homer and "concilliate" in relation to humans in Plato, whereas the sense "expiate" derives from the LXX and NT evidence. The more detailed studies cited below reinforce this conclusion.

38. Dodd, "*Hilaskesthai*, Its Cognates," 359.

39. The most extreme critique was that of Morris, who argued that the Greek terms, like Hebrew כִּפֶּר, refer to the propitiation of divine anger (*Apostolic Preaching*, 125–60; cf. Hill, *Greek Words*, 31–36). A useful summary can be found in Young, "C.H. Dodd, 'Hilaskesthai' and His Critics," 67–78. Cf. also Koch, "Translation of *kapporēt*," 65–75.

40. But they moderate some of Dodd's more drastic conclusions. For example, Young (ibid.) differs from Dodd in that the latter "granted to the LXX translators too great a con-sciousness in supposedly radically modifying the use of *(ex)ilaskomai*" (p. 77). See also Hill, *Greek Words*, 35–36. *hilaskomai* is attested in two Hellenistic sources with temples as its object. Though its sense is not entirely clear, it is most definitely not "entsühnt" as claimed by Breytenbach (*Versöhnung: Eine Studie zur paulinischen Soteriologie*, 85). For references, see the Liddell-Scott-Jones supplement, 74, where the editors suggest "respect."

41. Lang, "כפר," 291. He is referring to the Greek translation of Lev 4:26; 19:22.

In order to translate כִּפֶּר, the Greek translators used an unconventional syntax for the term whose conventional sense was "propitiate," yielding the sense "expiate." Surprisingly, nearly all scholars have failed to recognize that a similar semantic transition from propitiation to expiation had already taken place in the Hebrew כִּפֶּר.[42] Thus, the Greeks like the ancient Israelites, expressed the objectified notion of expiation by altering the syntax of the terminology of propitiation.

In several ways, the Latin translation of the Bible provides the antecedents to the later English translations and the theological ideas associated with it. First and foremost, we find the etymological sources for the terms "propitiation" and "expiation" in *prŏpĭtĭo, ex-pĭo* and their derivatives. In the Lewis and Short Lexicon, *prŏpĭtĭo* is glossed "to render favorable, to appease," while *ex-pĭo* is defined as "to make satisfaction, amends, atonement for a crime or a criminal." In general, the latter seems to be the more usual translation for the cultic uses of כִּפֶּר. One should note, however, that *ex-pĭo* is employed primarily in contexts that employ either כִּפֶּר or חָטָא to refer to the *purification* of people and sancta. Since this term was already used by Cicero (first century B.C.E.), centuries before Jerome's translation of the Bible, it seems that Latin already possessed an adequate terminology for the objectified notion of satisfying guilt. Thus, the Vulgate was better suited to provide later English translations with an appropriate vocabulary for this concept than the Hittite and Hebrew languages (of an earlier period), which were forced to lexically innovate when confronted with the objectified notion of expiating blood, or the Greek when translators were confronted with rendering Hebrew כִּפֶּר.

An additional line of continuity between the Vulgate and later English translations pertains to their theological premises. In particular, the Latin translators preferred to use derivatives of lexemes such as *rŏgo* ("implore")[43] and *de-prĕcor* ("avert by prayer")[44] to translate כִּפֶּר in many cases when the context implies a breach in the relationship between man and God. In other words, one detects a fairly clear distinction between a ritualistic-mechanical usage of כִּפֶּר, translated by *ex-pĭo*, and a personalized religious view, characterized by repentance and forgiveness, reflected in these latter terms. This distinction, apparently influenced by early Christian theology, served as a model for later translations.

Turning to the English translations of the Bible, one finds a general reticence to employ derivatives of "expiate," opting to translate כִּפֶּר with more personalized terms such as "atonement" and "reconciliation."[45] Nevertheless, at the turn

---

42. For a notable exception, see Barr, "Expiation," 281.
43. E.g., Lev 4:20, 26, 31, 35; 5:10, 13, 16; 10:17.
44. E.g., Exod 30:10; Lev 9:7; Num 6:11; 8:12.
45. These terms are avoided in the following translations: Geneva Bible (1599), KJV of 1611/1789, Webster Bible (1833), NKJV (1982), and NIV. These results and those following do

of the twentieth century and onwards, the terms "expiation"/"expiate" begins to appear. Although their use remains sporadic, an interesting pattern can be detected. Despite the numerous occurrences of כִּפֶּר throughout the Hebrew Bible, these translations employed "expiate"/"expiation" for only a handful of occurrences—all of which seem to depict an automatic process of satisfying guilt. Of these, a significant proportion pertains to the expiation of bloodguilt from the land. For example, among four appearances of "expiation" and "expiated" in the American Standard Version of 1901 we find Num 35:33 and Deut 32:43.[46] Writing at approximately the same period, S. R. Driver observed that the Authorized Version of the King James Bible employed "expiation" only once, in Num 35:33 and "expiate" in Isa 47:11, both in the margin. He observes that in the Revised Version "expiation" is incorporated into the text itself for Num 35:33 and Deut 32:43 and "expiate" in another handful of sources.[47]

These observations are by no means trivial. They show that at least some modern English translators have preserved the tradition of the Vulgate, whereby the terminology of "expiation" was reserved for an automatic process of satisfying guilt, to be distinguished from the notions of "atonement" and "forgiveness," which pertain to a personalized conception of the relations between humans and God. On this background, it is noteworthy, though not surprising, that the mechanized conception of sin and restitution was acknowledged in only a few biblical passages, of which the expiation of the land from bloodguilt remains prominent. Unknowingly, these translators have traced the biblical concept of "expiation" back to its pre-biblical source, namely, the depersonalized depiction of making compensation for spilled blood.

This brief survey permits some interesting conclusions regarding the role of ritual as an embodiment of cultural conceptions. The fact that verbal description of the blood rite required the invention of new linguistic expressions demonstrates that the nonverbal symbolism of blood enabled a unique type of conceptualization anterior to language that was only subsequently converted into words, albeit in somewhat clumsy forms. Contrary to the common practice of interpreting rituals in accordance with linguistic and textual analogies, this recognition reveals the importance of interpreting ritual on its own terms as a

---

not take into consideration translations of the NT.

46. The other two sources are Num 8:7 and 1 Sam 3:14. The NASB uses "expiation" only once, for Num 35:33.

47. Driver, "Expiation and Atonement," 653. The other sources are 1 Sam. 3:14; Isa 6:7; 22:14; 27:9. Similar results can be found in the JPS translation of 1917 and the RSV of 1952. The restricted usage of these terms, characteristic of the majority of modern translations, is particularly striking when compared with the NJB and the NJPS translation, which employ "expiation"/"expiate" regularly as a translation for cultic כִּפֶּר.

nonverbal medium. Finally, the process of translating the blood rite into verbal terminology presents an example of the primacy of nonverbal symbolism in cultural expression. Here a scheme that was originally conceptualized by means of a concrete embodiment in bodily praxis provided the basis for subsequent verbal articulation. Such a progression is analogous to metaphoric uses of language in which a concrete or embodied source domain provides a conceptual model for a more elusive or abstract target domain (see above, pp. 158–61).

An additional ramification of this survey of terminology pertains to the evolution in the function of ritual and the perceived source of its efficacy. In its original form, the blood rite seems to reflect a self-contained dynamic—an automatic process to remove transgression and avoid its consequences. In contrast, the Vulgate shows a tendency to interpret cultic כִּפֶּר formulas within the framework of personalized religion. According to this conception, ritual efficacy depends on the ability of the petitioner to sway the will of God.

The beginnings of this dramatic reframing of the function of the Israelite cult in general and the sin offering in particular can be found in the biblical period itself. Specifically, the beginnings of these fundamentally different approaches to ritual are represented in the Priestly sources of the Bible. Indeed, the traditions codified by P seem to reflect a decentralized notion of ritual efficacy, such that a rite has immediate effects based on its internal logic. This mechanical approach to ritual is evident in the Priestly use of the passive form נסלח ("be forgiven) to express the effects of the expiatory offerings. This form, unique to Priestly jargon, circumvents reference to divine or human agents, thereby implying that the cultic process itself effects expiation.[48] Although these texts imply a mechanistic dynamic, they need not be viewed as denying the involvement of God in the ritual process. They merely imply (from an analytical standpoint) that a divine lawgiver is not essential to give meaning to ritual. On the other hand, H demonstrates a clear tendency to provide rationales for rituals, including a self-conscious concern to emphasize the role of the Deity. This distinction corresponds with Knohl's observation that P lacks motive clauses, in contrast with H.[49] In terms of the scheme of a ritual's life cycle presented in ch. 5, we may

---

48. Attestations: Lev 4:20, 26, 31, 35; 5:10, 13, 16, 18, 26; 19:22; Num 15:25, 26, 28. It is hardly surprising that all thirteen biblical attestations of this form are found in P and H, since one can hardly imagine its use in natural language. Knohl notes the "technical-impersonal" character of blood expiation, understanding it as reflecting a tendency to reduce anthropomorphism in P (*Sanctuary of Silence,* 135). Though this interpretation is surely possible, one must also consider the broader tendency of cult officiants to view retribution and expiation as mechanical processes (see Feder, *"Mechanics of Retribution"*). For a different view, cf. Milgrom, *Leviticus,* 245; Eberhart, *Bedeutung der Opfer im Alten Testament,* 172.

49. Knohl, *Sanctuary of Silence,* 106 and n. 160. He cites the following rationales of H: Exod 25:8; 29:43–46; Lev 11:43–45; 15:31; Num 19:13, 20.

view P as representing the "codification" phase of rituals, whereas H represents the "reinterpretation" phase in which they are subject to new exegesis.

According to H, the rationale for ritual activity is related to the holiness of God. For example, the desire to dwell in God's proximity serves as the motivation for building the Tabernacle (Exod 25:8[H?]; 29:43–46) as well as the reason for maintaining the laws of purity (Lev 15:31; Num 19:13, 20). Likewise, according to the H redactor, the oil of Lev 14:16 and the blood of the red cow in Num 19:4 acquire their ritual efficacy by means of an act of sprinkling towards the Tabernacle (see above, pp. 65–67). Likewise, the principle of *imitatio Dei* serves as the basis for numerous laws (e.g.: Lev 11:43–45; 19:2). Although these rationales are inherently logical, corresponding to Frazer's principles of contiguity (contagious magic) and similarity (homeopathic magic), H takes pains to assert that God is the one and only point of reference for holiness and that this holiness is the exclusive basis for ritual efficacy. Consequently, H's concern for cult centralization is not limited to external institutionalized measures (Lev 17), but rather, it extends to this source's emphasis on God as the source of ritual efficacy—a centralizing view of the internal logic of biblical ritual.[50] By virtue of P's codification of the sin offering rite, the ritual became a relatively static object that could be transmitted to subsequent generations. However, as it was incorporated into the radically different cultural contexts of later Jewish and Christian tradents, the function of the ritual changed profoundly. The major stages of this transformation can be characterized as follows:

Stage	Object of Interpretion	Type of Interpretation
1. Blood rite	Physical action	Autonomous process for removal of guilt and impurity
2. H	Synthesis of action with canonical text	Process for reconciliation with God
3. Judaism	Canonical text	Legal exegesis
4. Christianity	Canonical text	Allegorical exegesis

As can be seen in this brief synopsis, the blood rite's transition from action to codified text set forth corresponding changes in its function within its changing cultural contexts. Whereas H's reinterpretation of the ritual still pertains in part

---

50. Another example worth mentioning is the standard passive formula ונכרתה הנפש ההוא ("that individual will be cut off"; e.g., Gen 17:14; Exod 12:15, 19; Lev 7:20, 21, 25, 27), which H has replaced in certain instances, apparently to emphasize the notion of God's wrath, with the personalized form והכרתי ("I will cut off"); e.g., Lev 17:10; 20:3, 5, 6.

to a living practice, the destruction of the Second Temple, among other changing historical circumstances, brought later Judaism and Christianity to focus exclusively on the canonical texts. While the legal exegesis of the Rabbis preserved the sin offerings' laws as part of their overall aspiration for the rebuilding of the Temple and Jewish commonwealth, Christian allegorical exegesis reflected the Christian view that this ritual was ultimately to be superseded in a non-sacrificial spiritual form.[51]

In essence, we find a continuously transforming dialogue between the objectified ritual and its changing cultural context in which the interpretation of the former is progressively subordinated to the concerns of the latter. Such a process could be described as one of increasing cultural mediation. The ritual in its original form is inherently motivated by means by the role of its signs in a particular concrete context of social interaction (expiating bloodguilt). Based on a self-explanatory (transparent) relation between signs and their use, rituals offer their practitioners the ability to affect the world from "inside." However, when this motivation is obscured and the connection between signs and their use is regarded as arbitrary, the understanding of a ritual's efficacy is changed dramatically. Its interpretation is progressively more influenced by its application to new cultural contexts and its incorporation into a broader system of cultural discourse.

In fact, this process could be viewed as just one particular type of a general cultural tendency towards conventionalism, that is, the recognition that social codes are culturally contingent. Indeed, regarding cultural beliefs in diverse areas such as language,[52] law,[53] and morality,[54] one can find similar transitions in which the belief in the innate truth of a phenomenon (the realist–essentialist view) gives way to a perception of its arbitrariness and conventionality. In all of these cases, the formalization of cultural codes acts as a catalyst for a process of recontextualization, invariably leading to a situation in which its underlying

---

51. An early example of the allegorical approach to biblical ritual is Origen's homilies on Leviticus. For a recent translation, see Origen, *Homilies on Leviticus 1–16*. For a survey of Christian exegesis of biblical ritual from the early Church to the present, see Klingbeil, *Ritual and Ritual Texts*, 91–124.

52. For example, the dichotomy of "nominal realism" (the view that names are divinely given and inherently connected to their corresponding referent) vs. "nominalism" (the belief in the arbitrariness of names); see Olson, *World on Paper*, 167.

53. In particular, the dichotomy of "natural law" (law is set by nature and of universal validity) vs. "positivism" (laws are human and possess no inherent validity).

54. Regarding morality, one can contrast "universal" and "conventional" conceptions. See Shweder, *Thinking Through Cultures*, 186–241 for an illuminating discussion of some issues pertaining to natural vs. conventional origins of morality and law. See also idem. et al., "Culture and Moral Development," 140–204.

code will no longer seem self-evident and natural.[55] In Bourdieu's terms, when a cultural phenomenon that was originally accepted as part of the *doxa*, that is, the universe of the undiscussed and undisputed, is forced into the field of explicit discourse, that is, the field of opinion, its hegemony has already been undermined. He writes: "It is when the social world loses its character as a natural phenomenon that the question of the natural or convention character (*phusei* or *nomo*) of social facts can be raised."[56] Applying this notion to ritual, we may observe that the moment a rite requires a verbalized rationale, such as H's rationales for cultic acts, it is clear that the original trust in the mechanics of ritual has been compromised.

In the face of these radical transformations, it seems almost futile to look for any form of thematic continuity in the transmission of the blood rite. Nevertheless, a core concept can be found that has survived the turmoil of translation—the metaphor of sin as debt. Interestingly, Anderson has recently gleaned abundant evidence in the Jewish and Christian traditions for the metaphorical notion whereby sin was viewed as a debt to the Deity.[57] Although this metaphor emerges as an increasingly influential conception in the Second Temple Period, Anderson finds no evidence that can be dated before the Babylonian exile. However, in light of the present analysis of the sin offering, it may be possible to trace this idea back to a much earlier period, stemming from the notion of repaying a blood debt. If the sin as debt literary motif is related to the tradition of the sin offering, it may turn out that the history of Western concepts of sin is more ancient than previously realized. Perhaps the nonverbal symbolism of the sin-offering, though relatively crude and unarticulate, was the seed from which all of these more elaborate theological discourses would emerge.

---

55. Cf. the distinction between natural law and legal positivism in relation to the Rabbis and the Qumran sectarians in Rubinstein, "Nominalism and Realism," 180–81.

56. *Outline of a Theory of Practice*, 168–69.

57. "From Israel's Burden to Israel's Debt," 9–30; *Sin: A History*, 43–74; see also Hoffmann, *Das Buch Leviticus* 1:188–89.

CONCLUSION

The first step of this investigation was to analyze the Hittite and biblical evidence, each on its own terms. In ch. 1, I surveyed the Hittite evidence for the blood rite. The abundant textual evidence, mostly originating from Kizzuwatna in southeastern Anatolia, provides a substantial basis for understanding the procedure and function of this rite. The *zurki* rite, named after the Hurrian term for blood, involves the smearing of an object with blood to remove sin, impurity, and the like. This act would serve to remove impurity or sin from the "owner" of the object by means of metonymic association. For example, the Papanikri Ritual involves the smearing of birth stools in order to remove divine anger against the parturient. The *zurki* rite is usually connected with the *uzi* rite, entailing the cooking of fat as an offering to the gods. Several factors indicate that the *uzi* and *zurki* rites were understood as a unity such as their frequent appearance together in the formula *uziya zurkia šipanti* ("one offers the flesh and blood") and the fact that the fat and blood are often derived from the same animal. This close relationship between the two rites seems to imply that the *zurki* rite, like the *uzi* rite, was conceived as a sacrificial offering. The circumstances that require the performance of the *zurki* rite include the appearance of a portentious omen, the occurrence of cultic desecration, the committal of an unintentional sin, and the preparation of a new cultic temple.

In ch. 2, the textual evidence for the biblical sin offering (חטאת) was surveyed. This ritual involves the smearing or sprinkling of blood on cultic appurtenances, most commonly the horns of the altar. The suet of the animal was then burned on the altar as an offering to YHWH. Although the sin-offering rites involve the smearing of blood on objects, not people, the accompanying goal formulas indicate that this rite serves to expiate or purify the offerer. This dynamic of action-at-a-distance can characterized as metonymy. The occasions that require the performance of a sin offering include the committal of unintentional sin (Lev 4; Num 15), defilement with severe bodily impurities (Lev 12; 14–15), desecration of the temple (Lev 16), and the initiation of new cult officiants and sancta (Exod 29; Lev 8; Ezek 43).

The diachronic analysis of the sin offering texts reveals a multi-stage process of historical development. In particular, the earliest texts feature goal formulas using כִּפֶּר עַל + personal pronoun, which seem to express the notion that the positive effects of the offering are accrued to the offerer. In comparison, in the later editorial layers of P and H as well as in Ezek 40–48, one finds the formulas כִּפֶּר אֶת and חִטֵּא אֶת with sancta as the direct object, which seem to express the notion of purging these objects. This diachronic distinction undermines the relative chronology of sources advocated by most source-critical scholars according to which Ezekiel represents the earliest phase of the ritual's development. On the contrary, the present analysis determines that Ezekiel represents a relatively late stage of Priestly tradition.

This growing emphasis on the purificatory function of the תאטח finds further support in the etymological development of the *piel* form חִטֵּא, usually glossed as "cleanse." Numerous modern scholars contend that the verb provides support for translating חטאת as "purification offering." However, the present study has arrived at a very different conclusion. Recognizing that the *piel* and *hitpael* forms of חט"א are found exclusively in cultic texts, it is clear that these terms originated as part of the technical jargon of the priesthood. Accordingly, a survey of the lexical evidence for these forms leads to the conclusion that the *piel* form in most cases refers to performing a rite of cleansing, whereas the *hitpael* form refers to being the recipent of a rite of cleansing. This recognition reveals the following path of semantic development for חִטֵּא: "to perform a sin-offering" → "to perform an act of cleansing" → "to cleanse." Accordingly, the verbal forms are denominative derivatives of the offering, correctly translated as "sin offering." At the same time, the emergence of the later sense of "cleansing" coincides with the later interpretation of the rite as "purging" sancta. By tracing the etymological development of חטאת, we also found indications of an earlier conception in which even severe bodily abnormalities, later understood as *impurities* (טמאת), may have originally been understood as divine punishments requiring the performance of a sin offering (cf. 2 Sam 3:29).

These findings have important ramifications for reconstructing the historical development of the sin offering. Although the present analysis accepts the methodology of source critics such as Elliger and Koch, it parts ways their historical assumption that the earliest textual evidence was composed during the Babylonian exile. Rather, the present analysis views P as a canonical form of earlier ritual instructions, which were used by the officiating priests at local cult sites throughout the pre-exilic period. Further early evidence for the existence of the sin offering can be found in Hos 4:8 and 2 Kgs 12:17 as well as the reference to the נשיא in the earliest layer of Lev 4 (vv. 22–35), which may stem from a period when tribal chieftains were still a socio-political reality. Moreover, the requirement for a parturient to bring a sin offering, outlined in Lev 12, is most plausibly understood in the context of a local cult.

After independenly analyzing the Hittite and biblical sources, the comparison between them is presented in ch. 3. In order to evaluate the possibility of a historical connection between these two cultural traditions, the present study borrows a methodological framework proposed by Meir Malul. According to these guidelines, the historical connection must be assessed by its uniqueness and by the existence of a viable medium for the transmission of ideas between the two cultures. Regarding the first of these criteria, it was observed that these two rites demonstrate striking similarities in terms of their 1) procedure, 2) dynamic, and 3) circumstances. In terms of procedure, both rites involve the smearing blood on an object, frequently cultic, to remove sin or impurity. Furthermore, just as the sin offering blood rite is accompanied by the burning of the suet as an offering, the Hurro-Hittite *zurki* rite usually appears in tandem with a fat-cooking rite, the *uzi* offering, which often comes from the same animal as the *zurki*. Furthermore, both the Hurro-Hittite and biblical blood rites employ a metonymic dynamic in which the smearing of blood on an object benefits the offerer by virtue of an associative connection between the object and offerer. Moreover, these rites are performed under similar circumstances, which include unintentional sin, sanctuary defilement, and the consecration of new cult structures.

The importance of these similarities is underlined by the virtual absence of a similar use of blood in adjacent cultures. Specifically, the relatively abundant evidence documenting ancient Mesopotamian and Greek blood rites all points towards the role of blood as food for chthonic deities. In this capacity, blood is placed in the doorposts of temples and other structures as an apotropaic measure to prevent the entry of demonic entities. Alternatively, in cases of severe illness, blood is applied to the body of the patient as a means of coaxing the possessing spirit to leave the patient's body. Although these themes appear sporadically in Hittite and biblical treatments of blood, they are not central to the treatment of either the *zurki* rite or the sin offering. This discrepency between these rites, on one hand, and the Hurro-Hittite *zurki* rite and the biblical sin offering, on the other, supports the conclusion that the latter two practices stem from the same distinct tradition. The single ostensible exception is the anointment of *sikkānu* stones with blood and oil as part of the Emar *zukru* festival. However, due to the Syrian provenance of the latter, one may also suspect that the Emar rite is also historically related to the Hurro-Hittite and biblical traditions, a possibility that is explored in further detail in ch. 7.

Furthermore, Malul's second criterion— a viable medium for the transmission of ritual traditions— poses no difficulty. The Kizzuwatnean provenance of the Hittite texts indicates that the *zurki* traditions were transmitted to the Hittites by the Hurrians of southern Anatolia in the Late Bronze Age. In fact, though it is one of the most persuasive examples, the blood rite is one of several ostensibly parallel traditions found in the Hittite sources and the Bible, many of which can be traced to the Syrian mileu. In searching for a context of transmission, we noted the evidence of the rituals from Ugarit, which were composed during roughly the same period as the Kizzuwatna texts. The Ugarit texts integrate the ritual traditions, pantheons, and terminology of the local Semites and Hurrians, thereby providing a vivid illustration of the cross-cultural exchange that could have allowed the blood rite to pass between southern Anatolia and Canaan.

The assumption of a historical connection between the Hurro-Hittite and biblical blood rites finds further support in a comparison of specific ritual texts. For example, the birth ritual KUB 9.22+ shows numerous points of similarity with the ritual for the purification of a leper described in Lev 14. These include the use of two birds in an elimination rite; the use of a stick bundle tied with red string for aspersions, and; a purificatory act of pouring oil on the head of the beneficiary. The comparison of the birth ritual KBo 17.65+ with Lev 12 is less conclusive. Although both texts depict differentiating periods of purification for male and female offspring as well as a similarly named rite several days after birth, these similarities may be coincidental. At the same time, a comparison of the Kizzuwatna birth ritual corpus as a whole with Lev 12 offers a more secure parallel. Specifically, the centrality of the blood rite in both cases, especially the use of the blood of birds, supports the assumption of a historical connection. As a result, although some parallels are more convincing than others, the examination of individual ritual texts reinforces our earlier conclusions regarding the existence of a shared tradition.

A final point of interest pertains to how these parallels can shed light on the interpretation of Lev 12. In particular, the requirement for a parturient to bring a sin offering has challenged commentators, who have struggled to understand why the Bible ascribes sin to the new mother. Some modern scholars even view this source as a proof-text that the חטאת is not a "sin offering" but a "purification offering" (see above). However, the identification of a series of similar birth rituals featuring the blood rite in the Kizzuwatna corpus reveals a somewhat more complicated picture. For example, the Papanikri Ritual views a negative omen as evidence that either the parturient or her parents have, in fact, sinned. Though we should not give inordinate weight to the Papanikri Ritual when interpreting other rituals, one cannot avoid the awareness that birth was approached with an exceedingly high level of apprehension in the ancient world. In fact, the possibility of a stillbirth appears in at least one of the other Kizzuwatna birth rituals containing the *zurki* rite. As a result, although the sin offering of the parturient in Lev 12 deals exclusively with ritual impurity, not sin, it may possibly (though not necessarily) reflect an earlier conception in which the period immediately before and after birth was accompanied by rites of penitence.

Chapter 4 engages the problem of ritual *meaning* and attempts to outline a viable methodology for understanding the expiatory use of blood. The basis for this approach is the recognition that ancient Near East rituals attribute to signs a unique capacity to influence metaphysical forces and alter the state of the world. Building on an insight of Wittgenstein, it is argued that ritual involves the creation of a language with which to influence these impersonal forces. A fundamental requirement of this language is that signs act as univalent media for expressing the ritual message. The rest of this chapter seeks to describe the process by which signs attain their ritual significance. Drawing upon a multi-disciplinary framework for analyzing the role of signs in culture, this chapter outlines an approach for analyzing the meaning attributed to ritual signs as determined by their roles in particular concrete sociocultural contexts. Accordingly, ritual symbolism is generally not an arbitrary interpretation imposed on a sign or gesture by a person or group wielding authority, but rather, emerges as a natural outgrowth of the sign or gesture's significance in the material existence of a culture. This realization provides the possibility for achieving a deeper understanding of the cultural context through analysis of ritual symbolism.

These insights are then applied to illuminate the profound connection, recognized by the earliest Jewish and Christian commentators, between blood and expiation (signified by כִּפֶּר), in the Priestly sources of the Bible. A survey of the biblical evidence reveals that the most prominent context by which one can account for the role of blood in the sin offering is that of homicide retribution. This significance seems to have originated in the early belief that the blood of the victim, containing the vital spirit screams out for vengeance. Although not all passages describe the blood in such personified terms, there is widespread evidence for the notion that unatoned blood could even threaten the community at large with retribution. To avoid such a calamity, the community was charged with ensuring that the murder was properly avenged by the "redeemer of blood." According to the strict requirement of vengeance, the Bible rejects the conventional ancient Near East practice of monetary restitution. This institutional background provides essential insight into the significance of blood in ancient Israelite society. In other ancient Near East cultures, such as Babylonia, where monetary compensation was accepted, the term "blood" (*dāmu*) was used as a term for payment, that is, blood money. This terminology also entered Mishnaic Hebrew through Aramaic influence, in the term דמים, meaning "damages" and, more generally, "payment." However, in biblical Hebrew, reflecting the view that only the blood of the perpetrator could expiate guilt, blood itself was characterized in monetary terms, as apparent from expressions such as וייקר דמם ("their blood is precious") in Ps 72:14.

The foregoing provides crucial background for understanding the semantic development of verbal and nominal derivatives of כפ"ר. Despite an abundance of earlier studies, often focusing on Semitic cognates and the assumption of an original concrete sense, scholars have yet to provide a clear account for the semantic development of these terms. A more productive approach, applied in the present study, is to identify concrete social contexts in which of כפ"ר derivatives were used, namely, A) appeasement of an adversary of judge to avoid a punitary action, and B) removal of culpability for bloodguilt.

Upon further consideration, one recognizes that B is simply a subset of A. Not surprisingly, this relation finds semantic expression in the nuanced use of כפ"ר terminology in the context of bloodguilt. In particular, the nominal form כֹּפֶר, whose original sense was "propitiatory gift" or "bribe," acquired the sense of "ransom." Similarly, verbal forms such as כִּפֶּר, which previously meant "appease," acquired the senses "compensate" and "expiate."

The social context for these semantic transitions can be found in sources such as Exod 21:29–30, 2 Sam. 21:1–6 and Deut 21:1–9. In these sources, one finds a transition from the idea of "appeasing" either the spilled blood or the kin of the deceased to a notion of "making compensation" for the spilled blood. Accordingly, the semantic transition of כפ"ר derivatives corresponds to a more fundamental conceptual transition from the notion of *propitiation* to that of *expiation*. Where as the former consists of placating the anger of the offended party, the latter pertains to undoing the ill effects of the wrong committed. The latter depiction seems to involve a more mechanistic, depersonalized conception in which bloodguilt automatically brings retribution unless it is properly addressed by the perpetrator and community.

In light of the role of blood in the context of expiating bloodguilt and corresponding semantic transitions of כפ"ר derivatives, one may understand the motivation of the sin offering's blood rite. Based on the function of blood as a "payment" that eliminates guilt in the context of the blood feud, the blood rite of the sin offering applies this significance in a cultic context, serving to remove guilt and avoid its consequences. This compensatory function of blood is stated explicitly elsewhere in Priestly materials such as Gen 9:6, Lev 17:11, and Num 35:33. This notion of compensating guilt is consistent with the broader Israelite cultural conception in which divine retribution is depicted in terms of a commercial metaphor of "payback" (הֵשִׁיב, שִׁלֵּם).

This line of inquiry also enables us to understand the role of the altar's horns in the sin-offering ritual. In relatively early sources, the altar served as an asylum for inadvertent murderers (cf. Exod 21:14; 1 Kgs 2:28–34), protecting them from avengers who demand their blood. In fact, Jeremiah mentions the altar together with protective amulets in his exhortation: "The sin of Judah is inscribed with a stylus of iron, engraved with an adamant point on the tablet of their hearts and on the horns of your altars" (17:1). This verse lends striking expression to the metonymic scheme—explicated by Milgrom in relation to the sin-offering texts—in which the Israelite's sins are projected onto the altar as a record of their transgression. Accordingly, the prophet asserts that these protective means will offer no "sanctuary" to Judah, as they only serve to remind the Deity of their misdeeds.

This approach and its conclusions diverge dramatically from those of prior research. In most earlier studies, the expiatory use of blood in the sin offering is explained on the basis of explicit statements that relate blood with נפש, frequently mistranslated as "life" (Gen 9:4; Lev 17:11, 14; Deut 12:23). Aside from the fact that נפש never means "life" in the abstract sense, a meaning reserved for חיים, a survey of these statements in their literary contexts reveals a very different understanding of the relationship between blood and נפש. Aside from Lev 17:11, the association of blood with נפש appears as a rationale for the prohibition of ingesting blood. These formulas are most simply understood if one translates נפש as referring to the "vital spirit" of the animal, which must not be ingested. Indeed, these formulas appear in conjunction with explicit references to the notion that spilled blood demands a reckoning (Gen 9:5; Lev 17:4). Accordingly, spilled blood must be covered with earth and laid to rest so as not to demand cosmic vengeance (cf. Ezek 24:7–8; Job 16:18). As implied by Lev 17:14, the same "vital spirit" (נפש) that demands revenge is that which must not be ingested.

The exceptional passage Lev 17:11 uses the association of blood with נפש as a rationale for understanding the sacrificial use of blood. However, two major considerations militate against the common application of this statement to the sin offering. First of all, nothing in the context of Lev 17 provides any indication that v. 11 refers to the unique blood rite of the sin offering. On the contrary, the content of the chapter warrants understanding v. 11 as referring to either the blood of the well-being offering or that of the sacrificial offerings in general, which is poured out at the base of the altar. Second, it is important to recognize that the rationale offered in Lev 17:11 represents a midrashic reinterpretation of the use of blood in the cult that conflates two distinct uses of נפש. When asserting that "the spirit of the flesh is in the blood" (כי נפש הבשר בדם הוא), this passage evokes the notion that blood contains the "vital spirit" of the animal as it appears in the prohibition of ingesting blood. However, by stating that "it is the blood that ransoms by means of the life" (כי הדם הוא בנפש יכפר), it is expanding upon the talionic formula "life for a life" in which נפש signifies "individual life" (Exod 21:23; Lev 24:18; Deut 19:21). Whether or not the author was deliberately exploiting this polysemy, it is clear that this interpretation is based exclusively on the synthesis of these two originally unrelated verbal formulas.

Aside from pointing out the inapplicability of this passage for interpreting the sin offering's blood rite, the examination of this passage fulfills an important heuristic function for distinguishing between varying approaches to ritual interpretation. Unlike the type of secondary verbal rationalization of ritual activity offered by Lev 17:11, the present study seeks to explore the original motivation of a ritual, as determined by its ancient sociohistorical context.

In ch. 6, the same methodology was applied to the Hittite evidence. However, in this case, it was necessary to consider four independent and coherent rationalizations for the blood rite. In these sources, blood appears as 1) a gift to chthonic deities; 2) a means of compensation; 3) an agent of purification; and 4) an agent of consecration.

In evaluating these various rationales, the distinction between texts originating from the ritual circle of Kummanni (representing rationales 2 and 3) and those from Šamuha (representing rationales 1 and 4) is of central importance. Of these two text groups, it seems that the former has preserved the more original of the rationales, whereas the latter contains secondary interpretations based on local traditions. This assumption finds support in the Muršili's explicit complaint in KUB 32.133 that the scribes and temple personnel of Šamuha had altered ritual traditions.

In order to better understand the rationale of "compensation," it was necessary to examine the use of the verb *šarnink-* ("compensate") and its metaphorical application to the realm of divine retribution. For example, in texts from the Old Hittite period, the compensation metaphor appears exclusively in the context of blood retribution. In situations of bloodguilt, the gods are described as demanding the blood (*ešḫar šanḫ-*) of the perpetrator. The compensation for this bloodguilt could be described using *šarnink-*.

However, this usage seems to have been expanded over the course of the following centuries. In the prayers of the Hittite monarchs from the end of the empire, the metaphor of compensation is applied more broadly to express the idea of making atonement for prior transgressions before the gods. Accordingly, *šarnink-* and similar terms were used to describe various means of paying back one's debt to the gods, including the death of the perpetrator as well as the performance of a sacrificial offering.

This evidence provides the background for understanding the application of the terminology of compensation to the blood rite. For example, Muršili II's First Plague Prayer describes a "ritual of blood" (*išḫanaš* SISKUR) that was used to expiate (*šarnink-*) his father's murder of Tudhaliya the Younger. Though appearing here with a Hittite name, this rite is probably to be identified with the *zurki* rite. Likewise, the Papanikri ritual employs *šarnink-* in relation to the blood rite in declaring that the parturient has made compensation to the gods for a prior sin. In light of the metaphor of debt and compensation that served as a model for divine retribution, the use of blood as a payment to remove guilt is readily understandable.

This rationale is consistent with the appearance of *zurki* in the Hurro-Hittite ritual corpus in general, in which bloodguilt is one of several forms of depersonalized evil, such as curses and broken oaths, that can defile an object or building and provoke punishment against a person. Unlike these other forms of evil, bloodguilt stands out due to the fact that it offers a fitting means for making restitution for the crime committed, namely making compensation for the spilled blood. Thus, the notion of compensation, which was associated with blood, could serve by analogy as a general means for making expiation and prevent the otherwise automatic mechanism of retribution.

From the foregoing discussion, it emerges that the semiotic motivation for the Hittite and biblical blood rites is essentially the same. The textual evidence from both cultures reveals a fundamental belief in the threat of retribution stemming for bloodguilt and the compensatory role of blood in this social context. This scheme was applied by analogy to other forms of guilt towards the gods, which without any act of restitution would bring retribution automatically on the perpetrator.

The assumption of a mechanical notion of bloodguilt and its expiation that spanned from Canaan to Anatolia finds further support in the striking parallel between the late revision to Hittite Law §6 and Deut 21:1–9. Both of these texts deal with a situation in which a person is murdered in an open field. In the absence of a suspect, the nearest community as a whole is incriminated by default, as determined by measuring the distance to the closest city. At this point, the texts diverge. Whereas the biblical text requires a ritual of expiation, the Hittite law requires monetary compensation. Nevertheless, the remarkable similarity between these texts seems to reflect a shared belief, common to the Levantine region, in the threat of automatic retribution posed to a community that is collectively culpable for homicide. This shared conception finds ritual expression in the expiatory use of blood.

In ch. 7 an attempt is made to integrate the results of the preceding discussions into a comprehensive picture and assess the ramifications of the present study for understanding the transmission of the blood rite in history as well as its role in evolving religious conceptions of the Judeo-Christian tradition.

In order to determine the ethnic origin of the blood rite among the various groups of the Levant, the possible connection between the Hurro-Hittite *zurki* rite and the term *zukru(m)* in texts from Mari and Emar was evaluated. The evidence for a linguistic borrowing between the Akkadian and Hurrian terms in either direction is found to be inconclusive. Consequently, the blood rite's original ethnic origins cannot be determined at present, and we must suffice by recognizing its southern Anatolian/northern Syrian provenance, where it originated no later than the Late Bronze Age.

Regarding the transmission of these traditions to the Israelites, several historical scenarios may be proposed depending on whether the Israelites were indigenous or exogenous to Canaan. Neither of these scenarios undermines the assumption of a shared tradition; nevertheless, the evidence points most directly to a Syrian context of transmission. In particular, the Ugarit ritual texts provide clear evidence for an open atmosphere for sharing ritual traditions between Hurrians and Semites during this period. Furthermore, the blood rite is actually one of several compelling ritual parallels connecting Israel with the cultures of Syria and Anatolia in the Late Bronze Age. These points may offer some support to viewing the biblical tradition regarding the Syrian ancestry of the patriarchs as being rooted in historical reality, as argued by Fleming based on the documents from Mari and Emar.

As intuited above, the present study poses many challenges to the dominant historical framework for understanding the Priestly sources of the Bible. In particular, several counterintuitive assumptions of the Wellhausenian paradigm have misled scholars from giving proper attention to the comparative evidence and its importance for form criticism. Specifically, the existence of non-canonical ritual instructions from throughout the ancient Near East indicates that the Priestly sources originated in a similar manner. Indeed, the diachronic analyses presented here support reconstructing the literary development of P and H from ritual instructions used by officiating priests at local altars or sanctuaries in the pre-exilic period, which were later adapted to a canonical narrative framework. When the development of Priestly materials is conceived in such a way, many of Wellhausen's arguments lose their strength, especially as pertains to the pre-canonical versions of these texts.

At this point, the focus of discussion turns to the transmission of the biblical sin offering traditions from late antiquity to the present, especially regarding the relationship between nonverbal symbolism and verbalized description and translation. Although the Hittite and biblical sources reveal the same mechanical notion of bloodguilt in which blood serves as a means of expiation, this idea was expressed differently by the scribes of the two cultures. Whereas the Hittites employed a metaphor of debt and compensation (*šarnink*), the Hebrew text expressed this notion by means of changing the syntax and sense of כפ"ר derivatives to effect a semantic transition from appeasement to expiation (see above). Interestingly, the latter strategy was also employed by the Greek translators of the LXX, who achieved this effect by adapting the syntax of *hilaskomai* and its derivatives. Unlike the domiant usage in ancient Greek in which deities appear as the indirect object of these verbs, expressing the notion of "propitiation," the lxx frequently employs this verb with sancta or terms for sin as the indirect object, representing a calque of Hebrew כִּפֶּר.

A precursor to modern English translations can be found in the Latin Vulgate. Most obviously, the etymological sources for "propitiation" and "expiation" can be found in *prŏpĭtĭo* and *ex-pĭo*. The latter is the more regular translation for כִּפֶּר, though it is employed primarily where the usage of כִּפֶּר or חָטֵא refers to the purification of people or sancta. However, the Vulgate often prefers translate כִּפֶּר with *rŏgo* ("implore") and *de-prĕcor* ("avert by prayer"), which emphasize the personalized aspect of man's relationship with God.

This personal emphasis is apparent in most modern English translations. A survey of these translations reveals a general reticence to employ derivatives of "expiate," preferring terms such as "atone" and "reconciliate." Interestingly, one does find "expiate" in several of the English translations of the Bible from the beginning of the twentieth century, particularly in the context of removing bloodguilt from the land (e.g., Num 35:33; Deut 32:43). These translators have unknowingly traced the notion of "expiation" back to its prebiblical source, namely, the depersonalized depiction of making compensation for spilled blood.

The fact that verbal description of the blood rite required the innovation of new linguistic expressions in Hittite, Hebrew, and Greek shows that the nonverbal symbolism of blood enabled a unique type of conceptualization anterior to language that was only later converted into words, albeit in somewhat clumsy forms. Aside from demonstrating the problem of interpreting rituals in terms of linguistic and textual analogies, this example provides testimony to the process of semiotic evolution in which an idea embodied in nonverbal practice provides the basis for subsequent verbal articulations. Likewise, the metaphor of debt and compensation that underlies the sin offering was developed in various ways by later Jewish and Christian theology.

In addition, this survey of translations reveals a process by which a ritual is continuously reinterpreted in light of new cultural contexts. This development is accompanied by new understandings of the ritual's source of efficacy. The tendency towards interpreting the biblical cult in personalized terms, found in the Latin and English translations, already finds an antecedent in the Priestly source H. Unlike P's tendency to depict cultic activity in depersonalized mechanical terms, H tends to supply rationalizations to these rituals that emphasize the participation of God as the basis for ritual efficacy. Though perhaps additional reasons can be adduced for the increasingly theistic focus represented by H, an important factor may be the need to reinterpret rituals after their meaning has been obscured by changing cultural contexts.

Closing Thoughts

In the previous chapter, we examined several dimensions pertaining to the transmission of the blood rite across cultures and its perpetuation across generations. Observing the historical processes of reinterpreting earlier traditions, one becomes sensitive to the disproportionate power of the interpreter over the object of interpretation. By submitting the blood rite to academic analysis, there is a fundamental imbalance between the empowered position of the scholar and the vulnerable state of the cultural phenomenon under examination. Without seeking to overturn this natural order, it is tempting to propose a reversal of this hermeneutic, if only in the spirit of fairness.

Perhaps the most viable way of carrying out such a project is to identify the core ideas that have to some extent managed to survive the processes of intercultural transmission and translation in order to see what they have to say to the modern interpreter. As shown above, two such themes include the mechanistic notion of "expiation" and the debt metaphor for conceptualizing guilt. These items share a common perspective that misdeeds leave a real impression on the world—a lasting effect that will not disappear unless a penitential act is performed. This view can even be taken as an expression of a comprehensive form of religious experience shared by the ancient Hittites and Israelites (among others). Perhaps there is something the modern Westerner can learn from this different set of beliefs, despite (or perhaps because of) its drastically different ontological premises regarding such fundamental notions such as freedom, truth and morality.

In these texts, we encounter a world where the humans are all too aware of the limits of their control over their own destiny. When suddenly overwhelmed by the chaotic forces that overturn the stability of ordinary life, the person turns inwards to make an accounting over that small domain that remains under his sovereignty. Under such circumstances, he is forced to face up to the objective consequences of his deeds, even at the risk of being villainized in his own autobiographical narrative. With the gods as witnesses, he cannot escape his fate by reconstruing the facts. But this recognition need not bring resignation and despair. In this world of ritual, actions take over where words reach their limitations.

BIBLIOGRAPHY

Aartun, K. 1980. "Studien zum Gesetz über den grossen Versöhnungstag Lv 16 mit Varianten. Ein ritualgeschichtlicher Beitrag." *Studia Theologica* 34: 73–109.

Abusch, T. 2003. "Blood in Israel and Mesopotamia." Pages 675–84 in *Emanuel: Studies in Hebrew Bible, Septuagint and Dead Sea Scrolls in Honor of Emanuel Tov*. Edited by S. M. Paul et al. Leiden: Brill.

Ambos, C. 2004. *Mesopotamische Baurituale aus dem 1. Jahrtausend v. Chr.* Dresden: Islet.

Andersen, F. I., and D. N. Freedman. 1980. *Hosea*. AB. Garden City, N.Y.: Doubleday.

Anderson, G. A. 2005. "From Israel's Burden to Israel's Debt: Towards a Theology of Sin in Biblical and Early Second Temple Sources." Pages 1–30 in *Reworking the Bible: Apocryphal and Related Texts at Qumran*. Edited by E. G. Chazon et al. Leiden: Brill.

———. 2009. *Sin: A History*. New Haven: Yale University Press.

Astour, M. 1972. "Hattušiliš, Halab, and Hanigalbat." *JNES* 31: 102–9.

Bakhtin, M. M. 1986. *Speech Genres and Other Late Essays*. Edited by C. Emerson and M. Holmquist. Translated by V. W. McGee. Austin, Tex.: University of Texas Press.

———. and P. N. Medvedev. 1985. *The Formal Method in Literary Scholarship*. Translated by A. J. Wehrle.Cambridge, Mass: Harvard University Press.

Bakhurst, D. 1991. *Consciousness and Revolution in Soviet Philosophy*.Cambridge: Cambridge University Press.

Barmash, P. 2005. *Homicide in the Biblical World*. Cambridge: Cambridge University Press.

Barr, J. 1961. *The Semantics of Biblical Language*. London: Oxford University.

———. 1963. "Expiation." Pages 280–83 in *Dictionary of the Bible*. 3rd ed. Edited by J. Hastings et al. Edinburgh: T&T Clark.

Barth, F. 1975. *Ritual and Knowledge among the Baktaman of New Guinea*. Oslo: Universitetsforlaget.

Barth, J. 1894. *Die Nominalbildung in den Semitischen Sprachen*. Leipzig: Hinrichs.

Bauer, H. and P. Leander. 1922. *Historische Grammatik der Hebräischen Sprache des Alten Testamentes*. Halle: Niemeyer.

Beal, R. 2002. "Dividing a God." Pages 197–208 in *Magic and Ritual in the Ancient World*. Edited by P. Mirecki and M. Meyer. Leiden: Brill.

Beattie, J. H. M. 1964. *Other Cultures*. London: Cohen and West.

Beaulieu, P. A. 2002. "Eanna = Ayakkum in the Basekti Inscription of Narām-Sîn." *NABU* n. 36.

Beckman, G. M. 1983. *Hittite Birth Rituals*. StBoT 29. Wiesbaden: Harrassowitz.

————. 1999. *Hittite Diplomatic Texts*. 2nd ed. SBLWAW. Atlanta: Society of Biblical Literature.

————. 2011. "Blood in Hittite Ritual." *JCS* 63: 95–102.

Bell, C. 1992. *Ritual Theory, Ritual Practice*. New York: Oxford University Press.

Benveniste, E. 1971. *Problems in General Linguistics*. Translated by M. E. Meek. Coral Gable, Fl.: University of Miami Press.

Berger, P. and T. Luckmann. 1966. *The Social Construction of Reality*. New York: Doubleday.

Bertholet, A. 1901. *Leviticus*. KHC. Tübingen: Mohr.

Black, J. A. 1991. "Eme-sal Cult Songs and Prayers." *AuOr* 9: 23–36.

Blank, A. 2003. "Words and Concepts in Time: Towards Diachronic Cognitive Onomasiology." Pages 37–66 in *Words in Time: Diachronic Semantics from Different Points of View*. Edited by R. Eckardt et al. Berlin: de Gruyter.

Blenkinsopp, J. 1988. *Ezra-Nehemiah*. OTL. Philadelphia: Westminster.

Block, D. 1997–1998. *The Book of Ezekiel*. 2 vols. NICOT. Grand Rapids, Mich.: Eerdmans.

Bordreuil, P. and D. Pardee. 2004. "Ougarit-Adana, Ougarit-Damas: voyage outremer, voyage outremont vers 1200 av. J.-C." Pages 115–25 in *Antiquus Oriens: Mélanges offerts au Professeur René Lebrun*, vol. 1. Edited by M. Mazoyer and O. Casabonne. Paris: L'Harmattan.

Bourdieu, P. 1977. *Outline of a Theory of Practice*. Translated by R. Nice. Cambridge: Cambridge University Press.

Boysan-Dietrich, N. 1987. *Das hethitische Lehmhaus aus der Sich der Keilschriftquellen*. THeth 12. Heidelberg: Winter.

von Brandenstein, C. G. 1939. "Ein arisches und ein Semitisches Lehnwort im Churritischen." *AfO* 13: 58–62.

Bremmer, J. N. 2001. "The Scapegoat between Hittites, Greeks, Israelites and Christians." Pages 175–86 in *Kult, Konflikt, und Versöhnung*. Edited by R. Albertz. AOAT 285. Münster: Ugarit-Verlag.

Breytenbach, C. 1989. *Versöhnung: Eine Studie zur paulinischen Soteriologie*. Neukirchen-Vluyn: Neukirchener Verlag.

Brichto, H. C. 1976. "On Slaughter and Sacrifice, Blood and Atonement." *HUCA* 47: 19–56.

Broyer, Y. 1986. "איסור טומאה בתורה." *Megaddim* 2: 45–53.

Bryce, T. 1998. *The Kingdom of the Hittites*. Oxford: Clarendon.

Büchler, A. 1967. *Studies in Sin and Atonement in the Rabbinic Literature of the First Century*. New York: Ktav.

Burkert, W. 1992. *The Orientalizing Revolution: Near Eastern Influence on Greek Culture in the Early Archaic Age*. Cambridge, Mass.: Harvard University Press.

Carmichael, C. M. 1979. "A Common Element in Five Supposedly Disparate Laws." *VT* 29: 129–42.

Carr, D. M. 1996. *Reading the Fractures of Genesis: Historical and Literary Approaches*. Louisville, Ky.: Westminster John Knox.

————. 2005. *Writing on the Tablet of the Heart: Origins of Scripture and Literature*. Oxford: Oxford University Press.

Cassuto, U. 1964. *A Commentary on the Book of Genesis*, part 2. Translated by I. Abrahams. Jerusalem: Magnes.

Chandler, D. 2002. *Semiotics: The Basics*. London: Routledge.

Chavalas, M. W. and J. L. Hayes, eds. 1992. *New Horizons in the Study of Ancient Syria*. Malibu: Undena.

Christ, H. 1977. *Blutvergiessen im Alten Testament: Der gewaltsame Tod des Menschen untersucht am hebräischen Wort* dām. Diss. Universität Basel, Basel: Komm. Friedrich Reinhardt.

Christiansen, B. 2006. *Die Ritualtradition der Ambazzi: Eine philologische Bearbeitung und entstehungsgeschichtliche Analyse der Ritualtexte CTH 391, CTH 429 und CTH 463*. StBoT 48. Wiesbaden: Harrassowitz.

Cohen, C. 1968–1969. "Was the P Document Secret?" *JANES* 1–2: 39–44.

Cole, M. 1996. *Cultural Psychology: A Once and Future Discipline*. Cambridge, Mass: Harvard University Press.

Collins, B. J. 2002. "Necromancy, Fertility and the Dark Earth: The Use of Ritual Pits in Hittite Cult." Pages 224–41 in *Magic and Ritual in the Ancient World*. Edited by P. Mirecki and M. Meyer. Leiden: Brill.

———. 2006. "Pigs at the Gate: Hittite Pig Sacrifice in Its Eastern Mediterranean Context." *JANER* 6: 155–88.

———. 2007. *The Hittites and Their World*. Atlanta: Society of Biblical Literature.

Cook, S. L. 2004. *The Social Roots of Biblical Yahwism*. SBLSBL 8. Atlanta: Society of Biblical Literature.

Cooke, G. A. 1967. *The Book of Ezekiel*. ICC. Edinburgh: T&T Clark.

Culler, J. 2001. *The Pursuit of Signs: Semiotics, Literature, Deconstruction*. Ithaca, N.Y.: Cornell University Press.

Dalglish, E. R. 1962. *Psalm Fifty-One: In Light of Ancient Near Eastern Patternism*. Leiden: Brill.

Daniels, P. T. and W. Bright, eds. 1996. *The World's Writing Systems*. Oxford: Oxford University Press, 1996.

Dardano, P. 2002. "'La main est coupable', le sang devient abondant'." *Orientalia* 71: 333–92.

———. 2006. *Die hethitischen Tontafelkataloge aus Ḫattuša (CTH 276–282)*. StBoT 47. Wiesbaden: Harrassowitz.

de Martino, S. and F. Pecchioli Daddi, eds. 2002. *Anatolia Antica: Studia in memoria di Fiorella Imparati*. 2 vols. Eothen 11. Florence: LoGisma.

Dennis, J. 2002. "The Function of the חטאת Sacrifice in the Priestly Literature: An Evaluation of the View of Jacob Milgrom." *Ephemerides Theologicae Lovanienses* 78: 108–29.

Dietrich, M. 1990. "Die akkadischen Texte der Archive und Bibliotheken von Emar." *UF* 22: 40–48.

Dietrich, M. and O. Loretz. 1993. "Der biblische Azazel und AlT *126." *UF* 25: 99–117.

——— and W. Mayer. 1995. "Sprache und Kultur der Hurriter in Ugarit." Pages 7–42 in *Ugarit: Ein ostmediterranes Kulturzentrum im Alten Orient*, vol. 1. Edited by M. Dietrich and O. Loretz. Münster: Ugarit-Verlag.

Dillmann, A. 1897. *Die Bücher Exodus und Leviticus*. Leipzig: Hirzel.

Dion, P.-E. 1982. "Deutéronome 21, 1–9: Miroir du développement légal et religieux d'Israël." *Studies in Religion* 11: 13–22.

Dijkstra, M. 1992. "The Altar of Ezekiel." *VT* 42: 7–32.

Dodd, C. H. 1931. "*Hilaskesthai,* Its Cognates, Derivatives, and Synonyms, in the Septuagint." *JTS* 32: 352–60.

Douglas, M. 1999. *Leviticus as Literature.* Oxford: Oxford University Press.

Dreyfus, H. L. 1991. *Being-in-the-World.* Cambridge, Mass: MIT.

————. 2001–2002. "Phenomenological Description Versus Rational Reconstruction." *Revue internationale de philosophie* 216: 181–96.

Driver, S. R. 1902. *Deuteronomy.* ICC. New York: Scribner's Sons. Repr. Edinburgh: T&T Clark, 1960.

————. 1911. *The Book of Exodus.* Cambridge: Cambridge University Press. Repr. 1953.

————. 1915. "Expiation and Atonement (Hebrew)." Pages 653–59 in *Encyclopedia of Religion and Ethics,* vol. 5. Edited by J. Hastings. Edinburgh: T&T Clark.

Duguid, I. M. 1994. *Ezekiel and the Leaders of Israel.* Leiden: Brill.

Durand, J.-M. 2002. "Cuneiform Script." Pages 20–32 in *A History of Writing.* Edited by A.-M. Christin. Paris: Flammarion.

Durkheim, E. 1995. *The Elementary Forms of Religious Life.* Translated by K. E. Fields. New York: Free Press.

Ebeling, E. 1971. "Färbestoff." *RlA* 3: 26–27.

Eberhart, C. 2002. *Studien zur Bedeutung der Opfer im Alten Testament: die Signifikanz von Blut- und Verbrennungsriten im kultischen Rahmen.* Neukirchen-Vluyn: Neukirchener Verlag.

Eco, U. 1976. *A Theory of Semiotics.* London: Macmillan.

Ehrlich, A. 1909. *Randglossen zur hebräischen Bibel,* vol. 2. Leipzig: Hinrichs.

Eisenbeis, W. 1967. *Die Wurzel šlm im Alten Testament.* Berlin: de Gruyter

Elliger, K. 1966. *Leviticus.* HAT. Tübingen: Mohr.

Ellis, R. S. 1968. *Foundation Deposits in Ancient Mesopotamia.* New Haven: Yale University Press.

Englund, R. K. 1998. "Texts from the Late Uruk Period." Pages 15–233 in *Mesopotamien: Späturukzeit und Frühdynastische Zeit.* OBO 160/1. Edited by P. Attinger and M. Wäfler. Freiburg: Universitätsverlag.

Faust, A. 2006. *Israel's Ethnogenesis.* London: Equinox.

Feder, Y. 2010. "On *kuppuru, kippēr* and Etymological Sins that Cannot be Wiped Away." *VT* 60: 535–45.

————. 2010. "The Mechanics of Retribution in Hittite, Mesopotamian and Biblical Texts." *JANER* 10: 119–57.

Feliks, J. 1968. *Plant World of the Bible.* Ramat-Gan: Bar-Ilan University. (Hebrew)

Fensham, F. C. 1964. "The Treaty between Israel and the Gibeonites." *BA* 27: 96–100.

Firth, R. W. 1973. *Symbols: Public and Private.* London: Allen & Unwin.

Fishbane, M. 1980. "Biblical Colophons, Textual Criticism, and Legal Analogies." *CBQ* 42: 438–49.

————. 1985. *Biblical Interpretation in Ancient Israel.* Oxford: Oxford University Press.

Fleming, D. E. 1998. "The Biblical Tradition of Anointing Priests." *JBL* 117: 401–14.

————. 2000. *Time at Emar: The Cultic Calendar and the Rituals from the Diviner's House.* Winona Lake, Ind.: Eisenbrauns.

————. 2002. "Emar: On the Road from Harran to Hebron." Pages 222–50 in *Mesopotamia and the Bible.* Edited by M. W. Chavalas and K. L. Younger. London: Sheffield Academic.

————. 2004. "Genesis in History and Tradition: The Syrian Background of Israel's

Ancestry Reprise." Pages 193–232 in *The Future of Biblical Archaeology*. Edited by J. K. Hoffmeier and A. Millard. Grand Rapids, Mich.: Eerdmans.

Forlanini, M. 2007. "Geographica Diachronica." Pages 263–70 in *Tabularia Hethaeorum*: *Hethitologische Beiträge. Silvin Košak zum 65 Geburtstag*. Edited by D. Groddek and M. Zorman. Wiesbaden: Harrassowitz.

Fox, J. 2003. *Semitic Noun Patterns*. Winona Lake, Ind.: Eisenbrauns.

Franz-Szabó, G. 2003–2005. "Öl, Ölbaum, Olive. B. In Anatolie." *RlA* 10:33–38.

Frazer, J. G. and T. H. Gaster. 1969. *Myth, Legend and Custom in the Old Testament*. New York: Harper & Row.

Füglister, N. 1977. "Sühne durch Blut—Zur Bedeutung von Leviticus 17, 11." Pages 143–64 in *Studien zum Pentateuch. W. Kornfeld zum 60. Geburtstag*. Edited by G. Braulik. Vienna: Herder.

Gabbay, U. 2007. "The Sumero-Akkadian Prayer 'Eršema': A Philological and Religious Analysis." Ph.D. diss. Jerusalem: Hebrew University.

Gammie, J. G. 1970. "The Theology of Retribution in the Book of Deuteronomy;" *CBQ* 32: 1–12.

Gane, R. 2005. *Cult and Character: Purification Offerings, Day of Atonement, and Theodicy*. Winona Lake, Ind.: Eisenbrauns.

Geertz, C. 1973. *The Interpretation of Cultures*. New York: Basic Books.

Gelb, I. J. 1963. *A Study of Writing*. Chicago: University of Chicago Press.

Gerleman, G. 1973. "Die Wurzel šlm im Alten Testament." *ZAW* 85: 1–14.

Gerstenberger, E. 1996. *Leviticus: A Commentary*. Translated by D.W. Stott. Louisville: Westminster John Knox.

Gese, H. 1981. "The Atonement." Pages 93–116 in *Essays on Biblical Theology*. Translated by K. Crim. Minneapolis: Augsburg.

Gibbs, R. W. 1999. "Taking Metaphor out of Our Heads and Putting it into the Cultural World." Pages 145–66 in *Metaphor in Cognitive Linguistics*. Edited by R. W. Gibbs and G. J. Steen. Amsterdam: Benjamins.

———. 2006. *Embodiment and Cognitive Science*. Cambridge: Cambridge University Press.

Gilders, W. K. 2004. *Blood Ritual in the Hebrew Bible: Meaning and Power*. Baltimore: Johns Hopkins University Press.

———. 2006. "Why Does Eleazar Sprinkle the Red Cow Blood? Making Sense of a Biblical Ritual." *JHS* 6. Online: http://www.arts.ualberta.ca/JHS/Articles/article_59.pdf.

Ginsberg, H. L. 1965. *New Trends in the Study of Bible*. New York: Jewish Theological Seminary of America.

———. 1982. *The Israelian Heritage of Judaism*. New York: Jewish Theological Seminary.

Giorgieri, M. 2000. "Schizzo grammaticale della lingua hurrica." Pages 171–277 in *La Civiltà dei Hurriti*. Edited by G. P. Carrratelli. Naples: Arte Tipografica.

Goetze, A. 1930. *Kleinasiatische Forschungen* I. Weimar: Böhlaus.

Gorman, F. H. 1990. *The Ideology of Ritual: Space, Time and Status in the Priestly Theology*. Sheffield: JSOT.

Greimas, A. J. 1987. "Towards a Semiotics of the Natural World." Pages 17–47 in *On Meaning: Selected Writings in Semiotic Theory*. Translated by P. J. Perron and F. H. Collins. Minneapolis: University of Minnesota Press.

Greenberg, M. 1984. "The Design and Themes of Ezekiel's Program of Restoration." *Interpretation* 38: 181–209.

Grintz, J. M. 1972. "Do not Eat on the Blood (Lev 19, 26)." *Annual of the Swedish Theology Institute* 8 (1972): 78–105.

Guiraud, P. 1975. *Semiology*. Trans. G. Gross. London: Routledge. 1975),

Güterbock, H. G. 1983. "Hethitische Götterbilder und Kultobjeckte." Pages 203–17 in *Beiträge zur Altertumskunde Kleinasiens*. Edited by R. M. Böhmer and H. Hauptmann. Mainz: von Zabern.

Haas, V. 1993. "Ein hurritischer Blutritus und die Deponierung der Ritualrückstände nach hethitischen Quellen." Pages 67–86 in *Religionsgeschichtliche Beziehungen zwischen Kleinasien, Nordsyrien und dem Alten Testament*. Edited by B. Janowski, K. Koch, and G. Wilhelm. Freiburg: Universitätsverlag.

———. 1994. *Geschichte der hethitischen Religion*. Leiden: Brill.

———. 1998. *Die hurritischen Ritualtermini in hethitischem Kontext*. ChS I/9. Rome: CNR.

———. 2003. "Betrachtungen zur Traditionsgeschichte hethitischer Rituale am Beispiel des 'Sündenbock'- Motivs." Pages 131–41 in *Hittite Studies in Honor of H. A. Hoffner on the Occasion of His Sixty-Fifth Birthday*. Edited by G. Beckman et al. Winona Lake, Ind.: Eisenbrauns.

———. 2003. *Materia Magica et Medica Hethitica: Ein Beitrag zur Heilkunde im Alten Orient*. 2 vols. Berlin: de Gruyter.

——— and G. Wilhelm. 1974. *Hurritische und luwische Riten aus Kizzuwatna*. AOATS 3. Neukirchen-Vluyn: Kevelaer.

Haase, R. 1995. *Beobachtungen zur hethitischen Rechtssatzung*. Leonberg: self-published.

Hacker, P. M. S. 2010. "Meaning and Use." Pages 26–44 in *The Later Wittgenstein on Language*. Edited by D. Whiting. Basingstoke, UK: Palgrave Macmillan.

Hagenbuchner, A. 1989. *Die Korrespondenz der Hethiter*, vol. 2. THeth 16. Heidelberg: Winter

Hallett, G. 1967. *Wittgenstein's Definition of Meaning as Use*. New York: Fordham University Press.

Halpern, B. 2001. *David's Secret Demons: Messiah, Murderer, Traitor, King,* Grand Rapids, Mich.: Eerdmans.

Hampe, B. 2005. *From Perception to Meaning: Image Schemas in Cognitive Linguistics*. Berlin: de Gruyter.

Haran, M. 1982. "Book Scrolls in Israel in Pre-Exilic Times." *JJS* 33: 161–73.

Harper, W. R. 1979. *Amos and Hosea*. ICC. Edinburgh: T&T Clark.

Heidegger, M. 1962. *Being and Time*. New York: Harper and Row.

Hill, D. 1967. *Greek Words and Hebrew Meanings: Studies in the Semantics of Soteriological Terms*. Cambridge: Cambridge University Press.

Hobart, M. 1982. "Meaning or Moaning? An Ethnographic Note on a Little-Understood Tribe." Pages 39–64 in *Semantic Anthropology*. Edited by D. Parkin. London: Academic.

Hodge, R. and G. Kress. 1988. *Social Semiotics*. Ithaca: Cornell University Press.

von Hoffman, J. 1859. *Der Schriftbeweis*, vol. 2/1. Nördlingen: Beck.

Hoffmann, D. 1905–1906. *Das Buch Leviticus*. 2 vols. Berlin: Poppelauer.

Hoffmann, I. 1984. *Der Erlaß Telipinus*. Heidelberg: Winter.

Hoffner, H. A. Jr. 1973. "The Hittites and Hurrians." Pages 197–228 in *Peoples of Old Testament Times*. Edited by D. J. Wiseman. Oxford: Clarendon.

———. 1974. *Alimenta Hethaeorum: Food Production in Hittite Asia Minor*. New Haven: American Oriental Society.

———. 1992. "Syrian Cultural Influence in Hatti." Pages 89–116 in *New Horizons in the Study of Ancient Syria*. Edited by M. W. Chavalas and J. L. Hayes. Malibu: Undena.

———. 1995. "Oil in Hittite Texts." *BA* 58: 108–14.

———. 1997. "On Homicide in Hittite Law." Pages 293–314 in *Crossing Boundaries and Linking Horizons: Studies in Honor of Michael C. Astour on His 80th Birthday*. Edited by G. D. Young et al. Bethesda, Md.: CDL.

———. 1997. *The Laws of the Hittites: A Critical Edition*. Leiden: Brill.

———. 2004. "Ancient Israel's Literary Heritage Compared with Hittite Textual Data." Pages 176–92 in *The Future of Biblical Archaeology: Reassessing Methodology and Assumptions*. Edited by J. K. Hoffmeier and A. Millard. Grand Rapids, Mich.: Eerdmans.

——— and H. Craig Melchert. 2008. *A Grammar of the Hittite Language, Part I: Reference Grammar*. Winona Lake, Ind.: Eisenbrauns.

Holland, D. and N. Quinn, eds. 1987. *Cultural Models in Language and Thought*. Cambridge: Cambridge University Press.

Holy, L. "Contextualization and Paradigm Shifts." Pages 1999 in *The Problem of Context*. Edited by R. Dilley. New York: Berghahn.

Hout, T. van den. 1998. *The Purity of Kingship: An Edition of CTH 569 and Related Hittite Oracle Inquiries of Tuthaliya IV*. Leiden: Brill.

———. 2006. "Muršili II's 'First' Plague Prayer." Pages 259–63 in *The Ancient Near East: Historical Texts in Translation*. Edited by M. W. Chavalas. Malden, Mass.: Blackwell.

Houtman, C. 1983. "Exodus 4:24–26 and Its Interpretation." *JNSL* 11: 81–103

Huehnergard, J. 1987. *Ugaritic Vocabulary in Syllabic Transcription*. HSS 32. Atlanta: Scholars Press.

Hulse, E. V. 1975. "The Nature of Biblical 'Leprosy' and the Use of Alternative Medical Terms in Modern Translations of the Bible." *PEQ* 107: 87–105.

Hurvitz, A. 1970–1971. "Linguistic Observations on the Biblical Usage of the Priestly Term *'Eda*." *Tarbiz* 40: 261–67.

———. 1982. *A Linguistic Study of the Relationship between the Priestly Source and the Book of Ezekiel: A New Approach to an Old Problem*. Paris: Gabalda.

Janowski, B. 1982. *Sühne als Heilsgeschehen: Studien zur Sühnetheologie der Priesterschrift und zur Wurzel KPR im Alten Orient und im Alten Testament*. Neukirchen-Vluyn: Neukirchener Verlag.

———, K. Koch, and G. Wilhelm, eds. 1993. *Religionsgeschichtliche Beziehungen zwischen Kleinasien, Nordsyrien und dem Alten Testament*. Freiburg: Universitätsverlag.

——— and G. Wilhelm. 1993. "Der Bock, der die Sünden hinausträgt: Zur Religionsgeschichte des Azazel-Ritus Lev 16,10.21f." Pages 109–70 in *Religionsgeschichtliche Beziehungen zwischen Kleinasien, Nordsyrien und dem Alten Testament*. Edited by B. Janowski, K. Koch, and G. Wilhelm. Freiburg: Universitätsverlag.

Jay, N. 1992. *Throughout Your Generations Forever: Sacrifice, Religion, and Paternity*. Chicago: University of Chicago Press.

Jenni, E. 1968. *Das hebräische Pi'el.* Zürich: EVZ.

Kaddari, M. Z. 2006. *A Dictionary of Biblical Hebrew.* Ramat-Gan: Bar-Ilan University Press. (Hebrew)

Kaiser, O. 1992–1994. *Grundriss der Einleitung in die kanonischen und deuteronkanonischen Schriften des Alten Testaments.* Gütersloh: Mohn.

Kammenhuber, A. 1976. *Orakelpraxis, Träume und Vorzeichenschau beiden Hethitern.* THeth 7. Heidelberg: Winter.

———. 1989. *Materialien zu einem hethitischen Thesaurus.* Lieferung 11. Heidelberg: Winter.

Kapferer, B. 2005. "Ritual Dynamics and Virtual Practice: Beyond Representation and Meaning." Pages 35–52 in *Ritual in Its Own Right.* Edited by D. Handelman and G. Lindquist. New York: Berghahn.

Kasher, R. 1998. "Anthropomorphism, Holiness and Cult: A New Look at Ezekiel 40–48." *ZAW* 110: 192–208

———. 2004. *Ezekiel: Introduction and Commentary.* 2 vols. Mikra Leyisrael. Tel-Aviv: Am Oved. (Hebrew)

Kaufmann, Y. 1960. *The Religion of Israel.* Translated by M. Greenberg; Chicago: University of Chicago Press.

Kellerman, G. 1980. *Recherche sur les Rituels de Fondation Hittites.* PhD dissertation. Paris: Université de Paris.

Kempinski, A. 1983. *Syrien und Paläestina (Kanaan) in der letzeten Phase der Mittelbronze IIB-Zeit.* Wiesbaden: Harrassowitz.

Kennedy, A. R. S. and J. Barr. 1963. "Sacrifice and Offering." Pages 868–76 in *Dictionary of the Bible.* 3rd ed. Edited by J. Hastings et al. Edinburgh: T&T Clark.

Kiuchi, N. 1987. *The Purification Offering in the Priestly Literature.* Sheffield: Sheffield Academic.

Klengel, H. 1965. *Geschichte Syriens im 2. Jahrtausend v.u.Z.,* Part I: *Nordsyrien.* Berlin: Akademie-Verlag.

Klengel, H. 1980. "Mord und Bußleistung im spätbronzezeitlichen Syrien." Pages 189–97 in *Death in Mesopotamia.* Edited by B. Alster. Mesopotamia 8. Copenhagen: Akademisk Verlag. 189–97.

Klingbeil, G. A. 1998. *A Comparative Study of the Ritual of Ordination as found in Leviticus 8 and Emar 369.* Lewiston: Edwin Mellen.

———. 2007. *Bridging the Gap: Ritual and Ritual Texts in the Bible.* Winona Lake, Ind.: Eisenbrauns.

Knohl, I. 1991. "The Sin-Offering Law in the Holiness School." Pages 192–203 in *Priesthood and Cult in Ancient Israel.* Edited by G. A. Anderson and S. M. Olyan. JSOTSup 125. Sheffield: JSOT Press.

———. 1995. *The Sanctuary of Silence: The Priestly Torah and the Holiness School.* Minneapolis: Fortress.

Koch, K. 1955. "Gibt es ein Vergeltungsdogma im AT." *ZTK* 52: 1–42. Repr. pages 130–80 in *Um das Prinzip der Vergeltung in Religion und Recht des Alten Testaments.* Edited by K. Koch. Darmstadt: Wissenschaftliche Buchgesellschaft, 1972.

———. 1962. "Der Spruch 'Sein Blut bleibe auf seinem Haupt' und die israelitische Auffassung vom vergossenen Blut." *VT* 12: 396–416. Repr. pages 432–56 in *Um das Prinzip der Vergeltung in Religion und Recht des Alten Testaments.* Darmstadt: Wissenschaftliche Buchgesellschaft, 1972.

————. 1983. "Is There a Doctrine of Retribution in the Old Testament?" Pages 57–87 in *Theodicy in the Old Testament*. Edited by J. L. Crenshaw. Philadelphia: Fortress.

————. 1995. "Some Considerations on the Translation of *kapporēt* in the Septuagint." Pages 65–75 in *Pomegranates and Golden Bells: Studies in Biblical, Jewish and Near Eastern Ritual, Law, and Literature in Honor of Jacob Milgrom*. Edited by D. P. Wright, D. N. Freedman, and A. Hurvitz. Winona Lake, Ind.: Eisenbrauns.

Kövecses, Z. 2005. *Metaphor in Culture*. Cambridge: Cambridge University Press.

Krapf, T. M. 1992. *Die Priesterschrift und die vorexilische Zeit*. OBO 119. Freiburg: Universitätsverlag.

Kronasser, H. 1963. *Die Umsiedelung der Schwarzen Gottheit: Das hethitische Ritual KUB XXIX 4 (des Ulippi)*. Vienna: Boehlaus.

Kuenen, A. 1886. *An Historico-Critical Inquiry into the Origin and Composition of the Hexateuch*. Translated by P. H. Wicksteed. London: Macmillan.

Kühne, C. 1993. "Zum Vor-Opfer im alten Anatolien." Pages 225–83 in *Religionsgeschichtliche Beziehungen zwischen Kleinasien, Nordsyrien und dem Alten Testament*. Edited by B. Janowski, K. Koch, and G. Wilhelm. Freiburg: Universitätsverlag.

Kümmel, H. M. 1980–1983. "Kummanni." *RlA* 6: 335.

Kurtz, J. H. 1980. *Sacrificial Worship of the Old Testament*. Translated by J. Martin. Grand Rapids, Mich.: Baker.

Labuschagne, C. J. 1982. "The Meaning of *beyād rāmā*." Pages 143–48 in *Von Kanaan bis Kerala*. Edited by W. C. Delsman et al. AOAT 211. Kevelaer: Butzon & Bercker.

Lafont, B. 1984. "Les prophètes du dieu Adad." *RA* 78: 11.

Lakoff, G. 1987. *Women, Fire and Dangerous Things: What Categories Reveal about the Mind*. Chicago: University of Chicago Press.

————. 1993. "The Contemporary Theory of Metaphor." Pages 202–51 in *Metaphor and Thought*. 2nd ed. Edited by A. Ortony. Cambridge: Cambridge University Press.

———— and M. Johnson. 1980. *Metaphors We Live By*. Chicago: University of Chicago Press.

————. and Z. Kövecses. 1987. "The Cognitive Model for Anger Inherent in American English." Pages 195–221 in *Cultural Models in Language and Thought*. Edited by Holland, D. and N. Quinn. Cambridge: Cambridge University Press.

Landsberger, B. 1967. *The Date Palm and Its By-Products according to the Cuneiform Sources*. Graz: Weidner.

Laroche, E. 1973. "Études de Linguistique Anatolienne." *RHA* 31: 83–99.

————. 1976–77. *Glossaire de la langue hourrite*. *RHA* 34–35.

Lawson, E. T. and R. N. McCauley. 1990. *Rethinking Religion: Connecting Cognition and Culture*. Cambridge: Cambridge University Press.

Lebrun, R. 1976. *Šamuha: Foyer Religieux de l'Empire Hittites*. Louvain-la-Neuve: Universite catholique de Louvain.

————. 1978. "Les rituels d'Ammihatna, Tulbi et Mati contre une impureté= CTH 472." *Hethitica* 3: 139–64.

————. 1996. "Rituels de Muwalanni à Manuzziya= CTH 703." *Hethitica* 13: 39–64.

————. 1999. "Fragment d'un rituel de Walkui, prêtre de la déesse de la nuit (KBo XXXII 176 = Bo 83/902)." *Archív Orientální* 67: 601–8.

Lee, B. 1985. "Intellectual Origins of Vygotsky's Semiotic Analysis." Pages 66–93 in *Vygotsky and the Social Formation of Mind*. J. V. Wertsch. Cambridge, Mass.: Harvard University Press.

Levine, B. A. 1965. "The Descriptive Tabernacle Texts of the Pentateuch." *JAOS* 85: 307–18.

———. 1974. *In the Presence of the Lord*. Leiden: Brill.

———. 1989. *Leviticus*. JPS Torah Commentary; Philadelphia: Jewish Publication Society.

———. 1993–2000. *Numbers*. 2 vols. AB. New York: Doubleday.

———. 2003. "Leviticus: Its Literary History and Location in Biblical Literature." Pages 11–23 in *The Book of Leviticus: Composition and Reception*. Edited by R. Rendtorff and R. A. Kugler. Leiden: Brill, 2003.

Levi-Strauss, C. 1966. *The Savage Mind*. Chicago: University of Chicago Press.

Licht, J. 1995. *A Commentary on the Book of Numbers,* vol. 3. Jerusalem: Magnes. (Hebrew)

Linke, U. 1985. "Blood as Metaphor in Proto-Indo-European." *JIES* 13: 333–75.

Linssen, M. J. H. 2004. *The Cults of Uruk and Babylon: The Temple Ritual Texts as Evidence for Hellenistic Cult Practices*. Leiden: Brill.

Lods, A. 1950. "Une tablette inédite de Mari, interessante pour l'histoire ancienne du prophétisme sémitique." Pages 103–10 in *Studies in Old Testament Prophecy*. Edited by H. H. Rowley. Edinburgh: T&T Clark.

Loewenstamm, S. 1971. "עגלה ערופה," *Enṣiqlopedya Miqra'it* 6: 77–79.

Leach, E. R. 1976. *Culture and Communication: The Logic by which Symbols are Connected*. Cambridge: Cambridge University Press.

L'Hour, J. 1963. "Une législation criminelle dans le Deutéronome." *Biblica* 44: 1–27.

Linnsen, M. J. H. 2004. *The Cults of Uruk and Babylon: The Temple Ritual Texts as Evidence for Hellenistic Cult Practises*. Leiden: Brill.

Löhr, M. 1925. *Das Ritual von Lev 16*. Untersuchungen zum Hexateuch-problem 3. Berlin: Deutsche verlagsgesellschaft für politik und geschichte.

Löw, I. 1909. "Der Biblische 'ēzōb." *Sitzungsberichte* 160: 1–30 (vol. 3; Akademie der Wissenschaften in Wien Philosophisch-Historische Klasse; Vienna: Hölder.

Lund, N. W. 1942. *Chiasmus in the New Testament*. Chapel Hill: University of North Carolina Press. Repr. Peabody, Mass.: Hendrickson, 1992.

Lust, J. et al. 1992. *A Greek-English Lexicon of the Septuagint*, vol. 1. Stuttgart: Deutsche Bibelgesellschaft.

Maccoby, H. 1999. *Ritual and Morality: The Ritual Purity System and Its Place in Judaism*. Cambridge: Cambridge University Press.

Machinist, P. 2009. "The Road Not Taken: Wellhausen and Assyriology." Pages 469–531 in *Homeland and Exile: Biblical and Ancient Near Eastern Studies in Honour of Bustenay Oded*. Edited by G. Galil et al. VTSupp 130. Leiden: Brill.

Malamat, A. 1955. "Doctrines of Causality in Hittite and Biblical Historiography: A Parallel." *VT* 5: 8–12

Malul, M. 1990. *The Comparative Method in Ancient Near Eastern and Biblical Legal Studies*. AOAT 227. Kevelaer: Butzon & Bercker.

———. 1992. "David's Curse of Joab and the Social Significance of *mhzyk bplk*." *AuOr* 10: 49–67.

de Martino, S. 2003. *Annali e Res Gestae antico ittiti*. StMed 12. Pavia: Italian University Press.

Marx, A. 2005. *Les Systèmes Sacrificiels de l'Ancien Testament*. Leiden: Brill.

Marx, K. 1953. *Das Kapital*, vol. 1. Berlin: Dietz.

Maul, S. M. 1994. *Zukunftsbewältigung*. BF 18. Mainz: von Zabern.

———. 1989. "ᴺᴵᴺᴰᴬGEŠTUG = *ḫasīsītu*, 'Öhrchen,' 'Brot in Ohrenform'." *NABU*, no. 7.

———. 1999. "How the Babylonians Protected Themselves against Calamities Announced by Omens." Pages 123–29 in *Mesopotamian Magic: Textual, Historical and Interpretative Perspectives*. Edited by T. Abusch and K. van der Toorn. Gröningen: Styx.

Mauss, M. 1935. "Les techniques du corps." *Journal de psychologie normal et pathologique* 32: 271–93. Repr. pages 364–86 in *Sociologie et Anthropologie*. Edited by M. Mauss. Paris: Presses Universitaires de France, 1968.

Mayer, W. 1996. "The Hurrian Cult at Ugarit." Pages 205–11 in *Ugarit, Religion and Culture: Essays Presented in Honour of Professor John C. L. Gibson*. Edited by N. Wyatt et al. Münster: Ugarit-Verlag.

McCarter, P. K. 1980. "The Apology of David." *JBL* 99: 489–504.

———. 1984. *II Samuel*. AB. New York: Doubleday.

McCarthy, D. J. 1969. "The Symbolism of Blood and Sacrifice." *JBL* 88: 166–76.

———. 1973. "Further Notes on the Symbolism of Blood and Sacrifice." *JBL* 92: 205–10

McKeating, H. 1975. "The Development of the Law of Homicide in Ancient Israel." *VT* 25: 46–68

Meier, S. A. 1991. "The Sabbath and Purification Cycles." Pages 3–11 in *The Sabbath in Jewish and Christian Traditions*. Edited by T. C. Eshkenazi et al. New York: Crossroad.

Melchert, H. C. 1979. "Three Hittite Etymologies." *Zeitschrift für Vergleichende Sprachforschung* 93: 262–71.

———. 1983. "Pudenda Hethitica." *JCS* 35: 137–45.

Merz, E. 1916. *Die Blutrache bei den Israeliten*. Leipzig: Heinrichs.

Milgrom, J. 1971. "A Prolegomenon to Leviticus 17:11." *JBL* 90: 149–56.

———. 1971. "Sin Offering or Purification Offering." *VT* 21: 237–39.

———. 1973. "The *Ḥaṭṭat* Offering and the Temple Cult in Jeremiah's Time." Pages 123–45 in *Studies in the Book of Jeremiah*, vol. 2. Edited by B. Z. Luria. Jerusalem: World Jewish Bible Society. (Hebrew)

———. 1978. "Priestly Terminology and the Political and Social Structure of Pre-Monarchic Israel." *JQR* 69: 65–81.

———. 1990. *The Book of Numbers*. JPS Bible Commentary. Philadelphia: Jewish Publication Society.

———. 1990. "The Modus Operandi of the 'Ḥaṭṭa'th': A Rejoinder." *JBL* 109: 111–13.

———. 1991–2001. *Leviticus*. 3 vols. AB. New York: Doubleday.

———. 2000. "Impurity Is Miasma: A Response to Hyam Maccoby." *JBL* 119: 729–46.

———. 2007. "The Preposition מִן in the חטאת Pericopes." *JBL* 126: 161–63.

Miller, J. L. 2004. *Studies in the Origins, Development, and Interpretation of the Kizzuwatna Rituals*. StBoT 46. Wiesbaden: Harrassowitz.

Miller, P. D. 1970. "Apotropaic Imagery in Proverbs 6, 20–22." *JNES* 29: 129–30.

Moldenke, H. N. and A. L. Moldenke. 1952. *Plants of the Bible*. Waltham, Mass.: Ronald Press.

Moraldi, L. 1956. *Espiazione sacrificale e riti espiatori nell'ambiente biblico e nell'Antico Testamento*. Roma: Pontificio Istituto biblico.

Morris, C. 1955. *Signs, Language and Behavior*. New York: Braziller.

Morris, L. 1955. *The Apostolic Preaching of the Cross*. London: Tyndale.

Mouton, A. 2004. "Le rituel de Walkui (KBo 32.176): quelques réflexions sur la déesse de la nuit et l'image du porc dans le monde Hittite." *ZA* 94: 85–105.

———. 2007. "Sur la différenciation entre rêve et *parā ḫandandatar* dans les textes hittites." Pages 523–31 in *VITA*. Edited by M. Alparslan et al. Istanbul: Ege Yayınları.

Moyer, J. C. 1983. "Hittite and Israelite Cultic Practices: A Selected Comparison." Pages 19–38 in *Scripture in Context II*. Edited by W. W. Hallo et al. Winona Lake, Ind.: Eisenbrauns.

Müller-Karpe, A. 2000. "Kayalıpınar in Ostkappadokien: Ein neuer hethitischen Tontafelfundplatz." *MDOG* 132: 363–64.

Muraoka, T. 2002. *A Greek-English Lexicon of the Septuagint*. Louvain: Peeters.

Na'aman, N. 1994. "The 'Conquest of Canaan' in the Book of Joshua and in History." Pages 218–81 in *From Nomadism to Monarchy*. Edited by I. Finkelstein and N. Na'aman. Jerusalem: Yad Izhak Ben Zvi.

Neu, E. 1996. *Das hurritische Epos der Freilassung* I. StBoT 32. Wiesbaden: Harrassowitz.

Norris, C. 1982. *Deconstruction: Theory and Practice*. London: Methuen.

Noth, M. 1965. *Leviticus: A Commentary*. OTL. Translated by J. E. Anderson. London: SCM Press.

Nöth, W. 1990. *Handbook of Semiotics*. Bloomington, Ind: Indiana University Press.

Nougayrol, J. 1968. "Textes Suméro-Accadiens des archives et bibliothèques privées d'Ugarit," *Ugaritica* 5: 1–446.

Olson, D. R. 1994. *The World on Paper: The Conceptual and Cognitive Implications of Reading and Writing*. Cambridge: Cambridge University Press.

Olyan, S. 1998. "What Do Shaving Rites Accomplish and What Do They Signal in Biblical Ritual Contexts?" *JBL* 117: 611–22.

Onians, R. B. 1951. *The Origins of European Thought About the Body, the Mind, the Soul, the World, Time and Fate*. Cambridge: Cambridge University Press. Repr. Cambridge: Cambridge University Press, 1988.

Oppenheim, A. Leo. 1977. *Ancient Mesopotamia: Portrait of a Dead Civilization*. Chicago: University of Chicago Press.

Origen. 1990. *Homilies on Leviticus 1–16*. Translated by G. W. Barkley. Washington D.C.: Catholic University of America.

Otten, H. 1961. "Eine Beschwörung der Unterirdischen aus Boğazköy." *ZA* 54: 114–57.

———. 1971. *Materialien zum hethitischen Lexikon*. StBoT 15. Wiesbaden: Harrassowitz.

———. 1976. "Bemerkungen zum Hethitischen Wörterbuch." *ZA* 66: 89–104.

Pardee, D. 1996. "L'ougaritique et le Hourrite dans les textes de Ras Shamra-Ougarit." Pages 65–80 in *Mosaique de langues, mosaique culturelle: Le bilinguisme dans le Proche-Orient ancient*. Edited by F. Briquel-Chatonnet. Paris: Maissonneuve.

Parker, R. 1996. *Miasma: Pollution and Purification in Early Greek Religion*. Oxford: Oxford University Press.

Parpola, S. 1993. *Letters from Assyrian and Babylonian Scholars*. SAA 10. Helsinki: Helsinki University Press.

Patai, R. 1939–1940. "The 'Egla Arufa' or the Expiation of Polluted Land." *JQR* 30: 59–69.

Peirce, C. S. 1931–1958. *Collected Papers*. 6 vols. Edited by C. Hartshorne and P. Weiss. Cambridge, Mass.: Harvard University Press.

Penner, H. H. 1985. "Language, Ritual and Meaning." *Numen* 32: 1–16.

Pentiuc, E. J. 2001. *West Semitic Vocabulary in the Akkadian Texts from Emar.* HSS 49. Winona Lake, Ind.: Eisenbrauns.

Pinker, A. 1994. "The Number 40 in the Biblical World." *JBQ* 22: 163–72.

———. 2007. "A Goat to Go to Azazel." *JHS* 7. Online: http://www.arts.ualberta.ca/JHS/Articles/article_69.pdf

Propp, W. H. C. 1993. "That Bloody Bridegroom." *VT* 43: 495–518.

———. 2006. *Exodus 19–40.* AB. New York: Doubleday.

Puhvel, J. 1978. "Remarks on 'two' in Hittite." *ZVS* 92: 98–107.

von Rad, G. 1963. *Genesis: A Commentary.* OTL. Translated by J. H. Marks. London: SCM.

———. 1963–1965. *Old Testament Theology.* 2 vols. Translated by D. M. G. Stalker. Edinburgh: Oliver and Boyd.

Rainey, A. F. 1970. "The Order of Sacrifices in Old Testament Ritual Texts." *Biblica* 51: 485–98.

Rappaport, R. A. 1999. *Ritual and Religion in the Making of Humanity.* Cambridge: Cambridge University Press.

Reiner, E. 1995. *Astral Magic in Babylonia.* Philadelphia: American Philosophical Society.

Rendtorff, R. 1967. *Studien zur Geschichte des Opfers im Alten Israel.* Neukirchen-Vluyn: Neukirchener Verlag.

———. 1985–2004. *Leviticus.* BKAT. Neukirchen-Vluyn: Neukirchener Verlag.

———. 1995. "Another Prolegomenon to Leviticus 17:11." Pages 23–28 in *Pomegranates and Golden Bells: Studies in Biblical, Jewish and Near Eastern Ritual, Law, and Literature in Honor of Jacob Milgrom.* Edited by D. P. Wright, D. N. Freedman, and A. Hurvitz. Winona Lake, Ind.: Eisenbrauns.

———. 1999. "The Paradigm is Changing: Hopes—and Fears." Pages 51–68 in *Israel's Past in Present Research. Essays on Ancient Israelite Historiography.* Edited by V. Philips Long. Winona Lake, Ind.: Eisenbrauns. = *Biblical Interpretation* 1 [1993], 34–53.

Reventlow, H. G. 1972. "Sein Blut Komme über Sein Haupt." Pages 412–31 in *Um das Prinzip der Vergeltung in Religion und Recht des Alten Testaments.* Edited by K. Koch. Darmstadt: Wissenschaftliche Buchgesellschaft. (=*VT* 10 [1960]: 311–27)

Rhees, R. 1982. "Wittgenstein on Language and Ritual." Pages 69–107 in *Wittgenstein and His Times.* Edited by B. McGuinness. Chicago: University of Chicago Press.

Ricoeur, P. 1967. *The Symbolism of Evil.* Translated by E. Buchanan. New York: Harper & Row.

Rieken, E. 2009. "Hethitisch *kāša, kāšma, kāšat(t)a*: drei verkannte deiktische Partikeln." Pages 265–73 in *Pragmatische Kategorien: Form, Funktion und Diachronie. Akten der Arbeitstagung der Indogermanischen Gesellschaft, Marburg, 24–26 September 2007.* Edited by E. Rieken and P. Widmer. Wiesbaden: Harrassowitz.

Robertson Smith, W. 1927. *Lectures on the Religion of the Semites.* London: Black.

Rodriguez, A. M. 1979. Substitution in the Hebrew Cultus and Cultic Related Texts. Dissertation, Andrews University.

Rofé, A. 1961–1962. "עגלה ערופה." *Tarbiz* 31: 119–43. (Hebrew)

Rubinstein, J. 1999. "Nominalism and Realism in Qumranic and Rabbinic Law: A Reassessment." *Dead Sea Discoveries* 6: 157–83.

Rupprecht, K. 1975. "Quisquilien zu der Wendung פלוני את-יד מלא (jemenden die Hand füllen) und zum Terminus מלאים (Füllung)." Pages 73–93 in *Sefer Rendtorff*. Edited by K. Rupprecht. Dielheim: self-published.

Sarna, N. M. 1989. *Genesis*. JPS Torah Commentary. Philadelphia: Jewish Publication Society.

Sasson, J. M. 1966. "Circumcision in the Ancient Near East." *JBL* 85: 473–76.

Schenker, A. 1982. "köper et expiation." *Biblica* 63: 32–46.

———. 1983. "Das Zeichen das Blutes und die Gewissheit der Vergebung im Alten Testament." *Münchener theologische Zeitschrift* 34: 195–213.

———. 2000. *Recht und Kult im Alten Testament: Achzehn Studien*. Freiburg: Universitätsverlag.

Schmandt-Besserat, D. 1992. *Before Writing*, vol. 1. Austin, Tex.: University of Texas Press.

———. 1996. *How Writing Came About*. Austin, Tex.: University of Texas Press.

Schmitt, R. 2004. *Magie im Alten Testament*. AOAT 313. Münster: Ugarit Verlag.

Schwartz, B. J. 1991. "The Prohibitions Concerning 'Eating' the Blood in Leviticus 17." Pages 34–66 in *Priesthood and Cult in Ancient Israel*. Edited by G. A. Anderson and S. M. Olyan. JSOTSup 125. Sheffield: JSOT Press.

———. 1994. "'Term' or Metaphor: Biblical נשא עון/פשע/חטא." *Tarbiz* 63: 149–71. (Hebrew)

———. 1995. "The Bearing of Sin in the Priestly Literature." Pages 3–21 in *Pomegranates and Golden Bells: Studies in Biblical, Jewish and Near Eastern Ritual, Law, and Literature in Honor of Jacob Milgrom*. Edited by D. P. Wright, D. N. Freedman and A. Hurvitz. Winona Lake, Ind.: Eisenbrauns.

———. 1999. *The Holiness Legislation: Studies in the Priestly Code*. Jerusalem: Magnes. (Hebrew)

Schwemer, D. 1995. "Das alttestamentliche Doppelritual *'alwt wšlmym* im Horizont der hurritischen Opfertermini *ambašši* und *keldi*." Pages 81–116 in *Edith Porada Memorial Volume*. Edited by D. I. Owen and G. Wilhelm. SCCNH 7. Bethesda, Md.: CDL.

———. 1998. *Akkadische Rituale aus Ḫattuša*. THeth 23. Heidelberg: Winter.

Scurlock, J. 2002. "Translating Transfers in Ancient Mesopotamia." Pages 209–23 in *Magic and Ritual in the Ancient World*. Edited by P. Mirecki and M. Meyer. Leiden: Brill.

Searle, J. R. 1995. *The Construction of Social Reality*. New York: Free Press.

Shweder, R. A. 1991. *Thinking Through Cultures: Expeditions in Cultural Psychology*. Cambridge, Mass.: Harvard University Press.

———, et al. 1990. "Culture and Moral Development." Pages 140–204 in *Cultural Psychology*. Edited by J. W. Stigler et al. Cambridge: Cambridge University Press.

———, et al. 1998. "The Cultural Psychology of Development: One Mind, Many Mentalities." Pages 865–937 in *Theoretical Models of Human Development*. Vol. 1 of *Handbook of Child Psychology*. 5th ed. Edited by W. Damon. New York: Wiley & Sons.

Singer, I. 1987. "Oil in Anatolia according to Hittite Texts." Pages 183–86 in *Olive Oil in Antiquity. Israel and Neighboring Countries from Neolithic to Early Arab Period*. Edited by M. Helzer and D. Eitam. Haifa: University of Haifa Press.

———. 1996. *Muwatalli's Prayer to the Assembly of Gods Through the Storm-God of Lightning (CTH 381)*. Atlanta: Scholars Press.

————. 1997. Review of *Religionsgeschichtliche Beziehungen zwischen Kleinasien, Nordsyrien und dem Alten Testament. JAOS* 117: 604–5.

————. 2002. "Danuḫepa and Karunta." Pages 739–52 in *Anatolia Antica: Studia in memoria di Fiorella Imparati*. 2 vols. Eothen 11. Florence: LoGisma.

————. 2002. *Hittite Prayers*. Atlanta: Society of Biblical Literature.

————. 2006. "The Hittites and the Bible Revisited." Pages 723–56 in *"I Will Speak the Riddle of Ancient Times": Archaeological and Historical Studies in Honor of Amihai Mazar on the Occasion of his Sixtieth Birthday*. 2 vols. Edited by A. M. Maeir and P. de Miroschedji. Winona Lake, Ind.: Eisenbrauns.

Sklar, J. 2005. *Sin, Impurity, Sacrifice, Atonement: The Priestly Conceptions*. Sheffield: Sheffield Phoenix.

Sokoloff, M. 2002. *A Dictionary of Jewish Palestinian Aramaic*. Ramat Gan: Bar-Ilan University Press.

Sommer, F. and H. Ehelolf. 1924. *Das Hethitische Ritual des Papanikri von Komana*. Boghazköi-Studien 10. Leipzig: Hinrichs.

Sperber, D. 1975. *Rethinking Symbolism*. Translated by A. L. Morton. Cambridge: Cambridge University Press.

Staal, F. 1979. "The Meaninglessness of Ritual." *Numen* 26: 2–22.

Stamm, J. J. 1940. *Erlösen und Vergeben im Alten Testament*. Bern: Francke.

Starke, F. 1985. *Die keilschrift-luwischen Texte in Umschrift*. StBoT 30. Wiesbaden: Harrassowitz.

Steiner, G. 1999. "Was bedeutet LUGAL-*zu-nu...ul-tam-li* im Aleppo-Vertrag?" *AoF* 26: 13–25.

Stol, M. 1987–1988. "Leprosy: New Light from Greek and Babylonian Sources." *Jaarbericht van het Voorariatisch-Egyptisch Genootschap* 30: 22–31.

————. 1993. *Epilepsy in Babylonia*. Gröningen: Styx.

————. 2000. *Birth in Babylonia and the Bible: Its Mediterranean Setting*. Gröningen: Styx.

Stowers, S. K. 1995. "Greeks Who Sacrifice and Greeks Who Do Not." Pages 293–333 in *The Social World of the First Christians*. Edited by L. M. White and O. L. Yarbrough. Minneapolis: Fortress.

————. 1998. "On the Comparison of Blood in Greek and Israelite Ritual." Pages 179–94 in *Hesed ve-Emet: Studies in Honor of Ernest S. Frerichs*. Edited by J. Magness and S. Gitin. BJS 320. Atlanta: Scholars Press.

Strauss, C. and N. Quinn. 1997. *A Cognitive Theory of Cultural Meaning*. Cambridge: Cambridge University Press.

Strauß, R. 2006. *Reinigungsrituale aus Kizzuwatna*. Berlin: de Gruyter.

Stuart, D. 1987. *Hosea-Jonah*. WBC. Waco, Tex.: Word Books.

Sürenhagen, D. 1981. "Zwei Gebete Hattušilis und der Puduhepa." *AoF* 8: 83–168.

Sweetser, E. 1990. *From Etymology to Pragmatics: Metaphorical and Cultural Aspects of Semantic Structure*. Cambridge: Cambridge University Press.

van der Toorn, K. 2007. *Scribal Culture and the Making of the Hebrew Bible*. Cambridge, Mass.: Harvard University Press.

Traugott, E. C. and R. B. Dasher. 2002. *Regularity in Semantic Change*. Cambridge: Cambridge University Press.

Trémouille, M.-C. 1996. "Une objet cultuel: le *šeḫelliški*." *SMEA* 38: 73–93.

————. 1997. *ᵈHebat: Une Divinité Syro-Anatolienne*. Eothen 7. Firenze: LoGisma.

————. 1999. "La religion des Hourrites: état actuel de nos connaissances." Pages 277–91 in *Nuzi at Seventy-Five*. Edited by D. I. Owen and G. Wilhelm. SCCNH 10. Bethesda, Md.: CDL.

————. 2001. "Kizzuwatna, terre de frontière." Pages 59–78 in *La Cilicie: Espaces et pouvoirs Locaux*. Edited by E. Jean et al. Istanbul: Institut francais d'etudes anatoliennes.

Tullock, J. H. 1966. "Blood-Vengeance among the Israelites in the Light of its Near Eastern Background." PhD dissertation. Nashville: Vanderbilt University.

Turner, V. 1967. *The Forest of Symbols: Aspects of Ndembu Ritual*. Ithaca, N.Y.: Cornell University Press.

de Vaux, R. 1964. *Studies in Old Testament Sacrifice*. Cardiff: University of Wales Press.

Veldhuis, N. 2004. *Religion, Literature, and Scholarship: The Sumerian Composition "Nanše and the Birds."* Leiden: Brill.

Vickers, B. 1973. *Towards Greek Tragedy*. London: Longman.

Voloshinov, V. N. 1973. *Marxism and the Philosophy of Language*. Translated by L. Matejka and I. R. Titunik. New York: Seminar Press.

Vriezen, T. C. 1950. "The Term *Hizza*: Lustration and Consecration." *OTS* 7: 201–35.

Vygotsky, L. S. 1986. *Thought and Language*. Translated by A. Kozulin. Cambridge, Mass.: MIT.

Wagenaar, J. A. 2003. "Post-Exilic Calendar Innovations: The First Month of the Year and the Date of the Passover and Festival of Unleavened Bread." *ZAW* 115: 3–24.

Wallis, G. 1981. "'Hand füllen': Einen Amtseid leisten lassen?" *Henoch* 3: 340–49.

Waltke, B. K. and M. O'Connor. 1990. *An Introduction to Biblical Hebrew Syntax*. Winona Lake, Ind.: Eisenbrauns.

Watts, J. W. 2007. *Ritual and Rhetoric in Leviticus*. Cambridge: Cambridge University Press.

Wefing, S. 1979. "Untersuchungen zum Entsühnungsritual am grossen Versöhnungstag (Lev 16)." Ph.D. diss. Bonn: Rheinischen Friedrich-Wilhelms Universität.

Wegner, I. 2000. *Hurritische: Eine Einführung*. Wiesbaden: Harrassowitz.

Weinfeld, M. 1964. 1972. *Deuteronomy and the Deuteronomic School*. Oxford: Clarendon.

————. 1983. "Social and Cultic Institutions in the Priestly Source against their Ancient Near Eastern Background." Pages 95–129 in *Proceedings of the Eighth World Congress of Jewish Studies*. Jerusalem: World Union of Jewish Studies.

————. 1993. "Traces of Hittite Cult in Shiloh, Bethel and in Jerusalem." Pages 455–72 in *Religionsgeschichtliche Beziehungen zwischen Kleinasien, Nordsyrien und dem Alten Testament*. Edited by B. Janowsky, K. Koch, and G. Wilhelm.Freiburg: Universitätsverlag.

————. 1964. "Towards the Concept of Law in Israel and Elsewhere." *Beit Miqra* 8: 58–63. (Hebrew)

Weiss, I. M. ed. 1946. *Sipra with Rabad's Commentary*. New York: OM.

Wellhausen, J. 1899. *Die Composition des Hexateuchs und der historischen Bücher des alten Testaments*. Berlin: Reimer.

————. 1905. *Prolegomena zur Geschichte Israels*. Berlin: Reimer.

Wenham, G. J. 1979. *The Book of Leviticus*. NICOT. Grand Rapids, Mich.: Eerdmans.

————. 1981. *Numbers: An Introduction and Commentary*. Leicester: Inter-varsity Press.

Wertsch, J. W. 1985. "The Semiotic Mediation of Mental Life: L.S. Vygotsky and M.M.

Bakhtin." Pages 49–71 in *Semiotic Mediation: Sociocultural and Psychological Perspectives*. Edited by E. Mertz and R. J. Parmentier. Orlando: Academic Press.

———. 1985. *Vygotsky and the Social Formation of Mind*. Cambridge, Mass.: Harvard University Press.

———. 1998. *Mind as Action*. Oxford: Oxford University Press.

Westbrook, R. 1988. *Studies in Biblical and Cuneiform Law*. Paris: Gabalda.

——— and R. D. Woodard. 1990. "The Edict of Tudhaliya IV." *JAOS* 110: 641–59.

Westermann, C. 1994. *Genesis 1–11*. Translated by J. J. Scullion. Minneapolis: Fortress.

Whitekettle, R. 1995. "Leviticus 12 and the Israelite Woman: Ritual Process, Liminality and the Womb." *ZAW* 107: 393–408.

———. 1996. "Levitical Thought and the Female Reproductive Cycle: Wombs, Wellsprings and the Primeval World." *VT* 46: 376–91.

Williams, M. 1999. "Vygotsky's Social Theory of Mind." Pages 273–81 in *Wittgenstein, Mind and Meaning: Toward a Social Conception of Mind*. London: Routledge.

Wittgenstein, L. 1991. *Remarks on Frazer's Golden Bough*. Edited by R. Rhees. Translated by A. C. Miles. Gringley-on-the-Hill, England: Doncaster.

Wilhelm, G. 1982. *Grundzüge der Geschichte und Kultur der Hurriter*. Darmstadt: Wissenschaftliche Buchgesellschaft.

———. 1999. "Reinheit und Heiligkeit." Pages 197–217 in *Levitikus als Buch*. Edited by H. J. Fabry and H. W. Jüngling. Berlin: Philo.

———. 2002. "Noch einmal zu Šamuha." Pages 885–90 in *Anatolia Antica: Studia in memoria di Fiorella Imparati*. 2 vols. Eothen 11. Florence: LoGisma.

———. 2004. "Hurrian." Pages 95–118 in *The Cambridge Encyclopedia of the World's Ancient Languages*. Edited by R. D. Woodard. Cambridge: Cambridge University Press.

———. 2006. "Die hurritischsprachige Tafel Kp 05/226." *MDOG* 138: 233–36.

Wolff, H. W. 1964. "Hoseas geistige Heimat." Pages 243–50 in *Gesammelte Studien zum Alten Testament*. Munich: Kaiser.

Wright, D. P. 1986. "The Gesture of Hand Placement in the Hebrew Bible and in Hittite Literature." *JAOS* 106: 433–46.

———. 1987. "Deuteronomy 21:1–9 as a Rite of Elimination." *CBQ* 49: 387–403.

———.1987. *The Disposal of Impurity: Elimination Rites in the Bible and in Hittite and Mesopotamian Literature*. Atlanta: Scholars Press.

———. 1992. "Day of Atonement." Pages 71–76 in *Anchor Bible Dictionary*, vol. 2. New York: Doubleday.

———, D. N. Freedman and A. Hurvitz, eds. 1995. *Pomegranates and Golden Bells: Studies in Biblical, Jewish and Near Eastern Ritual, Law, and Literature in Honor of Jacob Milgrom*. Winona Lake, Ind.: Eisenbrauns.

Yakubovich, I. 2005. "Were Hittite Kings Divinely Annointed? A Palaic Invocation to the Sun-God and Its Significance for Hittite Religion." *JANER* 5: 107–37.

Young, N. H. 1976. "C.H. Dodd, 'Hilaskesthai' and His Critics." *EvQ* 48: 67–78.

Zevit, Z. 1976. "The 'eglâ ritual of Deuteronomy 21:1–9." *JBL* 95: 377–90.

———. 2001. *The Religions of Ancient Israel: A Synthesis of Parallactic Approaches*. London: Continuum.

Zimmerli, W. 1983. *Ezekiel 2*. Translated by J. D. Martin. Hermeneia. Philadelphia: Fortress.

Zipf, G. K. 1949. *Human Behavior and the Principle of Least Effort*. Cambridge, Mass.: Addison-Wesley. Repr. New York: Hafner, 1965.

Zohar, N. 1988. "Repentance and Purification: The Significance and Semantics of Ḥaṭṭaʾth in the Pentateuch." *JBL* 107: 609–18.

Zohary, M. 1982. *Plants of the Bible*. Cambridge: Cambridge University Press.

GLOSSARY

Hittite and Hurrian Terms

ešḫar	blood
ešḫar šanḫ-	demand the blood
šarni(n)k-	appease, compensate
šarnikzil	compensation
uzi-	flesh (offering)
zurki-	blood (offering)

Hebrew Terms

דם	*dam*	blood
חטאת	*ḥaṭṭat*	1. sin; 2. sin offering
חִטֵּא	*ḥiṭṭe*	1. perform a sin offering rite; 2. cleanse
כִּפֶּר	*kipper*	1. appease; 2. expiate/compensate; 3. purge
כֹּפֶר	*koper*	1. appeasement gift, bribe; 2. ransom
נפש	*nepeš*	1. spirit; 2. seat of appetites, emotions; 3. individual, living being

Subject Index

Source Index

Author Index

www.ingramcontent.com/pod-product-compliance
Lightning Source LLC
Chambersburg PA
CBHW021809270326
41932CB00007B/115